FOOTNOTES

Footnotes: On Shoes

EDITED BY
SHARI BENSTOCK
AND
SUZANNE FERRISS

RUTGERS UNIVERSITY PRESS
NEW BRUNSWICK, NEW JERSEY, AND LONDON

A portion of our royalties from this book will be donated to Dress for Success to purchase shoes for its clients. As the organization's founder, Nancy Lublin, has said, "You can't pull yourself up by your bootstraps if you don't have any boots!"

Quotation from "Bad Morning," from *Collected Poems* by Langston Hughes, Copyright © 1994 by the Estate of Langston Hughes, reprinted by permission of Alfred A. Knopf, a division of Random House, Inc.

Quotations from "I Saw a Mountain," by Moses Schulstein, translated by Mindelle Wajsman and Bea Stadtler, Copyright © 1993 by Mindelle Wajsman and Bea Stadtler, reprinted by permission of Mindelle Wajsman and Bea Stadtler.

Quotation of an untitled poem, first line, "My every breath is a curse," by Abraham Sutzkever, from *A. Sutzkever: Selected Poetry and Prose,* translated by Barbara and Benjamin Harshav, Copyright © 1991 The Regents of the University of California, reprinted by permission of the University of California Press.

Quotations from "The Dachau Shoe" by W. S. Merwin, Copyright © 1970 by W. S. Merwin, reprinted by permission of W. S. Merwin.

Library of Congress Cataloging-in-Publication Data

Footnotes : on shoes / Shari Benstock and Suzanne Ferriss, editors.
    p.   cm.
   Includes bibliographical references and index.
   ISBN 0-8135-2870-4 (cloth : alk. paper) — ISBN 0-8135-2871-2 (pbk : alk. paper)
   1. Shoes—Social aspects.   I. Title: Footnotes.   II. Benstock, Shari, 1944–   .
III. Ferriss, Suzanne, 1962–   .

GT2130.F35   2001
391.4'13—dc21   00-034204

British Cataloging-in-Publication data for this book is available from the British Library

Manufactured in the United States of America

To our editor and friend, Leslie Mitchner

CONTENTS

$\mathcal{P}$erspective

$\mathcal{P}$resentation

ACKNOWLEDGMENTS

Those who love us know our passion for shoes—from strappy sandals to hiking boots. Our thanks to those who have indulged us over the years we were developing and completing this book by giving us shoes, shoe figurines, shoe books, calendars, notepads, images, articles, and all manner of "ped-abilia": Steven Alford, Lauren Berlant, Barbara Brodman, Isabelle de Courtivron, Douglas Flemons and Shelley Green, Tom Goodman, Linda Gordon, Pegram Harrison, Kitty and Martin Jacobs, Mary Jones, Annemarie and Thierry Jutel, Elizabeth McDaniel, Laura Mullen, Lulu Selby, Eric Shivvers, Rochelle Simmons and Mark McGuire, Lynn Wolf and Paul Joseph.

In loving memory of Bernard Benstock.

FOOTNOTES

Introduction

SHARI BENSTOCK AND SUZANNE FERRISS

*S*hoes are hot. They hang on walls in calendars. They grace the covers of coffee-table books and magazines, including at least one devoted entirely to footwear, *Shuz*. Shoe postcards are tacked to refrigerator doors with shoe magnets. Ivy dangles from shoe planters. Women accessorize with shoe bracelets and earrings encrusted with diamonds. Christmas trees—even fish tanks—are decorated with the Metropolitan Museum of Art's miniature replicas of famous shoe designs (each accompanied by a descriptive minihistory).

Footwear has assumed such prominence that an entire museum, the Bata Shoe Museum in Toronto, has devoted its collection to the history of shoes, as well as to the shoe as an aesthetic object. Not to be outdone, the Fashion Institute of New York recently mounted its own high-profile exhibition, titled *Shoes: A Lexicon of Style*, curated by fashion historian Valerie Steele.[1]

Consumers have established their own collections. Teens and twenty-somethings stockpile Steve Madden's platforms with the same fervor that thirty- and forty-somethings amass Prada boots and sandals. Long before they were born, Marie Antoinette set the standard, collecting over five hundred pairs of custom-made, gem-encrusted shoes, each carefully cataloged by her shoe wardrobe mistress.[2] The most infamous contemporary collector of shoes, Imelda Marcos, more than doubled Marie Antoinette's total, amassing over twelve hundred pairs of shoes before she and her husband fled the Philippines.[3]

While she may have stepped out of the international spotlight, her legend lives on. At Fetish, a store in Austin, Texas, customers automatically become members of the "Imelda Club": buy five pairs and the next is half price. Every one of us knows some- one who resembles Marie or Imelda: the woman in New Zealand who has shoes dis- played in her living room, the friend with the walk-in closet consisting of rows of cubbyholes, each containing a shoebox stapled with a Polaroid snapshot of the shoes inside.[4] So entrenched is the notion that women, in particular, have an insatiable desire for collecting shoes, that one major corporation once lured frequent fliers with the question "Was it a fetish?"—extending the invitation to gain air miles by augment- ing one's already overflowing collection (figure 1).

A proliferation of Internet sites caters to collectors with particular predilections for specific brands and distinct styles, including the Clog Page, Platform Diva, and Go-Go Boots Online. Others impart historical information about Viking footwear and footwear in the Middle Ages. There is even a site dedicated to the Bruno Magli shoe that figured so prominently in the notorious O. J. Simpson trial.[5] The Web serves as an industry resource as well as a virtual shoe mall: shoesonthenet.com bills itself as "the shoe store in every computer." A television commercial for nordstromshoes.com features a woman gleefully supervising the destruction of her husband's vintage car to make room in the garage for all the shoes she'll be able to purchase at "the world's biggest shoestore."

What is it in our culture that has led to this fascination with shoes?

FOOTNOTES: ON SHOES

The essays in this collection offer various answers to this question, from the per- spectives of art, film, literature, history, folklore, dance, psychology, and cultural stud- ies. Sometimes overlapping, sometimes contradictory, these analyses extend arguments drawn from the steadily growing body of work devoted to fashion. Reflecting the para- doxes inherent in shoes—in collecting, consuming, fashioning, representing, and wear- ing them—they are loosely organized into four sections: perspective, presentation, power, and perception. In a sense, such distinctions are arbitrary, for our contributors persistently identify the ambivalences and anxieties in the culturally constructed mean- ings of shoes.

PERSPECTIVE

At the Internet site Solemates: The Century in Shoes, visitors can "dial a decade" to learn how shoes "reflect the changing passions, perspectives, and ideals of our culture."[6] As fashion historians from Anne Hollander to Christopher Breward have demonstrated, not only does clothing have a history, it reflects cultural changes. Such is obviously the case with footwear, and the displays at the Bata Shoe Museum in Toronto trace its history across time and across cultures. But, as Julia Emberley argues, the museum presents shoes simultaneously as cultural or aesthetic artifacts and as commodities. The fragmentary nature of the museum's exhibits thus embodies our postmodern existence:

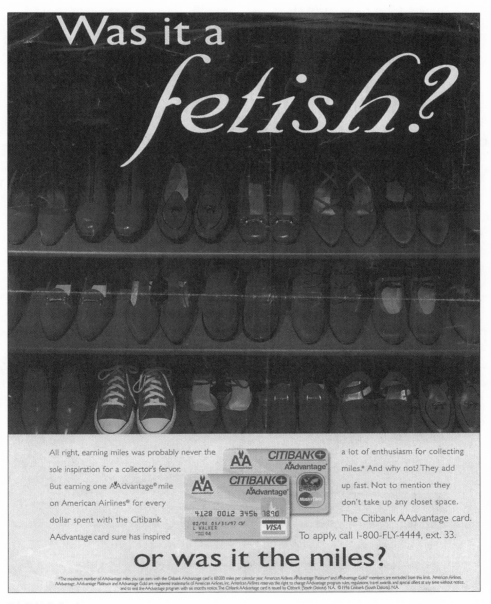

FIGURE 1

"In a postmodern age we no longer live in a world of different cultures, as people did in the nineteenth century, but in a culture of commodities. What the Bata Shoe Museum teaches us is knowledge about commodity culture and its capacity to resolve social contradictions and 'differences' into the mute eloquence of an object, a shoe."[7]

As an object of worship and adoration, the shoe has figured prominently in art, particularly since the eighteenth century. In *Seeing through Clothes,* Hollander notes that a new "delight in the lovely shape of the shod foot" could be seen in the works of Jean-Antoine Watteau, William Hogarth, and others. She explains their attraction:

> Female shoes had become very abstract, sophisticated objects by the
> eighteenth century. They were curved, pointed, and heeled and made of
> elaborate materials; and the new interest in legs undoubtedly occurred
> simultaneously with a new interest in feet and their clothing. Renaissance
> images of fully clothed ladies had usually hidden their feet. Elaborate shoes
> appeared for the first time below the hems of Jacobean ladies at the turn of
> the sixteenth century; but they are exactly like men's shoes, and anything but
> erotic. Later, women's shoes acquired some of the curved suggestiveness
> eventually to have such importance in the eroticism of feet and legs, and they
> came to be sharply differentiated from men's footwear.[8]

Janice West argues that shoes have been no less significant in twentieth-century art, from the works of the surrealists to those of the present day. Examining the works (and lives) of Andy Warhol, Jim Dine, and Lisa Milroy, West argues that shoes transcend barriers between art and design.

Film can also been seen as a "kinetic museum of . . . footwear history," according to Maureen Turim. In "High Angles on Shoes: Cinema, Gender, and Footwear," she argues that shoes are central to the representation of women and men. In silent movies, musicals, film noir, neorealist films, as well as contemporary comedies, "shoes take on a magic and even a life of their own."

PRESENTATION

Lorraine Gamman maintains that women's passionate attachment to shoes, women's particular pleasure in collecting and wearing them, is connected to the impulse for self-fashioning and self-presentation. The satisfaction we take in having purchased a pair of shoes that "is us," that represents us, reveals much about the constructedness of individual identity. As Elizabeth Wilson argues, "The fashionable dress of the Western world [is] one means whereby an always fragmentary self is glued together into a semblance of unified identity."[9] Shoes serve as markers of gender, class, race, ethnicity, and even sexuality.

Shoes have, historically, delineated clear class distinctions, for instance. Heels have, from the time they first appeared in Italy, signaled that the wearer—male or female— belongs to the leisure class. Chopines, popular in sixteenth-century Venice, boasted platform columns as high as thirty inches.[10] Incapable of walking without assistance, wearers were supported by two servants, one on each side. Lowering the sole in front transformed chopines into high heels. When Catherine de Medici wore them in Paris at her wedding in 1533, heels became indelibly associated with privilege. While we may now associate stilettos with "working girls," they remain in certain instances the sign of wealth. The trademark stilettos of Manolo Blahnik, the "high priest of the high heel," are called "limousine shoes," referring simultaneously to the fact that wearers never actually walk much in them and that devotees routinely shell out $450 for a pair. "Sensible shoes"—from moccasins to work boots—identify the wearer as a member of the laboring classes, feet planted firmly on the ground.

Class distinctions are intertwined with gender divisions. Fashion theorists have traced the emergence of clear distinctions between male and female dress to the nineteenth century, and sociological studies of shoes uphold this argument.[11] One study found that "shoes provide a means for applying sex-typed attributes, and that sex differences with respect to perceptions of shoes are consistent with traditional sex-role orientations."[12] Loafers, boots, and wing tips were easily classified as masculine, while a black high-heeled sandal was perceived to be the "most formal, the most feminine, the most fashionable, the most uncomfortable, the sexiest and most prestigious." Interestingly, shoes perceived as exclusively masculine fell into only one category, whereas those perceived as feminine fell into two: sexy and sexless (e.g., nursing shoes, career pumps). Thus shoes also reflect expectations for women's sexuality.

However, as Elizabeth Wilson argues, "modern fashion *plays* endlessly with the distinction between masculinity and femininity. With it we express our shifting ideas about what masculinity and femininity are."[13] In modern culture, for example, men redefined fashionable masculinity. Christopher Breward demonstrates how shoes came to signify status, "manliness," and nationhood at the turn of the twentieth century and into the 1920s, and how modernist aesthetics—defined in the theoretical writings of Adolf Loos and Le Corbusier and displayed in advertisements for shoes themselves—challenged traditional definitions of "masculine" design. The same challenges to traditional definitions of sexual and national identity were made by women. As Jaime Hovey notes, in Daphne Du Maurier's novel *Rebecca,* the shoes and other intimate belongings of the dead Mrs. De Winter are the focus of anxieties related to class, female homo-sexuality, and national identity.

Distinctions of class, gender, and sexuality often further overlap with ethnic iden-tification, as particular styles become synonymous with certain groups of wearers. Accord-ing to Tace Hedrick, spike heels (*tacones*) have come to be connected with the exotic beauty of Hispanic women. "Where would the Brazilian Carmen Miranda, Nuyorican Jennifer López, or Mexican-born Salma Hayek be without their seemingly requisite high heels?" she asks. Heels have become synonymous with "brownness."

Shoes can also be conceived of as talismans of their wearer, bearers of the power accrued to the absent being. In the magical thinking of American advertising, shoes have acquired a talismanic significance: ads for Air Jordans once extended the promise that the wearer could "be like Mike." Despite Michael Jordan's protest that "the shoes mean just shoes," young consumers were still willing to pay upwards of $200 to purchase a token of his success.[14] Vintage Air Jordans routinely go for $2,000 a pair in Japan, with patent leather prototypes commanding as much as $22,500, about as much as the retro VW beetle.[15] Jordan may have retired, but Nike's basic marketing strategy hasn't. A Lakota Indian says he runs the Sacred Hoop 500 for all Lakota (figure 2). Since, as he reminds us, "we belong to this land, to the spirit of Paha Sapa," we can all turn running a relay in our Nikes into a spiritual quest.

POWER

Such a gesture, of course, distracts consumers from the realities of shoe production, from the impoverished and brutal working conditions of laborers in sweatshops in the United States and in the exploited third-world markets favored by Nike and other first-world corporations. Recently, troubled athletic giant Reebok publicized the results of a study citing health and safety problems in the factories of its subcontractors in Indonesia and its suppliers in China, Thailand, Vietnam, and Brazil. Nike is reportedly inviting college students to investigate its labor practices in Indonesia and elsewhere. Students must, of course, possess a working knowledge of the country's language and regional dialects, so one wonders how many will actually be able to take advantage of this "opportunity."

As the manufacture of athletic footwear demonstrates, "the western fashion sys-tem goes hand-in-hand with the exercise of power,"[16] the power of late capitalism, to be precise. "Fashion *speaks* capitalism," according to Elizabeth Wilson. "Capitalism maims, kills, appropriates, lays waste." It is also "global, imperialist and racist" and "at the eco-nomic level the fashion industry has been an important instrument of this exploitation."[17]

Long before shoe manufacturers exploited workers in the third world, they abused black workers in the United States. As Anthony Barthelemy reminds us, from the late 1700s to the Civil War and beyond, shoe laborers in Massachusettes toiled to make rough unlined boots for southern slaves. Called "brogans," the boots have come to be synonymous with African American experience, symbolic of servitude in slavery and in the shoes' manufacture. They are "indisputable relic[s] of a hideous and degrading past."

Why do I run?

I am Lakota.

And this

is our church,

the Black Hills.

We run this relay,

the Sacred Hoop 500,

to make a statement.

We belong to this

land, to the spirit

of Paba Sapa.

I'm tired, I'm sore

and I'm cold, but

tonight I'm running

the sixth leg

out on rte. 40

for all Lakota.

nike

FIGURE 2

Ironically, shoes were once icons of worker rebellion. The word "sabotage" comes from *sabot,* the French wooden clogs that eighteenth-century workers threw into the machinery of mills as an act of defiance. In a less direct manner, shoes have served political and moral ends in the twentieth century. At a 1994 protest in Washington, D.C., for example, 38,000 pairs of shoes stood in for victims of gun violence in the United States. The same political statement has been borrowed in Paris and other French cities to symbolize the over 600,000 civilians killed by land mines. Shoes have also served as reminders of Holocaust victims in staged recreations of the aftermath of genocide. The pile of 4,000 shoes from death camps in Poland displayed at the United States Holocaust Memorial Museum recalls the "piles of corpses in the streets of the ghettos, in the death carts of the camps, in the mass graves." In "Empty Shoes," Ellen Carol Jones writes, "Abject survivors of the abjection suffered by the men and women and children killed in the Shoah, the shoes—derelict, decaying—figure the abandonment of European Jewry by the West, the decomposition of a people under the Nazis." Shoes—in

FIGURE 3a

photographs, paintings, poems, and survivor testimonies—serve as tangible reminders of Holocaust victims.

The impact of such images requires an imaginative leap: we envision the shoes attached to bodies that we ourselves invent to complete the effect. As such, the protests accrue a moral power. Shoes are employed to subvert class, race, and gender divisions, to remind us that each of us is human and mortal. One major shoe manufacturer, Charles David, has tapped into this realization, asking its customers to sign petitions in favor of Tibetan independence, to "give a voice to those who can't speak. And walk with us" (figure 3). Walk a mile in my shoes? It's hard to imagine Charles David pumps gracing the tired feet of Tibetan monks. In the hands of the advertisers, class and cultural divisions are enhanced, not erased.

"When we are interested in fashion, we are concerned with relations of power and their articulation at the level of the body."[18] This lesson is most powerfully demonstrated in Hans Christian Andersen's story "The Red Shoes." The infamous and autonomous

FIGURE 3b

red shoes subject Karen to pain at once spiritual and physical. To Erin Mackie, they possess a "fetish magic," functioning not merely as phallic substitutes but as vehicles for social ascendancy and bodily transcendence. Karen's desire to transcend her lowly status is embodied in the shoes, and they exact their revenge, her death.

PERCEPTION

The red shoes were perceived by others as excessive and inappropriate for a young girl in mourning for the death of her mother, but to Karen, "nothing else in the world was so desirable." Her story reveals the tension between appearance and sensation, between the visual and the tactile, between image and sensation. Shoes, of course, offer bodily pleasure and so, according to Elizabeth Wilson, "gratify women's highly developed sense of touch and pleasure in their own bodies."[19]

The effect of high heels on the body has been the origin of much speculation and controversy. When American women imported them from Paris, they created a scandal. The Massachusetts colony passed a law: "All women, whether virgins, maidens or widows, who shall after this Act impose upon, seduce or betray into matrimony any of His Majesty's male subjects by virtue of . . . high heel shoes, shall incur the penalty of the law now enforced against witchcraft, and the marriage shall be null and void."[20] This fear of the seductive power of stilettos has been traced to the shoes' effects on the female body. In *The Sex Life of the Foot and Shoe,* William A. Rossi delineates the various ways the high heel "adds new dimensions to the sensuousness and sex-attraction of a woman." The high heel elongates the leg and increases the arch of the foot, making it appear smaller. It raises the buttocks (as much as 25 percent, according to *Harper's Index*) and curves the back, pushing the chest forward. It also "feminizes the gait by causing a shortening of the stride and a mincing step that suggests a degree of helpless bondage" that "appeals to the chivalrous or machismo nature of many men." Added height may also provide women with "a psychological and emotional uplift that enhances sexual attraction."[21] The arched foot, for sexologist Alfred Kinsey, more simply and directly indicates erotic arousal: "Curled toes have, for at least eight centuries, been one of the stylized symbols of erotic response."[22] (Now we know why Barbie is always smiling.) Men have also periodically donned high heels to enhance their sexual attractiveness. King Louis XIV popularized them in the sixteenth century when male wearers discovered that "Louis heels" enhanced the muscles of the calves, making them seem more "masculine" in their short pants and hose.[23]

High heels find a counterpart in ballet slippers, which similarly display the dancer's arched foot *en pointe* and elongate the leg. Yet the ballet slipper is "a paradoxical signifier," according to Gerri Reaves, for it "unifies pain, restrained beauty, and control, and it clothes in glossy satin the wounded feet that make ballet beautiful." She contrasts the bound foot of the ballerina to the sensual freedom of the barefooted modern dancer. Isadora Duncan and Martha Graham "revolutionized our attitudes toward bare feet and woman's body, and their dance techniques offer a sensual counterpoint to the masochism of the ballet slipper." In contrast to the bound feet of the traditional ballerina, the modern dancer's bare feet represent "freedom, sexuality, and abandon." For this reason, as Janet Lyon notes, critics associated the naked foot with bestiality and moral degeneration, making the bare foot the object of a modern debate.

The tension between the foot and shoe is the origin of shoe fetishism. Much has been written about the mechanism of substitution inherent in fetishism, where the female shoe can serve as a tangible reminder of an absent female wearer or substitute for the body itself. In her highly accessible book *Fetish,* for instance, Valerie Steele recounts the story of a man who, while kissing one rose-colored slipper, ejaculated into the other.[24] Chuck Jones, Marla Maples's publicist, arrested for stealing fifty pairs of her shoes, admitted to having a "sexual relationship" with them.[25] In Freudian theory, the shoe (or foot) substitutes for the female body, as protection against the threat of castration. Sexual desire is thus redirected to a benign, inanimate substitute for the female body. This linkage between shoes and sexuality is surely more complicated, however, as feminist critics of Freud would be quick to admit.

These complex relations of power, desire, and shoes are evident in one of the most enduring stories about shoes, "Cinderella," where a perfect fit snags a prince (or the prince's penis). To the prince, the glass slipper stands for the ravishing and mysterious woman at the ball; finding the woman who fits the shoe means he will have recovered the object of his sexual desire. In a crude equation, the shoe, to the prince at least, equals sex.

But desire of an entirely other sort is at work for the women in the tale, for the prince himself represents certain wealth, leisure, and power. The glass slipper represents a prize so desirable that the stepsisters in the original version by Charles Perrault were willing to cut off their toes to attain it. The power accrued to the object is worthy of this sacrifice. In the original version of the story, desire was at issue for Cinderella, as Laura Mullen argues. She takes the mistranslation of Perrault's tale, the infamous substitution of "glass" (*verre*) for "fur" (*vair*) as symptomatic of the male misunderstanding and fear of feminine sexual pleasure, pleasure in touch more than sight.

The glass slipper's small size also speaks volumes about cultural definitions of femininity. Todd Lyon argues that the prince "was really looking for . . . the woman with the smallest feet in the kingdom. Those tiny feet were the very definition of refinement. It wasn't her sparkling conversation, fashion sense, or dancing skills that deemed Cinderella queenly and desirable. It was her teeny-weeny, eensy-beensy little feet." Her essay, the "Postcript" to our collection, defends "big feets" and, in the process, playfully invokes the ambiguities and ambivalences of shoes explored by the volume as a whole, the tensions between sight and touch, femininity and masculinity, conformity and rebellion, power and passion, sexual display and sensual pleasure.

————

We do not purport in this collection to have offered a definitive explanation to the enduring fascination of shoes, nor do we think it possible to do so, for the very reasons that our contributors repeatedly suggest: the cultural significance of shoes is tied up with complex issues of gender, race, ethnicity, sexuality, history, psychology, and aesthetics. Instead, this collection offers "footnotes," essays about shoes that leave a trail of footprints for readers to follow. Our contributors crisscross and double back on each other and by no means cover the entire path. We hope they guide you but also lead you to discover unexplored pathways.

Lace up your boots or strap on your sandals and wander with us.

NOTES

1. Steele also published a book, *Shoes: A Lexicon of Style* (New York: Rizzoli, 1999), in conjunction with the exhibition.

2. "Millennium Icon: The Shoe," *Miami Herald* Web site (http://www.herald.com), September 30, 1999.

3. Marcos now estimates her collection at three thousand or more (*Miami Herald,* August 19, 1999). The shoemaking capital of the Philippines, Marikina, is even establishing a museum on Shoe Street to display two hundred pairs from her collection.

4. We are grateful to Todd Lyon for giving us this glimpse into her friend's closet.

5. The Clog Page (http://members.aol.com/clogs01/index.htm), Go-Go Boots Online (http://www.geocities.com/FashionAvenue/2958/), Platform Diva (http://www.geocities.com/FashionAvenue/1495/contents1.html), A Basic Guide to Footwear in the Viking Age (http://www.spoon.demon.co.uk/vikes/vikshoe.htm), Footwear of the Middle Ages (http://www.pbm.com/~lindahl/carlson/shoe-home.htm), and Bill Elisburg, The Bruno Magli Shoes (http://www.geocities.com/CapitolHill/5244/article1.html).

6. *Solemates: The Century in Shoes* (http://www.centuryinshoes.com/home.html).

7. Jean Baudrillard's contention that fashion is a simulacrum, an arbitrary sign with no referent, has inspired a number of critics to contend that fashion itself is a sign of the postmodern. See Baudrillard, *For a Critique of the Political Economy of the Sign,* trans. Charles Levin (St. Louis: Telos Press, 1981); and Julia Emberley, "The Fashion Apparatus and the Deconstruction of Postmodern Subjectivity," Kim Sawchuk, "A Tale of Inscription/Fashion Statements," and Gail Faurschou, "Fashion and the Cultural Logic of Postmodernity," in *Body Invaders: Panic Sex in America,* ed. Arthur Kroker and Marilouise Kroker (New York: St. Martin's Press, 1987), 47–60, 61–77, and 78–93, respectively.

8. Anne Hollander, *Seeing through Clothes* (1975; reprint, Berkeley: University of California Press, 1993), 221–222.

9. Elizabeth Wilson, *Adorned in Dreams: Fashion and Modernity* (Berkeley: University of California Press, 1985), 11.

10. William A. Rossi, *The Sex Life of the Foot and Shoe* (1977; reprint, Ware, Hertfordshire: Wordsworth Editions, 1989), 131.

11. See Fred Davis, *Fashion, Culture, and Identity* (Chicago: University of Chicago Press, 1992) and Ruth P. Rubenstein, *Dress Codes: Meanings and Messages in American Culture* (Boulder: Westview Press, 1995).

12. Susan B. Kaiser, Howard G. Schutz, and Joan Chandler, "Cultural Codes and Sex-Role Ideology: A Study of Shoes," *American Journal of Semiotics,* 5, 1 (1987): 13–34.

13. Wilson, *Adorned in Dreams,* 122. Marjorie Garber also notes that female cross-dressers are advised to wear wing tips to appear more "masculine" (*Vested Interests: Cross-Dressing and Cultural Anxiety* [New York: Routledge, 1992], 44–45).

14. The *New York Times* reports that used sneakers have become a $10 million market in Tokyo ("The Nike Railroad," *New York Times Magazine,* October 5, 1997, 23).

15. Robert Sullivan, "Sneakers in Seattle," *Vogue,* March 1999, 246.

16. Jennifer Craik, *The Face of Fashion: Cultural Studies in Fashion* (New York: Routledge, 1994), x.

17. Wilson, *Adorned in Dreams,* 14.

18. Sawchuk, "A Tale of Inscription," 62.

19. Wilson, *Adorned in Dreams,* 100. Note that Wilson is referring generically to fashion as "women's pornography." Her argument applies equally to shoes, as fashionable objects.

20. "Millennium Icon: The Shoe."

21. Rossi, *The Sex Life of the Foot and Shoe,* 121.

22. Quoted in ibid., 9.

23. Ibid., 128.

24. Valerie Steele, *Fetish: Fashion, Sex, and Power* (New York: Oxford University Press, 1996), 98.

25. Ibid., 8.

Perspective

The Ends of Fashion; or, Learning to Theorize with Shoes in the Bata Shoe Museum

JULIA EMBERLEY

The centrality of postmodern fashion to the commodity culture of the museum is nowhere more obviously and daringly presented than in the recently erected Bata Shoe Museum in Toronto, Canada. The museum, which opened on May 6, 1995, is devoted exclusively to the history and culture of shoes. It is a privately funded corporate venture and the brainchild of Sonja Bata, chairman of the Bata Shoe Museum, renowned philanthropist, environmentalist, and the marriage-business partner of Thomas J. Bata, who owns and runs Bata Limited. Not surprisingly, the opening of a private shoe museum by a shoe manufacturer met with a mixture of praise and skepticism. Canada's national newspaper, the *Globe and Mail,* lauded the use of private money in support of cultural development in Canada, a country where the arts are traditionally funded by the state and public sectors. Alternative, radical media sources such as the *Socialist Worker* wanted to "Give Bata the Boot" and took the occasion of the museum's opening to raise an issue that has circulated in Canadian media for some time: the questionable labor practices of the Bata corporation in Guatemala, Indonesia, and, especially, South Africa.[1] The underlying problem expressed in these diverse media sources revolves around a desire to maintain borders—those of a geopolitical and material nature. What this privately funded museum has done by devoting itself exclusively to representing the diverse histories and cross-cultural life of shoes is to throw the boundary between *shoe as commodity* and *shoe as cultural or aesthetic artifact* into question.

In many respects, the Bata Shoe Museum is exemplary in dramatizing the increasing fluidity between aesthetics and commodification that Fredric Jameson notes is a telling sign of the condition of postmodernity. Aesthetic production, he writes, "has become integrated into commodity production generally," and the drive for "more novel-seeming goods" has become a structural influence in the desire to achieve "aesthetic innovation and experimentation."[2] It is the instability of what were once certain distinctions that, in my view, prompted the media contest over the meaning of the museum. "Boundary maintenance," to borrow a term from Donna Haraway, was high on the agenda.[3] This fluidity and instability between commodities and aesthetic objects provide an occasion to examine what new material values emerge from this categorical crisis. The ever increasing commodification of the artistic or aesthetic domains at the turn of the twenty-first century has raised concern among progressive art movements that worry about whether the creative and libidinal forces feeding the desire for social change will be compromised by their commodification. Equally disturbing for conservative purists is that the high cultural values and money invested in art will be undermined by the accessibility and reproductive capabilities of commodity production and distribution. The priceless will soon be subject to a readable and nonnegotiable price tag.

If, as Jameson argues, "every position on postmodernism in culture—whether apologia or stigmatization—is also at one and the same time, and *necessarily,* an implicitly or explicitly political stance on the nature of multinational capitalism today," then it must now be possible to theorize with the commodity form, to deploy it for various, and sometimes contradictory, political purposes.[4] With the ends of style come multiple departures for the commodity form, including its entry into the museum as a pedagogical tool for multinational capitalism. The Bata Shoe Museum represents just such an example of the historical shift in the material values attributed to the commodity by postmodernism, or the epistemic reconfigurations of turn-of-the-twenty-first-century global capital.

A   P O S T M O D E R N   (D I S) P L A Y

Postmodernism has often been characterized by a reverse millenarianism, a sense of "the end of this or that."[5] This dead-end logic appears to be more typical of modernity, with its heroic quest for origins and teleological historiographic narratives, than postmodernity. If, however, this sense of an end does indeed characterize postmodernism, such "ends," I would suggest, signify neither death nor new beginnings. The ends of postmodernity are best understood as the loose threads that dangle from the edge of the social textile, the remnants left on the seamstress's floor, usually swept away as so much rubbish and debris. These remainders signal the ends of theory; they are an invitation to play with the residual aspects of cultural production, the parts that have remained unconsumable and survived fetishization. Ironically, the subject of this loosely gathered social textile—fashion—is, perhaps, the most notorious object of consumption and fetishism the twentieth century has ever seen. Until the poststructural turn toward a deconstruction of "nature" and the "natural," fashion existed largely in its feminine and masked form, principally in terms of style and related modes of artifice, deception, and dissimulation. Rarely was it taken seriously as a subject of knowledge with the capability of denaturalizing and unmasking what has become "naturalized," canonic, fixed, and binding. In other words, while so much has been written about style, little attention has been given to its conceptual powers as something *to theorize with.*

Jameson's inquiry into the difference between modernism and postmodernism, on the other hand, unfolds the dialectical capacities of style. His analysis of this historico-epistemological break is entirely predicated on the changing nature of style. He asks, "Does [postmodernism] imply any more fundamental change or break than the periodic style and fashion changes determined by an older high-modernism imperative of stylistic innovation?" Furthermore, he concludes his critique of the "waning of affect"—a study in the aesthetic commodification of shoes in which Jameson juxtaposes Vincent van Gogh's *A Pair of Boots* with Andy Warhol's *Diamond Dust Shoes*—with a prognosis of the contradictory aspect of style under late capitalism: style is at once the very logic of late capitalism, and yet late capitalism is signaled by the end of style itself, "in the sense of the unique and the personal, the end of the distinctive individual brush stroke (as symbolized by the emergent primacy of mechanical reproduction)."[6]

The question of style lingers at the margins of (high) modern consciousness as something trivial, feminine, and mundane, of mere symbolic value but lacking real political, social, and economic significance. Postmodernism, however, takes seriously the material effects of symbolic or stylistic power and in so doing opens up the theoretical capacities of fashion and, in particular, the commodity form.

It is in the commodity form that fashion plays a specific role as bearer, producer, or inscribed object of meanings and values—meanings and values that are material, social, and ethical, as well as monetary. Although the commodity is primarily produced and put into circulation to make money, it also produces surplus and residual effects, sometimes unanticipated, sometimes contradictory. Erica Rand's groundbreaking analysis of Barbie is a case in point.[7] Here is an object whose status as a semipornographic icon of white femininity appears unparalleled and largely uncontested in feminist critique, yet in the hands of children—and in the cultural memory of some adults—it is an agent of freedom and fantasy. Do children learn best by being told what they should or should not play with or by being encouraged to exercise their imaginations in learning to play or *(dis)play* the objects the marketplace throws in their path? Learning to play with Barbie is like learning to theorize with fashion. It is my contention that feminist cultural materialist critique has a lot to gain from theorizing with fashion. Theorizing with fashion permits a transvestism of the spirit of the commodity; it allows us to turn it to other purposes, to inhabit its simulated flesh of sensation and uncertainty and see the world as products of our making and values, regardless of how the mainstream marketplace would like to contain and regulate our ways of seeing, knowing, and, of course, dressing!

To emphasize the act of theorizing with cultural objects is to dismantle a complex matrix of divisions among women. Within this matrix exists a set of all too common splits in the representation, for example, of middle-class women as objects or subjects of desire and working-class women or colonized women as objects or subjects of physical and material labor. The divisions are three-dimensional as it were, multi-layered, imbricated by differences of class, "race," imperialism, and bodily representation. Sometimes the lines are drawn between middle-class and laboring or colonized women. Sometimes the lines of difference emerge within middle-class women's bodies, whose sexuality is represented either as a commodity that can be produced, packaged, sold, or traded, or as a sign of power capable of representing and subjecting themselves and other women to acts of desire and desirability. Laboring and colonized women are similarly divided by a physical/symbolic material split. Their bodies are represented not by the vicissitudes of artifice but by the apparent muteness of nature, orality, and traditionalism. The inarticulateness of nature must then be brought into meaning as must the bodies of those women who represent it. To deconstruct hierarchical divisions among women does not create a unified field of women but reconfigures the field of difference in order to see and comprehend its complex and contradictory nature, to see, for example, that the bourgeois female consumer is at times laboring to secure her class and race interests and the laboring or colonized woman is often taking pleasure in securing her difference from those interests. Commodity culture is an arena in which such battles are fought.[8]

"AN IMAGINARY MUSEUM OF A NOW GLOBAL CULTURE"

In his seminal essay "Postmodernism; or, The Cultural Logic of Late Capitalism," Jameson writes about an "imaginary museum of a now global culture" in reference to the use of pastiche as the dominant mode of postmodern representation. Pastiche is constituted by a "random cannibalization of all the styles of the past" and "random stylistic allusion."[9] What Jameson imagined has been realized in the Bata Shoe Museum.

The museum opened with four exhibits: (1) *All about Shoes;* (2) *Inuit Boots: A Woman's Art;* (3) *The Gentle Step: 19th Century Women's Shoes;* and (4) *One, Two, Buckle My Shoe: Illustrations from Contemporary Children's Books about Shoes* (see figure 1).[10]

Several publications complemented the displays and were available at "The Shop," the museum's store. They included *All about Shoes: Footwear through the Ages,* published by the in-house publisher of Bata Limited, and *Our Boots: An Inuit Women's Art,* authored by Jill Oakes, professor in the Department of Native Studies at the University of Manitoba, and Rick Riewe, professor of zoology at the University of Manitoba.[11] Also available was the information booklet *The Gentle Step: The Ladies' Realm of Fashion, 1800 to 1900,* which acts as an explanatory guide to the exhibit. These texts are designed to re-present the shoe objects in the exhibits as well as provide additional information about related shoe artifacts and shoe culture. The books, along with the artifacts on display, are also commodities that are good to theorize with.

The Bata Shoe Museum represents an outstanding postmodern artifact in both its content, where shoes are displayed as much for their artistic as well as cultural value in fashion historiography, and its architectural design—the museum itself is in the shape

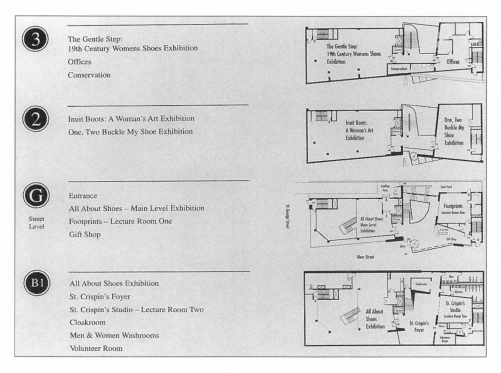

FIGURE I ↗ Courtesy of the Bata Shoe Museum.

FIGURE 2   ↝   Courtesy of the Bata Shoe Museum.

of a shoe box (see figure 2). Specific to the Bata Shoe Museum, however, is the question of the relationship between pedagogy and display, between knowledge and the representation of knowledge.

THE BATA SHOE MUSEUM

The purpose of The Bata Shoe Museum is to contribute to the knowledge and understanding of the role of footwear in the social and cultural life of humankind. It achieves this by acquiring, conserving, researching, interpreting, and exhibiting material evidence related to the history of footwear and shoemaking for the purpose of study, education and enjoyment.

(BSM Display Unit)

RESEARCH

Research plays a key role at the BSM. In addition to sponsoring publications and field studies, the Museum has a growing resource centre which incorporates a library and "hands-on" study facilities. The future promises computer access and CD-ROM capabilities.

(BSM Display Unit)

The Bata Shoe Museum clearly demonstrates the possibilities of thinking with commodity artifacts and, importantly, the relationship between the knowledge such thinking produces and multinational capitalism. Thus my questions include: How do these displays accomplish the task of making and exhibiting such knowledge? What is the relationship between information and the discrete representation of so-called facts or codes of information and an epistemological collective project? My main question concerns the pedagogical impulse that leads me to wonder—if not "to understand"— how the museum makes it possible to theorize with shoes as commodity artifacts, to theorize as a consumer of the museum experience, and to theorize as a feminist cultural critic.

Theorizing with the shoe commodity can only be accomplished in postmodernity because of the kind of rationality that has come to invade its circulation, in this case, as museum artifact. Characterizing this "rationality" must entail an emphasis on *information* and *pedagogical exchange.* On an advertising flyer for membership, which includes a gift of the book *All about Shoes,* the museum declares: "Shoes have been with us for millennia and are intriguing sources of information about human identity. . . . Fascinating information about shoes in history, titillating shoe trivia and wonderful full-color photographs are brought together in this educational and entertaining book—providing hours of enjoyment for the entire family." The museum's pedagogical impulse to provide information and act as an educational institution endows the shoe commodity with new material significance. What is the semiotic value of this new material signification? It is the value of difference.

WORLDING THE DIFFERENCE

I am particularly interested in two intersecting orders of difference—cultural difference and sexual difference—that inform the pedagogical rationality of the individual display arenas as well as the choices involved in the overall organization of the four exhibitions. The arenas of display in the Bata Shoe Museum are constructed along a particular enlightenment—and thoroughly "modern"—fault line: the division between the traditional and the modern. This division is artfully and carefully constructed to encode a series of "worlding" differences (i.e., first world/third world, East/West, classical/modern, Aboriginal/non-Aboriginal) in the production and consumption of shoes. The "worlds" narrativized by the displays tell us a great deal about the contemporary international dynamics of commodity shoe production.

In the signature exhibit, *All about Shoes,* a plurality of historical, social, and cultural codes are woven through the main-floor displays of shoes. The exhibit treads through history as if it were a well-worn path of progress from functional primitivism to the aesthetic maturity of the civilizing process. "The First Step" (see figure 3), which is the introductory display unit of the exhibit, represents an originary story of humankind's physical development, the moment of bipedalism, or the ability to walk upright: "3,700,000 years

FIGURE 3   ↗   Courtesy of the Bata Shoe Museum.

ago a group of bipedal hominids strolled through a field of volcanic ash, dampened by a recent rainfall. The prints [exhibited on the floor below] are thought to be of a young-ster, a male and a smaller male or female, the latter turning to look to its left. These hardened depressions in the earth are our oldest link to upright primates. Through our feet, we have come in closest contact with our history. On the floor below are copies of the earliest footprints dating about 3,700,000 years ago. Discovered by anthropolo-gist Mary Leakey in 1976 at Laetdi, Tanzania" (BSM Display Unit). Inscribed on the surface of the earth, the first markings of man (and possibly a woman), the first signs of feet appear and signal the origin story of shoes. The body of man—and possibly woman—is the first essential figure to this origin story.

Soon the body disappears as shoes take on a life of their own, apparently separate from and supplemental to the biophysical existence of man, and possibly woman. In the central plaque for the next display unit, "The Ancients/Nos Ancêtres," the follow-ing words are on show: "As humankind found social order and organized into tribes, set-tlements evolved. Footwear, first invented as protection from the elements and terrain, became more complex in both manufacture and meaning. Specialized artisans of the craft made footwear for specific rituals, social ranks and occupations. While still pro-tecting, footwear became representative of more more than basic needs" (see figure 4).

In the text *All about Shoes,* we find this additional explanation: "People have been wearing shoes for thousands of years, but the knowledge of who crafted the first shoe or where that creative act took place is lost in time. Still, it is not difficult to deduce why shoes came into being or why we continue to wear them. Nature in part necessi-tated their invention: since nature did not provide the human species with hard hooves, like the horse, or sturdy pads, like the cat, human ingenuity came up with the shoe—a means of protecting tender feet from cold. . . . Over time, shoes transcended purely practical applications and became, as objects of beauty in themselves, essential fash-ion accessories."[12]

The movement from simple tribe to complex society is imbricated by additional movements from the functional to the decorative, from basic needs to passion, desire, and beauty—from primitivism to civilization. These layers of teleological progress lie at the heart of twenty-first-century renditions of nineteenth-century life and, interest-ingly, are simulated by the contrast of the other two exhibits, *The Gentle Step* and *Inuit Boots: A Woman's Art,* a point to which I will return.

The line of progress from functional to commodity status is, thus, "historicized" within the exhibit by the "ancients" of the classical world—from the Ice Age, when "humans dressed in animal skins," to the development of civilization with the Egyptians, the Mesopotamians, the Greeks and Romans, and, in the Western Hemisphere, the Maya.

FIGURE 4   ⌐   Courtesy of the Bata Shoe Museum.

Several plaques tell the historical narrative. The display cases are filled with sandals: "This imposing bronze foot with an intricate Caliga sandal is about 20 centuries old. The statuary is from ancient Rome, where rulers and high-ranking military officials wore sandals such as these."[13]

The museum constructs its historical narrative for shoes through a discursive representation of the classical world and the apparent "universality" of the sandal. In the display area "Shoes and Religion/Chaussures et religion," it is the code of cultural tradition that constitutes this representation of historical knowledge:

ISLAM AND FOOTWEAR

Islam builds on Judeo-Christian beliefs, and is based on the Koran, the teachings and experiences of Mohammed, who was born in Mecca in 570. Islam united the Arab peoples and flourished during the Middle Ages, spreading throughout the Middle and Far East. To show respect and submission to Allah (God), footwear is removed before entering a mosque.

Throughout the Islamic world, this has resulted in styles that can be easily slipped on and off, most commonly resulting in the backless shoe or mule.

(BSM Display Unit)

SHINTOISM AND TRADITION

Followers of Japanese Shintoism honour the *kami* (dieties) and hold a deep respect for tradition. The *kami* are to be remembered and celebrated, and life enjoyed through numerous festivals and rites. Shinto traditions are responsive to natural and calendar events. The change of seasons and New Year are large festival occasions, although many celebrations vary from town to town, as each region has its own schedule of holidays.

(BSM Display Unit)

Shoes are ahistorical objects within this discursive representation of historical knowledge. They are deployed as signs of respected cultural traditions (see figure 5). The force of these seemingly timeless and transcendent cultural traditions provides the shoe concept, if not the contemporary shoe commodity, with a significance it would otherwise not have as mere fashion accessory.

The museum constructs meanings and values for shoes through the agent of historical narrative and the rhetoric of cultural and social codes of difference. Other display titles include "What's Their Line?/ Quoi de plus pratique?" and "Tools of the

FIGURE 5 ⟿ Courtesy of the Bata Shoe Museum.

Trade/Les Outils de l'artisan." In the "What's Their Line?/Quoi de plus pratique?" exhibit, an ascending series of box display cases contains some twenty-five shoes used for a specific purpose or job: specialty shoes such as wooden clogs from nineteenth-century France, used for tree pruning, and tall leather boots with wooden clog bottoms, used by eel fishermen in Quebec; Australian sheep-shearing shoes "from Rupert Murdoch's 'Boonoke' property, Riverina district, New South Wales, 1988"; and socklike *tabi* boots from Japan with soft rubber soles, used to secure workers' footing on tile roofs. It is the idea of working shoes that organizes this display. According to the explanation provided, footwear has at least two practical applications: "to protect and enhance performance" (BSM display unit).

In his discussion of van Gogh's *A Pair of Boots,* Jameson stresses the way van Gogh's painting engages the viewer in an activity of reconstruction, a reconstruction of the world in which the painted shoes existed: "In Van Gogh that content, those initial raw materials, are, I will suggest, to be grasped simply as the whole object world of agricultural misery, of stark rural poverty, and the whole rudimentary human world of back breaking peasant toil, a world reduced to its most brutal and menaced, primitive and marginalized state."[14] The activity of reconstruction creates a space for the viewer replete with sensations, what Jameson calls an "emergent sensorium" which "replicates the specializations and divisions of capitalist life at the same time that it seeks in precisely such fragmentation a desperate Utopian compensation for them."[15] From the raw materials of an everyday working life to the painterly materials of the artist, the shoes signify life, nature, world, and work.

In his comparison of van Gogh's *A Pair of Boots* with Andy Warhol's *Diamond Dust Shoes,* Jameson argues that a "waning of affect" has occurred in the late twentieth century. Warhol's imagery and technologies of representation flatten sensory experience. There is no way for the viewer to complete the speech act, to respond to the image by reconstructing "the larger lived context of the dance hall or the ball, the world of jet-set fashion or glamour magazines."[16] Like Warhol's fetishistic images of a collection of shoes all arranged in an orderly and serial fashion, the "What's Their Line?/Quoi de plus pratique?" display provides no opportunity to reconstruct the workplace in which the shoes were used. More important in both Warhol's image and the Bata Shoe Museum exhibit, the bodies that occupied these shoes have all but disappeared. To be sure, the shoes have outlived their owners, but this display would even seem to dispossess the original workers of such ownership.

What was once an object used to earn a living is now a museum artifact and as such endows the shoes with a uniqueness and special quality that they never exhibited when used for a practical purpose. As the French-language title indicates, the practical dimension of these objects has become fetishized as an aesthetic object in the museum display. The line between the practical and the aesthetic has dissolved; the middle-class viewer is called upon to contemplate the various shoes she owns for different "practical" purposes: special running shoes for tennis and aerobics, for example, special shoes for hiking and walking, shoes for the office, for parties, for summer, for winter. All shoes can be reduced to a practical purpose; and yet, in so doing, the working body recedes from the North American middle-class imaginary. What is left is an interesting pair of shoes that provides information on the history of work in other times and other countries. The current global division of labor separating the consumption and production of shoes goes unperceived.

A GLIMPSE INTO THE PRIVATE WORLD OF COMMODITIES

I am looking through the window of a shoe store in Lebanon. There is a display of Italian leather shoes for men. The prices range from $65 to $85 (U.S. dollars). I point enthusiastically and turn to my partner. "Look, only $85 for those shoes. We saw the same ones in Toronto and they were twice as much!" My partner puts his hands on his hips and smiles. He shifts his weight uncomfortably and lights a cigarette. I am watching him with curiosity. Why, I wonder, isn't he interested in the shoes? "Do you know," he says quietly, "what the average salary of a worker is in Lebanon?" "No," I say, "what is it?" The average worker in Lebanon makes $100 a month. In fact, my partner's niece works for a textile manufacturer. She works six days a week and more than forty hours per week. She is twenty years old and has undiagnosed pains in her legs. She is an artist and dreams of designing haute couture fashions. She makes $100 a month. I try to imagine looking at a pair of shoes in the Eaton's Centre in Toronto that are priced at 85 percent of my monthly salary as an academic. Could anything be more surreal and futile? I spend the afternoon reading Rousseau's *Discours sur l'origine et les fondements de l'inégalité parmi les hommes* and contemplating the nature of consumer resentment among an eighteenth-century emerging European bourgeoisie.

To return to the thread of cultural difference: the notion of cultural tradition is also, of course, present in the exhibit *Inuit Boots: A Woman's Art,* although this mode of cultural representation is contained within a different civilizational rhetoric. Whereas the cultural tradition of the ancients establishes the distant roots of European civilization as always already "civilized" (it is, perhaps, the French version—"Nos Ancêtres"—that more explicitly connotes the identification with a shared cultural heritage), the Inuit boot exhibit establishes the difference between primitivism and civilization, between nature and culture.

When you enter the exhibit, you enter a space of nature, a diorama of a full-size caribou, a kayak, and a dogsled. Stretched skins are poised against the wall of what looks like a building or someone's domestic dwelling, an internal space which houses eight display areas of different Inuit boots (see figure 6). The regions represented include: Iglulik, Baffinland, Ungava, Labrador, Caribou, Netsilik, Copper, and Mackenzie Delta Inuvialuit. The different styles of boots are arranged along with display units that exhibit the name of the region in English and in Inuktitut syllabics, a photograph of a woman, and a quote in English that is designed to look like a prose poem (see figures 7, 8, and 9). Other modes of picto-hieroglyphic display include a tapestry, sewing patterns, maps, and photographs of women sewing (see figure 10).[17]

The difference that lies between this exhibit and the exhibit of nineteenth-century bourgeois and largely female commodity culture that follows it on the third floor incorporates a culture/artifice opposition. In the gap between Inuit women's production and bourgeois women's consumption of shoes exists the competing historical fetishisms of desire and labor and the cultural fetishism of "traditionalism." The place "cultural difference" occupies, then, shifts according to the relations between or among the exhibits: bourgeois female commodity culture of the nineteenth century depended on the imperial exchange of raw materials and goods from the colonies; the Inuit boot making by women signals a romantic conception of Canada's colonial

FIGURE 6   ↶   Courtesy of the Bata Shoe Museum.

FIGURE 7 ～ Courtesy of the Bata Shoe Museum.

FIGURE 8 ～ Courtesy of the Bata Shoe Museum.

FIGURE 9 ᒧ Courtesy of the Bata Shoe Museum.

FIGURE 10 ᒧ Courtesy of the Bata Shoe Museum.

history. Today Bata shoe stores, located in the so-called third world, service the transnational needs of an indigenous bourgeoisie; their factories produce commodities for a global bourgeoisie.

With the end(s) of fashion comes the birth of style, an accumulation of "things" both textual and textile. The words on the page, the objects in the museum, are part of a new vocabulary and syntax of codes and signs that bespeak the postliteracy of global cultural exchange. But more than isolated, nonrelational, fixed elements, these codes and signifiers move with a certain fluidity; they are part of a transliteracy movement, where the apparently fetishized "differences" of culture, gender, race, and class cross over geopolitical and body/self boundaries, boundaries that were once exclusively subject to the hegemonic demands of bourgeois culture. In this exchange space of difference, a series of transactions take place, and the "worlds" divided by religious or cultural difference here or labor differences there become sites of other multiple differences unperceived by the makeup and design of transnational capital. Herein lies the dialectical potential of this museum. Its fragments of information, bits and pieces of knowledge, here and there, then and now, demand that we make connections between the objects and ourselves. How we do that as cultural consumers will vary enormously, depending on our experience and knowledge of commodity culture.

TO PHILOSOPHIZE WITH SHOES: AN ACCESSORY AFTER THE FACT

The museum brilliantly theorizes the historical forces and figures of postenlightenment commodity culture. I offer three examples taken from the museum's displays of shoe knowledge and artifact.

1. In the nineteenth century bourgeois women acquired "knowledge" through fashion. The pamphlet produced for *The Gentle Step: The Ladies' Realm of Fashion, 1800 to 1900* exhibit tells us that "The Gentle Step explores the influence of ladies' journals on fashionable 19th century women's footwear. . . . The American, French and Industrial revolutions dramatically restructured social order, setting the scene for the 19th century. A newly monied 'middle' class emerged, setting the standards of taste and decorum for all of society. Being stylish was a status symbol for women, who followed the latest modes through the information provided in fashion periodicals."[18]

Shoes do not contain nor disseminate knowledge, but their presence as commodities is a call to know about history, trade economies, and hybrid cultural formations resulting from the effects of colonization:

A WALK IN THE WILD

Naturalism was a movement which emerged from the writings of Jean
Jacques Rousseau in the mid-18th century and became a dominant force in
the early 19th century, manifesting itself in art, literature, artificially wild
"English" gardens and plenty of walks outdoors. English ladies were the first
to take to country promenades as the gentry resided in the country most of
the year. To protect stockings and dresses from brambles and mud spatters,
"spatterdashes" or "spats," as they are known today, were adapted from men's
18th century military dress.

A TASTE FOR THE EXOTIC

As European boundaries expanded through trade and colonialism, goods from
all over the world flooded the western market and a taste for the exotic
ensued. Embroidery, beading and other forms of decorative work were
adapted from foreign styles and incorporated into fashionable wares. . . . The
Russian and Ottoman empires came into conflict over control of the Crimean
Peninsula in 1854. Western Europe supported the Ottoman Turks bringing
numbers of soldiers into the Middle East not seen since the Crusades.
Mementos brought home by soldiers revived a taste for the Turkish and
Persian arts. One of the more popular imports were "khilim" tapestries. . . .
British India provided many textiles for the West's burgeoning taste for the
exotic. Slipper and shoe uppers were embroidered in India for export to
Europe, where they were made into the lastest styles of footwear.

NEW FRONTIERS

Europe's colonial expansion in the 18th and 19th centuries brought colonists
into contact with new peoples. This interaction often resulted in a marriage of
Native and European clothing styles, materials and decorative techniques. In
Canada, moccasins made by Native women were sold to colonists who often
added European-type leather soles for the express purpose of wearing the
moccasins outdoors, sometimes as galoshes over their own shoes. European
materials were supplied to Natives through missions and on reserves. In turn,
many of these materials were fashioned, with Native skill, into items for the
settler trade. With indigenous workmanship, floral motifs were often inspired
by European tastes.[19]

2. In the section "Status Symbols/ Symbole social" in the *All about Shoes* exhibit,
the life of Margaret Townsend is immortalized by her shoes:

One woman's life was remembered through the shoes she kept. Margaret
Townsend was born in about 1840 in New York City. The daughter of
socialites, she attended Mrs. O'Kills Female Boarding School, attended the
ball given in honour of the Prince of Wales's visit to New York in 1861, and
married Elias Plum in 1863. On her tenth wedding anniversary she was

presented with a pair of tin shoes to commemorate the occasion. All these events are represented by the shoes and boots she kept.

(BSM Display Unit)

In the display case we find Margaret Townsend's school certificate for excellence in conduct and recitation, her graduation certificate, an invitation to an alumni Christmas party on Thursday, December 23, 1858, and the imported French silk shoes she wore to the party; imported French silk shoes worn by Margaret to the ball given in honor of the visit of the Prince of Wales to New York City in 1861; more silk shoes, Turkish Khilim woven uppers made into fashionable shoes, probably made in the United States, and the tin shoes.

3. Shoes are an accessory to speech and presence. They are the bourgeois woman's passion, beyond need and beyond nature. They are a gesture, a sign, a way of signaling a bourgeois, philanthropic woman.

> Sonja Bata, Chairman of The Bata Shoe Museum, is the person whose vision, knowledge and drive have resulted in the first class assemblage of footwear which comprises the Museum collection. . . Over the years she became more and more fascinated by shoes, their history and the reasons why specific shapes and decorative treatments had developed in different cultures. During her travels, she realized that some traditional forms were being replaced with western shoes, reflecting changing lifestyles, to some extent influenced by the spreading Bata factories serving local markets. A combined interest in design and shoes led to a shoe collection, with examples from across the globe. Today that collection has grown to include almost 10,000 artifacts and Sonja Bata continues to hold an active position in all aspects of Museum operations. A strong belief that in a democratic country citizens should actively contribute their talents to community needs is reflected in Mrs. Bata's many philanthropic activities.[20]

The Bata Shoe Museum participates in a mode of writing, a graphic mode of writing in the style of the "supplement." Jacques Derrida fashions the supplement as follows: "The supplement supplements. It adds only to replace. It intervenes or insinuates itself *in-the-place-of*; if it fills, it is as if one fills a void. If it represents and makes an image, it is by the anterior default of a presence. Compensatory [*suppléant*] and vicarious, the supplement is an adjunct, a subaltern instance which *takes-(the)-place* [*tient-lieu*]. As substitute, it is not simply added to the positivity of a presence, it produces no relief, its place is assigned in the structure by the mark of an emptiness. Somewhere, something can be filled *up of itself,* can accomplish itself, only by allowing itself to be filled through sign and proxy. The sign is always the supplement of the thing itself."[21] The supplement teaches us about the value of the accessory. The language of explanation, of information and knowledge, in the exhibits is an accessory to the shoe displays—and the shoe displays are themselves accessories to nature. To accessorize is to dissimulate a signature, an identity, a style. Like the supplement, it is an addition, a piece of the nonessential and superfluous, something extra, the other, the "notself." The language that tries to fix the meaning of the shoes, to give them meaning, is an accessory before the fact and after the fact. The fact, the shoe, stays put and lets its accomplice do its work for it.

Shoes exhibit a kind of mute eloquence. They do not embody words but signify like a hieroglyphic *graphie,* which, writes Derrida, "is already allegorical." Furthermore, he writes, "the gesture which speaks before words [*dit la parole avant les mots*] and which 'argues with the eyes,' is the moment of savage writing."[22] This savage writing is, of course, the writing of "savages," a "primitivism" that is accessorized in the *Inuit Boots* exhibit by the symbolic values ascribed to the animal skin boots. It is also the writing that belongs to a postliterate language characteristic under late and global capitalism with the commodity and its transnational flow. Throughout the twentieth century, this savage writing, this writing that was simply and always an externality, a series of objects displayed in a museum of shoes, this was the language of the feminine, the language of "woman" as figure of desire and as consumer of fetishes. Here the figures of "woman" and "primitive" are cojoined as the dominant representatives in the nineteenth century of commodity and sexual fetishism. The twenty-first century is consumed by its desire to represent the nineteenth century through these two important figures; these accessories that adorn history and its otherness—hence the rise of femininity, the female consumer, and "woman" as object of material desire, and the rise of nativism, the reinvention of so-called traditional gatherer-hunter cultures.

Nature and Culture stand marked by a new primitivism, a reinvented Savage tattooed on the heart of the urban center, and linked to that nonessential figure of artifice, the Dissimulatress, who signifies the undoing of "nature." Both figures thrive in the Bata Shoe Museum's commodity culture, floating between that Gentle Step that treads softly in Rousseau's footsteps and the Inuit animal skin boots crafted in the mouths and orality of Inuit women.

The signature image for the *Inuit Boots* exhibit depicts a woman, Rachel Uyarasuak, chewing a piece of fur (see figure 11; see also images of women chewing fur in figures 7 and 9). A woman with fur in her mouth. The image gestures toward a series of connotations: nature, animal, orality. In this oral picto-hieroglyphic, the Inuit woman is mute, her mouth busy with the business of making an animal skin boot. Her mouth speaks through the object. The fur in her mouth is an accessory, a substitute for voice. It becomes an acoustic sign that takes the place of her voice. She is nature, and nature speaks for her. The language on display, the written work, accessorizes the image,

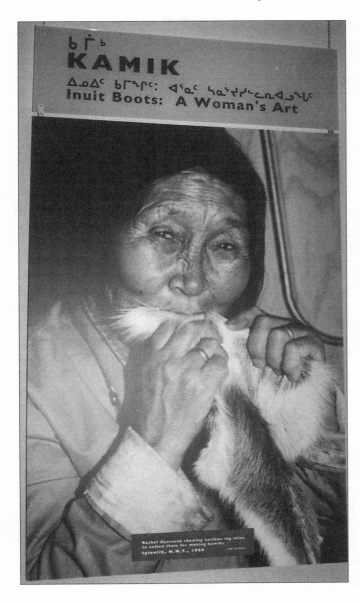

FIGURE II
Jill Oakes, *Iglulik* (1986).

adorns it, frames it. The image, like nature, is mute. It is made to speak the language of knowledge, information, explanation. The Bata Shoe Museum conquers the inarticulateness of nature through this image of a woman it does not know how to address, to speak to; rather, it speaks a functional discourse to the object, and the object, like all good fetishes, speaks back about nature, about woman, about primitivism.

The signs that direct the museum consumer through the exhibit duly supplement other signs such as the syllabics. Words that appear in roman orthography appear to have no exhibition value, for they constitute "real" language. The syllabics, on the other hand, have display value and create for the non-Inuktitut reader a graphic otherness that once again adorns the images of Inuit women making animal skin boots. The symbolic values attributed to the boots do not make meaning like language, but to the extent that the syllabics signify that "meaning" is present, it is to convince the cultural consumer that the meaningless materiality of the body and nature can have significance for colonial culture.

Language as knowledge fulfills an apparent need to extend colonial culture to all peoples and all natures. Language as accessory fulfills a desire to extend beyond nature and thrive in the domain of artifice, which is culture, which is civilization. The words, the syllabics, ensure meaning can be made for Inuit boot making, and they apparently record that "meaning" for posterity. Nature has meaning inscribed on the force of its existence. This making of meaning becomes a source of knowledge, a mode of transmission of information and poetic fragments of explanation. Style constitutes a breakdown into sentence fragments, graphics, words, objects—in short, pieces of the present disguised as an archaeological past.

Inuit woman's speech constitutes a "natural language," a language of need, of functionality and practicality. Bourgeois woman's speech, however, is an acquired one or an accumulated language, a language of desire (the desire for commodities), and a language of passion, jealousy, and possessiveness (to have what another has). The one represents society or civilization, the other its supplement, an accessory to the naked state of nature, a state that is close to the life of animals and animal language:

> Animal language—and animality in general—represents here [i.e., in Rousseau's *Essay on the Origins of Language*] the still living myth of fixity, of symbolic incapacity, of nonsupplementarity. If we consider the *concept* of animality not in its content of understanding or misunderstanding but in its specific *function,* we shall see that it must locate a moment of *life* which knows nothing of symbol, substitution, lack and supplementary addition, etc.—everything, in fact, whose appearance and play I wish to describe here. A life that has not yet broached the play of supplementarity and which at the same time has not yet let itself be violated by it: a life without difference and without articulation.[23]

Inuit woman's culture, then, represents a life without difference, a life of tradition that is close to nature and therefore without articulation, without language, only an orality that makes boots. The exhibit must establish the symbolic values ascribed to the boots, the tapestry, the sewing patterns, and other picto-hieroglyphics with its displays of written language, knowledge, information, and explanation.

The organization of the exhibits constitutes a well-planned resolution to the profoundly modernist dilemma of a breakdown in "universals"—universals that can no longer hold in a colonial age of immense spatial distance and social or cultural difference. The opposition of European bourgeois women and Inuit women is constructed around the apparent unity of the feminine love of finery that bonds all women. The difference between bourgeois women and Inuit women, however, distinguishes desire from need, culture from nature, and civilization from primitivism.

In my view, postmodernism is about coming to terms with the nineteenth century, its imperial project, its collective epistemological project to dominate the world through reason and enlightened knowledge. In a postmodern age we no longer live in a world of different cultures, as people did in the nineteenth century, but in a culture of commodities. What the Bata Shoe Museum teaches us is knowledge about commodity culture and its capacity to resolve social contradictions and "differences" into the mute eloquence of an object, a shoe. Ironically, it is this very capacity of the commodity to resolve differences that makes theorizing with shoes a possibility.

NOTES

Thank you to the Bata Shoe Museum for permission to reproduce the images in this essay and a special thanks to Suzanna Petti for her generous help in tracking down the images and providing important information regarding subsequent exhibits at the museum. I am also grateful to Shari Benstock and Suzanne Ferriss for their insightful editorial comments.

1. John Bell, *Socialist Worker*, May 17, 1995.

2. Fredric Jameson, *Postmodernism; or, The Cultural Logic of Late Capitalism* (Durham: Duke University Press, 1991), 4–5.

3. Haraway explains that "maintaining boundaries can no longer be rendered invisible, but boundary-maintaining is hardly proscribed. Far from it. Boundary maintenance, as well as splicing and joining, requires work, including, but not limited to, the semiotic, logical, and rhetorical work of convincing people who are both like and different from oneself; such labor is practice and culture in action." See Donna J. Haraway, *Modest_Witness@Second_Millennium. FemaleMan©_Meets_ OncoMouse* (New York: Routledge, 1997), 67.

4. Jameson, *Postmodernism*, 3.

5. See ibid., 1.

6. Ibid., 2, 15.

7. See Erica Rand, *Barbie's Queer Accessories* (Durham: Duke University Press, 1996).

8. For more on this subject, see an analysis of Inuit fur fashions and the figure of the bourgeois female consumer of fur in my *Cultural Politics of Fur* (Ithaca: Cornell University Press, 1997).

9. Jameson, *Postmodernism*, 18.

10. My discussion of the museum focuses exclusively on these opening exhibits. Since the opening of the museum, *All about Shoes* has remained on a semipermanent basis with minor changes. Other exhibits to follow included: *Shoe Dreams: Designs by Andrea Pfister* (May 1996–spring 1997) and *Tradition and Innovation* (June 1996–June 1997); *Rock and Sole (Raptors)* (February 1997–November 1997), *Loose Tongues and Lost Soles: Shoes in Cartoon and Caricature* (spring 1997–November 1997), and *Footwear Fantasia: Shoe Sculptures by Garry Greenwood* (April 1997–November 1997); *The Taming of the Shoe: From Attic to Exhibition* (November 1997–October 1998), and *Spirit of Siberia* (June 1997–June 1998); *Dance!* (March 1997–February 1999), *Little Feats: A Celebration*

of Children's Shoes (October 1998–May 1999), and *Footsteps on the Sacred Earth* (July 1998–June 1999); *Paduka: Feet and Footwear in the Indian Tradition* (July 1999–June 2000), *Japanese Footgear: Walking the Path of Innovation* (February 1999–January 2000), and *Herbert and Beth Levine: An American Pair* (June 1999–December 1999).

11. See *All about Shoes: Footwear through the Ages* (Toronto: Bata, 1994) and Jill Oakes and Rick Riewe, *Our Boots: An Inuit Women's Art* (Vancouver/Toronto: Douglas and McIntyre, 1995). *Our Boots* was published in association with the Bata Shoe Museum Foundation.

12. *All about Shoes,* 4.

13. Ibid., 6.

14. Jameson, *Postmodernism,* 7.

15. Ibid.

16. Ibid., 8–9.

17. The translation of the tapestry reads: "Part 1: (in the middle, at the right) Father and son: 'Come little son, we'll take the puppy and go hunting.' Father hauls out a square flipper seat; the boy and his dog are excited about the catch: 'Son, help me pull! Now we'll have plenty to eat.' 'Oh father, my dog and I will be happy to eat!' Part 2: (top centre) Mother scrapes the skin as daughter tends her baby brother. Mother sews the sealskin kamiks outside the tent because it is too dark inside. The kamiks are finished and the woman is very happy."

18. *The Gentle Step,* 1.

19. Ibid., 4, 5.

20. See "The Founder," *Footnotes: The Quarterly Newsletter of the Bata Shoe Museum* 1, 1 (summer 1995): 3.

21. Jacques Derrida, *Of Grammatology,* trans. Gayatri Chakravorty Spivak (Baltimore: Johns Hopkins University Press, 1974), 145.

22. Ibid., 237.

23. Ibid., 242.

The Shoe in Art, the Shoe as Art

JANICE WEST

To be carried by shoes, winged by them. To wear dreams on one's feet is to begin
to give reality to one's dreams.
—*Roger Vivier, quoted in Linda O'Keefe,* Shoes

Until the twentieth century, shoes were important in art only as part of costume
or as props in erotica. In this century, however, the shoe has become an iconic
subject in paintings, sculpture, and art installations. This does not mean that the shoe
no longer has a place in erotica—far from it. As shoes have become more affordable and
available to more people, so the erotic potential of the shoe has increased. But what is
new is that we also see the shoe as a fascinating object (or pair of fascinating objects)
in its own right. If we consider shoes in the work of such artists as Elsa Schiaparelli,
Meret Oppenheim, Andy Warhol, Jim Dine, and Lisa Milroy, we see how ideas about
fashion, the self, art, and the modern are concentrated in the shoe. What to some may
be no more than a necessary item has become, in the work of artists and shoe designers, a telling expression of modernity.

Shoes have figured in erotica since the Renaissance. The wearing or shedding of
certain kinds of footwear by women has been a source of titillation from the courtesans
of fifteenth-century Venice wobbling on their nine-inch (or higher) chopines, to the little

satin high-heeled mules falling from the feet of Boucher's or Fragonard's young women as they play on swings or sprawl on chaise longues.

Another theme of the erotic shoe in paintings is not unsteadiness or shoes falling from the feet, but shoes worn with very little else, shoes worn, therefore, to emphasize nakedness, as in Edouard Manet's *Olympia* (1863), or to emphasize the eroticism of underwear, as in his *Nana* (1877). In the latter the model wears pale blue embroidered stockings which match her blue corset; her only other garments are short white petticoats and black high-heeled shoes. The sexual frisson is created by the combination of underwear and outerwear.

Sexual power is articulated in a rather different manner in the many equestrian and military paintings and statues that feature soldiers, hunters, or simply men of fashion whose boots were cherished and their high gloss maintained at some expense. Beau Brummel, the ultimate arbiter of fashion for men in late Georgian England, had his boots cleaned, it is said, with a special mixture that included honey and champagne.[1]

The notion of footwear as a class of objects that deserves to be viewed as a subject in its own right seems to have occurred first to Vincent van Gogh, who painted a pair of laced boots (*A Pair of Boots,* 1886) that are battered, worn, and unpolished (figure 1). They are one of four pairs of peddler's boots that van Gogh bought at a flea market in Paris and wore until they were so broken down that they provided him with an interesting subject, representing the painter's task in modern life. The paintings by van Gogh of his boots have a narrative quality which makes them fascinating to us, and they are the precursors of the boots and shoes used by artists from the surrealists to the present.

ELSA SCHIAPARELLI AND MERET OPPENHEIM

Surrealism's relationship with the body—particularly the female body—and the unconscious meant that the shoe was the perfect object of fantasy. In 1937 Elsa Schiaparelli and Salvador Dali designed a shoe hat: a hat in the shape of a high-heeled pump with a red sole based on a shoe made for Schiaparelli by Andre Perugia. The shoe hat was part of an ensemble featuring a tailored black suit that emphasized the association between clothes and sexuality: pink, patent-leather lips appliquéd around the jacket pockets so that their openings suggested mouths effected a shocking displacement of body parts.[2]

In 1938 Schiaparelli and Perugia compounded the joke by creating boots decorated with long, thick, black monkey hair, which make the feet look as though they are wearing wigs.[3] As Valerie Steele points out, Schiaparelli considered herself an artist and

FIGURE 1   ↵   Vincent Van Gogh, *A Pair of Boots* (1886).
The Baltimore Museum of Art. The Cone Collection, formed by Dr. Claribel Cone and Miss Etta Cone of Baltimore, Maryland. BMA 1950.302

regarded fashion as art when it was concerned with the preoccupations of art, as indeed it was in her version of surrealism.[4]

In 1936 Meret Oppenheim created her sculpture titled *Ma Gouvernante, My Nurse, Mein Kindermadchen*. It consists of a pair of women's white, high-heeled kid leather shoes tied together and presented upside down on an oval meat serving dish, the heels crowned with the sort of paper frills used to decorate lamb cutlets. Marina Warner writes:

> Oppenheim is playing knowingly on this metonymy, substituting shoes for carnal knowledge. She was recognizing, with a certain mordancy, that the matched footwear leads to the bride's true recognition and thence to her wedding. . . . In *Ma Gouvernante* Oppenheim, through the symbolism of a pair of shoes, proposed an acerbic gloss on the preconditions a fairytale bride has to fulfill; she began to reverse the terms of value, to reject the groomed beauty (the golden blonde) for the dishevelled beasts she recognized and confirmed inside herself.[5]

The shoes Meret Oppenheim chose "became art" when they were used by an artist. But when they were simply being worn by their owner, Marie-Berthe Aurenche, the wife of Max Ernst, they were not art: "To some extent, then, clothing becomes an art form when exhibited *as art*. The contexts in which clothing is exhibited—on a body, on a mannequin, displayed in a case, or suspended from a ceiling like a modern art installation dictate different reactions and responses."[6] Whether shoes are the subjects of art, are presented as art by an artist, or are worn as created by a shoemaker, they maintain their status as exciting and challenging objects because of the specific relationship they have with the body and the self.

A N D Y   W A R H O L

[Andy Warhol is] the Leonardo da Vinci of the shoe trade.
—*David Bourdon, "Andy Warhol's 'Exhibition,'"* Art News *(October 1969)*

Although it is well known that Andy Warhol drew shoes in the early part of his career dedicated to advertising and commercial art, it is less widely known that his *first* commission was to draw shoes for *Glamour* magazine in 1949. This led to his distinctive work for the shoe manufacturer I. Miller in the 1950s. John Coplans recalls that:

> nobody had ever drawn shoes the way Andy did. He somehow gave each shoe a temperament of its own, a sort of sly, Toulouse-Lautrec kind of sophistication, but the shape and the style came through accurately and the buckle was always in the right place. The kids in the apartment [which Andy shared in New York] noticed that the vamps on Andy's shoe drawings kept getting longer and longer but I. Miller didn't mind. I. Miller loved them.[7]

Claire McCardell, one of the most important American fashion designers, designed for I. Miller during this period, and we can see the kind of shoes she designed in Warhol's work. Her shoes in the 1950s were high-heeled (she called them "spindly") and fragile, and she recommended that a woman choose her shoes to please her husband or lover.[8] This is a vision of footwear buying that reflects the back-to-the-home agenda of post–World War II reconstruction (exemplified in Doris Day movies) and one which contrasts strongly with McCardell's radical designs of the 1940s, such as a flat ballet-type shoe created jointly with Capezio expressly to provide women with elegant and comfortable shoes.[9]

Andy Warhol enjoyed drawing shoes and developed his "blotted line" technique for this work. Use of tracing paper and ink allowed him not only to repeat the basic image but also to develop endless variations on a theme—a working method which prefigures his better-known silk-screen pictures of the 1960s. Shoes became for a time not only his livelihood but a passion. In 1955 he published a portfolio of seventeen shoe drawings accompanied by text by Ralph Pomeroy. The drawings were of flat and brightly colored women's shoes in cerise, turquoise, shocking pink, pale green, pale blue, and orange, accompanied by aphorisms and quotations reworded so as to place shoes at the center of Western culture. The portfolio was titled *A la Recherche du shoe perdue* and included such words of wisdom as "See a shoe and pick it up and all day you'll have good luck." The text was written out by Mrs. Warhola, and indeed her decorative script enhances much of her son's graphics of this period.

Warhol started making three-dimensional shoe sculptures at about this time. He attached wooden heels to the lasts used for shaping women's shoes and decorated them in a similar fashion to his drawings using gold and silver leaf and painting motifs in the manner of the blotted line technique employed in his two-dimensional work.[10] These sculptures led to the exhibition *The Golden Slipper Show or Shoe Show in America* at the Bodley Gallery in New York in late 1956. An article titled "Crazy Golden Slippers," which appeared in *Life* magazine in January 1957, included illustrations of the shoe sculptures. There were high-heeled and long-vamped women's shoes and rather eighteenth-century louis-heeled men's riding boots styled fantastically with flowers spilling from them. The shoes are shown in profile without any reference to the body. Indeed, bodies seem irrelevant to Warhol's purpose, and shoes are never shown in pairs; to have done so would have led the viewer to consider the part of the body that shoes are designed to protect, enhance, and delineate: the foot. Warhol's shoes were always shoes of fantasy.

The early 1950s was the ideal time for the development of fantasy shoes. The exuberance and luxury of the period were a reaction against the austerity of the Second World War, and shoemaking, like car design or electronics, had its share of important technological and material advances. An interesting example of this is the development of the stiletto shoe. "Stiletto" was the term first used in 1953 for thin, high heels reinforced with steel.[11] It was taken to creative extremes by Roger Vivier, who worked for the couture house of Christian Dior from 1953 to 1963 and even designed some shoes for I. Miller in the 1950s.

Vivier invented the *aiguille* and the *choc* heels. The *aiguille* or needle heel became the model for the standard stiletto heel, the most popular women's shoe of the 1950s, but the *choc* or talon—on which the wearer balanced on a fine heel that curved precariously forward under the instep—while not as popular as the stiletto, was a masterpiece of shoe profiling. Vivier also played with the design of the toe box and the vamp, creating elongated tongues, square-toed shoes, and sharply pointed needle toes.[12] Not content merely with developing the structural possibilities of the court shoe, he worked with the Parisian embroiderers Rebe and Lesage to make shoes that were as decorative as possible. Some of his shoes drip with crystal and pearls; others are made of jewel-colored silks and velvets, feathers, and rare skins. Vivier was part of a tradition in which shoemaking is the creation of *objets de luxe*—and a fitting counterpart to Andy Warhol and his golden shoes. Indeed, a photograph of Roger Vivier sitting in a garden at the time of his 1987-88 Paris retrospective surrounded by examples of dozens of his shoes looks like a Warhol shoe picture *en pleine aire*.[13]

Roger Vivier's shoes were worn by celebrities and, therefore, gained public interest and notoriety through the charisma of such shoe enthusiasts as Marlene Dietrich and Catherine Deneuve, for whom the shoes were part of the construction of their dazzling star personae. The cult of celebrity, fueled by film and television in the 1950s, was an added inspiration to Warhol.

In 1956–57 Warhol collaged and drew a series of celebrity fantasy shoes for people he admired, such as Mae West, James Dean, Zsa Zsa Gabor, Julie Andrews, and Elvis Presley. These were published in the society pages of the *New York Times,* and the originals were for sale in a New York shop/gallery called Serendipity. His attitude toward his commercial shoe drawing was such that it took it out of the realm of the merely imitative and, like his use of the blotted line technique, prefigured the paradoxical blend of coolness and passion of his later work. Warhol moved away from commercial art in the early 1960s but continued to produce shoe pictures sporadically (e.g., the diamond dust pictures of 1980—figure 2); his interest in the subject waned but never disappeared.

In 1969–70, for instance, he worked on a project called *Raid the Icebox with Andy Warhol at* the Rhode Island School of Design. For this he chose items from the school's collection and decided how they should be arranged in the gallery. His choices and the way he arranged the work were controversial: some paintings were simply stacked together, as they had been while in storage, but the most startling for the staff was his attitude toward the shoes in the collection:

> He approached a large wooden cabinet and opened all five doors to reveal the museum's impressive shoe collection—an orderly arrangement of hundreds of pairs of shoes of all sorts: ballet shoes, boots, men's dress shoes, children's shoes, sabots, ladies dress shoes, most of them dating from the mid–nineteenth century to the 1950s. Warhol appeared mesmerized. . . . Warhol wanted the whole shoe collection. Did he mean the cabinet as well? Oh yes, just like that. But what about the doors? Would he allow people to open and close them? "Spectator participation," Warhol murmured.[14]

The museum staff were even more surprised when he insisted on having each pair of shoes fully cataloged, giving them the kind of provenance and importance that the museum—despite the name of the school—usually reserved for paintings and other fine art, rather than mass-produced objects.[15]

FIGURE 2   ↝   Andy Warhol, *Diamond Dust Shoes* (1980).
Copyright © 2000 Andy Warhol Foundation for the Visual Arts/ARS, New York

By using or choosing to display the collection in the gallery as closely as possible to the way in which it was stored—hidden from public view—Warhol shed particular light on the nature of collecting as well as on the nature of this particular collection. As Susan Stewart writes:

> the collection offers example rather than sample, metaphor rather than metonymy. The collection does not displace attention to the past; rather, the past is at the service of the collection, for whereas the souvenir lends authenticity to the past, the past lends authenticity to the collection. The collection seeks a form of self-enclosure which is possible because of its ahistoricism. The collection replaces history with *classification,* with order beyond the realm of temporality. In the collection, time is not something to be restored to an origin; rather, all time is made simultaneous or synchronous within the collection's world.[16]

This is the case not only within the collection's world but within the collector's world. Part of the fascination of collecting must surely be the ownership of so many similar objects at once; think of the serried ranks of Imelda Marcos's shoes. Whether she wore them, or kept them to gloat over, or used them as props in the myth that was her life in the Philippines, the possession of all those shoes at one time (we all wear and wear out many pairs of shoes in a lifetime) gave her collection character beyond mere consumption. As Linda O'Keeffe says, "The charismatic qualities of shoes have more to do with possession than use."[17] Professional curators can forget the simple fact that the collection is so much greater than the sum of its parts.

In *Raid the Icebox with Andy Warhol*, the artist worked with his customary obsession to include the eclectic, the current, the material, and the duplicated. Yet it seems that prior to the exhibition the staff had little idea of the work and preoccupations of the artist whom they had invited. The curator of the costume collection protested at the notion of displaying the entire shoe collection, telling him that it was unnecessary to show all the collection because some of it was duplicated. Warhol said nothing but simply raised his eyebrows and blinked at her.[18]

David Bourdon is informative about Warhol's personal choice of footwear: Warhol wore sneakers, but this did not always ensure comfort. He had an ingrown toenail on his left foot during the preparatory work on the *Icebox* project, and Bourdon tells us: "For relief he had cut open the tip of his left shoe and his big toe poking through the hole was a brilliant chartreuse, that being the color of the tights he was wearing under his brown suede pants."[19]

JIM DINE

When I got to that point, past the tie and I got to the suspender or the shoe, I think I was like on a roll of association. I would just say "shoe," and I made *Shoe* (1961). Now the reason I made that kind of shoe, that brown-and-white shoe, was because in those years a lot of us were talking about Art Deco in the 30s and talking about Fred Astaire and talking about haberdashery. I was trying to reconstruct a history for myself of whence I came from. . . . A personal mythology that I tried to make for myself, so that I am in this world, so that I am not of ether, I am not of vapor. I have two feet on the ground. I am trying to say it's me."
—Jim Dine, Jim Dine

Jim Dine's art is concerned with objects. His choice of objects is eclectic yet profound—the items of material culture that we choose and use everyday, items that we use to express ourselves and delineate our place in the world. In such works as the collage *Shoes Walking on My Brain* (1954), he incorporates real shoes into the piece that stick out with a real three-dimensional presence. They are not symbolic or metaphorical but are the artist's, albeit used by him in a specific artistic context. The shoes are battered brown loafers with the insoles hanging out and are shown as though shrugged off, on a ground of pink cloth with silver lame threads running through it. The shoes are at the bottom of the piece, while at the top a pair of brown painted eyes peer from under a band of red paint and an old red-and-white checked shirt. These rags and the shoes give poignancy to the image. They are so well worn, so impressed with the artist's body, that they become an extension of the subject rather than mere object. It is notoriously hard to wear secondhand shoes because the feet of the original wearer have so formed the shoes through use that they become a second skin for their first owner and instruments of torture for anyone else.[20]

Germano Celanti writes of Dine's work: "The object remnant replaces the artist's body, even while conveying its subjectivity. . . . the choice of thing as replica of the self forming a psychological 'twin' represents a doubling that makes transparent the artist's desire to pass from first-personhood to the otherness of his own being-in-time, a transition from the ego to its shadow."[21]

The objects that Dine returns to most often are clothes, and in this work he explores the preoccupations of fashion, identity, and of art. As John Harvey says: "Dress exists in a realm between flags and art. As art, dress is also performance art, for playing both safe and dangerous games. The clothed person is the persona we perform."[22]

The two-tone spectator shoe used in the painting *Shoe* harks back to the mid-1930s, when Dine was born into a first-generation Jewish-American family. This kind of men's decorative shoe dates from the late nineteenth century but became popular in the 1920s and 1930s. The contrasting colors and elegant shape echo the design of other products of the time such as radios and automobiles.[23] For working- and lower-middle-class men in the United States and Europe, the wearing of shoes instead of boots was an innovation and a mark of social and financial as well as sartorial progress. These white-and-brown shoes told the world that the wearer either enjoyed the luxury of not engaging in manual work, or, if he was a manual worker, he at least had the luxury of leisure in which to parade in these shoes. Modern design and mass production made these social changes and opportunities for conspicuous consumption through leisure possible in the 1930s.

Spectator shoes (also known as correspondent shoes) contrast with the battered and work-soiled loafers of *Shoes Walking on My Brain*. Yet in both these works, Dine is the artist of modern life, the flaneur, the man who displays and observes, creating and recording the spectacle of modernity. He knows how to dress appropriately, and clothing of all kinds is important to him. As he relates in a 1998 interview: "I used dress as a hedge against social fear. If one had a lot of clothes, one was armored against the world."[24] The shoes in Dine's work tell us about the public man, the artist in the world, and contrast with his series of dressing-gown self-portraits which reveal, yet paradoxically conceal, the inner man.

Dine's preoccupation with the public impact of clothing is reflected in *My Tuxedo Makes an Impression* (1965). This is a life-size mixed-media work that includes a black suit: trousers and a dinner jacket hang on wire coat hangers side by side on a gray-and-black canvas on which tools and legs are drawn in charcoal. On the floor below the trousers is a pair of men's black laced shoes. This suggests an incongruity because the shoes are Derbys, that is, the quarters are sewn over the vamp. The correct formal shoes for this outfit would be oxfords, with the vamp sewn over the quarters. I wonder if Jim Dine chose these shoes deliberately because they are not quite right. Evening dress is one of the most formal ways one can clothe the body, a uniform for occasions at which one may be judged by one's apparel; a wrong detail can be disastrous and may affect the wearer's standing in the eyes of observers. The impact of a sartorial blunder is perhaps less significant today than it once was. But the ghosts of Baudelaire and Beau Brummel hover over my shoulder and whisper that a man who cares so much about clothes must surely know what he is doing! Harvey argues that this formality is still important as signifier of worldly effectiveness, and he cites the "continuing tenacity of black (embodying continuing pieties of power) as it keeps its hold on evening dress."[25] Even in the twenty-first century one cannot overestimate the importance of dress, particularly shoes, in the search for style and identity.

Dine chose another iconic form of footwear for his first cast sculpture, *A Nice Pair of Boots* (1965). Here two biker boots are cast in bronze and enameled in silver and red, red being Dine's favorite color. Motorcycle boots have been part of popular culture since Marlon Brando showed us how to wear them in *The Wild Ones* (1955). They are a stripped-down version of the cowboy boot and have a resonance of freedom, of independence, and also of lawlessness.

Dine's images of alternative styles for women differ from those for men, and appear to have been influenced by the London fashion scene of the 1960s. In 1967 Dine and his family came to London and stayed in Chester Square near the Kings Road, the Chelsea end of swinging London. This led to such paintings as *Walking Dream with a Four Foot Clamp* (1967). Here, women's legs glimpsed in miniskirts parade in profile on a gray background. The legs are all the same shade of pink and appear to push through the background. The fashionable shoes with which the feet at the end of the legs are shod are carefully drawn and echo the precision and flatness of Warhol's commercial shoe drawings of the 1950s. However, the scale is quite different—they are life size—and the inclusion of legs gives a voyeuristic quality which is unusual in Dine's work.

Dine uses men's shoes as an adjunct to the self, part of his project of self-exploration and self-portraiture. The objects themselves are important as memento and talisman. He is interested in women's shoes but in a rather more decorative way.

Warhol and Dine seem entranced by the look, the image, of women's shoes but less interested in the shoes themselves.

Lisa Milroy, by contrast, shows her fascination with women's shoes as objects imbued with meaning when worn. Unlike Dine, she is not concerned with self-portraiture in an individual sense but rather with the shoes of everywoman.

LISA MILROY

Lisa Milroy's paintings indulge in the charm of beautiful things: a crisp, conservative painting style, always penetrating but the objects dwell in the casual, equilatrarian [sic], anti-hierarchical order (shoes, books, coats, skirts, etc.). In their cool existence, on a bland white background, in a world that has allowed them to move freely to shift characteristically in all directions without cultural obligation. This attitude of "secondarity" permits things, invented things to spread out. Lisa Milroy lays bare these methods by literally making them the contents of her paintings.

—*Jutta Koether, "Pure Invention,"* Flash Art *(April 1986)*

Her treatment of shoes in the paintings from the mid-1980s is notably different from the other objects that she paints. In her picture *Fans,* the fans are arranged across the canvas in a pleasing and decorative diagonal manner, and when viewing her picture *Sailor Hats,* one wonders who would have all those pristine and identical sailor hats except to paint them? But the shoes in her pictures have histories beyond the way they are arranged and the cool and restrained painting technique that she uses. They are all women's shoes, and they have all been worn, therefore presenting us with narrative possibilities. Milroy says she paints what the objects suggest to her rather than the objects themselves, and her pictures of shoes have this quality of the mystery of things unseen.[26]

Unlike Warhol and Dine, Milroy has only painted shoes as pairs, which has the effect of making it easier for the viewer to connect with the shoes in her paintings; two feet, after all, is the norm. (We also have two hands, but the wearing of gloves lost almost all social significance in the 1950s.) Our feet are our surest connection with terra firma, and this becomes a metaphor for connection with objective reality—hence the saying "s/he's got both feet on the ground." These feet are invariably shod, so the relationship is therefore between the body and the shoe and the shoe and the world. It is not simply a matter of the correct shoes for the correct occasion; shoes can be the site of ideological battles. Elizabeth Wilson cites the hostility of some feminists to high heels because they feel that such shoes indicate subservience and sexual stereotyping by men.[27]

Another reason for an obsessive interest in shoes is their visibility to the wearer. Without a mirror we can only have a restricted view of our body: the only areas we can see all of are the lower arms and hands, calves and feet. So it is not surprising that shoes are such a source of visual and sensual pleasure and that this fascination remains when they are taken off. This is a variant on the special consciousness that Alice White and Peter Stallybrass assign to the most sensual and potentially disruptive parts of the body, those that create the "grotesque body." These are the mouth, genitals, buttocks and anus, the stomach, the hands, and the feet: "'The grotesque body is emphasized as a mobile, split, multiple self, a subject of pleasure in process of exchange; and it is never closed off from either its social or ecosystemic context. . . .' The grotesque body, then, is the sensuous, material body signified as excessive and transgressive."[28] This analysis helps to account for the enthusiasm for shoes displayed by some people, the arousal felt by others, and the disgust of yet others. Feet are not neutral parts of the body, and our choice of shoes is a potent expression of the self.

In the largest and most varied of her shoe paintings, *Shoes* (1985), Milroy depicts sixteen pairs of women's shoes in four rows of four pairs each. Here are shoes for every quotidian social and work situation for which a woman might need to dress and perhaps several fantasy occasions, as well. From the top left-hand corner they are:

> Pink satin pointe ballet shoes with pink ribbons
>
> Green low-heeled pumps with black satin bows
>
> Gold, square-toed mules with embroidered vamps
>
> A very worn pair of flat, black Mary Janes
>
> Red pumps decorated with black-spotted white bows
>
> Peep-toed, sling-back, gold evening sandals with a woven leather vamp
>
> Black court shoes
>
> Bronze, closed-toed mules with white appliqué flowers on the vamp
>
> Pink satin slippers with elongated toes and fluffy fur decoration
>
> Sky-blue-and-gold Turkish slippers with turned-up toes and golden bells at the end
>
> Yellow court shoes with diamanté or cut steel buckles
>
> White fabric espadrillelike sandals with blue piping around the edges
>
> Tricolored sandals—royal blue, green, and yellow—with peep toes, ankle straps, and buckles
>
> Long-toed dark navy or black court shoes with navy fabric rosettes decorating the vamp
>
> Brown moccasins with fringing and tassels and beadwork on the vamp
>
> Flat, white canvas shoes with tie fronts
>
> Red court shoes
>
> Flat, brown lace-up shoes with black heels and soles, low-cut and laced, a kind of Oxford variant
>
> Flip-flops or thongs with thick soles, rather like Japanese *geta*, white with flecks of color.

It would be hard to assign a time or place to the owner of this collection of shoes. Some of the court shoes have the elongated and elegant fronts of shoes from the 1930s, a couple of pairs could come from the 1950s, and some, such as the moccasins, are timeless. The moccasins reflect a fashion for Native American handicrafts which emerged in the late 1950s, but may well be a reference to Milroy's Canadian background. The materials depicted range from bronze kid leather, satin, and canvas to rubber and plastic. But this is not a taxonomy of shoe styles. These shoes are all women's shoes, and they all look as though they have been worn; all have histories. As we look at the painting we want to ascribe narratives to them, although we do not know whether all or any of them were owned or worn by the artist. These shoes are in effect components of masquerade.

The shoes in this painting are components in many different costumes all denoting variations on the feminine and showing the instability of constructed femininity. Stephen Heath, writing about Joan Rivière, who developed this use of term "masquerade" in the 1920s, explains the implications of this sartorial behavior: "The masquerade says that woman exists at the same time that, as masquerade, it says she does not."[29] The seemingly endless variations of fashionable dress as represented by the shoes that Milroy paints express disguise but fail to disguise the anxiety within, an anxiety based on what it is to be a woman. "The display of femininity, the masquerade, hides an unconscious masculinity."[30]

Milroy's other multiple shoe picture, also generically called *Shoes* (1985), is of twelve pairs of almost identical low, black court shoes. In his book *Men in Black,* John Harvey discusses the contradictions of black in dress: "It is a colour that speaks loudly because it is conspicuous even if it says 'Don't see me! I efface myself.'"[31] These are exactly the contradictory sentiments expressed by Beau Brummel and Charles Baudelaire when they describe the appropriate dress for city life. In the Western world, black worn by women has historically been the color of abjection, mourning, service, and self-abnegation. It was worn by servants, widows, and nuns as they renounced—or were forced to renounce—the color and decoration of femininity. But these black court shoes provide a new reading of black for women. They are shoes for city life, smart, elegant but understated. They could not be mistaken for men's shoes but provide a version of female footwear that implies a performance of gender that is mediated by modernism. Harvey again: "Whereas in the new use there is no implication of lack, but rather, an allusion to the power-confidence in black which used to be associated especially with menswear."[32]

Silvie Fleury gives a very different view of women's shoes. Her installation *Untitled* (1992) consists of a luxurious pink-and-gray rug on which stands a padded, striped ottoman surrounded by shoes and shoe boxes from the most prestigious contemporary shoe designers. Opulent and high-heeled, these shoes are unworn and speak of a future self or a fantasy self rather than hinting at a past. (Although, of course, the past is as much a site of fantasy as the future.) These shoes are the trappings of conspicuous femininity, firmly fixed in the post–World War II period by the stiletto heels and silver boots. They are shoes designed deliberately to catch the viewer's gaze and take it down, down the body to the feet. They are the products of the consummate artist-shoemakers such as Manolo Blahnik, Maude Frizon, Jimmy Choo, all heirs to Salvatore Ferragamo, the "shoemaker of dreams."[33]

And yet these shoes spell frustration as much as pleasure. After all, one can only wear one pair of shoes at a time, and what if none of them succeeds in creating the wearer's ideal of her own feet? Caroline Evans writes of another of Fleury's works: "In Silvie Fleury's video 'Twinkle' (1992) the artist's feet are framed greedily and compulsively trying on and discarding fashionable shoes. Offering an ironic commentary on the convergence of fashion and art, the artist, a socialite and shopper, turns her life into a work of art. Fashion has more to tell us about life than we thought."[34] Fashion springs from life and is part of life, and, for women probably more than for men, fashion can be enabling as well as confusing. Not only does Lisa Milroy paint from memory, she paints memory.

CONCLUSION

Fashion and art in the twenty-first century can be considered equivalent because they deal with the same preoccupations: modern life and the redefinition and performance of the self. We can take this to be a legacy of Baudelaire's modernism in which the artist of modern life embraces fashion, because without it, there would be no progress in art: "This transitory, fugitive element, whose metamorphoses are so rapid, must on no account be despised or dispensed with. By neglecting it, you cannot fail to tumble into the abyss of an abstract and indeterminate beauty."[35] Salvatore Ferragamo certainly thought of his shoemaking in these terms: "One might say that my shoes are made, not for the modern woman but for the Modern Woman. In designing new styles I do not try to express the personality of any individual but rather the personality of the age, matching new styles with the changes of mood that one can always sense in advance."[36]

Aileen Ribeiro observes that it is the context in which clothing is seen that dictates our interpretation of it. Shoes seen in ordinary circumstances, therefore, are unlikely to be considered art by the viewer. But in the installation HG (1995) Robert Wilson and Hans Peter Kuhn used shoes to symbolize people killed in the Holocaust and also recalled the photographs of piles of shoes found at concentration camps in Europe.[37] The shoes were laid on the ground all facing the same direction, and the scene created a poignant sense of loss. The shoes in *HG* were elegant (supplied in the main by Manolo Blahnik), which had the effect of increasing one's sense of absence and doom. Primo Levi wrote about the importance of shoes, however poorly made, in the camps and the way that shoes gave a sense of dignity and humanity to the wearer. In *If This Is a Man* he wrote, "Death begins with the shoes."[38] He explained that if an inmate did not have shoes that fitted and protected his or her feet sufficiently, then death would not be far away.

Shoes used in such a work as *HG* obviously have a power beyond the functional and decorative, but what of the shoes by Jimmy Choo hung from the ceiling of the Victoria and Albert Museum in London (August 18, 1999)? They are disconnected from the body and from the ground, and this allows us to appreciate their forms and colors. But is this simply a sophisticated form of window dressing?

Peter Wollen, citing Anne Hollander's book *Sex in Suits,* argues that any debate about the overlapping roles of art and fashion is part of a blurring of the barriers between disciplines. Fine art is primarily visual, and fashion is visual and tactile. In an age where much of art and philosophy is concerned with the self, an appreciation of fashion as part of the performance of the self, and thereof part of art, is understandable if not inevitable.[39] Shoes can be said to transcend barriers between art and design more effectively than any other item of clothing because of their unique function and relationship to the body and because of their symbolic significance. They are a concentration and distillation of fashion, and, as Robert Radford reminds us: "Fashion sweeps imperiously on, conquering, infiltrating and colonizing all areas of social, cultural and (lest we forget) academic enterprise."[40]

NOTES

1. Colin McDowell, *Shoes: Fashion and Fantasy* (London: Thames and Hudson, 1989), 33.

2. Caroline Evans, "Masks, Mirrors, and Mannequins: Elsa Schiaparelli and the De-centred Object," *Fashion Theory: The Journal of Dress, Body, and Culture* 3, 1 (March 1999): 5.

3. These monkey-hair boots are illustrated in Mary Trasko, *Heavenly Soles: Extraordinary Twentieth-Century Shoes* (New York: Abbeville Press, 1989), 43.

4. Valerie Steele, *Women of Fashion: Twentieth-Century Designers* (New York: Rizzoli, 1991), 66.

5. Marina Warner, *From the Beast to the Blonde* (London: Chatto and Windus, 1994), 386.

6. Aileen Ribeiro, "Re-fashioning Art: Some Visual Approaches to the Study of the History of Dress," *Fashion Theory* 2, 4 (1998): 320.

7. John Coplans, *Andy Warhol* (New York: New York Graphic Society, 1978), 8–9.

8. Steele, *Women of Fashion,* 112.

9. Trasko, *Heavenly Soles,* 63. Not that flat shoes guarantee comfort. Ossie Clarke, the English fashion designer, recalls modeling for *Comme des Garcons:* "The left shoe I got on OK. The right one was so rigid it could have been made of bakelite and designed as an instrument of torture" *(The Ossie Clarke Diaries,* ed. Lady Henrietta Rous [London: Bloomsbury, 1998], 337).

10. Marco Livingstone, "Do It Yourself: Notes on Warhol's Techniques," in *Andy Warhol: A Retrospective,* ed. Kynaston McShine (New York: Museum of Modern Art, 1989), 64.

11. Lee Wright, "Objectifying Gender: The Stiletto Heel," in *A View from the Interior: Feminism, Women, and Design,* ed. Judy Attfield and Pat Kirkham (London: Women's Press, 1989), 10–11.

12. Trasko, *Heavenly Soles,* 76–85.

13. There is an illustration of Vivier surrounded by his shoes in McDowell, *Shoes: Fashion and Fantasy,* 191.

14. Michael Gober, "Warhol's Closet," *Art News* 55, 4 (winter 1996): 44.

15. Ibid., 45.

16. Susan Stewart, *On Longing: Narratives of the Miniature, the Gigantic, the Souvenir and the Collection* (Durham and London: Duke University Press, 1993), 151.

17. Linda O'Keefe, *Shoes: A Celebration of Pumps, Sandals, Slippers, and More* (New York: Workman, 1996), 13.

18. David Bourdon, "Andy Warhol's 'Exhibition,'" *Art News* 68 (October 1969): 57.

19. Ibid.

20. Some people, such as the English artist Derek Jarman, collect secondhand shoes.

21. Germano Celanti, "I Love What I'm Doing," Jim Dine, *Jim Dine: Walking Memory, 1959–69* (New York: Guggenheim Museum, 1999), 19.

22. John Harvey, *Men in Black* (London: Reaktion Books, 1995), 18.

23. Ken Baynes and Kate Baynes, *The Shoe Show: British Shoes since 1790* (London: Crafts Council, 1978), 56.

24. Dine, *Jim Dine,* 56.

25. Harvey, *Men in Black,* 27–28.

26. Judith Higgings, "Painted Dreams," *Art News* 87, 2 (February 1988): 122.

27. Elizabeth Wilson, *Adorned in Dreams: Fashion and Modernity* (London: Virago Press, 1985), 234–235.

28. Alice White and Peter Stallybrass, *The Symptom of Beauty,* ed. Francette Pacteau (London: Reaktion Books, 1994), 128.

29. Stephen Heath, "Joan Rivière and the Masquerade," in *Formations of Fantasy,* ed. Victor Burgin, James Donald, and Cora Kaplan (New York: Routledge, 1989), 54.

30. Ibid, 55.

31. Harvey, *Men in Black,* 15.

32. Ibid, 225.

33. Silvie Fleury, *Untitled* (1992) is illustrated in Jeffrey Deitch, *Post Human* (Pully/Lausanne: FAE Musée d'Art Contemporain, 1992), 92–93.

34. Caroline Evans, "Mutability and Modernity," in *Addressing the Century:100 Years of Fashion and Art* (London: Hayward Gallery, 1998), 97.

35. Charles Baudelaire, *The Painter of Modern Life and Other Essays* (London: Phaidon, 1964), 12.

36. Salvatore Ferragamo, *Salvatore Ferragamo, the Art of the Shoe, 1898–1969* (New York: Rizzoli, 1992), 32.

37. *HG,* an installation by Robert Wilson and Hans Peter Kuhn at the Clink Street Vaults, London, September–October 1995, produced by Artangel.

38. Primo Levi, *If This Is a Man,* trans. Stuart Woolf (London: Abacus, 1987), 40.

39. Peter Wollen, "Addressing the Century," in *Addressing the Century,* 18.

40. Robert Radford, "Dangerous Liaisons: Art, Fashion, and Individualism," *Fashion Theory: The Journal of Dress, Body, and Culture* 2, 2 (June 1998), 162.

High Angles on Shoes: Cinema, Gender, and Footwear

MAUREEN TURIM

From *The Gay Shoe Clerk* (Porter/Edison, 1903) to recent films such as *Clueless* (Heckerling, 1995) and *High Heels* (Almódovar, 1996), shoes have been central to representation of gender difference and gendered interactions in the cinema. From the "once over" look that begins at a woman's shoes to tilt up across her body to her face (or the inverse movement that slinks down from her face to her feet), to the close-up that uses the well-turned ankle in the high-heeled pump to signify the desirability of a woman, cinema has often looked at women through their shoes. While male shoes do not necessarily garner the same visual attention, in key instances they do become the focus of film imagery, often in a manner quite different from women's defining footwear. In this essay I will examine the particular inscription of shoes in selected films as a key image in the cinema's use of metonymy. Metonymy focuses on the part for the whole, a process which in film often finds expression through the close-up but may be indicated through other framing devices.

Metonymy, as I will explore in detail later, functions within visual expression to introduce much more than the signification of the whole object by a part of that object. This is particularly true when the part shown is a part of the human body or an article of clothing that covers that part. Shoes become a privileged metonymy, one that portrays much about sexuality, desire, class, and culture. Films explore the sexuality implicit in close-ups of shoes with humor and with reference to the Cinderella fairy tale.

Their initial focus is on the fetishized female foot. Increasingly women's shoes are seen in relation to men's shoes. Scenes in silent film develop an interaction between gendered footwear that establishes power and class hierarchies. The emergence of the flapper that precedes the transition to sound film conjoins with the dance film that sound film makes possible to create increased attention to this dance of gender roles. Two subsequent genres of film—film noir and neorealism—create a curious dialogue on shoes. More recent films maintain, satirize, or blend gender associations with footwear.

CINDERELLA STORIES

Some early examples from silent film stage tableaux in which women try on shoes. The moment of trying on shoes directly or indirectly recalls Cinderella's trial by shoes, suggesting a link between earlier folklore magic and the commercial ritual of shoe sales that emerges in the late nineteenth century.

Porter's comic film *The Gay Shoe Clerk* enters the arena of the shoe salon to examine the behavior of a male clerk toward his female patron in an age when the adjective "gay" meant "abounding in social or other pleasures" or even licentious. Fetishism, sexual display, and sexual flirtation reside in this space of the shoe store. Punishment for untoward behavior transforms such transgressions into both a joke and a morality lesson, as we will see. The film was not distributed at the time of its production,[1] but has since become well known as a surviving print from the Edison studio; what we say of its use of shoes, then, has nothing to do with its impact at the time, but rather tells us something symptomatically about the moment in consumer culture when it was produced.

The focal incident involves an attractive and fashionable young woman who comes shopping with an older female companion who acts as her chaperone. In an economically articulated three-shot film lasting one minute, we see the threesome first set against a backdrop of the neatly stacked rows of closed boxes on the storage racks above cabinetry in the shoe store, as the clerk on his low bench sits before his customer on the specially designed shoe trial chair; the other woman sits off to the left side reading a magazine. The second shot (figure 1) is an evocative close-up on the woman's pattern-stockinged leg and foot, which she exposes by hiking up her long skirt, as the clerk's hand fits her with a sleek-styled black pump with a two-inch heel.

These shots offer us a view of everyday commercial life in turn-of-the-twentieth-century New York, which is interesting to compare with still photos of specialty and department stores from this period. As Charles Musser notes, the close-up shot is set against a plain white background rather than the cabinet, which should have been the background

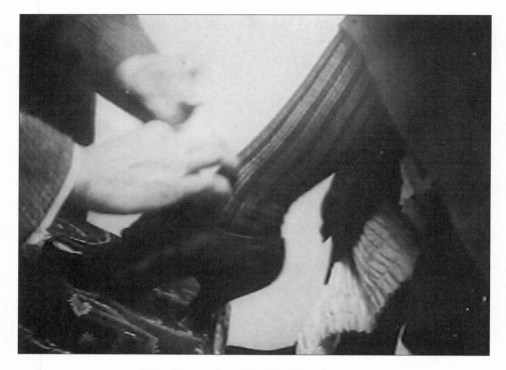

FIGURE 1 ↩ This close-up from *The Gay Shoe Clerk* (Porter/Edison, 1903) focuses on the shoe salon as site of an attempted seduction. The woman exposes her pattern-stockinged leg and foot by hiking up her long skirt, as the clerk's hand fits her with a black pump with a two-inch heel and sleek styling, as prelude to a stolen kiss.

as established in the previous long shot; a change of this type would become a common device for accentuation of the objects of interest in the filmic close-up. The petticoat of the client that frames the leg is suddenly white-pleated material, whereas in the long shot only dark garments are visible, a change in costuming that also serves to accent the dark-stockinged leg and ankle, making this close-up even more emphatic. This close-up reveals how even a short narrative provides shoe imagery with a gendered story and a fetishistic focus.

The clerk takes advantage of his job to move his hands up the calf of the woman. When we return to the long shot, this sexual move is followed by a "stolen" kiss. This sexual liberty earns the clerk an umbrella thrashing from the older woman, which ends the film. Such a quickly administered censor brings to rapid conclusion the progression from foot and leg exposed, seen, and touched, to the kiss.

This short comic film from early film history inscribes the erotic clasp for which the fashionable shoe seems to be destined. Offered to the audience for titillation without the punishment meted out to the clerk, this close-up offers itself to the male gaze, as the film "savors the spectatorial position of the male cinematic voyeur."[2] It seems simultaneously to instruct women on the power of shoes as fetish and to predict such montage patterns for future films. In many ways all the scenes of shoes I will analyze in this essay follow from this now famous, though once lost, prototype of shoe imagery. Shoes figure social situations, imbued always with sexual aspects, even when not so directly eroticized.

This film can be seen in relationship to the early adaptations of "Cinderella" such as the Méliès film of 1899 and Pathé film of 1905, each bearing the French title *Le Cendrillon.* This famous fairy tale reverberates in European culture in numerous forms: the Charles Perrault story of 1697 (the English translator mistakenly translated the white fur slipper of the original as a glass slipper); the Isoaurd opera, *Cendrillon,* of 1810; *La Cenerentola,* the Gioacchino Rossini opera presented in Italian in London in 1820; and Gustave Doré's illustrations of the 1850s—to cite major versions preceding these early films. So by the time of the Méliès film of 1899, the traditional tableau pose of Cinderella being fitted into her lost slipper by the prince's cavaliers has undergone numerous permutations. Musser notes that the Méliès film was a remarkable success and a notable spectacle for its time, while the later Pathé film marks the close of the fairy-tale genre in silent film.[3] *The Gay Shoe Clerk,* which is made between these two French *Cinderella*s, may be seen as imaging the relationship between the Cinderella tableau and the everyday experience of shoe shopping at the turn of the century; the trying on of shoes holds within its intertextual universe a fairy-tale trial by shoes, a testing of the woman by what fits her feet. Grace and sexuality are all calibrated in proportion to shoe size, and a singular identity verified by a uniquely small and adorable foot that fits this shoe, a holdover perhaps of the fetish of *pied mignon* celebrated in the art of Honoré de Fragonard. By extension through *The Gay Shoe Clerk* and consumerist fantasies, the fairy tale promises that every shoe has the potential to be a glass slipper. If the brazen clerk, who dares caress the foot as prelude to kissing the lips of the fair lady who chances into his realm, pays for his transgression rather than reaping princely rewards, this comic treatment still speaks to the magical fetishism of the shoe that the fairy tale exposes.

THE CLOSE-UP AND THE FETISH

Shoes are shown from these earliest films to be sites of inscription, a way of writing the body. They should be considered alongside such significant and far more recognized sites as the face, the eyes, the hat or hair, and the hand. In fact, the comparison is instructive, for the foot is far less frequently shown in close-up than the parts of the body mentioned above, and this is undoubtedly due to its location at the other extreme from the face. The foot immediately connotes either baseness, or sexuality, or both. Best associated in emphatic function perhaps with the hand, the foot differs in having no proximity to the face, no role in most conventions of gesture and greeting. While the hand may be gloved or bejeweled, it is far more often exposed nude than is the foot. The shoe, however, is a required covering for the foot in public and civilized circumstances. The opposition of shoes to bare feet is central, then, to significations of wealth, public space, and civilization itself. Shoes are, in fact, one among many contingent coverings of body parts assigned the role of emblematizing the body, its placement and social position, its activity and movement, its roles.

Yet the shoe bears a particular relationship to the fetish, dependent on the role of the foot, best described by Georges Bataille, who narrows his focus to even a smaller part of the foot, the big toe. He sees the big toe is the most abject part of body, first because it belongs to the foot, the body part in direct contact with the dirt and assigned the role of support. Further, Bataille suggests, the big toe is a phallic displacement, but one which is a bit absurd, carrying over to this phallic role its abject connotations. Bataille posits that we have a "secret horror" of our feet, which leads us to cover them, concealing their length and shape, using heels to disguise "the foot's low and flat character."[4]

Bataille's essay, then, extends Freud's argument in "Fetishism."[5] Freud demonstrates how the base associations with sexuality in European culture find their mutation as the fetish, both as the fixation on a part object and as a displacement of sexual desire from genitalia and flesh to elegant accoutrements. The history of cinematic inscription of shoes coincides with the reception of Freud's essay, which introduces theoretical connections that begin to shape mass culture. Not only did Freud's ideas help explain the shoe fetish in certain filmic narratives, his essay disseminated concepts that led to self-conscious representations of shoes. Films display a psychoanalytic awareness in presenting the shoe as the object of sexual gazing. Men have been conditioned to link shoes with desire and with the denial of castration; the films mark women wearing heels as the gift of European culture, as an answer to male anxieties. Bataille's essay adds to the theory of fetishism a very dark side of fetishist desire, one that seems steeped in masochism, in debasement, in the ideal having its appeal in direct proportion to a base seduction, as even the ideal foot "still derives its charm from deformed and muddy feet."[6]

Even more interesting for my purposes, Bataille's essay helps us to understand cinematic editing, as Pascal Bonitzer points out in his seminal essay on the close-up.[7] Bonitzer traces the special historical attention that the introduction of close-ups receives in accounts of early cinema. Bonitzer argues that close-ups become the supplement that emphasizes the fragmentary nature of cinematic editing. He then argues that, as supplement, the close-up demands a reading of films through a syntax of shots. Bonitzer focuses on the role of the close-up in foregrounding filmic enunciation and fragmentation, rather than as a metonymic detail enlarging the film's presentation of the effect of reality (fiction understood *as* reality) or as an element of filmic symbolism.

In a parallel theoretical move we can see the close-up of the shoe as a particular case that doubly inscribes what is involved in most close-ups. Linked not only by form, but by association to the bare foot or the big toe, the close-up of the shoe grounds filmic enunciation in the earthy and the sexual, encouraging spectatorial participation in shoe fetishism. The close-up can give us shoes that stand in for the body, but it almost always charges them with excess and supplementarity. The close-up of the shoe is rarely a simple detail of the fiction, and its effects go beyond enriching the realism. The fetishistic elements of the shoe in film are shown in many close-ups, and perhaps any mise-en-scène, such as the Cinderella tableau, that offers the shoe as focal point of the composition. Yet the fetishistic elements of shoe representation are often less apparent than the metonymic aspects of such close-ups, which stand in for the movement of a body as a whole.

A REVOLUTION IN METONYMY

To illustrate how close-ups on shoes carry multiple meanings of the fetish, of realist detail, and of gender and class , I now turn to examples of shoe close-ups in two Russian films that surround the Bolshevik Revolution of 1917, one produced under czarist rule and the other commemorating the revolution ten years later. *The Girl in the Big City* by Evgeni Bauer (1913) explores the decadence of big-city life in a narrative of a golddigger/vamp preying on an upper-middle-class man, a narrative typical of Italian films of that period, and one which will eventually play a prominent role in U.S. and other European cinemas. Once the vamp has exploited the fortunes of her sugar daddy and abandoned him, we see her in a Poiret-style dress dancing the tango in her newly acquired luxurious apartment. This dance of foreign importation fulfills the role of her sexy fashions by allowing her beautiful black ankle-strapped high heels to show in its dramatic turns. This dance excludes the very man she ruined in order to arrive at such luxury. We see him, through crosscutting, committing suicide on the steps outside her apartment. The film offers a close-up of her high heels as she steps over the corpse of her former lover and benefactor as she descends the stairs (figure 2). Here the shoe signifies female cruelty and the fickleness of emotions in a modern urban capitalist environment that prizes personal wealth accumulated by any means necessary.[8]

The second film, made fourteen years later, Eisenstein's *Battleship Potemkin* (1927), echoes this staircase image. The splendid rhythmic montage of its famous Odessa Steps sequence establishes a visual refrain that focuses on boots and shoes. The czarist

FIGURE 2 ⁓ The medium shot shows the disdain of the femme fatale as her laced high-heel sandals step over the corpse of her former lover and benefactor as she descends her stairs in *The Girl in the Big City* (Evgeni Bauer, 1913).

soldiers' booted legs are used to signify their repressive descent on the protesters in equal measure to their pointed rifles, at first in long shot, but toward the end of the sequence in increasingly closer views. The counterpoint to such focus on the relentless crush of the booted soldiers begins prior to the first shot of their descent, with shots of some Odessa residents waving to encourage the sailboats taking supplies to the mutineers. One angle focuses on a double amputee, who moves sideways along the stairs between the elegant shoes of two women on stairs above and below. As an example of Eisensteinian montage within the frame, this shot ironically couples the elegant heels with a particularly ironic image of a member of the lumpen proletariat who is perhaps a veteran or accident victim. The elegant shoe here is contrasted not to bare feet but to one who has lost his feet altogether. This shot sets up a series of angles to follow on the victims' shoes as they fall after the czarist soldiers fire repeatedly at the crowd. One is a particularly striking shot of a woman in high heels who, having tripped, sits on the stairs as the legs of another woman and man cross the frame left to right. She then stands again, lifting her skirt above her ankles to cross the frame on the opposing diagonal, right to left (figure 3). This shot begs comparison to the close-up in *The Girl in the Big City,*

FIGURE 3a
The legless man is a contrast to the high-heeled ladies waving their greetings to the mutineers in the Odessa Steps sequence of *Battleship Potemkin* (Sergei Eisenstein, 1927).

FIGURE 3b
Battleship Potemkin includes among its shots focusing on shoes this one of a woman who stands and flees again after having snagged her heel on the stairs and fallen. She lifts her skirt above her ankles to cross the frame on the opposing diagonal, right to left (Odessa Steps sequence).

FIGURE 3c
The fallen child's hand is crushed by a foot of a fleeing man in *Battleship Potemkin*'s Odessa Steps sequence.

for while the Bauer film associates the high heel with the callous power of the woman who rises to the middle class by any means necessary, Eisenstein shows the high-heeled women here as perhaps unwittingly sacrificing their class privilege. They become victims of an indiscriminate repression, visually represented by the boots of the czarist soldiers. The women's high heels are liabilities in the revolutionary situation that unfolds symbolically on the steps of Odessa.

When a child falls—the one whose mother will later protest his death in one of the segment's most poignant moments—his body is seen trampled in several shots, as the shoes of others press into his foot, his hand, his chest. Toward the very end of the sequence we see the soldiers' boots in a tight shot as they point their rifles downward to fire at bodies on the step below. This shot, as well as an earlier one of a row of soldiers seen from behind stepping over corpses as they descend the staircase, also begs comparison with Bauer's film. It reverses the gender associations of Bauer's close-up, while it uses similar enunciatory power with new ideological resonance. It attaches this visually rendered act of disdain for the victim to violent czarist political repression.

GENDERED SHOES,
GENDERED DISCOURSE

The enunciatory power assigned the close-ups of shoes in these Russian films finds another inscription in Victor Seastrom's *The Wind* (1928). Throughout the film, dusty cowboy boots contrast with the city heels that the displaced eastern heroine Letty (Lillian Gish) brings to the foreboding landscape of the Texas plains, as well as with the polished shoes of a traveling salesman, Roddy (Montagu Love). This metonymy of expression, poetic and concise, also carries with it a discourse on gender and footwear. Forced into an unwanted marriage with Lars, Letty resists his advances on their wedding night. A series of shots traces their actions through high-angle shots on their feet, giving this serious and central scene a dynamic representation. We see Lars's boots pacing the floorboards outside the locked bedroom, a shot intercut with one framing the wind at the window and then another of Letty's black bowtie-decorated pumps pacing in parallel inside the bedroom. Lars's forcing of the door is shown by his emphatic boots on the threshold, followed by a cut to Letty's black pumps, recoiling. Finally the two pairs of shoes briefly share a shot, but only to remain apart, as Letty refuses Lars's affections and withdraws (figure 4). The rest of the scene returns to their facial reactions and to intertitle dialogue.

This silent ballet of the shoes, then, presents in symbolic terms the conflict between a female urban culture embodied in the elegant shoes and the rough ways of those who

FIGURE 4 ◠ The silent ballet of the shoes in *The Wind* (Victor Seastrom, 1928) presents in symbolic terms the conflict between a female urban culture embodied in the elegant shoes and the rough ways of those who wear cowboy boots.

wear cowboy boots. Comic scenes throughout the film augment the roughness of cowboy ways through similar high-angle close-ups on shoes. Early on a minor character, Sourdough, expresses his disdain by spitting on the pitchman's shiny shoes, shown in close-up as the spit hits its mark. Later Sourdough's spit figures once again as he launches it unthinkingly at Letty's cabin floor, but he apologizes through an action in high-angle close-up as his boot rubs out the spot.

Finally, the emphasis on shoes is linked to the incessant wind and dust storms that torment the plains. A high-angle shot shows Letty's now dust-covered shoes as she tries to sweep the dirt from her cabin while Lars's boots cross the threshold to brave the storm. More dramatically, this shot is echoed as Letty attempts to bury Roddy, whom she has shot after he made unwanted sexual advances toward her; we see her pumps now nearly buried in dust as she makes a futile attempt to dig a grave. While *The Wind* is often heralded as a late flowering of silent film expression and as an example of Swedish psychological film symbolism infused into the American Western, attention to footwear reveals another reason for its significance in the history of filmic expression. In addition to the stunning shots of the dust storms and the superimposition of the white horse representing the power of the wind, the close-ups on shoes play their role in creating a symbolic dynamism to the narrative conflict. Through its metonymic narration of gendered difference in the myth of the West, this film establishes a paradigm for how shoes mark sexual difference in American culture. The opposition is between elegant shoes of urban culture (associated with the feminine) and practical shoes of the frontier (associated with the masculine). Resolution of the conflict entails wedding the two, the ballet of the East and the West, the cultured and the wild, into a pairing and accommodation of difference soon to be eradicated by change.

THE HEELS OF THE MODERN WOMAN

Perhaps no other silent film dares develop so much of its narrative through the metonymic shots of shoes as does *The Wind*. However, the high angle on the shoe and ankle, often as part of a "once over" subjective shot of the heroine, is common, as are narrative instances in which shoes gain central focus. The history of silent film chronicles a transition from high-button boots peeking out from under long skirts to a similar view now marked by the pump or court shoe and the exposed heroine's ankles.[9] In *The Gibson Goddess* (Griffith, 1909), fashionable boots worn with a high-styled suit at the beginning of the film help establish the heroine's allure. Later, to fend off "the mashers," she develops a ruse dependent on the fashion of bathing costumes that includes tights worn with heels. She has stuffed the tights so that they reveal unsightly legs. The hobble skirt scene in *Intolerance* (Griffith, 1916) has the heroine accommodate modernity and compromise her outdated appearance, if not her old-fashioned sensibility, by binding the hem of her skirt with string. The shot depicting this process emphasizes how the homemade version, like the high-fashion look, draws considerable attention to ankles and shoes as objects of male interest. In both of these examples shots of shoes and ankles show heroines manipulating the details of fashionable footwear for their own purposes.

Male and Female (Cecil B. DeMille, 1919) contrasts the elegant drawing-room shoes of the film's opening with the homemade sandals later sported by all after a yachting wreck forces the wealthy and their servants to survive together on an island. The film also contains a fascinating image of class envy embodied in the image of a shoe. The maid Tweenie's subjective close-up on her mistress's embroidered shoe (figure 5), seen as the wearer relaxes languidly on a settee, is offered as visual testimony of how the maid wishes to trade places with the woman, who enjoys both wealth and leisure, and whose splendor makes her the object of the butler's affections, a man Tweenie her-

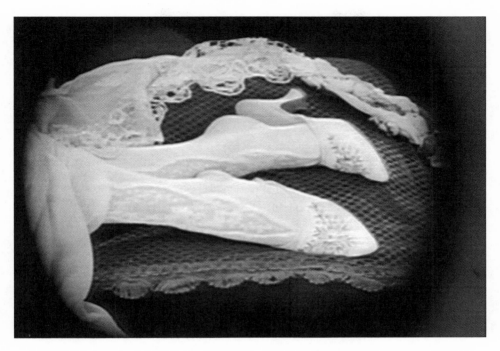

FIGURE 5 ↵ A subjective close-up on her mistress's embroidered "court" shoe embodies the class envy of the maid in Cecil B. DeMille's *Male and Female* (1919).

self desires. The close-up on the shoes emblematizes this relay of desire in which jealousy is linked to class envy. The fetishistic framing on a woman's shoe engages both the female and male audiences.

Another Cecil B. DeMille film, *The Ten Commandments* (1923), introduces the designs of Salvatore Ferragamo, beginning his years as Paramount's top footwear designer and private supplier to such stars as Mary Pickford, Lillian Gish, and Gloria Swanson.[10] The film's dual narratives of a modern story of sexual competition and corporate corruption framing a biblical epic provide images of elegant Egyptian sandals in the biblical segments and extravagant heels to complement the female costumes that represent luxurious modernity. This attention to shoes is accented by dialogue offered in the written intertitles, as when the pharoah says, "Thinkest thou the curse of thy God can destroy the son of pharoah—whose golden sandals have been beaten from the crowns of conquered kings?" Later, the sacrilegious son, Dan, of the modern story tells his brother, John, "I'd like your ten commandments better if they could mend this sole instead of the one mom's worried about," a remark that is followed by a close-up on the worn sole of Dan's shoe as he toys with a matchstick, emphasizing a gap at the toe. His mother retorts, "If you're setting a pair of shoes above your God, Dan McTavish—you'll get just what the Children of Israel got, when they worshipped the Golden Calf!"

To place shoes above God becomes an obsession of the film's visual imagery. These proclamations establish a context through which to read a series of shots on sandals and shoes. During the orgy surrounding the worship of the Golden Calf, a man pours wine onto the outstretched sandaled foot of a woman, only to lean over and lick it, an indication of all manner of decadence. Similarly, a high-angle close-up of Dan's and Mary's feet as they dance to celebrate their engagement is prelude to Dan's mother chastising them for dancing on the Sabbath, an incident that leads to Dan's break with his mother. Finally, a close-up of Mary's elegant heels slipping on a crumbling concrete platform becomes the first visible sign that her husband is illegally substituting a cheaper and unsafe mix of concrete in the church he is constructing. The film is typical for its period in its paradoxical display of the sexuality and power of rich shoes and costumes, even as the narrative seeks "to guide her feet into the straight and narrow path" (as the mother says of Mary). While the strict puritanical position of the mother is modified by the film's end, the film is clearly nervous about the seductive power its imagery grants the foot and shoe.

In silent films, seduction is often the province of a diva, queen, or vamp whose exotic footwear symbolizes her sexual power, as we saw in Bauer's *The Girl in the Big City.* Babylonian, Egyptian, Arab, Chinese—the ancient kingdoms or the "exotic" Others provide styles that foreground a sexuality through sandal laces, curved-toe slippers, fanciful and flamboyant decorations for the feet. Seduction cedes to style fully coded as American when the flapper's shiny pumps of the 1920s usurp the role of emblematic seductive shoe. The flapper's shoe is typically styled with an eye-catching reflective surface such as satin, rhinestone, or glitter and represents an increasing focus on heels as defining young women as aspirants to class ascendancy and exuberant, romantic, and fun adventures.

The on-screen shoe wardrobes of such stars as Clara Bow and Joan Crawford make fascinating examples. *Our Dancing Daughters* (Henry Beaumont, 1928) begins with a shot of Diana (Joan Crawford) in the mirror; the image pans down to her sparkle shoes accenting the exuberance of her impromptu Charleston (figure 6). Contrast this with the film's final scene of retribution that punishes the woman who stole Diana's boyfriend by pretending to be more modest and wholesome, and who has now become an unfaithful wife dressed in full flapper regalia. Diana's rival trips on the stairs, falling to her death, dying because she is too drunk to manage her flapper heels. This accident permits Diana to be reunited with her love. In such flapper films, the bow-tied or sparkled pump becomes the very image of a carefree modernity that flirts with immorality, yet, in order to survive, the flapper must learn to plant her feet sensibly on the ground. Thus Clara Bow in *It* (Clarence Badger, 1927) plays a clerk whose desire to marry the owner

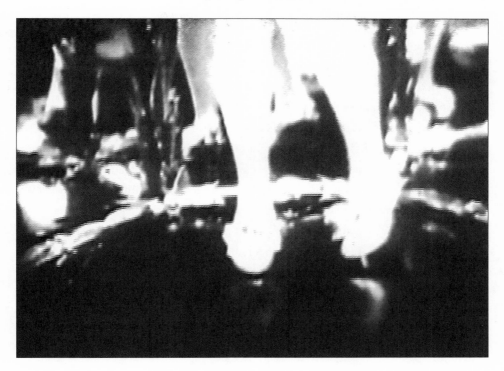

FIGURE 6 ⌇ This medium high-angle shot from the beginning of *Our Dancing Daughters* (Harry Beaumont, 1928) shows Diana's reflection in the mirror as her sparkle shoes accent the exuberance of her impromptu Charleston.

of the department store in which she works is coupled with a sexual energy that is first manifest when a high angle on her feet as she dresses shows her high heels bouncing in an impromptu dance of glee.[11] These tales of flappers focus on key instances of shoes as emblems of the historical moment. Dancing girls signify modernity. Films glorify their rituals of urban night life, which in the sound musical will mean renewed concentration on the gendering of footwear, even as the masculine side of the opposition becomes equally linked to culture, the East, and elegance.

FANTASIES
OF SHOES AND DANCE

In the only film I have found whose narrative is devoted to a shoe designer, *Pointed Heels* (Paramount-Famous Players-Lasky, 1929), William Powell plays a fashion designer with a particular interest in high heels. The film offers us a stunning tight close-up in which a young Powell, wearing a beret and mustache, looks pointedly at a pair of white high heels and well-turned ankles that share the frame with him. This early sound film makes the tantalizing connection between the coming of sound and the fashion for pointed heels, and the increasing association of American men with fashion and elegant shoes.

With the coming of sound, shoes are increasingly tied to dance, be it tap, soft shoe, or ballroom. As we are told in *Forty-second Street* (Lloyd Bacon, 1933), "Come and see / those dancing feet." In the Busby Berkeley dance numbers, rows of shoes on the silk-stockinged legs of chorines set up a duplication of the fetish in a mise-en-abîme of ornate patterned repetition. Notable are the medallion coin-decorated glitter heels that match the coin-covered bras and huge coin loincloth constructions of the "We're in the Money" number from *Gold Diggers of 1933* (Mervyn LeRoy) and the rows of black T-straps that accompany the black transparent lace bathing suits in *The Kid from Spain* (Leo McCarey, 1932). In fact, the high heel is a most uncanny accessory to the bathing suit and its tap dance equivalent, setting off with high style the nudity of the matching legs. *Gold Diggers in Paris* (Ray Enright, 1938) provides in its homage to the can-can recognition of this Montmartre dance as the predecessor in establishing the high heel and exposed leg as the quintessential image of the chorine, the chorus line dancer. "Pettin' in the Park" from *Gold Diggers of 1933* treats the fetishism of the chorine costume reflexively through a narrative of everyday exposure. Identical chorines lie on their backs with their lovers, the couples scattered across a lawn. The ensuing crane shot highlights the exposed garter belt, silk stockings, and high heels of each. Later, the camera aims through the dancers' spread legs, turning the image into a triangular abstraction, heels anchoring the shape to form a shiny white path.

The fetishism and visual puns of Berkeley's use of heels contrasts with the elegance associated with Astaire and Rogers's dance films of the 1930s. Such elegance represents a hope of extending the high life of the 1920s beyond its death in the depression. Shoes were integral to this fantasy, as were ever more flamboyant dance steps. Astaire and Rogers each specialized in elegant shoes, although in fact when one considers that each film includes at least one comic or "dressed down" dance for variety, the stars do dance in more than their trademark formal footwear. It is, however, their formal combinations of her white heels complemented by his black patents that we most readily associate with these stars dancing across the great white sets of Van Nest Polglase.

In fact, the flexible, shiny black dance shoes of Fred Astaire may not get mentioned in "Top Hat and Tails," which has the most famous song lyrics about sartorial accessories, but they do receive an homage in the line from the title number of *Shall We Dance* (Mark Sandrich, 1934) when Astaire sings, "put on your dancing shoes."[12] His black patents are in fact a necessary element for "Steppin' Out with My Baby," part of the resurgent image of male elegance. Visually they allow us to follow his feet across a partnership built on the charms of symmetry contrasted with asymmetry. We are constantly seeing the pair as a match, a couple, and as entrancingly different, highlighting gender difference as a magnetic charm. Given that all the plots are romances in which Ginger is hard to get, or the two are tangled in webs of misunderstandings, the dance scenes help resolve conflicts. These scenes highlight bodies, and especially the characters' elegant feet, as working through difference toward symmetry and unity.

Surprisingly, perhaps, there are relatively few close-ups of the dancing feet themselves. Exceptions are certain opening credits: in *Top Hat* (Sandrich, 1935), a row of the legs, shoes, and canes of formally dressed male dancers is featured across the top of the image, followed by the entrance of Rogers's legs and heels in the foreground to the right above her credit and finally Astaire's legs on the left above his. In *Shall We Dance,* by contrast, toe shoes adorn the row of ballerinas, establishing the high-art contrast to tap and ballroom dancing that will structure the narrative.

In the formal dance numbers, such as "Cheek to Cheek" and "Piccolino" (*Top Hat*), "Let's Face the Music and Dance" (*Follow the Fleet,* Sandrich, 1936), "Waltz in Swing Time" and "Never Gonna Dance" (*Swing Time,* George Stevens, 1936), "Night and Day" and "The Continental" (*The Gay Divorcee,* Sandrich, 1934), contrasts between Astaire's black tuxedo and black patent shoes are provided by Rogers's variety of full-length white or sparkling silvery dresses accompanied by white or glittery heels, most with some sort of bow or T-strap, that peek out from her long and flowing skirts at key moments of kicks and turns (see figure 7 from *The Gay Divorcee*). Since the sweeping gestures of the dresses draw our attention, a dissymmetry appears between the dancers even in moments when symmetrical matchings occur in the choreography. Astaire provides the articulated exactness of each rhythm, while Rogers's moves are more abstracted, their kinetics evidenced as broader effects. The intermittent vision of her shoes, then, reintroduces articulation, the recognition that the dancer's legs and body produce these abstracted swirls of radiant light.

In the contrasting novelty or casual dance numbers, the variety of costumes and footwear is great: the pair tap-dances and glides on roller skates in "Let's Call the Whole Thing Off" (*Shall We Dance*), and Rogers dances in low black boots to match her riding habit in *Top Hat*'s park impromptu "Isn't It a Lovely Day to Be Caught in the Rain," while Astaire wears the shoes that fit his disguise as a Central Park horse cabby. Occasionally, Astaire's shoes are white in these casual dance scenes, but these are usually solo numbers. Perhaps the most delightful delineation of Astaire's solo prowess is in *Top Hat*'s "No Strings (I'm Fancy Free)" number, which begins with Astaire tapping in his hotel room, disturbing Rogers in the room directly below, then resumes once Astaire has thrown sand from a large hallway cigarette receptacle onto the floor to turn his

FIGURE 7   ↗   Fred Astaire's and Ginger Rogers's elegant shoes are key to the
dance aesthetic in "The Continental" number in *The Gay Divorcee* (Mark Sandrich, 1934).

dancing into a gentle soft shoe to ease her back to sleep. Here the film concentrates
our attention on the relationship between the image of the shoe touching the floor and
the sound effect as rhythmic punctuation in a manner present in all tap numbers, but
here accentuated by the great vertical pan between floors that narrativizes the effect
of sounds of shoes meeting surfaces.

THE HEELED
AND THE BAREFOOT:
NOIR AND NEOREALISM

It is interesting to compare Rogers's white heels with those found in Italian films
of the fascist period—known as the "white telephone" films for their display of the lifestyle
of modernity designed as a fantasy of white elegance, epitomized by an object few Italians owned, the telephone, and certainly not in decorator white. These films might as
easily be called the "white high-heeled pump" films, although often these pumps are
fur-trimmed mules. All this whiteness of shoe design seems to desire differentiation of
these 1930s urban sophisticates from the image of the street-walking prostitute—one

can certainly walk the streets in heels, but white heels seem reserved for yachts, ballrooms, elegant restaurants, salons, and boudoirs.

Film noir of the postwar 1940s then turns toward the shadows, and the seductive femme fatale, whose heels play an integral role in telling her story. Her heels might well be black, but in key moments of early seduction, they are just as likely to be white, thus retaining her link to the associations white shoes garnered in the 1930s. For example, in *Double Indemnity* (Billy Wilder, 1946) Phyllis Dietrichson (Barbara Stanwyck) wears white pumps when she first descends the stairway to greet Walter Neff (Fred MacMurray), the insurance agent she will ensnare. The film underlines the seductive power of her shoes with a close-up from Walter's point of view. In a later scene in which Phyllis sits crossways in her armchair, she is wearing black sling-back pumps augmented by an ankle bracelet. As she dangles her feet, her flirtation becomes a visual footsie to Neff's verbal one. These two scenes have become legend to film noir devotees for symbolizing the attraction of the femme fatale in her adorned and displayed legs and feet.

In *The Postman Always Rings Twice* (Tay Gannettt, 1946), the white open-toed heels are the first image of Cora Smith (Lana Turner), followed by a sweep up her body

FIGURE 8 ☞ The white open-toe heels are the first part seen of Cora Smith (Lana Turner) in this famous shot from *The Postman Always Rings Twice* (Tay Gannett, 1946).

(figure 8). Later, when the couple runs away, a shot of Cora's heels on the highway being dirtied in a puddle calls the end to their escape; at that moment she insists on turning back. Later, Cora is lying down polishing her white shoes, as her lover Frank Chambers (John Garfield) spies through a window on her interaction with her husband. Finally, she struggles in heels on the rocks after the couple's first attempt at murdering her husband. The heels in these two noir films seduce, yet in *Postman* they become the emblem of Cora's desire for wealth and comfort, the femme fatale's true driving force. The seductive qualities of such shoes serve as illusion, misleading the male to the actual signification they hold for their wearer.

In contrast to film noir with its high-heeled femme fatales, Italian neorealism might seem a barefoot film genre. Actually, an alternation between the barefoot and the high-heeled marks several films, and more connection exists between the women of neorealism and the femme fatale than is sometimes acknowledged. This is especially true if we broaden neorealism to include more films than the Italian critics and filmmakers of the immediate postwar period recognized as part of the movement. The tie to hard-boiled fiction that was the root of film noir is at the root of neorealism. Luchino Visconti's *Ossesione* (1942) was an unauthorized adaptation of James M. Cain's novel *The Postman Always Rings Twice,* made four years before the Tay Gannett film discussed above. While Visconti's film provides on many levels a striking contrast to noir style, it also points to certain similarities between its proto-neorealism and film noir. The way it depicts its female protagonist's footwear parallels Gannett's depiction of Cora Smith's heels.

The wife, Giovanna (Clara Calamai), in *Ossesione* is introduced in a shot as striking as that which introduces Cora Smith, and her shoes do play a role, but the differences are instructive. In a shot from the point of view of the stranger who will become her lover, Giovanna, framed through a doorway, sitting on the edge of a table, rapidly swings her legs back and forth as she sings and paints her nails. She wears plain, dark bedroom slippers that have slipped off her heels, accentuating the bareness of her legs and feet. To augment the effect, her future lover enters the shot to fill the right half of the doorway frame, so that only her bare legs, feet, and dangling slippers are seen beyond his body. Later, Giovanna, like Cora, turns back from her escape with her lover, ostensibly because of her shoes. She tires of being on the road in her high heels, a situation marked by a shot that shows her sitting down to remove her heels and rub her feet before making her decision to return. These two shots present the fundamentally barefoot, earthy quality of Giovanna, images that are echoed toward the end of the film by a shot of Giovanna crossing a wet terrain near the sea as she searches for her lover, who abandoned her the night before after a brief reunion in which he learned she was pregnant. He meets her in the midst of this marshy desolate terrain, lifting her into his arms so that he, protectively, may transport her over the wet landscape. In death at the end of the film, Giovanna is once again carried up from the cliff after their car has crashed. In the ironic ending of the crash that spoils the happiness of the newly reunited couple, the spectator may not notice that her corpse has one bare foot and one dangling black heel, but this detail is the perfect encapsulation of Visconti's use of shoes for characterization throughout the film. He depicts Giovanna as a poor woman of earthy sensuality, lured by a desire to escape her meager background, but who ultimately has been broken by the force of circumstances.

The first scene of Fellini's *Le Notte di Cabiria* (*Nights of Cabiria*, 1957) introduces similar imagery as Cabiria's (Guiliana Massina) rescuers carry her shoeless from the water into which her boyfriend had pushed her as the culminating gesture of a robbery. Humiliated, she struggles with the men and boys who just rescued her, demanding her shoes, wriggling out of the arms that attempt to restrain her, and insisting on curtailing any further discussion by hurriedly walking home, alone. That she does so with one shoe on and one shoe off (figure 9) repeats, fifteen years later, the image of Giovanna's death scene, just as neorealism as a specific historical movement is waning.

FIGURE 9 ↝ After Cabiria walks home humiliated with one shoe on and one shoe off, she knocks helplessly, striking a tragicomic pose at her front door in *Le Notte di Cabiria* (*Nights of Cabiria*, Federico Fellini, 1957).

Throughout the rest of the film Cabiria's anklets and flats offer a sharp contrast to the heels of fellow prostitutes, female and transvestite, and especially to the fashionable women she encounters walking the Via Veneto. At a time when the Italian fashion and shoe industries were establishing the 1950s look in consort with Paris and New York, when the Via Veneto had regained in postwar Italy its trend-setting upscale ease, Cabiria represents the other side of the city. Though Cabiria sports blond hair, a fuzzy bolero sweater, and a tight skirt, she wears anklets and flats as she is forced to run through a broad puddle to escape the police chasing herself and her fellow prostitutes, who brave rainy nights and dangerous streets to work on their own terms.

The terms of the opposition between the barefoot woman and the high-heeled woman in Italian films of this period would not be complete without consideration of *Riso Amaro* (*Bitter Rice,* 1948), directed by Giuseppe De Santis, who coscripted with Carlo Lizzani. The film's star, Silvana Mangano, and its complicated murder plot led many critics at the time to argue that it was the antithesis of neorealism. Yet its framing by radio reportage of migrant female labor performing Italy's rice harvest recalls the documentary feel of the voice-over in *Paisa* (*Paisan,* Roberto Rossellini, 1946). *Riso Amaro*'s story of betrayal and gangsterism is in many ways so like film noir, its women protagonists, Silvana and Francesca, so like the molls we might see in heels, that the film is surprising in its insistence on them as barefoot working women. Of course, the gangsterism here is on a scale so small, desperate, and petty that its ultimate goal is to steal the harvested rice. These women are shoeless from the opening of the film, a medium shot of their legs as they step down barefoot to the rice paddies. The women are barefoot not only while working but while dancing, relaxing in their barracks, or surreptitiously meeting men in the rice storage loft. Both Silvana and Francesca are given the role of sexualized Cinderellas without fairy godmothers in sight. Italian films of this period emphasize shoes and shoelessness as defining tropes of sexuality and class. But these tropes are open to reversals, as if to speak to a cultural desire to resist the postwar consumerism that will return Italy to sexualized women in high heels, women whose feet no longer touch the earth.

ENCHANTMENT: RED SHOES AND RUBY SLIPPERS

Technicolor provided filmmakers with an additional tool for highlighting shoes, including their magical powers drawn from fairy-tale myth. Dorothy's ruby slippers in *The Wizard of Oz* (Victor Fleming, 1939) that the good witch Glinda magically moves to her feet from those of the deceased wicked witch of the East are perhaps the first pair of shoes that come to mind when people think of shoes and film. For others, though, another pair of famous enchanted shoes, the red ballet slippers of Michael Powell's *The Red Shoes* (1948), perhaps fill this role. The two make for a fascinating comparison.

In L. Frank Baum's novel *The Wizard of Oz,* Dorothy's enchanted shoes were silver.[13] The decision to make them red-sequined was a design decision linked to the Technicolor process, which is capable of rendering reds vividly. Much has been written on Oz and the slippers, but nothing so eloquent as Salman Rushdie's discussion of the film as a profound influence on his writing, as a story of an exile who learns that if "there is no place like home," home is where you make it. Rushdie creates his own fiction, "At the Auction of the Ruby Slippers," in which he imagines that "orphans arrive, hoping the ruby slippers might transport them back through time and space, and reunite them with their deceased parents," giving us a metaphor for the primal longing attached to the fetishism of these particular shoes.[14] We can see the power of the shoes as an emblem of the fantasy entree to Oz itself, for they are wedded by a marked close-up to the beginning of the journey down the yellow brick road and are an integral part of the skipping dance of Dorothy and each of the four companions she gathers en route to the Emerald City.

FIGURE 10 ✒ *The Wizard of Oz* (Victor Fleming, 1939) offers this famous high-angle medium close-up on Dorothy's feet as the act of transformation is completed with Glinda's magic star wand pointing at the shining slippers.

As such, the ruby slippers are to be understood in relation to the shoes of Kansas, the solid and dusty oxfords worn with anklets that play a major role in the series of traumas that precipitate her exile. The Kansas shoes balance precariously on a rail before slipping, sending Dorothy falling into the pigpen, only to be rescued by the frightened hired hand, chastised by her Auntie Em for diverting the adults on the farm from the tasks at hand. Then the Kansas shoes try desperately to pound open the door to the storm shelter as the tornado approaches, a futile effort. Dorothy lands in Oz with her sensible shoes, which contrast with the landscape, and with Glinda's sparkling magnificence, when she arrives to whisk the magic slippers off the evil witch of the East. The progression of shots here is from the shoes on the dead witch extending beyond the Kansas house, to a high-angle, medium close-up on Dorothy's feet as the act of transformation is completed, Glinda's magic star wand pointing to the shining slippers (figure 10). We should note that these are fantasy evening slippers, but Dorothy wears them with her blue anklets, an image which indicates adolescence. She is still a child, almost a woman; her footwear marks the magic of that moment of transition, trauma, and promise, the condensing of the two Kansas traumas. *The Wizard of Oz* is a magic shoe tale, in which the clicking of shoes is tied to a wish, tied to a return, tied to knowledge.

Far more perverse are the dancing shoes of *The Red Shoes,* adapted from the fairy tale by Hans Christian Andersen, whose obsession with the bloodlines of footwear is apparent in his tale "The Little Mermaid." To Anderson's tale of a ballerina's contract with the devil in the form of a shoemaker, Powell's film adds a manic energy, a perverse delight in the recognition of the grotesque that informs the tale. Dancing faster, dancing onto death, the red shoes become in the film a celebration of the perversity of art, as the film's rhythms accelerate toward a strange, sacrificial binding to endless, obsessive performance.

It is significant, then, that Amy Heckerling chooses red heels that match a red Azzedine Alaia dress as the party adornment of her high-fashion adolescent heroine, Cher (Alicia Silverstone), in *Clueless.* This red outfit and another similar white Anna Sui creation are the two gowns coupled with their matching satin shoes that place Cher as a contemporary reincarnation of the flapper of the 1920s and the streamlined dance goddess of the 1930s.[15] In fact her eye for fashion creates a number of shoe references across the film. She answers a critique of her driving by replying, "You try driving in platforms," and when asked by her father what she did in school today, she replies, "I broke in my purple clogs." Given Cher's preoccupation with footwear, it is perhaps not surprising that the subjective shot of the teacher, Miss Geist, whom she and her pal, Dionne, are sizing up for a makeover, begins as a high angle on ill-fitting black pumps slipping off her heels and continues up over the other fashion faults that make the teacher such an appropriate target of their skills at transformation.

In this world of exacting consumerist fashion expertise, the central red outfit becomes the perfect object for sabotage. First the red heels and later the dress are the objects of mishaps. At a Valley party, coke is spilled on the heels, which causes Cher to shriek, "Ruin my satin shoes, why don't you," as she rushes to the sink to repair her fashion emergency, and then lament, "This is so not fixable." Later that same evening, Cher is mugged at gunpoint, and this time it is the designer dress itself that is threatened by the thief's insistence that she lie down on the ground while he escapes. By the film's end Cher has lost the red high heels of an adolescent rushing past youth into a precocious consumerist adulthood. The film flirts with a comforting return to old-fashioned teenage romance, as she wears sneakers and jeans as she embraces Josh in the penultimate scene. Perhaps all narratives fixated on young women in red shoes are narratives of return, or, even stronger, deathly cautionary tales of the danger such shoes signify.

The high heel with its impracticality, its sensual curves and pointed form, is used in films to signify the modern woman molded into icon, into the iconicity of sexual object. The high heel accrues meanings across the history of film through associations with the nightclub but also with the brothel. When the high heel appears in the business world, it becomes the refusal of a more practical, nearly male attire, a transvestitism on the part of the female entrepreneur that is meant to indicate her sexual neutrality. *Smoldering Fires* (Clarence Brown, 1925) depicts its businesswoman in flats until she is made newly aware of her feminine desires, changes her suits to gowns, and converts to heels. *Female* (Michael Curtiz, 1933) depicts its female executive breaking the codes that demand masculinization of female bosses, appearing in gowns and heels to seduce her male employees at private sessions at her mansion. When the heel appears in the workplace, it carries with it the full threat of female sexual power combined with intelligence; recent films such as *Fatal Attraction* (Adrian Lyne, 1986) and *Disclosure* (Barry Levinson, 1994) have exploited a fear that historically has been associated with the heel-wearing female executive. Films like *Baby Boom* (Charles Silver, 1987) suggest, on the other hand, that the high-heeled executive may find redemption by trading her city shoes for country casual.

Spike heels have come to signify a female power in dominatrix pornography, and one can hardly imagine *The Seven Year Itch*'s famous image (Billy Wilder, 1955) of Marilyn cooling off at the subway grate without her white sling-back heels. So it is significant that Joseph Losey chooses the polar opposite to represent contemporary perversity in his remake of *M* (1951). He moves the tale of Fritz Lang's famous silent film to postwar Los Angeles and shifts the representation of the pedophile to a fixation on plain flat oxfords like the pair Dorothy wore in Kansas. The murderer collects the shoes of his child victims. Rather than the high heels that signify female sexual power, the worn, plain flats emblematize these girls as victims of a particular urban environment. Perversity, then, is contextual, taking the form of an inversion that has its specific relation to power and powerlessness. If male masochism is perverse, more perverse is the desire for a child not yet sexualized. Still more perverse is collecting the shoes of child victims, which represent their powerlessness and innocence. These collected shoes recall the Nazi stockpiling of the shoes of their victims, their worn nature a testament to everyday lives cut short by forces of evil seeking power over the powerless.

THE MAN IN HEELS

If the culture remains nervous about fancy clothes on a young woman, one of its oldest jokes, the man in heels, in drag, is still the object of comedy, but also of increasing fascination and respect. The high heel functions as a central component of transvestitism in film, be it the comic treatments of Billy Wilder's *Some Like It Hot* (1959), Paul Morrisey's *Women in Revolt* (1971), Sydney Pollack's *Tootsie* (1982), or Stephen Eliot's *The Adventures of Priscilla, Queen of the Desert* (1994), the horror of Brian de Palma's *Dressed to Kill,* or the drama of Luchino Visconti's *The Damned* (1969). In fact, a classic exchange on the physical difficulties heels pose for men in contrast to women's adaptation to towering heels is among the funniest exchanges in *Some Like It Hot*: the question "How do they ever manage to walk in these things?" is answered, "I guess their weight is distributed differently."

Yet it is in the work of Pedro Almódovar, who intermixes comedy and drama, that the high-heeled transvestite earns a unique role. She doubles female attributes, maintaining a maternal and sisterly presence that unsettles familial and sexual relations. Femme Lethal (Miguel Bosé), the transvestite performer of Almódovar's *Tacones lejanos* (*High Heels,* 1991),[16] impersonates the songstress, Becky (Marisa Paredes). With Becky's daughter, Rebecca (Victoria Abril), the two form a high-heeled triangle. The film pursues its concentration on shoes in brilliantly composed tableaux as it explores a love-hate relationship with the high heel as an emblem not only of female sexuality but of the memory of the mother.

The first shot emphasizing heels as such chronicles the arrival of a guitar on an airline baggage ramp. The camera pans right with the guitar as it slides down the ramp, then continues to pan right and tilt up to show first the bright red heels of Becky and her coordinated red Giorgio Armani suit and red hat. Becky, a famous Spanish pop singer, has just returned to Spain after a fifteen-year self-imposed exile in Mexico. Her daughter, Rebecca, who has been waiting at the airport to greet her, is dressed in a white Chanel suit (of the Karl Lagerfeld miniskirt period) and sling-back spectator pumps. The clothing opposition of Armani to Chanel will define mother and daughter throughout the film, as the daughter tries to assume a feminine, seductive appearance, a sophistication, an adult sexual identity equal to her mother's, but ends up locked instead in a battle for attention with her mother. Rebecca's struggle for acknowledgment seemingly is doomed by the older woman's greater sense of command.

The next high-heel shot graphically defines their unequal relationship. It occurs when Becky stops the limousine outside a basement apartment she has purchased. A tightly framed close-up shows her red heels as Becky approaches the casement window whose shape echoes the horizontal rectangle of the film's European frame, as she reminisces about her childhood experience growing up in this poor apartment, the daughter of the building's janitors: "The windows. I watched people's feet through them." The daughter's spectator sling-back pumps then appear in the frame (figure 11). This tableau visually aligns two generations engaged in transferring the legacy of a hard-won

FIGURE 11 ✐ A tightly framed close-up shows Becky, the mother, in elegant heels, followed by her daughter, similarly shod, as they approach the casement window. The framing serves as a background for Becky's reminiscences about her childhood experience growing up in this poor apartment, as the daughter of the building's janitors, in Pedro Almódovar's *Tacones lejanos* (*High Heels,* 1996).

class ascendancy, as both Becky and her daughter now occupy the privileged position of urban sophisticates that Becky as a janitor's daughter once envied from the other side of the window. For Becky, clothes and matching shoes provide her with a sexual power sanctioned by their new wealth. Rebecca echoes her attitudes by adopting a regime that awkwardly mixes mimicry with a desire for rebellious differentiation.

In this context the film introduces Femme Lethal, the transvestite performer whose career is based on her imitation of Becky, and who has befriended daughter Rebecca. We first see her as she performs her act at a Madrid club to an audience that includes mother and daughter as well as a group of three other transvestites who imitate her moves as an off-stage chorus from their front-row table. Lethal too is dressed in shades of red, a red bolero, a tight sequined minidress, and red platform shoes with ankle straps. Lethal later remarks that she has captured Becky's look of an earlier period, hence the dated platforms. Lethal has inserted herself in Becky's shoes, substituting herself as confidante of Rebecca in Becky's absence. However, unlike Becky's remote love, Lethal's love for Rebecca is charged, immediate, and sexual. In the dressing-room scene that follows, Lethal seduces Rebecca as she swings comically from an exposed pipe, until Lethal engages her in cunnilingus, so that one of Rebecca's high heels is now wrapped around Lethal's bare back. The imposition of lover through a mother impersonation, then, is sealed with a series of heel images. They trace a female legacy of desire using the image of the performative female, the female who establishes herself through the masquerade of a fetishized wardrobe. Lethal is finally only impersonating the impersonator; he is actually a judge sent into this narrative to precipitate its next convoluted move.

Almódovar's comedy veers off in the direction of a murder mystery as the husband of Rebecca and former (and renewed in the present) lover of Becky is found murdered, which results in Rebecca being incarcerated for the crime. As the film crosscuts from the jail to Becky's comeback concert, the film frames a shot on Becky's tear dropping onto the lipstick mark of the kiss she had earlier planted on the stage, a mark that is itself enclosed between the red pointed toes of her high heels. Only in the final scene, in which mother and daughter reconcile in acts of confession and sacrifice, does Rebecca point out that all the high-heel imagery is as much about her childhood memory as it is about her mother Becky's childhood. As the shadow of a pair of heels cast from the casement window seen earlier plays on the wall behind them, Rebecca says, "When we still lived together I couldn't sleep till I heard your heels clicking, disappearing down the hall after your looking in on me." So mother and daughter are bound by a shoe fetishism, tied, as Freud tells us shoe fetishism might always be, to inscriptions of desire in childhood, remembered and reanimated in the present. Almódovar stylishly frames their fetish as his own, creating comic characters whose psyches become his alibis for a masterful boutique window mise-en-scène, where display reflects its own meanings, the aesthetic of the fetish. As such, the film comments less on the function of the fetish outside the film than it plays with its aesthetics, a fiction constructed through objects that relay associations.

THE SHOES OF HISTORY AND FANTASY

It is tempting, by way of moving toward a conclusion, to link Almódovar back to *The Gay Shoe Clerk,* to imagine a remake in which the clerk is indeed gay in the contemporary sense of that term, but the scene of shoe trial fetishism leads to a complex set of seductions between customer, clerk, and chaperone, and perhaps others. The point of playing with such fantasies, of rearranging representations, is to learn comparatively something of the historical inscription of images. Film history is shadowed by a self-consciousness of shoe symbolism as regards the fetish, the relationship to gender, power, and class. However, self-consciousness of shoe representation reaches new levels in films such as Heckerling's and Almódovar's. This in turn permits them to re-inscribe quite familiar imagery and meanings with renewed appeal, to revisit the close-up inscription of the high heel as fetish.

Eisenstein's sequence on the Odessa steps may represent the most radical inscription of shoes from the standpoint of class and power. However, one could also argue that Eisenstein's dialectical confrontations of shoes on this symbolic stairway still depend on reading what shoes signify in entirely conventional ways. One could argue that the opposition between shoes and bare feet in film noir and neorealism has a different kind of implication, asking us to think about our relation to the cultural accoutrement of the high heel and about our ambivalent feelings about bare feet. Perhaps the film noir/neorealist dialogue suggests that though we have a lingering disdain for bare feet, we trust them more than fancy shoes. This premise informs a recent Iranian film whose style owes much to neorealism, *Children of Heaven* (Majid Majidi, 1997). Close-ups on shoes structure the entire narrative after a poor brother loses the newly repaired shoes of his sister in the opening sequence. As the two now have only a pair of weathered boy's tennis shoes between them, they resolve to share these shoes in order to each attend their respective schools while keeping the loss secret from their parents. The tennis shoe trade-off serves as a refrain that punctuates their ingenious attempts to survive poverty in Teheran. Though the boy longs for fancy running shoes while the girl covets bow-trimmed party shoes, they each envy the footwear of their richer classmates. Yet the film celebrates their barefooted grit and determination. It ends on a shot of the boy's bare and blistered feet soaking after he wins a long-distance race in the same worn tennis shoes. The film finds its moral center in children with their feet on the ground.

Children of Heaven also makes an intriguing comparison to our earlier exploration of shoe fantasies. If we, considering *The Wizard of Oz* alongside *The Red Shoes,* can imagine magic slippers as powerful vehicles for fantasy, these narratives, taken together, indicate that we are suspicious, if not moralistic, about the ethics of investments in the miraculous object. If the gendering of footwear is undergoing new cycles of transformation, such as the glam-rock glitter boots memorialized in *Velvet Goldmine* (Todd Haynes, 1998), much of the feminine-masculine polarity of footwear remains intact at the beginning of the twenty-first century, in films as in consumer culture, though "actual" women and men may choose their identities anywhere along the continuum that unites those polarities.

Films such as *Velvet Goldmine* fixate on the design detail of footwear as part of a larger scheme in which flamboyance colorfully accompanies the plea for sexual liberation. This tendency is part of a larger renewal of theatricality in film style, deeply connected to literature and theater, and which revisits the costume drama with new attention to politics.[17] Consider, for example, the splendid deviation taken by Pier Paolo Pasolini's adaptations of *The Decameron* (1971) , *The Canterbury Tales* (1974), and *1001 Arabian Nights* (1974). These films present flamboyant fantasies set in the past, or in purely imaginary baroque realms, where shoe design favors the decorated, the exaggerated, or even the bizarre. Yet Pasolini's *Salo, or The 120 Days of Sodom* (1975) dares to explore the fascist potential of both this flamboyance and this sexual liberation, presenting its fashionable shoes of the captors in stark contrast to the naked feet of the young victims of torture, and renewing the oppositional debate between the high heel and the bare foot in Italian film in the most unsettling of ways.[18]

Another sign of recent renewal of interest in elegant footwear is the residual influence on shoe fashion of Asian shoe designs. Western fascination with Asian shoes has a long history, but certainly Bernardo Bertolucci's *The Last Emperor* (1987) and Steven Spielberg's *Empire of the Sun* (1987) coupled with the popularity of costume films by Chinese directors seem to have brought about a revival of Asian-influenced styles in recent years. Given the historical specificity and diversity of Asian footwear, fashion seems to absorb from this filmic display simply a predilection for a return to silk, satin, embroidery, and beadwork.[19] Only the more adventurous high-fashion shoes have sought any fidelity to the specific historical shapes of East Asian shoes. Instead, the shoe industry amalgamates various Asian influences into an exotic alternative to European traditions of luxury.

Perhaps it is the context of a movie theater audience largely dressed in athletic shoes that these films reviving the elegance of handmade footwear seem a most astounding assertion that the fetish of the aristocratic shoe will not die once an aristocracy is impractical and politically detestable. Even if Hollywood stars offscreen are as likely to be seen in casual shoes as in the footwear associated with Fred and Ginger, the return of the costume drama in its various guises suggests a hunger on the part of audiences for shoe splendor. If these sorts of elegant shoes imply a world of carriages and footmen rather than the subways of our mean streets, they seem to connote that wearers today are of a class to take taxis or limos, or use valet parking. Seeing such elaborate and elegant styles appear in art films and museums serves as a reminder of times in which the shoe was a prime marker of social standing, determining what paths one was even allowed to dream of taking.

Film will be our kinetic museum of this footwear history, to preserve not the actual objects but their glorious traces in motion. Cinema helps to narrate and even to create meanings for footwear, as shoes take on a magic and even a life of their own. If Bonitzer is right to link the cinematic close-up with Bataille's emphasis on the big toe, it is by extension that we might say that shoes not only fulfill a special role in the close-up but become privileged points of kinetic interest in all shots in which they appear. Like the white lines that Etienne-Jules Marey fixed on his black-clothed figures in order to study motion through multiple-exposure photography, these shoes trace a kinetic pattern dear to the cinema, by using certain images in relationship to others in order to trace out the patterns of cinematic poesis.

NOTES

1. Charles Musser, *The Emergence of Cinema: The American Screen to 1907* (Berkeley and Los Angeles: University of California Press, 1990), 349.

2. Ibid.

3. Ibid, 288, 413.

4. Georges Bataille, "The Big Toe," in *Visions of Excess: Selected Writings, 1927–39,* ed. Allan Stoekl (Minneapolis: University of Minnesota Press, 1989), 21. Originally published in French as "Le Gros Orteil," *Documents* 6 (1929): 297–302.

5. Sigmund Freud, "Fetishism," in *The Standard Edition of the Complete Psychological Works of Sigmund Freud,* vol. 21 (London: Hogarth Press and the Institute for Psychoanalysis, 1953–74), 129–155.

6. Bataille, "The Big Toe," 23. Valerie Steele's chapter on shoes in her book *Fetish: Fashion, Sex, and Power* cites both Bataille and a similar argument from Ernest Becker's *The Denial of Death*: "The foot is its own horror; what is more, it is accompanied by its own striking and transcending denial and contrast—the shoe." Steele paraphrases, inserting her own description of the fetish shoes she studies in the chapter: "Whereas the foot is a low and dirty 'testimonial to our degraded animality,' the shoe—made of soft and shiny polished leather with an elegantly curved arch and pointed toe, lifted above the ground on a hard spiked heel— 'is the closest thing to the body and yet is not the

body'" (*Fetish: Fashion, Sex, and Power* [New York: Oxford University Press, 1996], 106). This echo of Bataille in Becker becomes useful to Steele as she examines hard-core foot fetishism as a cultural phenomenon. Given that in all the films discussed in this essay, foot and shoe fetishism is both less direct and less exaggerated than hard-core representations, we are still wise to hold on to this limit case in order to understand how narrative inscription often justifies our desire to see the foot and/or the dramatic or gorgeous shoe. The fetish shoe represents not only its wearer but our own desire as well.

7. Bonitzer cites Bataille in his title, "Le Gros Orteil: Réalité de la dénotation" (The big toe: reality of denotation), though the essay was relabeled "Le Gros Plan: Supplément de scène" (The close-up: supplement of the scene) on the cover of the *Cahiers du cinéma* issue, providing a less enigmatic and more descriptive title. See Pascal Bonitzer, "Le Gros Plan: Supplément de la scène," *Cahiers du cinéma* 232 (1972): 14–23.

8. Let me express my gratitude to Yuri Tsivian for his work in making this film and other Russian films from this period available to U.S. scholars and for his book *Early Cinema in Russia and Its Cultural Reception,* trans. Alan Bodger (London and New York: Routledge, 1994). According to Tsivian, the shoes worn in this film by the indifferent lover were known in Russia as "tango slippers," which gives us a sense of how this film marks significant trends in prerevolutionary popular culture and fashion.

9. In an earlier article I looked at how films' struggle with the moral dilemmas of modern and extravagant fashion coexists with a celebration of sartorial elegance in all its seductive power. In fact several of the films I examined contain remarkable images that trace the historical significance of changes in women's shoe design. See Maureen Turim, "Seduction and Elegance: The New Woman of Fashion in Silent Cinema," in *On Fashion,* ed. Shari Benstock and Suzanne Ferriss (New Brunswick, N.J.: Rutgers University Press, 1994), 140–158.

10. Nigel Cawthorne and Angela Pattison focus on this film as key to the success of the sandal in American fashion: "Salvatore Ferragamo brought the sandal from Italy to the United States. His sandal techniques were honed by his work on Cecil B. DeMille's movie, *The Ten Commandments.* In 1923, DeMille commissioned Ferragamo to make over 12,000 pairs of sandals for the movie in less than two months. After a trip to a local library, Ferragamo discovered that very little was known about ancient Egyptian footwear so he based his designs on some Victorian illustrations. During the same period Ferragamo invented his Roman sandal. It fastened around the ankle with a single thong. The revolutionary steel reinforcement he used in his shoes allowed him to create dainty pedestals to show off the foot. In the warm climate of California, his creations quickly caught on as evening wear. And when the movie stars wore them on screen, the fashion for elegant sandals took off around the world" (*A Century of Shoes: Icons of Style in the Twentieth Century* [Edison, N.J.: Chartwell Books, 1997], 65).

11. This foot gesture is typical of Bow's filmic heroines; *Mantrap* (Victor Fleming, 1926) and *The Wild Party* (Dorothy Arzner, 1929) also feature Bow playing young women who enjoy "kicking up their heels," but whose apparent wildness is only an energetic display of liveliness reserved for the dance floor, and tamed entirely by the films' end. *Mantrap* begins with a medium close-up of a divorcee playing footsie by stroking her heel against her divorce lawyer's pants. The divorcee in question is not Clara Bow, who plays a manicurist from Minneapolis not introduced until much later in the film. However, this opening shot establishes the shoe as tool of seduction, preparing us for the manicurist's Charleston-like footwork through her day at the upscale barber shop. Later, after her marriage to a backwoodsman, she exhibits the same exuberance in her cabin home, captivating the very New York lawyer who resisted the divorcee's seductive gesture at the film's opening. So the shoe motif links these two women, setting up the contrast between the evil man trap and the innocent, playful flapper figure. Like *The Wind, Mantrap* will show its high-heeled heroine eventually becoming acclimated to her rural life, renouncing a desire to return to an urban culture where high heels might be more appropriate.

12. Later this line echoes in David Bowie's "Let's Dance."

13. L. Frank Baum, *The Wizard of Oz* (New York: Grosset and Dunlap, 1956).

14. Salman Rushdie, *The Wizard of Oz* (London: BFI, 1992).

15. The dress in question is indeed a white Anna Sui slipdress chosen by costume designer Mona May. Cher's father remarks on the dress by asking, "What the hell is that? It looks like underwear," to which she simply replies, "It's a dress." Her father persists, "Who says?" Cher counters, "Calvin Klein."

16. The title of the film is translated as *High Heels* for its English-language release, though the Spanish actually means "Distant Heels," setting up the sound of heels in the distance in its connection to the distance between mother and daughter. Femme Lethal then mediates this distance by imitating the mother to solve the lingering family secrets of guilt and pain to reach the daughter with a love she never received from her own mother.

17. Shoe designers for film, particularly those specializing in creating the shoes of past periods, are the mediators who facilitate this process. Designers whose work affected the future of Italian shoe design include Salvatore Ferragamo, Stefania Ricci, and Edward Maeder (*Salvatore Ferragamo: The Art of the Shoe, 1890–1960* [New York: Rizzoli, 1992]). While most shoes for most films are today bought off the rack, be it one at an exclusive boutique, there is still a role to be played by the shoe designer in film production, whose major challenge is the re-creation of historical footwear. The Atelier Pompeï, which since 1932 has been the designer of shoes for Cinecitta, the hub of the Italian film industry, plays a role parallel to that of Ferragamo and other studio designers in influencing the revival of historical styles. This specialty shoe production company continues to be the most important contemporary shoe designer for costume films, as well as La Comédie Française, La Scala, L'Opéra Garnier, and L'Opéra Bastille. See Marie-Josèphe Bossan, ed., *Chaussure et Cinema: Créations de l'Atelier Pompeï* (Romans, France: Musée International de la Chaussure, 1996).

18. In contrast to the shoes in these films, consider Pasolini's earlier films, *The Gospel according to Saint Matthew* (1967), *Oedipe Rex* (1967), and *Medea* (1970), in which the ancient and the classical sandals were produced with less splendor and more authenticity. The proletarian emphasis of Pasolini's *Gospel* helps us understand the political implications of this shift in design philosophy and both borrows from and reifies the popularity of the sandal among members of the 1960s counterculture. Yet we should note that these sandals were the product of the Atelier Pompeï, as were the baroque shoe designs of Pasolini's later films. The Atelier Pompeï provided the shoes that propelled the revival of the ancient costume drama in the 1950s and 1960s; among its credits were both Italian and American films, films often connected through use of Cinecitta sets in *Rome: Quo Vadis?* (Mervyn LeRoy, 1951), *The Last Days of Pompei* (Mario Bonnard, 1959), *Ben Hur* (William Wyler, 1959), *Spartacus* (Stanley Kubrick, 1960), *Samson vs. Hercules* (G. Parolini, 1960), *Cleopatra* (Joseph L. Mankiewicz, 1963), and *The Bible* (John Huston, 1966). Golden shin-high sandals made of calfskin and those made of red kid with golden calfskin appliqué trim, both decorated with embossed lion heads, were the footwear of Robert Taylor and Peter Ustinov in *Quo Vadis?* They were matched or perhaps exceeded in elegance by the golden platform sandals made of calfskin that Elizabeth Taylor wore in *Cleopatra,* designs whose influence may be seen in the platform revival in fashion and popular culture of the 1970s. The connection of these ancient fantasy designs to Ferragamo's work for DeMille is obvious, but we need to also note that Ferragamo's boutique was instrumental in popularizing platform shoes in the 1940s, especially his cork-sole cloth espadrilles. In 1948–50 Ferragamo featured a gold kid sandal that, while it was part of a line that introduced a Chinese-inspired curved heel, has enough similarity to the *Cleopatra* sandal to support a claim of design dialogue between Ferragamo's high-fashion establishment in Florence and the Atelier Pompeï film and theater design house in Rome. So in giving Cleopatra platforms, Atelier Pompeï revives the 1940s and marks its relationship to Ferragamo. This relationship is also evident in the high heels Atelier Pompeï deigned for Federico Fellini's *La Dolce Vita* (1960) and *8 1/2* (1963); these stiletto heels are similar to the 1958–60 Ferragamo line of pumps and court shoes bearing slim elevated heels and pointed toes, enhanced with impeccable design detail. The play between contemporary fashion, revival aesthetics, and historical reference creates a filmic shoe design marked by fantasy.

Characterized by its outstanding use of color, the work of Atelier Pompeï was a perfect addition to the exploitation of color film design possibilities, as the house has a willingness to mix the historical with the self-consciously current trends of high-fashion design.

19. There is a contemporaneity to even the most historically accurate of Atelier Pompeï styles. Consider the great fun the house had with the medieval poulanes it created for Jean-Marie Poiré's *Les Visiteurs* (1996); although we now associate these pointed elongated toe fashions with elves and jesters, their exaggerated length was once a mark of court standing. Given the film's reinscription of the medieval as a fantasy sci-fi visitation from the past, the narrative actually inscribes what I take to be the Atelier Pompeï's design principle, rendering the past ever more spectacular, bearing within it an edge of fantasy, but retaining within the spectacular much serious work on the politics of this history. Witness Atelier Pompeï's designs for Bernardo Bertolucci's *The Last Emperor* (1987), for Jost Iacob's *Rouge Venise* (1988), for Patrice Chereau's *La Reine Margot* (Queen Margot, 1994), for Gérard Corbiau's *Farinelli* (1994), for Jean-Paul Rappeneau's *Le Hussard sur le Toit* (*The Horseman on the Roof,* 1995), and for Patrick Leconte's *Ridicule* (1995). These films take both the elegance and the specificity of historical periods as their point of departure, but their rendering of opulent shoe design, especially those worn by men, prolongs something of the 1970s glam and transvestite fashion explosions into a filmic fixation on glamorous historical footwear. Perhaps it helps to speak of the new theatricality informing film design in general, and certainly the design of footwear in these historical dramas, as we enter a new century.

Presentation

Self-Fashioning, Gender Display, and Sexy Girl Shoes: What's at Stake— Female Fetishism or Narcissism?

LORRAINE GAMMAN

Grand Hotel, Brighton, 1995: "Girl heaven" equals cream cakes from room service and boxes of new girl shoes to open and admire.[1] Shopping done, the art exhibition on "fetishism"[2] we had come down especially to see not quite gone from our minds—all eyes focus now on turquoise sandals. Why? (Why not?)

Shoes are so *easy.* It doesn't matter how many cakes you eat, there is usually a sexy pair somewhere that looks as if it will fit and cheer you up. Of course, women's shoes—like pumps, slingbacks, and mules[3]—involve fragmented fantasies of the feminine. They also offer potent symbols of gender and sexuality, but are they always worn and bought with men in mind? Self-fashioning and gender display through shoes are popular activities even with feminists. Questions about objectification, female masquerade, female narcissism, and fetishism through consumerism raise different theoretical issues about women's self-fragmentation and ultimately the human-object relation. Indeed, some shoe shopping by women might be viewed as a search for lost envelopes of the imagination, and allow us to move beyond phallocentric arguments—based on psychoanalytic notions of "lack"—to consider broader issues about "loss" in relation to shoe fixations by women.

FROM OBJECTIFICATION TO FRAGMENTATION:
BEST FEET FORWARD . . .

While objectification of the female body was common practice in paintings of the female nude well before the twentieth century, the sort of cropped fragmented-body-part imagery we associate with photography is essentially a twentieth-century phenomenon. It has been described as a metaphor of modernity, partly because the sense of dislocation implicit in a fragmentary vision is itself an evocative metaphor for the alienated modern condition.[4] Of course, not all images of body fragments, or of shoes, originate with photography.

Linda Nochlin, in her book *The Body in Pieces,* discusses a wide historical span starting with Henry Fuseli's red-chalk-and-sepia-wash drawing *The Artist Overwelmed by the Grandeur of Antique Ruins* (1778–79) as well as a number of late-nineteenth-century drawings and paintings of legs and feet. Eugene Disderi's 1860 photomontage showing the feet of the ballerinas at the Paris Opéra and a group of provocative drawings of legs and feet by Eduoard Manet are among the fragmented images Nochlin looks at.[5] When discussing Edouard Manet's *Masked Ball at the Opera* (1873), *Note to Mme Guillemet* (1880), and *At the Café* (c. 1880), Nochlin suggests that "gender difference is the major factor in constituting the meaning of the cut/off feet and legs. That is to say, the fact that these are *women's* legs, not men's, is of great significance, since the male fragmented leg obviously signifies very differently from the female one."[6]

Manet's drawings have fetishistic dimensions, not least because of erotic accentuation (the Victorians were obsessed with ankles), and this is quite common to images of body fragments.[7] Yet by the early twentieth century, photographs of hands and eyes, as well as nude female legs and feet, had become a "viable option."[8] The visual fragment superseded much earlier cultural practices (such as foot binding) and literary forms (such as the blazon)[9] as an acceptable mode of female representation. It was twentieth-century developments in anatomy, x-ray technology, and refined lithography and color printing techniques,[10] among other innovations, that contributed to the emergence of the visual fragment. Consequently, the nude fragment became very central to the work of the German "new objectivity" photographers of the 1920 and 1930s, as well as to so many subsequent art movements.[11] Often, the body fragment works as erotic synecdoche, where a part is featured to hint at the sexual attractiveness of the whole body. Today, similar images of fragmented female parts have almost become a photographic cliché of advertising and erotic representation.

According to James M. Ferreira, fragmented body parts were certainly found in naive early-twentieth-century erotic "barbershop" magazines.[12] Later nude magazines, as well as subsequent postwar lifestyle soft porn (such as *Playboy*) and the emerging market for fetish magazines, also featured nude fragments. As clothing gradually disappeared from the models in mainstream erotic male magazines, attention shifted from the whole body and personality to the breasts, buttocks, and crotch. Even advertising and fashion photography drew upon erotic codes and conventions. Lips for toothpaste and mouthwash ads were commonplace, as was the photographic fixation on buttocks and hips to sell jeans. Of course, these shots were a little more subtle than in porn magazines. For example, crotch shots in advertising are unusual and more often suggested instead by images that accentuate the feet via high heels (to sell stockings and panty hose) and that provide alluring views up the skirt, which don't quite reach the panties. These photographic clichés have effortlessly permeated popular culture as acceptable visual imagery. Consequently, such "modern" accentuation and mass production of photographic images have operated to objectify women's bodies far more than the paintings by Manet and his contemporaries ever did.

WOMAN AS "OBJECT"

The modern fixation on the female body fragment provoked a whole debate about "women as object." Betty Friedan, Germaine Greer, and Sheila Rowbotham, among other second-wave feminists, complained about women being forced, by social and mass media representations controlled by men, to see themselves in fragments through male eyes—often as a good pair of tits, lips, or legs.[13] Indeed, many subsequent feminists have argued that fashion and cosmetics are part of a male conspiracy to oppressively regulate the internalization of "femininity" and thus keep women in their place. Naomi Wolf, for example, has suggested that a covert feminist backlash, articulated via stereotypical images of female beauty, operates to sabotage women's advancement by making them psychologically hooked on "inexhaustible but ephemeral beauty work."[14] More recently, Natasha Walters has made similar arguments about appearance.[15]

In the 1970s, many feminists, particularly Germaine Greer in *The Female Eunuch*, argued that magazines, fashion, and advertising images featuring the sexual objectification of women were designed to address phallocentric male fantasies (oblivious to authentic female desires) and were oppressive to women.[16] Gloria Steinem made similar arguments and in particular complained about the Bunny Girl as a cultural icon presented for the pleasure of men. She went undercover as a Playboy bunny to achieve her journalistic assignment and complained about having to stand for long periods in bunny shoes: "and atop my three inch black satin heels, my feet were killing me." Unsurprisingly, her day ended with "swollen feet."[17] No wonder high heels were viewed very unsympathetically by feminists, many of whom saw them as titillating "man-made" objects, literally involved in crippling women, or at least slowing them down when the need to run away from male violence and oppressors arose.[18] While feminine shoes may mean many different things to different women, a site where class and ethnic fantasies (as well as gender identities) may be transformed, Susan Brownmiller points out "the unifying factors may be pared down to these: the shoe must make the foot look smaller, it must be light and flimsy in construction, it must incorporate some stylish hindrance that no man in his right mind would put up with. None of this is accidental."[19] She goes on to observe, "A feminine shoe imposes a new problem of grace and self consciousness on what otherwise would be a simple act of locomotion, and in this artful handicap lies its subjugation and supposed charm."[20]

Although shoes with stilettos went out of fashion in the late 1960s, high heels and fad fashions like platform shoes of the 1970s were also demonized because of their symbolic connotations. So much so, in fact, that Lee Wright could observe in 1989 that "the stiletto has been widely accepted as symbolizing female subordination," a comparable successor to foot binding and the tight-laced corset as a perverse regulatory objects for molding the feminine.[21]

Eventually, the feminist rejection of fashion started to lose much of its grassroots support in the postmodern context of the 1980s. The idea that fashion, cosmetics, and/or sexy shoes were not simply oppressive, but offered pleasure to women, became more widely accepted: feminist critics began to point out that "fashion can be an experiment with appearances, an experiment that challenges cultural meanings."[22] This change of heart about high heels perhaps was provoked by countercultural street fashions of the early 1980s, as well as by a feminist debate about pleasure and female desire in the context of what film theorists of the 1970s had defined as the "controlling" male gaze.[23] These events indirectly changed the way the fashion system was understood in certain quarters. So-called lipstick lesbians (gorgeous creatures who differentiated themselves from media constructions of dungareed dykes), as well as a band of "keep on shagging" material girls, made it clear to their more hard-line sisters that feminists could be glamorous. Dressing up, grooming, and playing around with identity could not be regarded as a response to oppression or the "male gaze" when sisters said they were doing it for themselves. Perhaps it took punk's semiotic warfare and reclaiming of women's fetish fashions, including dominatrix boots, to explain why attitude and appropriation were significant. In a context where fashion meanings were found to be polysemic rather than fixed,[24] it was hard to make the case stick that women's fashion shoes were linked to female subordination when so many strong (so-called phallic women) wore them. As Elizabeth Wilson observes, in some circumstances, "sexual display functioned as a kind of 'touch me not armour.'"[25] Whether it was punk stilettos worn with a garbage bag or early 1980s Doc Martens worn with a tutu and leather jacket, fashion met feminism on a journey toward empowerment through the purchase of consumer products.

Of course, throughout the 1980s and 1990s when fashions were changing, there were ideological contradictions about whether female empowerment could ever be really promoted by the marketplace. Also, the specter of anorectic models continued to haunt feminism, particularly when surveys of the early 1990s found children as young as seven overconcerned with body weight. A crude "moral panic" (did Twiggy and Kate Moss "cause" anorexia?) about thin models and what was termed "heroin chic" emerged. Concern about fashion "victims" was exacerbated by later spectacles like Naomi Campbell falling off Vivienne Westwood platforms, and saw the newspaper columnists raising all the tired old questions about "slaves" to fashion. Nevertheless, liberal feminist arguments that emerged at the end of the 1980s—that women need to take charge of their own self-esteem and image to feel good for themselves—eventually colonized about female adornment in the 1990s. Individualism ruled in stereotypical new-woman discourse about the need for women to make choices in their lives. Consequently, a girl wearing the kind of shoes "she wants to" became almost prototypically 1990s "feminist"—although anxieties were such that she probably would have chosen not to use the F-word.[26]

The historical argument that feminism had not empowered all women—that sisterhood should at least try to be inclusive—was overlooked in this 1990s consumer-magazine focus on aspirational images addressed to new female markets. In the battle that ensued between "bad girls" versus "nice girls"—kitten heels versus stilettos—young feminists wearing spikes seemed to win the fight. Emma Peel fashions once again became all the rage—even with 1990s new women. How so? High heels on pumps, slingbacks, and mules clearly connote feminine sexiness,[27] and at a moment when some feminists decided to reclaim female desire and lead a rebellion against neutered sexuality (read compliant femininity and "niceness"), high heels were almost seen as politically correct attire for desiring subjects. Fetish shoes and fashion spoke sexiness and caused category confusion—because signs of commodity fetishism and of erotic and sexual fetishism may look exactly the same. This led to questions about "sheep in wolves' clothing" and footwear. There were commercial reasons, too, why sexy girl shoes became popular. Manolo Blahnik's high-heel shoes were seen everywhere on the catwalks as new young designers of the 1990s revalued his work, and perhaps started to rethink the role of fashion accessories.[28] Designers who helped create the very tall heels of the 1990s, such as Jimmy Choo and Emma Hope, rode into that decade on this profitable new wave of interest in shoes. So did Tom Ford of Gucci, who suggested high heels were popular again because "it's hard not to be sexy in a pair of high heels." Simon Doonan, creative director of Barney's in New York, on the other hand, suggested the success of high heels was linked to power dressing: "High heels create a level of authority."[29]

Despite the success of high heels in the 1990s, a time when some obsessives claimed that a well-made four-inch Jimmy Choo was more comfortable than a badly made two-inch chain-store heel, some "strong" women were left behind wearing sneakers. Since my feet are not like Barbie's, it took me a long time before I let myself realize that the expensive heeled objects of my desire would never be more than a one-night stand. So I paid the price and kept my Manolo Blahnik snakeskin and patent shoe collection—featuring the odd pair of Sabrina heels—primarily in a closet. They were meant for the big outing or more often for private viewing or admiration purposes only. Finally, I got bored with the masquerade and even the fantasy of wearing them, and have recently developed a penchant for black suede hybrid shoe-sneakers (known as "Merrills") instead.[30] The only high heels I now spend money on are displayed as "Art." These are not obvious collectibles, such as the miniature design history shoe classics that can be bought at museum shops, but perhaps have more ironic sign value.[31] The fragile ceramic version of life-size red court shoe slip-ons made by printmaker Hedley Roberts found safe display room in the fish tank in my living room.[32] These shoes as aesthetic objects have given me and my goldfish a lot of pleasure, and perhaps have extended the private space the masquerade of femininity inhabits in my home.

THE MASQUERADE OF FEMININITY

The idea of consumer objects and style, from haircuts to jewelry, from heels to dresses, being central to gender masquerade is not a new idea. But there is a difference in recognizing that there is no authentic feminine behavior or that today generations of women enjoy playing with gender signs (if not always sexual orientation). So perhaps it is worth recapping the theory of masquerade in order to comprehend the significance of sexy girl shoes.

In her definitive article "Womanliness as Masquerade," Joan Rivière writes about clients who use feminine presentation itself to hide anxieties about being perceived as masculine.[33] Her overall point is that femininity is not real, but rather it is a simulacrum because there is no authentic feminine behavior to which it makes reference. Stephen Heath paraphrases her thinking as follows: "In the masquerade the woman mimics an authentic—genuine—womanliness, but then authentic womanliness as such a mimicry *is* the masquerade ('they are the same thing'). . . . the masquerade is a representation of femininity but then femininity is representation, the representation of the woman."[34] Rivière's account includes descriptions of a career woman who puts on a masquerade of femininity—literally flirting with her audience—in order to rebuke the charge of masculinity. Rivière relates masquerade to feminine lack, and this is compatible with Lacan's account too.[35] Women masquerade *as* the phallus (the signifier of desire) because they do not *have* it. Jacqueline Rose suggests that "for Lacan, masquerade is the very definition of 'femininity' precisely because it is constructed with reference to a male sign."[36]

Louise Kaplan in *Female Perversions* takes up Rivière's argument and the insights of Lacan, although she goes farther in her descriptions of the motivations underlying the female masquerade. Indeed, she makes the point that "just as not everyone who cross dresses is a transvestite, not everyone who dresses in the clothes of his or her own sex is of course a homeovestite."[37] She seeks to differentiate so-called perverse behavior from normal behavior. She suggests that when the element of feminine overcompensation in self-display is extreme, the behavior is perverse. Kaplan goes on to define female homeovestites as women who dress in stereotypical ways and whose homeovestism is driven by extreme fear of being perceived as masculine. She cites Flaubert's fictional heroine Emma Bovary as well as "Lillian" (a patient who was documented by the psychoanalyst George Zavitzanos) as typical of women who are so ill at ease with their femininity that they literally impersonate women. She says "a woman who dresses up to exhibit herself as a valuable sexual commodity" should be understood not in terms of "exhibitionism" (because "such women are as dominated by their sexual scenarios as the men they captivate") but in terms of homeovestism.[38] She says this is a more useful term for explaining the behavior of such women.

I must say I am reluctant to use the term "homeovestism," not least because the discourse of perversion tends to problematically pathologize individuals rather than femininity itself. Yet it does make sense that some women get more caught up in anxieties about gender performance than others. Perhaps we do need to hold on to the idea of homeovestism as an extreme, in order to consider what really is at stake in the female masquerade. E. L. McCallum in her excellent book *Object Lessons: How to Do Things with Fetishism* suggests that "masquerade offers reassurance to another" whereas "fetishism offers reassurance to oneself."[39] It's a nicely put distinction—and appears to differentiate women who masquerade from those who fetishistically exhibit themselves—but is it true that the female masquerade is always for the gaze of others? I would problematize such a notion, not least because exhibitionism is a form of masquerade that is clearly fetishistic.

Many women involved in the masquerade of womanliness don't appear to "go for it" completely, at least not the whole way in terms of grooming their appearance. Jennifer Patterson was the famous sixty-something British "fat lady" TV chef who was never seen without beautifully painted nails, even when cooking. On TV she appeared to accentuate one part of her body rather than others in her grooming rituals. Before she died, she was known for pleasing herself, not minding her waistline, and indulging in "forbidden" foods. Similarly, fifty-something Conservative politician Ann Widdicome always has exquisitely painted nails, but when interviewed says she is not interested in self-presentation or excessive grooming for male viewers; she is frequently called "Doris Karloff" or "Boris" by colleagues and opponents who wish to bait her.

Using these random examples, and my own experience, I want to suggest two things. First, that "intensities" of masquerade need to be identified in a way that parallels the intensities of fetishism formulated by Paul Gebhardt. In trying to differentiate individuals who get a sexual charge from objects (stage 1) from those who prefer the object to sex with a partner (stage 4), Gebhardt came up with the following description of intensities of fetishism:

Level 1: A slight preference exists for certain kinds of sex partners, sexual stimuli or sexual activity. The term "fetish" should not be used at this level.

Level 2: A strong preference exists for certain kinds of sex partners, sexual stimuli or sexual activity. (Lowest intensity of fetishism.)

Level 3: Specific stimuli are necessary for sexual arousal and sexual performance. (Moderate intensity of fetishism.)

Level 4: Specific stimuli *take the place of* a sex partner. (High level fetishism.)[40]

Freud said all women are clothes fetishists,[41] and I make the point that an element of fetishism (certainly commodity fetishism) is present in the contemporary feminine masquerade. Self-display as it affects the feminine masquerade may be informed by cultural differences between women, including those based on geograpic location, age, and generation, as well as race, sexuality, and class. Lisa Balmaseda's observation makes this point very astutely when she says, "It was the heels that distinguished the Latinas from the Americanitas. We were the chicks in the seven-inch, custom-designed platforms."[42] But questions about cultural difference and interpretation of gender display are not the only issues raised by the idea of measuring intensities of fetishism. Extreme behavior within groups becomes noticeable, even within groups and subcultures whose behavior challenges the dominant culture, and if there are four levels of self-display, it is clear to me that "homeovestism" linked to *extreme* exhibitionism would be level four, the strongest "perverse" intensity. It is also compatible with orthodox sexual fetishism. It should be noted, however, that the first three levels perhaps suggest more levels of agency for the shoe wearer than orthodox sexual fetishism, defined as level four, and I think it is important to retain a sense of female agency in relation to notions of female masquerade before invoking ideas about orthodox sexual fetishism.

My second suggestion is that fetishism and narcissism are constellatory interarticulations that inform the masquerade. They may drive other aspects of self-fragmentation and self-objectification by women, particularly when the women in question say they do it for their "own" sake. Such self-absorption and self-objectification may also be compatible with the sort of dislocated modern alienation Nochlin describes.

SHOE FIXATIONS AND WOMEN

Some female images may inspire individual women in their everyday life to buy high-heeled shoes that contort the body and enable them to perform to exaggerated types of femininity. For example, Beatrice Faust in *Women, Sex, and Pornography* argues that high heels have a physiological effect that make women's buttocks undulate and thus transmit sexual sensations throughout the female body; the "jiggle" walk that follows from wearing high heels apparently appeals particularly to men. "Tread on Them Heels" and "Fuck Me Shoes" may even inspire women to conform to male definitions about what is sexy, and to "the male gaze."[43] Yet many women who love shoes say they really don't buy them with men in mind or to titillate in the way fetish magazines such as *Footsy* require, and that their partners are not particularly interested in their footwear. Suzanne Moore maintains her shoes are "not worn just for the benefit of men. Most of the pleasure [of buying shoes] involves a private fantasy that starts with me and ends at my feet. Men don't get a look in."[44]

Why shouldn't women who have nice legs enjoy wearing shoes that make their legs look longer? Indeed, I suspect shoe fixations by women are connected to a different set of understandings altogether than men's shoe fixations. They demand a different reading of the feminine masquerade than is simply offered by the idea that the pursuit of womanliness is driven by making oneself into an object in order to appease the male gaze.

As a cultural sign, the reading of the female shoe has been dominated by the idea that the heel is a penis substitute and symbolizes phallic replacement. For example, Hilary Radner comments: "Feet and the foot fetish, of course, evoke even to the populace at large, a paradigm of sexual perversion in which, in the most literal sense, the man can't get it up unless the woman is wearing appropriate footgear."[45] Yet the shoe could also be read as swallowing or enveloping the foot, a symbolic "vagina," a metaphor, according to Bruno Bettelheim, absolutely central to analysis of the meaning of Perrault's "Cinderella" and her slipper.[46] However, Lisa Tickner once pointed out that "the stiletto heel . . . as an object . . . is seen as being exclusively female,"[47] and in the twenty-first century many drag queens, male transsexuals, and other camp icons,[48] as well as biological women, are aware of this and delight, for example, in tall Vivienne Westwood creations for the feet. They are also aware of the fact that our clothes and our shoes are all part of gender drag because as Ru Paul describes the transformation from he-male to she-male: "How tall am I? Honey, with hair, heels and attitude I'm through the damned roof."[49] High heels are such a crucial component of exaggerated femininity, that Alexander McQueen, the latest "enfant terrible" of British fashion, ensured his ready-to-wear collection for Givenchy in 1997 featured tall wigs and very high heeled shoes, in order to create a deliberately frightening look. Evidently, these women were so aggressive and Amazonian in the way that they were presented that the word "super-women" was used to describe them.[50]

Many women—post-Madonna—enjoy playing with their own signs of feminine identity, in the way Cindy Sherman has done in her photographs. Sometimes this playfulness may be part of a recontextualization by those with a keen fashion eye. "I have a few pair of shoes that I can actually only even wear in bed or at a push, if I'm sitting down," comments Suzanne Moore with some irony.[51] Shoes that don't function may work as perverse signage about female compliance, a joke shared by those in the know who are able to recognize a Jimmy Choo and appreciate a retro aesthetic when displayed on the feet. Wearing shoes such as this, or even dysfunctional shoes, may be the oppo-site of looking one's best, but then being fashionable is not necessarily the same thing as wearing comfortable clothes that flatter the body; to be fashionable often involves trying to look different from everybody else. It may also involve an avant-garde reading of gender display.

Wearing flattering, rather than avant-garde or fetish, fashions may offer a coping strategy that involves both elements of narcissistic masquerade and fetishism. Indeed, feet and shoes may be potent sexual symbols, but they are also easy fragments of the body to groom and dress. The question to consider is whether estrangement features in the pleasures on offer.

Lucie Russell's 1999 drawings of feet and shoes are worth looking at in order to raise such a debate because they seem to reveal the way some women have learned to live with objectification and fragmentation, and illustrate the pleasures grooming offers to women. The accentuation of feet, above other body parts, to those who do not value feet may suggest self-estrangement or alienation from the holistic body. Like

F I G U R E 1 ☙ Lucie Russell, *Are You Sitting Comfortably?*

the fragments Nochlin discusses, Russell's drawings dislocate the holistic image even if they don't convey the alienation and fetishism of some fragmented mind-sets. (Allen Jones's images of shoes, for example, appear to me rather more alienated than either Manet's or Russell's.) Indeed, Russell's drawings appear to reflect familiarity and ease with women's body parts and rituals (figures 1 and 2). Is this because her drawings focus on pleasures that appear perversely female and directed at the self rather than the outside viewer, or is there something else going on? Russell's images conjure up the sensuous pleasure of looking down at freshly painted toenails in nice sandals or at silky stockinged legs (figures 3 and 4)—serious pleasures enjoyed not necessarily for the reflection in the mirror but for the physical enjoyment and fulfillment of the task.

Yet this is not necessarily the opposite of alienation, as Sophie Davies explains about her shoe habit: "I was putting on weight but my feet were always a perfect size five. If a pair of trousers felt too snug around the hips, I'd leave the changing room hating

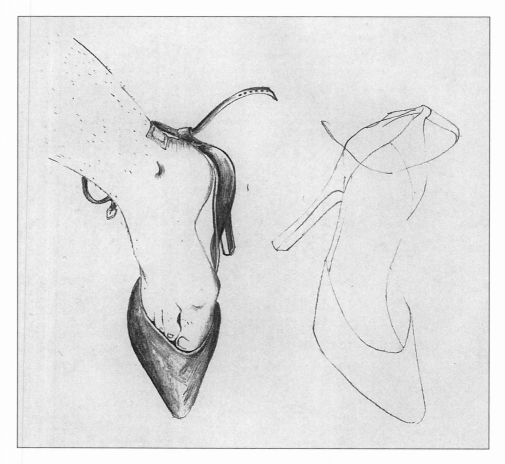

FIGURE 2   ↬   Lucie Russell, *Saturday Night and Sunday Morning.*

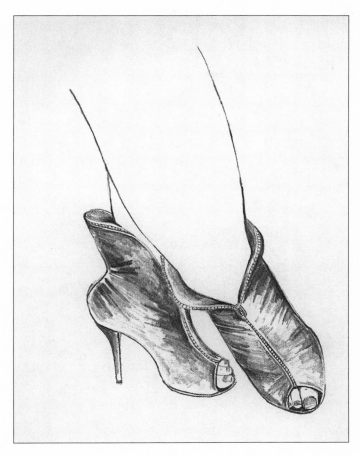

FIGURE 3
Lucie Russell, *Peep Toe.*

myself. But when I tried on shoes, I didn't even have to look above my knees. I could just focus on how slim my ankles looked—which meant that in the no-frumps fashion scene I socialized in, at least I could click my heels with pride."[52]

When we look at our own feet, the estranged body part, particularly if it is pleasing to the eye, may compensate for the whole image in the mirror image not being as perfect as we would like it to be. This is comparable to the way Renaissance painters would choose "bits" from various models in order to create the perfect nude. In making herself into an artwork through plastic surgery, the artist Orlan has also adopted a similar strategy to surgery on her own body. Parveen Adams observes that her "cosmetic surgery aims at a refiguration of the face of figure. To this Orlan adds the constraint that the image to which refiguration is directed comes from her choice of features from old Masters paintings. She is turning herself into an art historical 'morph.'"[53] Here, Orlan's work is disturbing, not only because her artwork and videos provide a chilling visual critique of the casual use of plastic surgery by women who wish to appear more feminine

FIGURE 4   ↙   Lucie Russell, *Everything and Nothing (to Wear)*.

but also because Orlan virtually turns herself into "an image trapped in the body of a woman."[54]

Taking care of one bit of yourself—be it feet or nails—may well be a coping strategy enjoyed by women—who find all the repetitive demands of maintaining the whole feminine body facade far too stressful and alienating to bother with. Lucie Russell's generously proportioned female line drawings in this context appear to show a female gaze at self-fragmentation and masquerade that may not necessarily involve anyone else (figure 5). Unlike Jenny Saville's wistful paintings of larger women, Russell's drawings of women and shoes appear to do two things at once: to show women subjects engaging with objectification or self-fashioning while reveling in its pleasures.[55] Whether this is the opposite of the alienating effects of modernity or a compounding of them (postmodern estrangement) is hard to tell. Silvie Fleury, in her video *Twinkle,* occupies clearer ground. The artist's feet are framed compulsively trying on and then discarding shoes, clearly unable to find "satisfaction."[56] The effect of self-absorption, literally gorging on

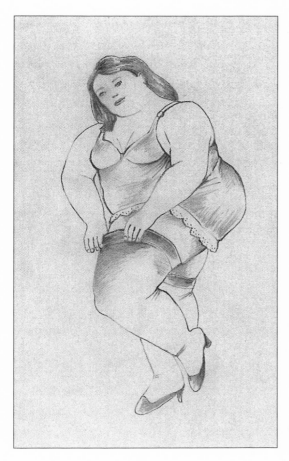

FIGURE 5
Lucie Russell, *Feels Good to Me, Lady.*

shoes, is a lot more uncomfortable than the sort of self-absorption Russell's drawings of women grooming display. Yet in very different ways both artists use female shoes and feet to reflect how femininity itself is a social fabrication, one that is inherently perverse and compelling, and framed by rituals of repetition.

FEMININITY AS PERVERSION

This idea of femininity as perversion is not a new one but has been discussed at length by Louise Kaplan.[57] In recent years it has been put forward to explain why eating disorders in women are prevalent and have reached epidemic proportions. Obsessive concern with physical appearance by women has become a cultural fixation that is troubling, but the practice of grooming itself is neither natural nor unnatural. Every culture uses adornment, and time spent grooming to attract a lover, or just for the pleasure of it, is not necessarily a waste of time or "oppressive." Grooming per se is certainly not fetishistic, even though narcissistic strategies regarding the purchase of grooming products may well be perverse and compounded by the consumer scenario. Valerie Steele, in her book *Shoes: A Lexicon of Style,* points out women often say that buying shoes gives them a lift, makes the feel good. One woman interviewed said buying shoes constitutes "the highest form of shopping";[58] another woman said she had run up credit card debts of over six thousand pounds on shoes she "didn't even like."[59] This raises questions about what is at stake for women in shoe shopping.

SHOPPING FOR SHOES: REVIEWING FEMALE NARCISSISM AND FETISHISM ARTICULATED THROUGH CONSUMERISM

Shopping for shoes may be about pleasure and linked to gender display, but it is also often connected to status issues. The first thing I bought with my "Saturday Girl" (part-time shop assistant) paycheck savings was an expensive pair of navy Gucci style flat casuals to wear to school. In retrospect I can see I couldn't afford to feel poor— my family lived too close to that reality—so I appeared, like some of the Afro-Caribbean girls who went to my school, to need the status only expensive leather can bestow. It obviously wasn't a matter of needing to protect my feet; shopping for the shoes themselves made me feel like a member of an exclusive school club (all the fashionable girls at school had casuals) as clearly as the noble red heels worn by Louis XIV and his courtiers to demark their status.

Shoes, based on the experience described above, clearly have a role to play in articulating status needs or consolidating border identities or even ideas about belonging. Shoe shopping, nevertheless, for most women can feel like pleasing themselves rather than others, encompassing both gender play as well as meeting ego and self-esteem needs, even if it appears to serve the demands of conformist feminine display.[60] Yet shoe shopping for pleasure can certainly be defined as healthy in a cultural context where women are often expected to service others before themselves or risk being defined by the obvious misogyny of what Hilary Radner has described as the "Shrew story."[61] Yet there are few psychoanalytic texts that connect the words "healthy" and "narcissistic." This may be because when Freud wrote his first treatise, "On Narcissism: An Introduction" (1914), he said "narcissism had the significance of a perversion."[62] What he went on to explain in this and in later articles was that omnipotent self-love unmediated by concepts of the "self" and "other" is regressive if the infatuation with one's own image is not grounded by the ability to love others.

THE NARCISSISTIC BODY

The history of the concept of "narcissism" is marked by revision, both by Freud and by subsequent theorists. Freud's original account explains narcissism as a response to the loss of the omnipotent ego ideal of childhood, rather than simply as a theory of autoeroticism or excessive self-esteem. The original story of Narcissus goes like this: When Narcissus sees his reflection in the water, he does not know he sees himself (the subject) and falls in love with his reflection. Consequently, he does not see that Echo, the fair Maiden, loves him too, and for this cruelty Nemesis punishes Narcissus to contemplate his own face in a pool of water. Fascinated by his own image, he pines away and dies. Freud's theory of narcissism uses the metaphor of Narcissus to conceptualize how self-love impacts the infant's ego through earlier stages of autoeroticism, gradually being transformed by the infant's ultimately recognizing the limits of his/her omnipotence and the significance of others. This account was revised by Lacan when writing about the imaginary and the mirror phase.

Freud saw narcissism as a stage all infants passed through. He went on to argue that, as infants, we eventually transfer narcissistic love from ourselves, and from an identity that is fused with someone else, to a love object that we experience as separate. As we separate, we retain some potential for love based on narcissism, and the original loss that separation signifies. In response to this discussion, Lacan suggests "there is something originally, inaugurally, profoundly wounded in the human relation to the world. . . . This is what comes of the theory of narcissism Freud gave us." The response to this "loss" is conceptualized differently across the sexes. In women, sometimes the original narcissistic wound is connected to penis envy and "lack," centered on the idea that the little girl imagines all children have penises and somehow hers has been lost (possibly as a punishment for misbehavior) and the wish or hope it will grow back. As Rosalind Minsky points out, "Penis envy may be experienced by some women as an enduring narcissistic sense of lack . . . as dissatisfaction with a self experienced as overwhelming narcissistic dissatisfaction . . . with a self experienced as imperfect or lacking . . . a sense of imperfection or inferiority beginning in early childhood."[63]

In such a scenario compulsive shopping for status shoes by women could be construed—if the material reality of class division and objects as status symbols was ignored—as an attempt to symbolically overcome feelings of inferiority inflicted by the already wounded female body. Or spending money on objects that men often fetishize, like high-heeled shoes, could be construed as part of the masquerade that involves women in reinforcement of what Lacan has described as the phallic term (that is engaged with through entry into the Symbolic). Yet there is another reading that could be made of shoe shopping, which doesn't fix it to a link with penis envy and which relates to notions about "loss" (of the mother's body and/or ego ideal) rather than "lack" (of a penis). Here, ideas about loss—or even the lost envelopes of the female imagination I referred to at the beginning of this article—are linked in theory with primary memories of the mother's body, and the deep mourning for this intimate closeness to the mother which we lose as we grow up.

Freud connected ideas about narcissism to loss in his essay "Mourning and Melancholia" (1917). Such rereading of the Freudian account has already been discussed by feminist critics, including Judith Butler, Teresa de Lauretis, Lorraine Gamman and Merja Makinen, and Peggy Phelan, among many others.[64] These feminist critics each take different objects of study: the body, lesbian desire, objects of fetishism, grief. From different perspectives they all suggest that ideas about female agency may be undermined by certain psychoanalytic explanations, which they try to help reformulate. While none of them directly discusses shoes, their work does seem pertinent. Having watched a friend grieve over the death of her mother by going to bed weeping, cradling one of her mother's shoes, I found myself moved but also reflective. Aren't primary memories of the mother's body significant in regard to ideas about narcissism and masquerade, and/or psychic loss? Could such ideas, and memories of the idealized mother of infancy, be relevant to the account of women's relationship to shoes, which nevertheless are more frequently interpreted as "phallic"—rather than vaginal—metaphors? Indeed, according to Bettelheim, "we must remember that the golden shoe was borrowed from the bird which represents the spirit of the dead mother, which Cinderella had internalized, and which sustained her in her trials and tribulations."[65]

Given such a reading, perhaps it's not outrageous to suggest that some (if not all) shoe fixations by women may conceal a masked melancholic aspect and unconscious address to separation and loss. Teresa de Lauretis describes such a scenario as follows: "What is disavowed must be the loss of something which the body has knowledge of pain, and pleasure, and something to which she has instinctual aims. This is not, cannot, be a penis, but is most likely to be her body itself (body image and body ego) although the symbolic structure rewrites that loss as lack of a penis."[66]

Indeed, there is surprisingly little discussion of the concept of loss and narcissism in relation to fashion, even though the theory of narcissism has been subject to many controversial revisions. Certainly, feminists might consider that fuller critical formulations of narcissism and loss may be warranted in the account of women's relationship to grooming, adornment, clothes, and shoes than is possible within the scope of this essay and by respected Lacanian explanations of sexual difference.[67]

COMMODITY FETISHISM
AND THE EROTIC

Naomi Schor is probably right when she points out that we may not recognize forms of female fetishism by simply looking for the same objects that men fetishize.[68] Yet there are always "exceptions" to be found in the psychoanalytic case studies. Take the woman who was obsessed with fur-lined shoes or the bulimic who revealed a fetish for feet in plaster. These accounts demonstrate that female sexual fetishism embraces many objects including feet, and in the case of the bulimic, this fetishism clearly equates with orthodox sexual fetishism: "She could not look at a foot in plaster without getting aroused and masturbating. . . . 'When I am alone at home, I stand in front of the mirror, I get out some stockings, which must always be white and have the toe piece cut out, I put them on and look at them until I am aroused, I become "another" and then masturbate.'"[69] Of course, most women who may like their own feet and love shoes don't *prefer* them to sexual partners but often buy many pairs of them to satisfy their consuming passions that may or may not have a conscious erotic dimension.[70] Advertising has clearly been used to sell everything, including women's shoes, and so shopping provides access to objects, which, as part of the process of consumer fetishism, become overlaid with erotic meanings. In this context, it may not be completely possible to differentiate narcissistic from fetishistic articulations involved in women's shoe-shopping habits outside of the therapy room; shoe fetishism by women may even involve a disavowal of narcissism. Yet the cultural reality of shoe shopping as an enjoyable and specifically *female* pastime that women share does need some explanation as to specifically what drives female desire toward new shoes.

Consumer fetishism and consumer narcissism are fused in many messages to buy things "because," as the L'Oreal advertisements remind us, "you're worth it . . . because *I'm* worth it." Consequently, the Lacanian reformulation of ideas about the masquerade that "it is woman herself who assumes the role of the fetish" through the feminine performance is very persuasive when trying to explain the consequence consumer messages may have on the female psyche. Such logic would probably construe women enjoying shoe shopping together as a collective opportunity for peers to create normative categories about how to be a "woman." Yet, as I have already mentioned, ideas about female agency are often undermined by such psychoanalytic explanations. Female desire is explained in terms of a response to sexual difference or the male gaze rather than to ideas about a melancholic response to the loss of the ego ideal of childhood and/or primary identification with the mother's body.[71] There are a number of possible causes for the masquerade involving shoes: narcissistic female desires and consumer fetishism, for example. So it may be simply inappropriate to "fix" readings of the female masquerade to the phallic term without first considering the significance of identifications that occur prior to entry into what Lacan calls the Symbolic.

CONCLUSION

As this analysis suggests, female objectification of the self is complex, and further dislocations than those noted by Nochlin as characterizing the modern period inform the feminine masquerade and may drive women's consuming passions for shoes. Symbolically, high heels have been connected by psychoanalysis to the "missing" penis, but some shoe shopping by women should be viewed as looking for lost envelopes of the female imagination, rather than in terms of phallic replacement. So we need to be more attentive to different intensities of the feminine masquerade and to the fetishistic dimensions of the perverse shoe scenarios enacted by some women. Also, we should remember that there has yet to be a useful or systematic analysis of the role of narcissism in fashion, and that understanding shoe fixations by women requires a more thorough understanding of narcissistic scenarios. Meanwhile, cream cakes and new shoes remain worthy objects of female desire. They deserve full critical investigation both inside and outside of "girl heaven" or even this book.

NOTES

1. According to Deb Orr at least. See her account in "Say Grace," *Weekend Guardian,* July 22, 1995, lead story.

2. Catalog to exhibition by A. Shelton, ed., *Fetishism: Visualising Power and Desire* (London: Lund Humphries, 1995).

3. Valerie Steele, *Shoes: A Lexicon of Style* (London and Hong Kong: Scriptum Editions, 1998). Steele points out "these shoe styles are worn almost exclusively by women" (63).

4. Linda Nochlin, *The Body in Pieces: The Fragment as a Metaphor of Modernity* (London: Thames and Hudson, 1994).

5. Ibid. See discussion on Eugene Disderi on 38.

6. Ibid., 38–39.

7. Anne Hollander, *Seeing through Clothes* (Berkeley: University of California Press, 1993), 221–222.

8. W. A. Ewing, *The Body: Photoworks of the Human Form* (London: Thames and Hudson, 1994), 3.

9. Jonathan Sawday, *The Body Emblazoned: Dissection and the Human Body in Renaissance Culture* (London and New York: Routledge, 1995), 191–192. Sawday argues that the notion of "blazon," which derives from a device worn on a heraldic shield, gave its name in the sixteenth century to poetic blazons. This literary form was addressed to female body parts (lips and breasts, etc.), and male authors were allowed to vie with one another in the production of verse that spoke their desire to women. Sawday also mentions there was a homoerotic element to this sort of banter between men.

10. Ewing, *The Body,* 3.

11. Ibid. See full discussion, 32–59.

12. R. B. Browne, *Fetishism in Popular Culture: Objects of Special Devotion* (Ohio: Bowling Green University Popular Press, 1989), 33–34.

13. Betty Friedan, *The Female Mystique* (Harmondsworth: Penguin, 1963); Germaine Greer, *The Female Eunuch* (London: Paladin, 1971); Sheila Rowbotham, *Women's Consciousness, Man's World* (Harmondsworth: Penguin, 1973).

14. Naomi Wolf, *The Beauty Myth* (London,Chatto and Windus, 1990), 6.

15. Natasha Walters, *The New Feminism* (London: Virago Press, 1999), addresses broader issues about women's oppression than Wolf.

16. Greer, *The Female Eunuch,* 62.

17. Gloria Steinem, "We Are All Bunnies," in *Outrageous Acts and Everyday Rebellions* (London: Jonathan Cape, 1983), 50.

18. High heels, in particular, have been identified not only as essentially feminine but as erotic and inappropriate for work. See Susan B. Kaiser, Howard G. Schutz, and Joan Chandler, "Cultural Codes and Sex-Role Ideology: A Study of Shoes," *American Journal of Semiotics* 5, 1 (1987): 13–34.

19. Susan Brownmiller, *Femininity* (London: Paladin, Grafton Books, 1986), 144–145.

20. Ibid.

21. Lee Wright, "Objectifying Gender: The Stiletto Heel," in *A View from the Interior,* ed. J. Attfield and P. Kirkham (London: Women's Press, 1989), 7–19. She also mentions that the "stiletto—the name given to the heel—has since 1953 become a generic title."

22. Caroline Evans and Minna Thornton, *Women and Fashion: A New Look* (London: Quartet, 1989), 15.

23. Laura Mulvey, "Visual Pleasure and Narrative Cinema," *Screen* 6, 3 (autumn 1975): 6–18. For a full discussion of appropriations of gaze theory, see Caroline Evans and Lorraine Gamman, "The Gaze Revisited, or Reviewing Queer Viewing," in *A Queer Romance: Lesbians, Gay Men, and Popular Culture,* ed. P. Burston and C. Richardson (London: Routledge, 1995), 13–56.

24. Dick Hebdige, *Subculture: The Meaning of Style* (London: Methuen, 1979).See also discussion of women and punk in Evans and Thornton, *Women and Fashion,* 17–26.

25. Elizabeth Wilson, "Fashion and the Postmodern Body," in *Chic Thrills: A Fashion Reader,* ed. J. Ash and E Wilson (London: Pandora, 1992), 12.

26. Caroline Evans notes that in the interwar years the sexually independent new woman was a source of much anxiety; and the definition of "newness" is often an anxious state. See "Masks, Mirrors, and Mannequins: Elsa Schiaparelli and the Decentred Subject," in *Fashion Theory: The Journal of Dress, Body, and Culture* 3, 1 (March 1999).

27. Kaiser et al. argue in "Cultural Codes and Sex-Role Ideology" that people tend to categorize shoes into one of several cognitive clusters: (1) feminine and sexy, (2) masculine, (3) asexual or dowdy, and (4) young and casual.

28. When I interviewed fashion theorist Caroline Evans, in October 1999, she suggested that this rethinking of fashion accessories may be explained by the fact that in a period of recession people buy accessories to freshen up existing outfits ("less money means status shifts to accessories"). For example, Prada—which originally made bags—has since blossomed as a fashion house financed by accessories.

29. Steele, *Shoes,* 16, 27.

30. Ibid., 63. Steele argues that "athletic shoes and boots were formerly regarded as masculine" but subcultural reappropriations changed their classification.

31. The Metropolitan Museum of Art in New York sells miniature stylized shoes with a brief description of design and period.

32. Hedley Roberts created his red ceramic molded stilettos for his show at Central St. Martins College of Art, London, in 1994–95, in connection with earning his B.A. in printing.

33. Joan Rivière, "Womanliness as Masquerade," reprinted in *Formations of Fantasy,* ed. V. Burgin et al. (London: Methuen, 1986), 33–44.

34. Stephen Heath, "Joan Rivière and the Masquerade," in *Formations of Fantasy,* 38.

35. Jacques Lacan, *Ecrits,* trans. Alan Sheridan (London: Tavistock, 1977), 289–290.

36. Jacqueline Rose, "Introduction II," in *Feminine Sexuality: Jacques Lacan and the Ecole freudienne,* ed. Juliet Mitchell and Jacqueline Rose, trans. Jacqueline Rose (New York: Norton, 1985), 43.

37. Louise Kaplan, *Female Perversions: The Temptations of Madame Bovary* (London: Pandora, 1991), 251.

38. Ibid., 260–262.

39. E. L. McCallum, *Object Lessons: How to Do Things with Fetishism* (New York: State University of New York Books, 1999), 62.

40. Gebhardt quoted in Lorraine Gamman and Merja Makinen, *Female Fetishism: A New Look* (London: Lawrence and Wishart, 1994), 38.

41. Sigmund Freud. "Freud and Fetishism: Previously Unpublished Minutes of the Vienna Psychoanalytic Society," ed. and trans. Louis Rose, *Psychoanalytic Quarterly* 57 (1988): 147–166.

42. Liz Balmaseda, "Seduced by Spikes," *Latina,* September 1997, 82–83. Quoted in Tace Hedrick, "Are you a *Pura Latina*? or, Menudo Every Day: *Tacones* and Symbolic Ethnicity," in this volume.

43. For a full discussion of appropriations of gaze theory, see Evans and Gamman, "The Gaze Revisited, or Reviewing Queer Viewing."

44. Suzanne Moore, "Help, I'm Addicted to Shoes," *Red,* autumn 1997, 60.

45. See Jim Collins, Hilary Radner, and Ava Preacher Collins, eds., *Film Theory Goes to the Movies* (New York: Routledge, 1993), 67.

46. The slipper is vaginal, according to Bruno Bettelheim, although the heel itself, particularly the stilletto, is often positioned as phallic (*The Uses of Enchantment: The Meaning and Importance of Fairy Tales* [London: Thames and Hudson, 1975], 265, 270).

47. Lisa Tickner quoted in Wright, "Objectifying Gender," 7–19.

48. See discussion by Majorie Garber, *Vested Interests: Cross-Dressing and Cultural Anxiety* (New York: Routledge, 1992).

49. Ru Paul quoted in Linda O'Keefe, *Shoes: A Celebration of Pumps, Sandals, Slippers, and More* (New York: Workman, 1996), 125.

50. Caroline Evans, forthcoming.

51. Moore, "Help, I'm Addicted to Shoes," 60.

52. Sophie Davies, "Manolos, Mastercard, and Me" *Minx,* September 1999, 83.

53. Parveen Adams, *The Emptiness of the Image: Psychoanalysis and Sexual Difference* (London: Routledge, 1996), 143.

54. Ibid., 144.

55. Lucie Russell's drawings first came to my attention at her show in June 1999 at the Royal College of Art, Kensington, London, in connection with earning her M.A. in printing.

56. Silvie Fleury, *Twinkle,* 1992.

57. Kaplan, *Female Perversions,* 14.

58. Steele, *Shoes,* 8.

59. Davies, "Manolos, Mastercard, and Me," 83.

60. See discussion in Steele, *Shoes,* 8.

61. Hilary Radner, "Speaking Out—Shrewish Behavior," in *Shopping around Feminine Culture and the Pursuit of Pleasure* (New York and London: Routledge, 1995), 1–33.

62. Sigmund Freud, "On Narcissism: An Introduction," in *The Standard Edition,* trans. James Strachy in colloboration with Anna Freud, vol. 14 (London: Hogarth Press, 1957), 73–102.

63. Rosalind Minsky, *Psychoanalysis and Gender: An Introductory Reader* (London and New York: Routledge, 1996), 53.

64. Judith Butler addresses Freud's discussion of narcissism in his "Mourning and Melancholia" (1917) when she points out that as "part of the incorporative strategy of melancholy. . . . The mask thus conceals this loss, but preserves (and negates) this loss through its concealment. The mask has a double function which is the double function of melancholy. The mask is taken on through the process of incorporation which is a way of inscribing and then wearing a melancholic identification, in and on the body: in effect it is the signification of the body in the mold of the Other who has been refused." See discussion of Judith Butler in Evans, "Masks, Mirrors, and Mannequins," 13. Teresa de Lauretis makes an interesting argument about narcissism and loss being connected to pre-Oedipal desire. She suggests that loss not lack drives female narcissism: "What is disavowed must be the loss of something which the body has knowledge of pain, and pleasure, and something to which she has instinctual aims. This is not, cannot, be a penis, but is most likely to be her body itself (body image and body ego) although the symbolic structure rewrites that loss as lack of a penis" (*The Practice of Love: Lesbian Sexuality and Perverse Desire* [Bloomington: Indiana University Press, 1999], 288). In Gamman and Makinen, *Female Fetishism,* we put forward the idea that female fetishism is not rare and has been overlooked because of the focus on "lack" rather than loss. We suggest that fetishism can be understood in women if we move back the arguments about phallic castration to an earlier stage of ego development, namely, separation from the mother. Here fetishism is a strategy designed to renegotiate the loss occurring through individuation. Peggy Phelan discusses "militant narcissism" in *Mourning Sex* (New York and London: Routledge, 1999).

65. Bettelheim, *The Uses of Enchantment,* 270.

66. de Lauretis, *The Practice of Love,* 288.

67. Adams, *The Emptiness of the Image.*

68. Naomi Schor, "Female Fetishism: The Case of George Sand," *Poetics Today* 2 (1985): 301–310. She specifically suggests "wounds" rather than "shoes" should be looked at.

69. Quoted in Gamman and Makinen, *Female Fetishism,* 102.

70. "The average American woman has twelve pair of shoes . . . many women have over a 100 pairs and counting," says Steele, *Shoes,* 38.

71. Evans, "Masks, Mirrors, and Mannequins," 13.

Fashioning Masculinity: Men's Footwear and Modernity

CHRISTOPHER BREWARD

I have never lost sight of what I consider to be the most material object to be gained from a publication of this nature, namely, the imparting of a moral feeling to the gratification arising from a taste in leather. Great Britain is the most wealthy, and politically speaking, perhaps the most powerful kingdom upon earth. Considered in a domestic point of view, here are thousands of large and affluent families; it follows of course, that there is scarcely a young man who enters upon life without being able to furnish himself with shoes. Nay, most have an opportunity of gratifying their tastes and passions in the purchase of great variety; and I am greatly deceived, if experience does not prove, that much more than half the misery of the world arises either from ill-directed taste in the purchase of shoes, or from the entire want of them. The objects to be obtained in such a dispute are of a most important and substantial character. Religion, patriotism, public and private virtue, pure and fixed principles of taste, intellectual and corporeal refinement, all—all depend upon the choice of shoes.

—*Reverend Tom Foggy Dribble, "The Street Companion; or, The Young Man's Guide and the Old Man's Comfort in the Choice of Shoes,"* London Magazine *(1825)*

Contrary to popular knowledge (which erroneously suggests that masculinity and clothes shopping are irreconcilable states), the acquisition of a pair of good shoes has long been held to be one of the most important considerations undertaken by any self-respecting male follower of fashion. Indeed for most men, regardless of their

position on the seriousness of dress, the shodding of the feet in appropriate attire constitutes a commercial transaction deserving of at least their limited attention, if only for
those reasons of comfort and value that tend to impinge less directly on the consumption of other items of clothing. The improbably named Reverend Tom Foggy
Dribble certainly held no reservations regarding the status of the man's shoe as an indi-
cator of civilized values, economic well-being, and impeccable taste. His robust confidence in the potential of British producers and consumers is unsurprising, coming as
it does in a period when fashionable London goods and their promoters dictated the
rules of sartorial aesthetics for those men with a disposition for the arts of the dressing room across the globe. The reverend's faith in the moral supremacy of the man's shoe
has been sustained across the intervening two centuries, offering a model for aesthetic
discernment that stretches beyond the humble realm of the foot to embrace broader
issues of taste, modernity, and gender.

The original tenets of dandyism, formed from the 1790s onward, focused on the
impeccable wardrobe of the English aristocrat, presenting a fiercely controlled style of
dressing and behavior that would prove resistant to those accusations of effeminacy, profli-
gacy, and that unhealthy attachment to surfaces that were associated with the decadence
of France.[1] These were practices that might otherwise be used to critique the values
of an emergent consumer culture, even when the acquisitive and self-aggrandizing performance of the dandy sometimes appeared to embrace the very same phenomena. Thus,
in its mannered disavowal of the vagaries of fashion, the dandy's wardrobe stood as a
cipher for fashion's spectacular excesses.

Nowhere has this irony been truer than in the long-term status accorded to the
discreet and unchanging form of the masculine shoe. While the philosophical meanings attached to the complex knotting of the linen cravat or the dense black pile of the
velvet swallowtail coat have, like the Brummels and the D'Orsays who sported them,
faded into a romantic past, traditional male footwear maintains a clear connection with
the sartorial debates and rhetorical styles of the early nineteenth century. In the delicate
balance between function and aesthetics that continues to dictate the pattern of stitching on a black Oxford or the number of eyelets on a brown brogue, there still resides the
residue of older discourses on manliness, nationhood, and class. Where the hosiery and
outerwear of previous generations of men lay revealed as mere temporal fashions, their
shoes seem more grounded, immune to the indignities imposed by a shifting sense of
la mode but subject to intense deliberation regarding fitness for purpose and occasion.

Part of the reason for the endurance of the man's shoe as a peculiarly progressive
symbol of aesthetic conservatism must lie in the manner through which its forms were
celebrated by propagandists for an equally dandified modernism at the opening of the

twentieth century. Le Corbusier, writing in his manifesto *L'Art decoratif d'aujord'hui* (1925), presented a moral and aesthetic vision that deliberately contested the social value of those feminized and fashion-led items that dominated the displays of the international Paris exhibition of the same year.[2] In a polemic that recalls the renunciatory posturings of the regency dandy, the rising architect looked to the functional and "innocent" surfaces of utilitarian "industrial" goods as a means of exposing the "shaming" and "dishonest" veneer of the moderne "bric-a-brac" beloved of the housewife consumer.[3] As the black-coated, exquisitely booted citizen of the 1820s ridiculed the lace-bedecked and high-heeled courtier of the *ancien régime* while covertly pursuing the pleasures of fashionable consumption with equal energy, so the modernist arbiter of taste critiqued the modishly ephemeral while fetishizing a myth of durability and the supremacy of the "moral" object that still prioritized surface impressions. What better illustrative vehicle for such a position than the contents and meanings of the dandy's wardrobe? Among many suggestions for aesthetic and design reform, Le Corbusier presented at least five desiderata that comfortably find their most potent exemplars in the polished seams and supple leather offered in the modern footwear catalog. Their pithy statements of intent provide an entry into further understanding the particular dynamics of the male shoe.

The first of these desiderata was an insistence on utilitarian need as a motor for the production of domestic goods:

> Utilitarian needs call for tools, brought in every respect to that degree of perfection seen in industry. This then is the great programme for the decorative arts. Day after day industry is turning out tools of perfect utility and convenience that soothe our spirits with the luxury afforded by the elegance of their conception, the purity of their execution, and the efficiency of their operation. This rational perfection and this precise formulation constitute sufficient common ground between them to allow the recognition of a style.[4]

Clothing as tool was an idea that had underpinned and smoothed the rise of the English gentleman's wardrobe as a paradigm of civilized taste in the nineteenth century. The utilitarian textiles associated with dressing for the country estate found an easy translation into the more relaxed tailoring associated with Savile Row.[5] And with them the waxed and toughened leather goods of the race track or the grouse moor were directly reflected in the craftsmanship labored on the gloves and galoshes of the city financier. To celebrate the elegant cadence of a new shape in toe caps for its own sake ran the risk of inviting ridicule for effeminacy, but when that form could be discussed in terms of its resistance to wear or rain, or the perfection of its construction, then the right of its owner to accrue a reputation for his impeccable style remained unquestioned. Yet the taint of the aristocrat imbued such objects with the problematic gloss of old-fashioned elitism. Le Corbusier was forced to look to a more self-consciously "modern" and proletarian role model, who could celebrate the bright patina of the mass-produced in as effortless a manner as that in which the old-style milord pulled on his bespoke hunting boots:

> Lenin is seated at the Rotonde on a cane chair; he has paid twenty centimes for his coffee with a tip of one sou. He has drunk out of a small white porcelain cup. He is wearing a bowler hat and a smooth white collar. He has been writing for several hours on sheets of typing paper. His inkpot is smooth and round, made from bottle glass. He is learning to govern one hundred million people.[6]

Similarly, if the genealogy of the gentleman's shoe lay in the leisured pursuits of the aristocracy, then any claim made on its democratic appeal was fraught with difficulty. Thus from Lenin's embodiment of a banal yet revolutionary modernity, Le Corbusier extended his celebration of utility to an account of the potential of the functional object to free the user from older notions of service and hierarchy. In his third proposition the adaptability of the demotic industrial product is commended as a metaphor for a utopian vision of social equality: "The objects of utility in our lives have freed the slaves of a former age. They are in fact themselves slaves, menials, servants. Do you want them as your soul-mates? We sit on them, work on them, use them up; when used up, we replace them. We demand from such servants precision and care, decency and an unassertive presence."[7]

Once again, it is possible to read a surviving variety of dandyism between the lines: the justification for consumption wrapped up in a reverence for unfettered performance. In the eighteenth century patriotic pamphleteers and caricaturists had often contrasted the well-shod, stockinged feet of John Bull with the naked ankles and callous-inducing clogs of the French peasant.[8] The belligerent freeborn Englishman sported the products of early mass production as trophies of his superiority. Plain speaking, plain living, and utterly efficient, the old self-deluded male consumer morphed effortlessly into the new. Le Corbusier's twentieth-century John Bull hid behind the democratizing promises of labor-saving commodities as an excuse to consume. Machine-turned lasts and uppers put together on sewing machines had replaced the notion of the bespoke, but the cheaper shoes that resulted offered all comers the promise of functional and elegant footwear.

If by the 1920s political reform and internationalism were causing the specter of class strife and the ideal of the nation-state to seem slightly outdated as philosophical motors for justifying or condemning the pleasures of consumption, a deeper-rooted misogyny held out as a retreat from which the compromised dandy could play fashion against function and still emerge with footwear unsullied. Le Corbusier certainly made full use of the contrast between plain, functional "masculine" objects and decorative, debased "feminine" ones in his push for a standard of taste that combined the mass-produced with the bespoke in its seeking after modern beauty:

> Trash is always abundantly decorated; the luxury object is well made, neat and clean, pure and healthy, and its bareness reveals the quality of its manufacture. It is to industry that we owe this reversal in the state of affairs: a cast iron stove overflowing with decoration costs less than a plain one; amidst the surging leaf patterns flaws in the casting cannot be seen. And the same applies generally. . . . This surface elaboration, if extended over everything, becomes repugnant and scandalous; it smells of pretence, and the healthy gaiety of the shop-girl in her flower patterned cretonne dress becomes rank corruption when surrounded by . . . Japanese umbrellas . . . Bichara perfumes, bordello lampshades, pumpkin cushions, divans spread with gold and silver lame . . . linoleum printed with Louis XVI ribbons.[9]

Here the disavowal of the purely decorative was visceral in its condemnation. Fashion in its purest form is "repugnant," "scandalous," "rank." It is illustrated through recourse to a description of all that is soft and sensuous, nowhere better suggested (for our purposes) than through the juxtaposition of a padded and delicate satin slipper with a sturdy walking boot.

In a final example Le Corbusier drew on the rhetoric of the healthy body and the corrupting effects of sexual desire to heighten his sense of terror at the threat posed to a rational universe by the excesses of female culture:

> Not only is this accumulation of false richness unsavoury, but above all and before all, this taste for decorating everything around one is a false taste, an abominable little perversion. I reverse the painting; the . . . shop-girl is in a pretty room, bright and clear, white walls, a good chair—wicker work or Thonet . . . some crockery of white porcelain, and on the table three tulips in a vase. . . . It is healthy, clean, decent. And to make something attractive, as little as that is enough. . . . We assert that this art without decoration is made not by artists but by anonymous industry following its airy and limpid path of economy.[10]

A stress on hygiene joined utility, a celebration of contemporary modernity, democratization, and a rejection of useless decoration on the modernist's agenda for the reformation of popular taste.

That these values were explicitly masculine in orientation and implicitly sartorial in character was most clearly communicated in the illustrations selected to accompany the text of *L'Art decoratif d'aujord'hui*. In juxtaposition with the more familiar icons of modernism—which included American office furniture, Peugeot automobiles, ocean liners, and commercial tableware—Le Corbusier chose images drawn from the world of the gentleman's closet: Hermès luggage, Saderne straw boaters, briar pipes, galoshes, and the classic leather shoe. Embodied in the latter objects lay a code for the proper appreciation of the modern commodity that found its origins not in the promises of Fordism or the hard technology of the industrial workshop, but in an older set of rules and practices engineered for the social display of the "clothes wearing man."

Representing the commercial application of such practices, the 1907 catalog of John Piggott, a typical gentleman's outfitter trading in the City of London, incorporated in its listing of men's shoe styles all of those desiderata dreamed up by Le Corbusier twenty years later, and similar publications must have inspired the architect in his search for the ideal modern "type-form" (figures 1–3). Here the discerning consumer could peruse mosquito boots for the tropics, morrocan leather Grecian slippers in black, scarlet, or maroon, patent leather Oxfords "for dancing" with low heels and single soles, together with specialized shoes for cricket, tennis, yachting, and boating. A whole department specialized in footwear for cycling and walking, boasting such items as the new century cycle shoe with "no unsightly hook or lace." For football the "never miss," "goal kicker," and "surekick" models ensured that function and appearance were elided. Hand-sewn boots "most elegant in style . . . suitable for town or country wear" fulfilled the company promise that "all our footwear is easy fitting, made on the very latest and improved lasts, and fits like a glove."[11]

Le Corbusier's enthusiasm for the arcane ephemera of the footwear department was not entirely original. The older Austrian architect Adolf Loos had also looked to the masculine wardrobe as a source of inspiration in the formulation of his own creative philosophy, finding in clothing and its relationship to the body a clear metaphor for the social and aesthetic responsibilities of architecture. Indeed, Le Corbusier had reprinted Loos's most influential essay, "Ornament and Crime" (which in 1908 had drawn on the surface embellishment of women's fashions and the tattooed bodies of "primitive" peoples for evidence of the "barbaric" effects of pattern), in the first issue of his journal *L'Esprit Nouveau* in 1920. As architectural theorist Mark Wigley has pointed out, Loos believed that male clothing had reached a state of standardization and functional convenience through a process of evolution and the beneficial effects of physical action. This placed it on a more rational plane than the cyclical and corrupting dress of women, whose constant style changes were, according to Loos, driven by the necessity for sexual display. In this sense "in as much as men's clothing is standardized, it is able to act as a mark behind which the individual is shielded from the increasingly

FIGURE 1 ~ John Piggott Ltd., London. Clothing Catalogue, 1907, p. 99.
Reproduced by kind permission of the Museum of London.

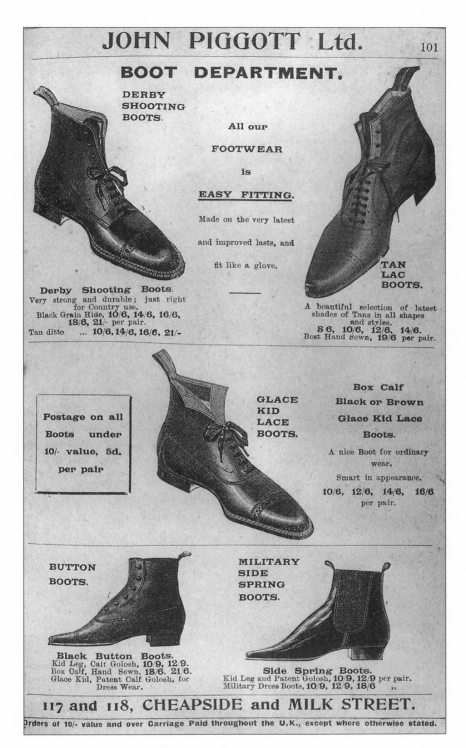

JOHN PIGGOTT Ltd.

CYCLING AND WALKING BOOT AND SHOE DEPARTMENT.
ALL SOLID LEATHER.

B 1.
Black Royal Calf Walking, 10/6, 12/6, 14/6
Box Calf, Black or Brown, 9/6, 11/6, 12/6.
Extra Value, Brown at 4/11.

B 43. Youth's Kid, Leg Calf, Golosh.
Size 2 to 5, 7/9 Boys. Size 11 to 1, 6/9
Box Calf, 2 to 5, 8/11. 11 to 1, 7/11
Postage 4d.

THE NEW CENTURY CYCLE SHOE.
Combination Walking and Cycling. No unsightly
Hook or Lace. Black and Brown, 4/11, 5/11
Willow Calf, Brown and Black, 8/6

KING EDWARD.
Combination, Walking or Cycling. The best Shoe
for the double purpose, especially for Cycling
Tourists. With best fastening, doing away with
hook or lacing; it does not leave part of foot
exposed to dust or wet, as the front is completely
covered; made with extra stout soles. Made in
Black or Brown, 6/6; in Black or Brown Willow
Calf, 8/11. Postage 4d.

Horse Skin Cycling Shoe. Strength and
durability guaranteed.
Made in Black and Brown, 6/6
Also in Box Calf, Brown Willow Calf, 8/6
Postage 4d.

THE FREE AND EASY CYCLE SHOE.
Veldtschoen Sewn.
With an improved strap and elastic garter
fastening, being a neat buckle at side.
Light in weight and flexible,
Made in Black and Brown, 6/11.
Postage 4d.

MEN'S CYCLING BOOTS, 8/6

FAMOUS PEDAL GRIPPER CYCLING SHOE.
Superior Quality, cut all in one piece. Made in
Horseskin upper, Butt leather sole.
Brown and Black, 4/11. Postage 4d.

THE PARKHURST CYCLE SHOE.
Light, Durable and Ventilated. This shoe is made in
Black and Brown, 6/6
Also Box Calf, Willow Tan Calf, 8/6 Postage 4d.

Cycling Boots, with Heel or no Heel.
Black or Brown 8/6
Superior Quality 10/6
Extra Fine Chamois 12/6

117 and 118, CHEAPSIDE, and MILK STREET.

Orders of 10/- value and over Carriage Paid throughout the U.K., except where otherwise stated

FIGURE 3 ⌒ John Piggott Ltd., London. Clothing Catalogue 1907, p. 103.
Reproduced by kind permission of the Museum of London.

threatening and seemingly uncontrollable forces of modern life (forces that were themselves understood as feminine)." Like modern architecture itself, the male wardrobe was engineered to act as a physical and psychological buffer against confusion.[12]

Loos's most explicit debt to men's shoes in the formation of these ideas was first worked out in a series of review articles published in *Die Neue Freie Presse* during the summer of 1898. As Le Corbusier's polemic in *L'Architecture* had been partly inspired by the exhibits of a decorative arts exhibition, so Loos's observations arose from his attendance at the Vienna Jubilee Exhibition of the same year. Three preoccupations worked their way through Loos's often short-tempered but constantly witty prose. First, changes of style in the male shoe could be accounted for in the "natural" processes of evolution. Second, cultural phenomena such as fashion caused the "natural" function of footwear to be compromised. And, finally, the increasing speed of modern life demanded a style of shoe that placed considerations of health and hygiene in paramount position. Under the title "Footwear" Loos flew the motto "*Tempora mutantur, nos et mutamur in illis*: Times change and we change with them. Our feet do the same."[13]

At the outset he set up a distinction between the craft of the shoemaker and that of the tailor, the former restricted by the intended function of his wares to produce items that followed the "natural" form of the foot, the latter freed to manipulate the given form of the body:

> Of course the form of our feet does not change from season to season. That often requires several centuries, at the very least a generation. A large foot cannot get smaller with the snap of a finger. Here the other clothing artists have it easier. . . . Changes can easily be made by means of a new cut, cotton padding and other aids. But the shoemaker must adhere closely to the form which the foot has at the particular moment. If he wants to introduce the small shoe, he must wait patiently until the race of men with large feet has become extinct.[14]

Loos next addressed the mechanisms by which the ideal size and shape of foot was arrived at through the sociological demands of changing forms of human activity and the inevitable process of distinction through which one social group defined its power over another. The forces of competition thus gave rise to fashions in shoe size and style, which undercut any rational or biological development. However half crazed his thesis now seems, it laid out clear parameters for arriving at the supremacy of the modern man's shoe, in terms of not only function and aesthetics but also the uncomplicated relationship between the two, which Loos identified as the defining paradigm of a successful object:

> But of course the feet of all men do not have the same form at the same time.
> . . . What is the shoemaker to do about this? Which type of foot should be his

standard? For he will be intent on producing modern shoes. He too wants to be progressive; and he too aspires to acquire the largest possible market for his products. And he sets about it the same way as all the other trades do. He keeps to the foot type of those who have power in society. . . . All those who thought and felt modern in the last century wore English riding shoes and boots, even if they did not own a horse. The riding boot was the symbol of the free man, who had won a final victory over the buckled shoe, the air of the court, and the glistening parquet floor. . . . The high heel, useless for the horseback rider, was left behind. . . . The whole of the following century . . . was taken up with the pursuit of the smallest possible feet.[15]

In his summing up, Loos saw in the frenetic rhythms of contemporary life the opportunity for reform in the design of men's shoes, a process that could be applied across all facets of material culture. Doubtlessly recalling those images of men that appeared in the fashion plates of nineteenth-century tailoring journals, he recoiled at the effeminate and dainty little pumps that ventured forth from under the trouser legs of otherwise hirsute and muscular models. It would seem that the form of the foot betrayed the enervating lifestyles and decadent attitudes of the European bourgeoisie, hinting at the torpor within. On the eve of a new century it was necessary to look to younger societies and new leisure activities as a means of inculcating a vigor sapped by the demands of fashion:

Nations with a more highly developed culture walk more quickly than those that are still backward; the Americans walk faster than the Italians. . . . In fashionable circles feet are no longer as small as they used to be because of pedestrian activity. They are constantly increasing in size. The big feet of English men and women no longer summon up our mockery. We too climb mountains, have bicycles, and—horrible dictu—now have acquired English feet. But let's take comfort. The beauty of the small foot is slowly beginning to fade, especially for men.[16]

Although Loos's articles were clearly rhetorical and not to be taken at face value, his overwhelming sense of disgust at the effects of "feminine" culture and female sexuality, together with his willingness to imbue everyday commodities with baleful sociological theory, threatens to undermine their value as an impartial record of the production and consumption of men's shoes at this pivotal moment in the history of the industry. Loos's direct intellectual descendants in this respect would appear to be those who have positioned footwear as sexual fetish at the expense of any understanding of its role in adjacent fields, as economic product, anthropological marker, semiotic sign, or indeed as art-object.[17] Yet despite their deliberately provocative tone, the 1897 publications find some strong echoes in the concerns of writers from within the shoemaking trades at the time.

For example, James Pond, a bootmaker of Norwich (a center for the manufacture of British dress shoes in the nineteenth century), completed "a practical treatise upon the natural care of the feet and their treatment in deformity" a year before Loos's journalism. In its concentration on the hygienic clothing of the feet, the book contributes to a more general discourse on links between health, aesthetics, and fashion, which engendered such reforming projects as that pioneered by Gustav Jaeger and maintained some parallels with those debates on decoration, style, and surface that were preoccupying writers on architecture and urbanism in the same period. Like Loos, Pond advocated a theory of design driven by rational utility, and which was resistant to the effects of fashion:

> The shape, cut and whole formation of the boot or shoe should be such as to give the best protection and the greatest freedom to all parts of the foot and leg; but fashion, unfortunately, is so mixed up in this question, as in all other questions of clothing, that all endeavours for the comfort of the feet are stifled. . . . The tailor, dressmaker and hatter may conform to fashion, however ridiculous, without inflicting serious injury upon their customers. This is not the case, however, with the shoemaker, he makes his boots the shape of the last given him, often not knowing, or even thinking about the construction of the foot or leg and its uses.[18]

Besides the effects of fashion, Pond was worried about the influence that sweated manufacture dictated over standards of finish and an attention to the orthopedic function of footwear. It is interesting that in their fetishization of the gentleman's wardrobe, both Le Corbusier and Loos were also attracted to bespoke items, to the handmade and the finely crafted. Here the iconic man's shoe was distinguished from those other items of mass production: the porcelain cup and the Thonet chair. Standardized workmen's clothing was overlooked in favor of the products of the traditional tailor or the master cobbler. As far as fitness for purpose was concerned, the individually fitted, hand-sewn shoe was clearly superior to the factory riveted clog, as Pond concurred:

> There is no doubt that hand sewn bespoke boots and shoes are preferable to ready-made ones as they are more carefully constructed, more pliable to the feet, stronger and more easily repaired. . . . A riveted boot in whatever form is worse than a wooden bottom or clog. It is rigid, hard and unyielding, and in whatever shape it is made the foot must adapt itself to it . . . as they are cheap they are very much worn, causing an enormous quantity of distorted and crippled feet, especially flat feet.[19]

In this manner, through recourse to contemporary debates on physical and moral degeneration among city dwellers, shoe manufacturers were able to promote the cause of the bespoke industry above that of the sweated trades.[20]

If commentators on aesthetic issues relied on the fear of feminization in the field of popular taste as a means of furthering the modernist cause, other interests were best served by focusing on the dire state of the national body. From the soles of the feet upward, critics from the fields of medicine, religion, and politics viewed the physiques of men in all walks of life as damaged by the rise of sedentary occupations, by an increased interest in the pursuit of leisure, and by exposure both to the real pollution of urban industry and to the polluting effects of commercial culture. Moral and health panics of this nature crossed geographic boundaries, fueling eugenicist research in the United States, Britain, and Europe and extending a set of arguments that were already well established in literature pertaining to military strategy from the period of the Boer War through to the advent of the First World War.[21]

So it was no coincidence that discussions surrounding the appropriate form of the modern shoe should relate closely to patriotic texts on strategies for the improvement of the physique of conscripts to the armed forces. In 1912 Edward Lyam Munson, a major in the medical corps of the U.S. Army, wrote on the design of the military shoe, employing a rhetoric that took civilian concerns about health a step farther:

> It is rare to find in civil life a shoe that even approaches the normal foot in shape and contour. Few manufacturers make them, as they are not saleable to the general public, whose choice is swayed rather by considerations of fashion than comfort. . . . Bad feet, especially in city-bred applicants, have come to be one of the chief causes for rejection for enlistment. . . . In civil life average conditions tend to be against rather than for foot development. But the soldier at the very outset represents the physically elect of the class from which he comes and is better in this respect than its average; moreover, all his parts, including the feet, undergo development in strength and size under the active life, weight carrying and systematized exercise which it falls upon him to perform.[22]

The panacea for the failings of the civilian shoe designer thus lay in the example set by the soldier's foot and its ideal casing. Beyond its functional prerequisites, which were to provide comfort, support, protection, durability, and ceremonial neatness at minimal cost, the military shoe embodied a celebration of fitness, vitality, and adaptability that held the potential to reenergize the flagging esteem of the urban office worker as much as it contributed to the success of martial campaigns. Following the First World War, several medical and industrial training texts drew on the expertise of the battlefield, bridging the requirements of the mainstream shoemaking trade and the quartermaster.[23] On a more intimate and private scale, the quiet pride taken by countless demobilized soldiers in maintaining a parade-ground polish on the surface of their oxfords bore testament to the pervasive influence of militarism on the relationship between men and their clothing.

In addition to all of this, the proselytizing of army medical officers remained extra-ordinarily close to the rhetoric of Loos and Le Corbusier in its fetishizing of function and fear of fashion:

> There can be no question but that of all the protective coverings which the foot soldier wears, his shoes are by far the most important from a strategic standpoint; since upon their shape, durability, use and comfort of fit, pliancy and lightness depends his military efficiency. Next to his armament, the shoe is probably the most important item of the equipment of the soldier. The construction of shoes for civilians is influenced almost wholly by consider-ations of fashion and style. These are irrational and are changed frequently in the financial interest of the shoe trade.[24]

Military and hygienic concerns were further acknowledged by Loos in his com-ments on the production of shoes that also appeared in *Die Neue Frei Presse* in the sum-mer of 1898. Here he championed the cause of his compatriot shoemakers, quoting the English trade press in its assertion that the Austrian footwear industry ranked above all others in the health-giving quality of its product. (Viennese shoe shop windows still dis-play a competitive range of paraphernalia for the care of the lower limbs, unmatched in other European capitals.) Loos retained less admiration for compatriot consumers, crediting the rise in deformities of the feet to the willingness of those who could not afford bespoke shoes to patronize the merchandise of "foreign" mass producers in their search for an elusive fashionability. In a ferocious passage of barely concealed anti-Semitism, Loos praised the rational impulses of Austrian craftsmen for setting the nation back on a footing appropriate to the needs of the forthcoming century: "We Austrians will be able to step out smartly in our shoes in the upcoming century. And good shoes will be necessary in the next century because we are going to be on the march. . . . The ancient Germanic blood still flows in our veins, and we are ready to march forward. We will do our best to help change the world of sitters and standers into a world of work and marching."[25]

Loos's implication that "good shoes" are those that reflect the heightened craft of the maker ("it is not by chance that the greatest poet and the greatest philosopher to have been bestowed on us by the artisan class were shoemakers")[26] and the discern-ing taste of the consumer is again an older one that leads us into the final area for con-sideration with regard to the broader meanings of the male shoe. Having focused on aesthetics and function, on the contribution of the dandy, the doctor, and the soldier in formulating a metaphorical rule of taste in respect to the modernity embodied in mas-culine footwear, it only remains to assess the ways in which the craft of shoemaking, the circumstances of production, can be read directly from the surface of the product (or indeed, obscured by it). For ultimately the signifiers of what constitutes a "good shoe" lie beyond questions of style and use. As any shoemaker or retailer would attest, they reside in the literal meeting of leather and thread. The male shoe is very much the sum of its parts, a physical object whose weight, texture, and smell bespeak the skill of its maker and point to its intrinsic value. The way in which a prospective buyer will "manhandle" his purchase as he raises it from the shop display for close inspection suggests as much. Textile commodities, trousers and shirts that derive their worth from the extrinsic values of fashionability, rarely receive such reverential treatment.

That shoe manufacturers have constantly been cognizant of this materiality is clearly evident from the texts of early advertisers. Elias Moses, a pioneering London clothing wholesaler of the mid–nineteenth century, traded on the concrete character of his wares in his evocative promotion:

> Two boots (quite unlike in their style and their leather)
> Were heard very recently talking together.
> It appears, from the facts which the journals record,
> That one was a Wellington fit for a lord,
> A boot such as very few houses can show,
> With a truly smart Heel and a truly flat Toe.
> The other one differ'd from this altogether:
> As ugly production—a mere waste of leather.
> 'Twas a dumpy, and lumpy and stumpy concern,
> Such as any respectable "trotter" would spurn.
> This queer piece of "craft" (who was all on the rip)
> Was the first who attempted to open his lip.
> "My friend (said his Ugliness, cover'd with mildew),
> Will you tell me the maker who happen'd to build you?
> For I certainly think you're a smart looking beau,
> And I find that our master thinks equally so.
> Since I first met with you Sir (oh, cutting disaster!)
> Believe me, I've not had one walk with my master.
> The service I've rendered is now all forgotten,
> And I'm pitched to and fro, just as though I were rotten."
> "I'm sorry to say (said the smartly made boot),
> You were never obtained at a house of repute.
> With regard to myself, I am smart to a point,
> And that's why your nose has been put out of joint."[27]

Moses's efforts at advertising the qualities of his wares came at a moment when the British shoe industry was undergoing a period of profound transition both in the organization of its labor and in the nature of its product. It is ironic that Moses, one of a new breed of wholesaler, should have puffed the attractions of his boots using the language of bespoke tradesmen, for it was precisely the business of entrepreneurs like him to undercut older methods of making-to-order with ready-made mass-produced goods at lower prices. As labor historian James Schmiechen has confirmed, the 1830s and 1840s saw the traditions of an established artisan trade in shoemaking eclipsed by sweated production. Adolf Loos drew on the older myth of the pipe-smoking, clean-shirted, intellectual cobbler at the end of the century, but by 1849 London shoemakers complained of their lack of work, money, and food. Aside from orders from elite consumers, traditional artisans found their professional practice invaded by cheaper female, child, and immigrant labor and the bulk of their customers drawn to "inferior" goods. In some respects this "labor aristocracy" had priced itself out of the market. While a reputation for trade-union activism had earned shoemakers valuable status and working conditions in the early nineteenth century, the reorganization of trade in Northampton on the lines of a factory system meant that the newer London retailers could look beyond London manufacturers to source their goods. The repeal of trade tariffs in 1842 also opened up contact with suppliers across the English Channel who were willing to supply fashionable French styles at low cost. Moses and his competitors, whose shops grandly answered to the names of Magazine, Depot, and Emporium, served a rapidly expanding population, insatiable for the "latest thing" with thousands of pairs of provincial and foreign shoes manufactured under sweated conditions.[28]

Beyond the shifting and fickle tastes of consumers, the actual process of manufacture remained fairly unaltered until fuller mechanization in the 1890s. The first stage in the manufacture of a shoe was "clicking," or cutting out the various parts of the product from the leather. The intricacy of this practice demanded great skill and so was initially least affected by the incursions of sweating and home-working. But by the 1860s the introduction of new cutting tools enabled some division of labor, where several unskilled hands could take on the work previously undertaken by one or two highly trained artisans, instantly increasing the speed of output but undermining an attention to detail.

The second stage of production was "closing," or stitching the upper part of the shoe together. The invention of the sewing machine caused this process to be the first to become fully mechanized and thus sweated, so that by the 1890s both branches of the trade, ready-made and bespoke, relied on machine closing.

The third stage of "making" the shoe incorporated the attaching of the sole and heel to the upper around the mold of a last. The first step of joining the insole and upper was a complex maneuver which relied on skilled hand-workers until 1891, when an automatic lasting-machine was patented with female operatives in mind. The fixing of insole and upper to sole was automated thirty years earlier with the introduction of the McKay shoe-sewing machine, enabling up to six hundred pairs of shoes to be "made" by one machine-hand in a working day. The development of heeling machines took longer, and the attachement of heels continued to be performed by hand-workers until the mid-1890s.

Finally, the finishing of the shoe involved cleaning, lining, accessorizing, and pack-ing, a highly subdivided process that had always entailed a high degree of subcontracting and home-work, but which nevertheless underwent a massive expansion in scale once the industry transformed itself to meet a frightening growth in demand.[29]

By the opening of the twentieth century, then, the classic man's shoe, whether bespoke or ready-to-wear, was a complicated organism. In terms of style, its basic look didn't differ greatly from the forms of shoe that had attracted consumers more than a hundred years before. It was this supposed "stability" that interested modernist critics. Yet the modern shoe was variously crafted through several industrial processes by hand and machine; it was probably manufactured in parts on separate sites; and it incor-porated in its makeup the history of a much-altered profession.

Despite the accusations of decline that mass production attracted, Edward Swaysland, principal of technical training in Northampton, was able to put a positive gloss on the fruits of his industry in 1905, drawing together those issues of hygiene, func-tionality, and aesthetics that made the man's shoe such a suggestive example for pro-gressive aestheticians. The shoe factories of the English midlands were some distance both geographically and intellectually from the ateliers of Vienna and Paris that framed the writings of Loos and Le Corbusier. But the discipline that Swaysland's trade demanded and the seemingly superior polish of its product opened that obscure amal-gam of leather, thread, blacking, and tin tacks up to surprising critiques and connec-tions, positioning it as a sign for something quite "other" than a simple shodding for the feet. It may not be in the nature of most male consumers to draw overt attention to them-selves, but all are surely aware of the wealth of information it is possible to read about a man in the simple choice of his shoe:

> Modern designs appear to trend towards severe simplicity and the perfect
> fitting of the foot. . . . But several developments of designs have been
> made from styles long in use, and provisions made for the requirements of
> modern manufacture that have raised the art of the shoe designer to a higher
> eminence than ever before attained. The demand for perfect fitting footwear,
> for an elegant appearance, the exactitude of the process of machine methods,
> and the rigid economy required, form a complication of problems that make
> boot and shoe design more than ever difficult. . . . The ideal pattern cutter is a
> scientific artist. The condition under which he produces his designs makes it
> indispensable that he be accustomed to great precision in measurement; that
> he make provision for the alteration in shape and dimensions of the materials

that his designs are produced in; and certainly not least, that he produces footwear that are artistic in shape. He therefore has to be scientific in his calculations, and artistic in his method of providing for them.[30]

NOTES

1. Ellen Moers, *The Dandy: Brummel to Beerbohm* (London: Secker and Warburg, 1960).

2. Nancy Troy, *Modernism and the Decorative Arts in France: Art Nouveau to Le Corbusier* (New Haven: Yale University Press, 1991).

3. Penny Sparke, *As Long as It's Pink: The Sexual Politics of Taste* (London: Pandora, 1995).

4. Le Corbusier, *The Decorative Art of Today,* trans. James Dunnett (London : Architectural Press, 1987), xxiii.

5. Christopher Breward, *The Hidden Consumer: Masculinities, Fashion, and City Life, 1860–1914* (Manchester: Manchester University Press, 1999).

6. Le Corbusier, *Decorative Art,* 7.

7. Ibid., 8.

8. Diana Donald, *The Age of Caricature: Satirical Prints in the Age of George III* (New Haven: Yale University Press, 1996).

9. Le Corbusier, *Decorative Art,* 87.

10. Ibid., 90.

11. John Piggott, Outfitter's Catalogue (London, 1907), 99–106. Museum of London Ephemera Collection.

12. Mark Wigley, *White Walls, Designer Dresses: The Fashioning of Modern Architecture* (Cambridge Mass.: MIT Press, 1995), 90–91.

13. Adolf Loos, *Spoken into the Void : Collected Essays, 1897–1910,* intro. Aldo Rossi (Cambridge Mass.: MIT Press, 1982), 55.

14. Ibid.

15. Ibid.

16. Ibid., 56–57.

17. William A. Rossi, *The Sex Life of the Foot and Shoe* (1977; reprint, Ware, Hertfordshire: Wordsworth Editions, 1989), 101–114.

18. James Pond, *The Foot and Its Covering* (London: Leather Trades Publisher, 1896), 17.

19. Ibid., 18–20.

20. Mark Anderson, *Kafka's Clothes: Ornament and Aestheticism in the Hapsburg Fin de Siecle* (Oxford: Clarendon Press, 1992).

21. Joanna Bourke, *Dismembering the Male: Men's Bodies, Britain, and the Great War* (London: Reaktion, 1996).

22. Edward Lyman Munson, *The Soldier's Foot and the Military Shoe* (Fort Leavenworth, Kans.: U.S. Army War Department, 1912), 35–39.

23. Captain C. W. Sewell, M.C., *A Resume on Weak and Tired Feet with Prescriptive Directions for Improving Function, Shape, and Structure* (London: C. W. Daniel, 1924).

24. Munson, *The Soldier's Foot,* 34.

25. Loos, *Spoken into the Void,* 61.

26. Ibid.

27. Elias Moses, *Fashion's Favourite; or, The Mart of the Many* (London, 1847), 18. Museum of London Ephemera Collection.

28. James Schmiechen, *Sweated Industries and Sweated Labour: The London Clothing Trades, 1860–1914* (London: Croom Helm, 1984), 9–12.

29. Ibid., 29–31.

30. Edward Swaysland, *Boot and Shoe Design and Manufacture* (Northampton, 1905), 8, 39.

Are You a Pura Latina? or, Menudo Every Day: Jacones and Symbolic Ethnicity

TACE HEDRICK

In the September 1997 issue of the women's magazine *Latina,* Liz Balmaseda muses on the "mystique" that high heels seem to hold for Latinas: "I remembered in high school, in the 1970s, it was the heels that distinguished the Latinas from the *Americanitas.* We were the chicks in the seven-inch, custom-designed platforms."[1] In the same article, Balmaseda quotes Herlinda de Armas, the "once-famous Havana cabaret dancer and Hotel Capri star," on the Latina penchant for wearing high heels: "Girl, I did it all on spikes. . . . They lift you up. It's a thing of greater fantasy. . . . We do everything in heels. I have this friend who wears her *puyas* [spikes] to the Calle Ocho street festival each year. She even wears them to the beach." Just recently, the Smithsonian Museum's Latino collection was enriched by the addition of Cuban singer Celia Cruz's famous platform heels. This is not to say, of course, that every Latina (Cuban American or Puerto Rican) or Chicana (Mexican American) wears high heels constantly; however, the connection of heels with the exotic beauty of certain Latin American and Hispanic American women has been part of the United States' collective imaginary for decades.[2] Where would the Brazilian Carmen Miranda, Nuyorican Jennifer López, or Mexican-born Salma Hayek be without their seemingly requisite high heels?

The question of an authentic ethnic and/or racial identity, when imagined in terms of ethnic markers such as clothing and style, is in fact now entangled with the possibility, made more and more accessible by increasingly sophisticated marketing

135

strategies, of gaining (or reinforcing) a cultural identity at the point of market consumption. In the process of my work in ethnic studies, I have become interested in
the ways in which popular self-representations of a certain kind of Latina femininity include a negotiated acceptance of certain stereotypes. Is an accommodation to
stereotype merely one more example of the ways in which an oppressed subject
buys into, internalizes, and reproduces the elements of her own objectification, in this
case the popular (white) male U.S. stereotype of the sexy, bombshell spitfire Latina
perched precariously on high heels? Or can appropriations of stereotypes, for example
of the high-heel-wearing Latina, constitute part of a "belly-down epistemology" of cultural survival (or even of ethnicity) itself, part of a subordinated culture's complex of
negotiations, resistances, and adoptions?

In contemporary U.S. mass or mediated culture, fashion occupies a peculiar, and
shifting, space in these debates and representations of the ethnic, of culture, and even
of race as well as, of course, gender.[3] Moving around and down the (cultural) body, from
stomach to butt to feet, and finally shoes, gives us an opening for some preliminary
thoughts on these terms and their received meanings. What interests me is not just the
cultural marker high heels (and whose cultural marker these are is, as we will see, itself
up for question) for a certain way of imagining *Latinidad*. I am also interested in
exploring how style, particularly for women, comes to be the site for contradictory impulses
toward femininity and ethnicity. These questions will not be comprehensively answered
by any means, and my choice of texts with which to examine them is small in number
and eclectic; this means my conclusions must necessarily be offered up as partial and
situated ones. But two spaces where I find these contradictory impulses operating are
in popular bilingual women's magazines aimed at Latinas and Chicanas, such as *Latina*
and *Moderna,* and contemporary Latina and Chicana fiction, which when successful
is often marketed to Anglo audiences as offering an excursion into a space of authentic "Hispanic" experience. Popular women's magazines remain important in women's constructions of themselves, and since the nineteenth century they have also provided an
important space for race or ethnic resistance, uplift, and affirmation. As we will see, these
magazines (unsurprisingly) present a commercialized sense of ethnic femininity. This
sense is simultaneously more rigid, homogenous, and contradictory than the sense of
Latinidad the reader derives from, for example, the Chicana author Sandra Cisneros's
work in *Woman Hollering Creek*. However, these texts represent a spectrum of, rather
than diametrically opposed alternatives to, the debate over authentic cultural identity
and its presumed opposite, stereotypical images of cultural identity.

As the spring 1997 issue of *Moderna* tells us in its article "Just How Latina Are
You?" the clothes—including shoes—you buy and the way you wear them let people

know "just how Latina" you are (although for the magazine *Latina* "meltproof *maquil-laje*" is equally important). To underscore the point, question number four from *Moderna*'s quiz, "Are you a Pura Latina?" allows the reader to choose, as "favorite shoes," clogs, Chuck Taylor Converse tennis shoes, high heels, and flats. High heels is the "correct answer," and if you choose it you are on your way to being "brown and proud": "Your awareness of current events and political issues doesn't stop you from doing or using what you want (you wear makeup tested on animals)," with a personal style that is "sexy and colorful."[4] Here "brownness" (the models they use to illustrate the two kinds of Latinas—one politicized, one urban and fun-loving—are in fact both quite light-skinned) and pride in that brownness are linked with style, specifically with shoes and makeup, two items which both *Moderna* and *Latina* emphasize as essential to a certain kind of "pura Latina."

It seems to me that any discussion about women's high heels and their relationship to certain constructions of ethnicity is of necessity concerned—both literally and metaphorically—with the lower regions of the body and the "lower" functions of the body. But rather than start from the ground up with the shoes, I'd like to start my thinking from the stomach down, with what Frances Negrón-Muntaner calls a "belly-down epistemology."[5] This is an epistemology, a way of knowing, that is of particular concern in ethnic and cultural survival. It involves, among other things, the ways that cultural products—food, clothing, everyday useful items—are called upon to perform in a group's sense of (ethnic) culture.

The Chicano lawyer and 1960s revolutionary icon Oscar Zeta Acosta's thoughts on *menudo* (tripe stew) demonstrate how in zones of contact the production of certain culturally coded "things" can be shifted and can be accommodated to changing circumstances.[6] Menudo is thought of by Anglos as low food, but for many Chicanos it is a valuable food connected intimately to certain cultural rituals and remedies. In his 1973 autobiographical novel *The Revolt of the Cockroach People,* Zeta Acosta describes a "Chicano power" march in Los Angeles in the late 1960s:

> A thousand young Chicanos and I are marching together . . .
> "Viva Zapata!" through the bullhorn.
> "¡Que Viva!" roars the crowd.
> "Viva Pancho Villa!"
> "¡Que Viva!"
> . . . A thousand kids streaming through a barrio of palm trees and Mexicatessens.
> "MENUDO EVERYDAY," the signs say.
> And then I remember that menudo is the stew made only on holidays, at Christmas time, for a wedding, a baptism and on those days that the fathers

have tripe, corn and lime for the morning-after hangovers. But here they make
it *everyday* [sic]. It would make a good title for a short story. Not just on
Saturday and Sunday, but *everyday*.[7]

What Zeta Acosta is really talking about is a practice of cultural survival sometimes referred
to as *rasquachismo,* the belly-down epistemology of using up, making do, appropriating,
and even accommodating (though not completely assimilating) oneself and one's cultural values to the requirements of the prevailing, dominant culture.[8] This is the belly-
down survival skill of those people considered by the dominant culture to be exotic maybe,
always in some way foreign and strange, but ultimately low. Zeta Acosta's remarks about
the ways the production and presentation of menudo, a special food, is accommodated
to the demands of living in the midst of a more dominant culture is a small example of
the ways a group's cultural self-articulation meets up with and is porous to the historical, social, and economic politics both of domination and of location.

    The efforts at cultural survival (and revival) of the kind employed by what's often
called the cultural nationalism of the U.S. black and Chicano power movements of the
1960s and 1970s have often been criticized for their overly reductive and essentializ-
ing notions of group identity and cultural survival. My reading of the connections
between a contemporary United States' sense of ethnicity and the ways it manifests itself
through representations of women's shoes has to be done through some of the entanglements produced by a relatively new understanding of ethnicity. The new understanding of this term is driven in large part by the changes wrought in the United States's
sense of itself during, and in the aftermath of, the civil rights movement. The newer
sense of race and ethnicity has been the center of a debate that, more than three decades
later, continues to concern itself with issues of identity, community, culture, and consensus. This debate also circles on the by now familiar tension between the realness
or authenticity of a cultural identity and a less well defined falseness of identity. Everyone knows, seemingly, what an authentic identity is, but what is a fake identity? The
Latina women's magazine *Moderna* has an answer: a "Wannabe Latina" is a "clueless
but well-intentioned Anglicized Latina trying to find [her] way in life. . . . all the passion, fun, and beauty could be [hers] if [she] hook[s] up with the right teachers."[9]

    Yet a closer look at some of the central cultural nationalist fictions of the time,
such as Zeta Acosta's, reveals that the impulse toward cultural nationalism and symbolic ethnicity was more afflicted with doubts about identity, and conceived more in
relational terms vis-à-vis Anglo or dominant culture than is generally thought. The material symbols of a group's cultural sense of itself are often fluid and adaptable, with boundaries that are leaky or porous, especially at the points where this sense of identity meets
up with the necessities of dealing with a more privileged group.

It's clear at the same time that this very fluidity and adaptability may, especially under marketing forces, in turn congeal into stereotype. For example, the oft-cited fact that U.S. citizens now buy more salsa than ketchup is offered up as evidence of the "Hispanicization" of the United States, perpetuating the hot and spicy stereotype of the Hispanic character. However, the notion of stereotype as an unequivocably fixed image, forcibly imposed from above and consciously rejected by the stereotyped Other, is itself a reductive way in which to view either constructions of ethnicity or the power relations between groups that are unequal in privilege. It's been suggested by the postcolonial critic Homi Bhabha that "the stereotype is a complex, ambivalent, contradictory mode of representation";[10] the eradication of stereotypes is not just a matter of educating one's thoughts away from wrong notions, because the stereotype itself is ambivalent and constantly in process, mutating to suit new circumstances. The point that ethnic studies scholars make, however, and one that is central to the study of ethnic fiction and ethnic self-representation, is that ethnicity is often (as Benedict Anderson notes of nations) a matter of mapping out communal imaginings.[11]

If debates around either the divisiveness or the diversity of ethnicity (and race) in the United States can be read in terms of how people (communally) *imagine* the performance of those terms, then the narratives and stories of ethnicity and race, how they're told, and what images accompany them become important. I want to show the reciprocal activities of imagining, mapping, and narrating ethnicity onto bodies—especially women's bodies—with the aid of certain kinds of style and fashions that both produce and complicate popular, often stereotypical, notions of ethnicity, femininity, and culture.

What is meant by "culture" in an ethnic studies context more often than not entails a complex interplay of give and take at the juncture where two (or more) cultures meet. Oftentimes, this juncture is one of both domination and accommodation, as has happened in the United States between Anglo culture and the Hispanic cultures within and on its borders. Attempts to read this interplay of cultural "emulation and imperialistic imposition"[12] have been made under the headings of mestizaje, hybridity, syncretization, transculturation, and border studies, to name just a few.

It is the point at which boundedness crosses over with (cultural, boundary) disarticulation that interests me; whether through imposition, kidnapping, stealing, or borrowing, the things—material objects, often enough—of culture sometimes end up functioning as areas of porosity, or points of relative leakiness, embedded throughout the broad area that constitutes the "contact zone" of different cultures. At these spots, different levels of mixing (up) happen between groups that see themselves, or that have been constructed, as different from each other. Sites of exchange and leakiness include, of course, the bodies of women, who, through their status as gifts, translators, or negotiators have been made to function as go-betweens and bridges from one culture to another since before the Spanish, French, and British arrived in the Americas. This is not to say that more privileged or more violent cultures don't simply carry off, then consume, what they want (including women) from dominated groups. Indeed, in contemporary U.S. mass culture, those things that can be identified and unhooked, taken away, or broken off from their proper place in a particular group's everyday functional and representational systems—foods, clothing, craft or artwork, music, religious or spiritual icons, *and* I would add (representations of) women—can be made to operate in precisely this way; this is what black feminist writer bell hooks has termed "eating the other."

Discussing an overheard conversation between white boys for whom "fucking was a way to confront the Other, as well as a way to leave behind white 'innocence,'" hooks maintains that this serves as an illustration of the extent to which (mostly white) popular culture looks for liveliness to the fantasies generated by its consumption of bits and pieces of (darker) Otherness.[13] Hooks notes that in the United States "mass culture is the contemporary location that both publicly declares and perpetuates the idea that there is pleasure to be found in the acknowledgment and enjoyment of racial difference."[14]

The fact is that since the nineteenth century the observation that *cultures* mix has often been conflated with *race*-mixing (or hybridity), and has served as a vehicle for the expression of *both* fears and desires about certain (racialized) kinds of women and their role in families, economies, and nations.[15] Toward this end, images and metaphors of marriage, love, and (hetero)sexual union have been pressed into the service both of unifying as well as of exclusionary social and political projects throughout the nineteenth and twentieth centuries. The romance with the Latin image, and its availability to stand in for several different exotic Others (Caribbean, Latin American, Brazilian, Native American, Mesoamerican), has a relatively long history in the United States: the islands of Puerto Rico and Cuba (especially Cuba) represented in the U.S. popular imagination of the 1930s through the 1950s "an accessible paradise, foreign and familiar at the same time,"[16] and the presentation of Latina actors and stars such as Talisa Soto, Jennifer López, and Gloria Estefan continues to provide an avenue for white United States to picture to itself the right way in which the always "heterocultural" romance should be conducted with the Hispanic Other it finds in its midst.

For example, Cuban writer Gustavo Pérez-Firmat looks for a unifying principle to explain why there is such a mixing when two cultures meet, and thinks he finds it in what he calls "heteroculturalism." For him, the answer to what to do about the presence of the cultural and/or racial Other is to be (heterosexually) attracted to it. As an example of the way in which "love" and sexual union (presumably) solve the problem of cultural differences, he points to the *I Love Lucy* TV show: "Ricky [Ricardo] thrives on unlikeness . . . the opposite sex is the apposite sex. The opposite culture is the apposite culture."[17] It is no surprise to discover that what Pérez-Firmat calls the "mindless agglutinizing energy"[18] of heteroculturalism is best illustrated by a 1940 film called *Too Many Girls* starring Desi Arnaz, where without actually meaning to he points to the violence, and the masculine privilege, involved in popular culture's consumption of those it constructs as Other:

> An Argentine Desi, dressed in a football uniform, with a *tumbadora* slung around his neck, lead[s] a conga in the New Mexico desert. . . .Never mind that [Ann Miller] plays a Mexican girl with the unlikely name of Pepe. Never mind also that a close-up of Desi's conga drum shows that it is decorated with Indian motifs. . . . All of the principal American cultures are there—black, white, Indian, Hispanic; but everyone is caricatured and distorted. Yet . . . jitterbugging to a conga, as some of the dancers do, is to treat the Afro-American jitterbug with no more respect than is bestowed on Cuban music or Amerindian art. In the throes of conga-fever . . . the town plaza becomes a melting pot.[19]

Pérez-Firmat's enjoyment of this scene (and I agree, there are ways it can be enjoyed) rests on the problematic assumption that all that "agglutinizing energy" is simply blissful ignorance in the service of an overtly sexualized (multi)cultural and egalitarian union. No one art form, according to him, is privileged in this scene, though he forgets the intended white U.S. audience will (paradoxically) see jitterbugging as "civilized" white dancing while the other dancers are "primitive" or "exotic."

Pérez-Firmat's perhaps inadvertent point, however, is useful for my point about Latina women's magazines. That is, a subordinate group (Latinas in general) is represented also as being unproblematically part of the larger, fairly homogeneous consuming community—Revlon advertises its darker shades in the pages of *Latina*, General Motors and Sears advertise (in Spanish) in *Estylo*, and Elizabeth Arden's makeup appears in *Moderna*, to name only a few corporations targeting Hispanic markets. But the very homogenizing impulse so essential to capitalism's push for as large a market as possible, combined with the melting pot push of U.S. nationalism, works against a magazine like *Latina*'s own efforts at ethnic resistance or empowerment.

For example, Puerto Rican actor and model Talisa Soto tells the story (complete with photos of her posing in six-inch heels—see figure 1) in *Latina*'s January 1998 issue of how she broke into modeling with the new agency Click, which, tired of the "blond and blue-eyed thing," wanted the kind of "different, exotic look" she could provide. Without a trace of irony, the article goes on to detail her work on the TV show *Harts of the*

FIGURE I   ⌒   Puerto Rican actor Talisa Soto posing in high heels.

West where she plays a "Native American," while simultaneously emphasizing that she "relishes her Puerto Rican heritage."[20]

Thus those gestures toward resistance, such as celebrating brownness or discussing Latina lesbianism or showcasing Latinas who have been successful, often seem to do nothing but "reduce protest to spectacle"[21] with the same kind of "mindless agglutinizing energy" as Pérez-Firmat points out in *Too Many Girls.* Additionally, the already-familiar role of women as consumers par excellence is joined, as in all women's magazines, with the self-inscription of the female body as mirroring, monitoring, and reproducing its own place within the now-commodified spaces of (mostly white) masculine privilege.

So is a magazine like *Latina* just the latest in a long history of the merchandising of exoticized women's bodies by ethnic sell-out "coconuts" (brown on the outside, white on the inside)? Is it the ethnic self-catering spice to the "dull dish that is white mainstream culture"?[22] Images and texts that seem to emulate or even cater to the often fearful desires of white mass culture coexist uneasily with those that strive, sometimes in radical fashion, to "love brownness" in all its shades on the pages of magazines like *Moderna* and *Latina.* To paraphrase hooks, who is "eating" whom in these magazines?

Apart from their promotion of a general image of the Latin(a) spitfire who is invested in a particularly urban and artificial self, the magazines of course serve their own economic interests in promoting *maquillaje* and fashion, since their primary advertisers are makeup and clothing manufacturers. This produces an interesting paradox, one where what would seem to be the superficiality of a certain kind of ethnic femininity—the use of lots of external devices such as makeup, jewelry, clothes, hair products—in fact is posited as revealing the *realness* and *depth* of the ethnically feminine: "You are a Latina by blood, and you can't change that no matter how much you try to deny it."[23] Cultural critic Stuart Hall has noted that "cultural identity" is often thought of "in terms of one, shared culture, a sort of collective 'one true self,' hiding inside the many others, more superficial or artificially imposed 'selves,' which people with a shared history and ancestry hold in common."[24] In an interesting twist, true Latina identity is only enhanced, not hidden, by the products the magazine offers, to produce not just a successful and therefore pleasurable femininity but a successful and therefore pleasurable *ethnic* femininity. What "successful" means here, however, is a complex and often contradictory set of codes both of femininity and of ethnicity.

RACE, *CULOS,* AND *TACONES*

As Negrón-Muntaner says in her essay on the *puertorriqueña* butt, for "[North] American image gatekeepers," a big Latina *culo* (butt) is "a sign for the dark, incomprehensible excess of 'latino' and other African diaspora cultures . . . through the three deadly vectors of miscegenation, sodomy, and a high-fat diet."[25] Although her point can be extended from Afro-Hispanic bodies to the perceived exotic attributes of the mis-cegenated, voluptuous mestiza or Indo-Hispanic body, for now we will stay with the vaguely Cuban/Caribbean connotations of the popular use of the term "Latina," where the exotic lure of the big butt is propped up (so to speak) by that other staple of the "Latina" image, *los tacones.*

Although it is not just dark "Latinas" who wear high heels, the popular image of the generic, high-heel-wearing Latina is often racialized. For example, Liz Balmaseda's essay "Seduced by Spikes" in *Latina*'s September 1997 issue (figure 2) describes her experience walking in spike heels: "I could even feel my backside more round and free with each stride, as if responding to the roll of ancient drums."[26] The next two pages of this particular issue are devoted to Celia, the Afro-Cuban singer whose signature style since the 1950s includes the butt-enhancing *bata cubana,* a traditional long, tight Cuban dress that flounces out around the feet, and high heels that "defy gravity" (fig-ure 3). Not only do they defy gravity, but "on top of these heels, you have this volup-tuous body moving around, dancing around. Those heels are *her* [Celia]."[27] Turning back to the previous pages' musings on the "mystique" of the high heel for Latinas, we find that the image of the Cuban singer Celeste Mendoza also connects race with high heels. In a 1961 video clip from Havana, she dances the *guaguancó* "in white spiked pumps . . . turning smooth, seductive circles with her hips, an African goddess beau-tifully dancing."[28]

The image of the dancing, big-hipped, and big-butted African goddess should alert us to the conjunction of several histories converging on the (racialized) body of the Latina. *Latina* tells us that "Latinas aren't afraid to look dramatic," and the "1940s Hollywood starlet" look it offers features "meltproof *maquillaje*" on a model whose broad nose and bee-stung lips gesture suggestively toward the imagined pleasures of miscegenation in the same way that high heels make big (dark) Latina butts even bigger, rounder, and more "primitive."[29] The reference to Hollywood starlets of the 1940s provides, upon closer reading, a partial context for such images: as Gustavo Pérez-Firmat notes, the popularity in the mid-1930s to the mid-1950s of movies with a "Latin" theme was "of a piece with Hollywoood's efforts to promote Roosevelt's Good Neighbor policy toward Latin America."[30] Stars such as the Spanish-Irish Rita Hayworth (born Margarita Cansino, whose process of Anglicization included losing weight, heightening her fore-head, and dying her hair to become the "all-American girl"), (Brazilian) Carmen Miranda, Lupe Vélez (the "Mexican Spitfire"), and (Cuban) Xavier Cugat, (Cuban) Desi Arnaz, and (Mexican) Ricardo Montalbán all appeared as "Latin," often vaguely Cuban,

Seduced by spikes

BY LIZ BALMASEDA

Carlos slid back upon my bed, crushing pillows along the way, and hissed a command.

"Put on your heels, *Mami.*"

I caught his deep *cielo* eyes checking me out between wisps of hair. I glanced down at my bare toes, then dubiously at the shoes he had pulled out for me, black spike-heeled pumps. I slipped one reluctant foot into one daunting spike, then the other, and I studied myself from the shoes upward—the spikes, the short black skirt, the black tapered jacket—a sober ensemble he had extracted from the carnival that was my closet. He tossed aside the prints, the flower patterns, the stripes. "Never wear these again!" he barked with some credibility. He was, after all, an artist famous in the hippest strata of South Beach for conjuring an air of Armani on a thrift-shop budget.

"Aha. Like that, baby. Now, walk. Walk to me."

It was not a difficult thing to do, to walk toward a guy chosen that year by *People* magazine as one of the 50 most beautiful people in the world. So I walked across the room in my spikes, feeling a strange power as he hooted and writhed playfully. "Yeah! *Así! Así!*"

I could feel my calves lift and tighten, my quads swell upward and outward. I could even feel my backside more round and free with each stride, as if responding to the roll of ancient drums. Out of some primal instinct, I tucked in my belly, smoothed back my shoulders, and took a cool walk in my spikes.

Something important happened that night. I actually became one of those women in *tacones:* tall, taut, and daring.

For a decade I lived the cautious existence of a girl in flats, rarely venturing beyond the comfort of *vieja* shoes. High heels? They were a thing

of my early twenties, a casualty of my better judgment in the postdisco age. Unwilling to recognize their hidden power, I dismissed them as borderline bimbo wear. I nodded in approval when the American Orthopedic Foot and Ankle Society chastised shoe manufacturers years ago for producing foot-deforming shoes. I shook my head in disgust when I learned that 88% of women wear shoes that are too small, in the name of vanity. I felt safe and smug within the prudent 12%.

But that night I decided to take the big plunge. I would no longer be the butt of my sister's jokes—"Liz actually wore sensible shoes to her own wedding!"

"You must wear these always," Carlos, my stylist pal, told me. "Always."

Well, I thought, outta my way! Me and my spikes are strutting through.

It was all coming back to me. I remembered in high school, in the

FIGURE 2   ↶   "Seduced by Spikes."

Spun sugar

"Who says she's not blond? Spun sugar, honey! I love it. I love her audacity. She's an original."

"¿Quién se atreve a decir que Celia no es rubia? Me encanta su audacia".

Yo soy Cuba

"Here she is saying, 'Yo soy Cuba.' She most certainly embodies Cuba. That's why she can wear the flag.... She's beyond risk; she is so secure in her position, that she doesn't worry what people think. That's what fashion is all about."

"Está tan segura que hasta se viste de bandera cubana y no le preocupa lo que diga la gente. De eso se trata la moda".

Extravagant

"I prefer the more extravagant styles: Her headpieces remind me of Patti LaBelle or Tina Turner. A Puerto Rican does her wigs."

"Prefiero los estilos más extravagantes de sus pelucas. Quien se las arregla es puertorriqueño".

a kind'

"Her dresses are all a variation on the *bata cubana*, the traditional Cuban dress. She's one of a kind. No one has come out that can touch her yet. Her image evolves from her persona and her stage presence. She knows who she is. She knows where she came from. She knows how to carry herself."

"Sus vestidos son variantes de la tradicional bata cubana. Su imagen surge de su personalidad y de su presencia en escena".

Prrrrr

"Sleek. Coy. Prrrrr. She breaks the monotony of the blue hair and blue dress with the red lips and nails. It brings the focus to her mouth and her hands, her most beautiful features."

"Lo único que no es azul son los labios y las uñas; sus atributos más bellos".

Since the fifties

"If you don't know whose shoes these are, you're not Latino. Shoes are Celia's signature. She's been wearing this style since the fifties. They defy gravity. On top of these heels, you have this voluptuous body moving around, dancing around. Those heels are *her*."

"Estos zapatos son un desafío a la gravedad. Ella los usa desde los años 50. Y todos reconocen que este es su estilo".

Fabulous

"Looking at Celia's nails, it's quite obvious that she's never had to do the dishes. And there is that fabulous emerald ring on her finger. She wears it all the time."

"Esas manos fabulosas revelan que Celia nunca ha tenido que lavar los platos".

Golden goddess

"She's a golden goddess. She's beyond showgirls. A showgirl is one of a group; she's in a class all her own. I love the outrageousness. The sky is the limit for Celia. She's not limited by anything. Age, weight, ethnicity. She plays with all of it."

"Es una Diosa Dorada sin par. Nada la cohíbe. Ni edad, ni peso, ni raza. Ella juega con todo eso".

La esencia tropical

Above, center: "This dress looks like a Thierry Mugler [French designer]. It reflects her status as an international icon. She has inspired many designers. She's *la esencia tropical*. The dress is built around a corset. I wonder if it's hard to breathe in that...."

"Celia es la esencia tropical. Este vestido está montado sobre una faja. ¿Podrá ella respirar?"

FIGURE 3 ✌ Cuban singer Celia Cruz, her famous *bata cubana* dresses, and her platform shoes.

sometimes "Mexican," and even at times Native American exotics (regardless of their real countries of origin) in innumerable films of this genre. As Clara Rodríguez notes, these images taught (white) North Americans not about Latin America so much as about what Latin America's "proper relationship should be to the United States."[31]

At the turn of the twenty-first century, we witness a similar (though differently motivated) impulse toward producing a homogenous Latina image for U.S. commercial consumption. Negrón-Muntaner remarks that, for example, "in this marketing and audience-building trajectory, Selena [as represented in the movie *Selena*] went from being a Tejana (a territorialized 'regional' identity) to being a Latina (an 'ethnic minority'). 'Latino' . . . does not refer to a cultural identity, but to a specifically American national currency for economic and political deal making; a technology to demand and deliver emotions, votes, markets, and resources on the same level as other racialized minorities."[32] Although the term "Latino" can work as a tool for political and economic recognition when it is delivered as a "cohesive identity and as a market," it also works to obscure the fact that so-called Hispanic groups have differing historically and regionally based senses of themselves, and that often political and economic power is usually achieved more locally, even more ethnically, and sometimes at the cost of coalition building.[33] Magazines like *Moderna* and *Latina,* in fact, are not unaware of this problematic. *Moderna,* for example, cites Angelica, a "Mexican American from Phoenix who has perfect command of the Spanish language," on the ideological and political splits within Latina/Chicana "communities": "It's not like we hate each other—we just joke and make fun if someone speaks Spanish with an accent, because in the larger scheme of things we are all *hermanas.* When it counts, we'll be there for each other."[34]

Hermanas or not, the problematic of forming coalitions across different "Hispanic" groups or across different experiences of what it means to be "Hispanic" in the United States is not in fact erased in these magazines but instead is first raised as a problem and then redirected in more appropriately feminine ways. When it comes to women's looks, the problem of differences among Hispanic Americans is in fact redirected toward a presumably more private, individual, and less politicized discourse of ethnic styles, which in turn is taken to be pointing to the realness of a pan-Hispanic or Latina sisterhood.

In magazines such as *Moderna,* the image of the "brown and proud" Latina perched in her short skirt and high heels, while appropriating the black pride slogan of the black power movement,[35] also owes much to U.S. white imaginings of the sexuality of mixed-race peoples. But it is important to note that these imaginings find their counterpart in constructions of the mixed-race female body in Hispanic Caribbean nationalist and independence movements. As Vera Kutzinski points out, in the pan-Caribbean negritude movement of the 1940s and 1950s, and even before then in the earlier *poesía negra* or *poesía mulata* movements of the turn of the century through the 1920s, the image of the Afro-Hispanic *mulata* has often served to encode national identity in the Hispanic Caribbean. Although these movements arose in part in reaction to U.S. domination and racism, North American racist fears both paralleled and reinforced long-standing Caribbean *criollo* (or Creole, that is, white, native-born, but of Spanish descent) fears of their large black populations. Kutzinski notes, for example, that Afro-Cubanism's emphasis on blackness as well as on *mulatez* (Afro-Hispanic mixing) in the 1920s through the 1930s "contained and defused potential ethnic threats to national unification by turning [blackness and *mulatez*] into original . . . contributions to Cuban culture." This was especially effected through the iconic image of the *mulata,* (supposed) sign of black/white love and unification under the sign of Afro-Cuban ritual, dance, and music. The fact that the very body of the *mulata* was symbolically as well as literally connected to the (slave) production of Cuba's wealth through its two main crops, sugar and tobacco, only made the material signs of her production more useful for independence or for nationalist desires.

The Puerto Rican *poesía negra* poet Luis Palés Matos gave voice to such nationalist impulses in his 1937 "Plena de menéalo" (Full of shakin' it):

> Dale a la popa, mulata,
> proyecta en la eternidad
> ese rumbo de caderas
> que es ráfaga de huracán, y menéalo,
> de aquí payá, de ayá pacá,
> menéalo, menéalo,
> ¡para que rabie el Tío Sam!

> Shake that butt, mulata,
> project into eternity
> this beat of your hips
> that's the hurricane's gale, and shake it,
> back and forth, forth and back,
> shake it, shake it,
> to piss Uncle Sam off!

The Cuban anthropologist Fernando Ortíz's 1930s study of the steatopygia of African women meets up with these 1937 verses, which, in spite of their avowed resistance to U.S. hegemony, in turn find their slightly whitened-up counterparts in the bodies of Hollywood Latina stars such as Carmen Miranda (famous for her butt-enhancing platform shoes) in Hollywood conga musicals, in Havana-locale movies of the 1940s (see Pérez-Firmat's partial list of such movies in his *Life on the Hyphen*), and the contemporary emphasis on Jennifer López's butt. Finally, they are completely consonant with the sentiments expressed in the September 1997 *Latina*: high heels make the "backside more round and free with each stride, as if responding to the roll of ancient drums," while the "African goddess" Celeste Mendoza turns "smooth, seductive circles with her hips . . . beautifully dancing" in white pumps. In the context of mostly masculine Caribbean "celebrations" of *mulatez,* Kutzinski maintains that "most saliently contradictory . . . is the symbolic privileging of a socially underprivileged group defined by its mixed race or phenotype, its gender, and its imputed licentious sexuality. In the case of the mulata, high symbolic or cultural visibility contrasts sharply with social invisibility."[36]

The appropriation of the "high symbolic or cultural visibility" of the high-heeled Latina by magazines such as *Latina* and *Moderna* constitutes an interesting reworking of the constellation of historical, social, ideological, and political specificities that surround the Hollywood Latina and her Caribbean counterparts within the space of popular and mass constructions of ethnicity. Here, the stereotype is presumably no longer employed, at least consciously, at the expense of "social invisibility" but rather crosses paths with a very real attempt to form an oppositional and highly visible social/ethnic body.

LA LUCHA/COPING: RESISTANCE

As we have briefly seen, both of the Latina women's magazines I've discussed offer points of accommodation with, as well as points of resistance to, the racism, sexism, and ethnocentrism of the Anglo majority. Much as *Essence* does for black women, *Latina* and *Moderna* regularly offer their readers examples of Latina/Chicana success stories, from actors to writers, artists, and politicians. (In fact, *Essence* is *Latina*'s parent magazine.) Both magazines offer Latina-oriented advice to women on child care, careers, money matters, as well as on fashion and men—those *papis chulos* ("Our Finest Men") figured in each *Latina* issue. One of the acts of resistance for such magazines, which try for a national rather than regional market, is that they are not just bilingual (though English tends to dominate) but engage to some extent in cultural code switching, a linguistic act that still carries connotations even in Hispanic populations of sociolinguistic ignorance, which flies in the face of the sentiments expressed in the growing English-only movement.

Latina also carries sections titled "La Lucha (The Struggle)/Coping" (right after "Belleza/Beauty") and "Triunfos/Successes." In its January 1998 "La Lucha," for example, *Latina* reprinted a piece (originally written by Puerto Rican reporter Juan Carlos Pérez for the *Philadelphia Inquirer*) on Lolita Lebrón. Lebrón was a Puerto Rican nationalist;

in 1954 she entered the U.S. House of Representatives along with three others and pro-
ceeded to open fire on the Senate, shouting, "Free Puerto Rico!" She served a twenty-
three-year prison sentence until she was pardoned in 1979.[37] *Latina* has also featured
articles on Los Angeles girl gangs (Fusco and Cobo-Hanlon), a rapist's right to marry
his victim in Peru (Rivera), an "homage" to the various shades of *mestizaje* embodied
in mothers and daughters (Aranda-Alvarado), and even, more daringly for a magazine
that caters to peoples of largely Catholic background, a pair of articles by Cuban
American author Achy Obejas and Tejana college student Leticia Villareal where they
discuss their lesbianism and cultural/familial reactions to it.

   Latina and *Moderna* do not represent, nor do they actually link themselves with,
a clear-cut oppositional or political stance. We can see operating in these magazines what
Dominick LaCapra calls the "assimilative and assimilating capacity of mass culture" and
its tendency to be a "dominant force." He also points to the fact that "a mild and readily contained level of social and cultural criticism is the price of access to the mass
media."[38] But social change and social resistance do not flow only from politically committed sources; on a popular and now increasingly mass-mediated level, social change
moves in jerky, confused, and often ambivalent ways as everyday people work out how
best to imagine themselves in relation to others. This is not my plea for an idealized pop-
ulism; the point here is that magazines like *Latina* clearly see themselves, in ways that
magazines aimed at white female audiences cannot, as ethnically oppositional simply
by celebrating brownness and Latina-ness. Bell hooks continually keeps before her readers the problem of the fear and hatred experienced by both black and white folks in the
United States, a fear which creates a social *and* commercial space where loving blackness (or, in the case of my essay, brownness) as a political stance rather than as a heterocultural impulse or market ploy can be "deemed suspect, dangerous, and threatening."[39]
To risk that threat, however ameliorated it might be by these magazines' self-positioning
within the framework of commodified feminine beauty and fashion, means taking
"loving women's brownness" seriously.

"HISPANIC" CULTURE:
WOMAN HOLLERING CREEK

   The 1991 collection *Woman Hollering Creek* was written while the Chicana
writer Sandra Cisneros, who is from Chicago, was living in Texas. These stories also take
loving women's brownness as a political stance while they more consciously complicate
the ways in which both culture and ethnic women are objects of consumption.

By now it should be clear that contemporary U.S. marketing forces have profoundly influenced and even modified both the public, Anglo reception of Hispanic ethnicity as well as vice versa. In the case of ethnic women, ethnic concerns with style and fashion—such as high heels—teeter on the border between dominant cultural and gender-imposed meanings and ethnic resistance to such meanings. In particular, the conflation of what I call geohistories and the role in that conflation played by a Latina exotic and sexualized beauty which is often marked by high heels impels the ambiguity we have seen in mass-market attempts to represent the ethnic woman. This is the case, for example, in the implicit assumption that the exotic nature of Talisa Soto's Puerto Rican looks will suffice to portray a Native American woman on TV. Such an assumption in effect conflates the materiality of very different bodies, locations, and histories for the sake of demographic appeal, and actually erases from the public mind the particularity and difference of those bodies as well as of their histories, which are often ones of dislocation and oppression. In her short stories, Cisneros critiques both dominant cultures' practices of historical erasure as well as the ways in which this erasure is accepted and even internalized by members of subordinate cultures.

The new reader coming first to Cisneros's short story collection *Woman Hollering Creek* might be drawn by the blurbs on the front cover. The *Houston Chronicle,* for example, maintains that while "the voices in her stories are uniquely Chicana" the emotions "are universal." Added to this comforting marketing twist on identity politics (different, but not too much) is the contention that this collection "offers . . . the chance to taste deeply of Hispanic culture while accompanied by a knowing and generous guide." Ironically, it is just this kind of invitation to consume a piece of a homogenized, yet vaguely exotic and sexy, Hispanicism that Cisneros critiques so devastatingly in the collection itself, especially in her final story, "Bien Pretty."

In this story, Lupe Arredondo, a Chicana, comes to Texas to house-sit, work on her art, and get over a failed love affair. While in Texas, Lupe falls in love with Flavio, a Mexican whom she first meets when he comes to her house to exterminate cockroaches. Eventually, Lupe and Flavio argue about fashion and authenticity:

> I said, "What *you* are, sweetheart, is a product of American imperialism," and plucked at the alligator on his shirt.
> "I don't have to dress in a sarape and sombrero to be Mexican," Flavio said. "I *know* who I am."
> I wanted to leap across the table, throw the Oaxacan black pottery pieces across the room, swing from the punched tin chandelier, fire a pistol at his Reeboks, and force him to dance. I wanted to *be* Mexican at that moment, but it was true. I was not Mexican.[40]

The references to the Oaxacan black pottery, punched tin chandelier, and Zapata-like pistol-dancing at first glance seem to act like the ethnic stuff in Werner Sollors's "ethnic rooms," serving as indicators of Mexicanness. The "veneer of Southwest funk" in the house Lupe is taking care of, however, also resonates with the "agglutinizing energy" of Pérez-Firmat's *Too Many Girls,* though with a different twist: clearly the decorative ethnic items covering every surface in the house are now only meant to provide a backdrop of Mexican realness for the New Age material success of the homeowners, a Texas poet and her "Huichol" husband.

Lupe, too, searches for the answers to her sense of cultural bifurcation—neither Mexican nor North American—in a mishmash of world culture and New Age beliefs, including crystals and many consultations of the *I Ching.* This desire for a cultural home manifests itself in her hope that Flavio will somehow transmit the realness of his *Mexicanidad* to her: "'My grandma taught me the dances,' Flavio tells Lupe, 'el chotis, cancán, los valses. . . .' 'Don't you know any indigenous dances?' I finally asked. 'Like el baile de los viejitos?' Flavio rolled his eyes. That was the end of our 'dance lesson'" (151).

In the argument between Lupe and Flavio over his clothes, Flavio's shoes operate in ways that are both like and unlike the "mindless agglutinizing energy" embodied in the women's magazines' use of the high heel as a sign of a pan-*Latinidad.* Flavio's Reeboks are ambivalently reminiscent of the kinds of practices entailed, for example, in the cinematic packaging and selling of Jennifer Lopez's urban Nuyorican butt as that of Selena's country Tejana, "like the people's" *culo* in the movie *Selena.* Indeed, Flavio's Reeboks—the way Flavio *wears* those Reeboks (Flavio is the "real" Mexican in the only superficially ethnic room)—confound or at least complicate the quest for authentic identity, in part because he wears them unselfconsciously, "mexicanly"; he "*knows* who he is" without resorting to style to prove it. But even this seemingly unproblematic fashion identity shows us the complex ways corporate interpenetration between Mexico and the United States begins to constitute a commodified "culture" all its own.

The title of Zeta Acosta's novel—*Revolt of the Cockroach People*—emphasizes his point that in the United States black and brown bodies are indeed more often than not "cockroach" bodies, despised and disposable. Ironically, Cisneros's Mexican Flavio is a cockroach exterminator. But, in fact, the real "cockroach" in this story is the Mexican American cashier who compliments Lupe on her shawl (which is Peruvian but was purchased in New York or Santa Fe, Lupe can't remember) while she is buying *Vanidades,* a Spanish-language romance and fashion magazine. The encounter between the two women critiques the ways in which "Latina" women are interpellated by the ideologies of love, fashion, and romance in magazines like *Vanidades* (on the cover: "Julio Confesses He's Looking for Love." "Still Daddy's Girl?—Liberate Yourself!" "15 Ways to Say I Love You with Your Eyes"), but also points up the class difference between them. This is a class difference that gives Lupe an *opportunity* to pick and choose an identity for herself, an opportunity the cashier will never have.

Although both women share a moment over the cover of *Vanidades,* which pictures Libertad Palomares, Argentinian star of the *telenovela* (soap opera) *Amar es Vivir* (To love is to live), the cashier's exclamation "*Bien* 'spensive!" when she sees the price of the magazine clarifies the distance between the image of the sexy bombshell Latina and the material conditions of poverty and even abuse that often mark female ethnic bodies. The Mexican American cashier bears markers of ethnicity different from those we normally see in *Latina* or *Moderna*: "Plastic hair combs with fringy flowers. Purple blouse crocheted out of shiny yarn, not tucked but worn over her jeans to hide a big stomach. . . . She's my age, but looks old. Tired . . . those creases from the corner of the lip to the wing of the nostril from holding in anger, or tears" (162). High heels are not part of this woman's everyday attire.

Cisneros's insertion of the nameless Chicana cashier into the story of Lupe's more fashionable quest for an identity one could put on like a pair of high heels, her use of Spanish code switching without the translations readily available in *Latina* and *Moderna,* and her critiques of both Anglo and Hispanic commodification of ethnic style mean that she takes resistance one step farther than the magazines do. In this and other stories in the collection, Cisneros points to the ways female pleasure is constructed through marketing images and stereotypes of a successful (ethnic) femininity, while she acknowledges, lovingly and subversively, that in a "belly-down epistemology" of cultural survival, the politics of ethnic women's real material existence necessarily accommodates but must move beyond the "seduction in spikes" of commercial Latina and Chicana representations.

NOTES

1. Liz Balmaseda, "Seduced by Spikes," *Latina,* September 1997, 82–83.

2. Throughout this essay, I will use the terms "Latino/a," "Chicana/o," and "Hispanic." Though I use "Hispanic" for brevity's sake, because of its Nixon administration overtones (this administration instituted the term for the Federal Consensus Bureau) and its conflation of different histories, this term is a contested one both inside and outside academic circles. Following academic practice, I use "Latina" to designate Cuban American, Puerto Rican, and Nuyorican (New York Puerto Rican) identities; "Chicana" refers to Mexican Americans. For all three of these terms, I am assuming populations of people who were born in the United States but who look back to a Latin American heritage.

3. Here I have found helpful intellectual historian Dominick LaCapra's distinctions among various "kinds" of culture in his *Soundings in Critical Theory* (Ithaca, N.Y.: Cornell University Press, 1989), "Culture and Ideology: From Geertz to Marx." LaCapra notes that mass culture is "culture" dependent on mass media for dissemination, and further that this dependency means it is especially

in nonsocialist countries a commodified culture: "culture further mediated by the market and converted into a commodity bought and sold in accordance with market criteria" (141). Mass culture through television has, he maintains, become a "primary culture" which to some extent has "passed beyond the status of a technology and now assimilates or modifies various forms of elite and popular culture to become a culture in its own right" (141).

4. Christine Granados, "Just How Latina Are You?" *Moderna,* spring 1997, 24–27.

5. Frances Negrón-Muntaner, "Jennifer's Butt," *Aztlán: A Journal of Chicano Studies* 22 (fall 1997): 192.

6. I use the vague and unscholarly term "things" purposely here, because I have yet to discover a way of talking about the material nature of "culture," what Clifford Geertz calls "an historically transmitted pattern of meanings embodied in symbols" (quoted in LaCapra, *Soundings in Critical Theory,* 133); I find that such notions as "symbol" do not completely serve to get at either the physical or always-negotiated nature of those objects, rituals, behaviors, and other odds and ends that on an everyday level people take to "mean" or signify what they share with a certain number of other people.

7. Oscar Zeta Acosta, *Revolt of the Cockroach People* (New York: Vintage, 1973), 40–41.

8. Rasquachismo is, culturally speaking, a Chicano, or Mexican American, term; I am using it here in a more general sense.

9. Granados, "Just How Latina Are You?" 28.

10. Homi K. Bhabha, *The Location of Culture* (New York: Routledge, 1994), 70.

11. Benedict Anderson, *Imagined Communities: Reflections on the Origin and Spread of Nationalism* (London: Verso, 1991).

12. LaCapra, *Soundings in Critical Theory,* 136.

13. bell hooks, *Black Looks: Race and Representation* (Boston: South End Press, 1992), 23.

14. Ibid.

15. Robert Young connects contemporary notions of race mixing, racism, and sexuality to nineteenth-century anthropological and scientific debates on hybridity: "The debates about theories of race in the nineteenth century, by settling on the possibility or impossibility of hybridity, focussed explicitly on the issue of sexuality. . . .Theories of race were thus also covert theories of desire" (*Colonial Desire: Hybridity in Theory, Culture, and Race* [London: Routledge, 1995], 9).

16. Gustavo Pérez-Firmat, *Life on the Hyphen: The Cuban-American Way* (Austin: University of Texas Press, 1994), 61–63.

17. Ibid., 41.

18. Ibid., 54.

19. Ibid.

20. Mandalit del Barco, "Talisa Soto," *Latina,* January 1998, 47–49.

21. hooks, *Black Looks,* 33.

22. Ibid., 21.

23. Granados, "Just How Latina Are You?" 28.

24. Stuart Hall, "Cultural Identity and Diaspora," in *Colonial Discourse and Post-Colonial Theory: A Reader,* ed. Patrick Williams and Laura Chrisman (New York: Columbia University Press, 1994), 393.

25. Negrón-Muntaner, "Jennifer's Butt," 189.

26. Balmaseda, "Seduced by Spikes," 82.

27. Julian Asion, "Style by Celia," *Latina,* September 1997, 85.

28. Balmaseda, "Seduced by Spikes," 84.

29. Belén Aranda-Alvarado, "Meltproof Maquillaje," *Latina,* July 1997, 62.

30. Ibid., 63. As Clara Rodríguez notes in her introduction to *Latin Looks,* Hollywood's history with "Latinos" "has also been in part a reflection of larger political and economic relationships between the United States and Latin America"; for example, images of "Latinos" improved during both world wars because of the importance of unification against the Axis powers, and the greater importance of Latin American markets with many European markets closed to the United States. In addition, Alfred Richard's *Censorship and Hollywood's Hispanic Image* argues that Clause 10 of the Production Code of the movie industry required that neither foreign nationals nor the history of their countries be defamed (drawn from *Latin Looks: Images of Latinas and Latinos in the U.S. Media,* ed. Clara E. Rodríguez [Boulder, Colo.: Westview Press, 1997], xvii); although this was not applied across the board, the Good Neighbor policies of the 1930s through the 1950s ensured that it was applied to "Latin" roles and representations.

31. Ibid., 12.

32 . Negrón-Muntaner, "Jennifer's Butt," 184.

33. Ibid.

34. Quoted in Granados, "Just How Latina Are You?" 25.

35. Werner Sollors somewhat crustily remarks that "in contemporary America ethnic revivalists who want to defy assimilation often adopt black American styles rather than white ones—which makes cultural sense, though it does little to support claims for authentically indigenous ethnic styles" (*Beyond Ethnicity: Consent and Descent in American Culture* [New York: Oxford University Press, 1986], 17).

36. Vera M. Kutzinski, *Sugar's Secrets: Race and the Erotics of Cuban Nationalism* (Charlottesville: University Press of Virginia, 1993), 7.

37. Juan Carlos Pérez, "Lolita Lebrón sigue p'alante," *Latina,* January 1998, 26–29.

38. LaCapra, *Soundings in Critical Theory,* 145.

39. hooks, *Black Looks,* 10.

40. Sandra Cisneros, *Woman Hollering Creek* (New York: Vintage Books, 1991), 151–152. Subsequent page references to this work are given in the text.

In Rebecca's Shoes:
Lesbian Fetishism in
Daphne Du Maurier's Rebecca

JAIME HOVEY

By the 1930s, the new "companionate" marriage demanded heterosexual enthu-siasm from women as its litmus test. Conversely, sexually suspicious women were viewed as foreign and detrimental to the smooth functioning of this national hetero-sexuality.[1] Thus a kind of sexual nativism emerged whose function was to banish per-verse femininity from modern national and domestic life. Sexual nativism is reflected in the paranoid atmosphere of British novelist Daphne Du Maurier's 1938 enduring mystery-romance novel *Rebecca,* where the Rebecca of the novel's title possesses tradi-tional womanly attributes of beauty, taste, and social flair that help to disguise a sex-ually poisonous nature. Indeed, much of *Rebecca*'s tense atmosphere stems from the struggle of its narrative to advocate female heterosexual expressiveness as a function of normal married life while at the same time pathologizing excessive female sexual expression as lesbian, deviant, and destructive. The precarious balance that respectable married women had to negotiate in this era between heterosexual normativity and sex-ual propriety is reflected in the novel's anxieties surrounding unhusbanded femininity, women who want to know too much, and girls who should have been boys. This anxiety is managed at several key moments in the novel by having the narrator focus instead on the intimate, gendered accessories that help women pass in everyday life for femi-nine, normal, and heterosexual, accessories such as women's shoes and other apparel. Rebecca, the first Mrs. De Winter, although dead for almost a year when the novel's

156

unnamed young narrator comes to Manderley, still seems to her to be everywhere: "Her footsteps sounded in the corridors, her scent lingered on the stairs. . . . Her clothes were in the wardrobes in her room, her brushes were on the table, her shoes beneath the chair, her nightdress on her bed."[2]

Employing what at first appears to be a classic Cinderella plot, *Rebecca* begins as the story of how a plain, middle-class girl with no family or fortune meets and marries the dashing Maximilian de Winter, lord of Manderley, recent widower of legendary hostess and famed beauty Rebecca. Maxim is attracted by her helplessness and girlish innocence; she is attracted by his social status and patriarchal authority.[3] Although Du Maurier's novel never explicitly refers to Charlotte Brontë's nineteenth-century gothic classic *Jane Eyre, Rebecca* shares many elements of its predecessor: a young woman of liminal class position comes to an estate owned by a Bluebeard husband, who falls in love with the girl but whose marriage to her is haunted by the ghostly presence in the house of his discarded, sexually indiscreet first wife. Early drafts of the novel ended the story with the crippling of the husband, as Rochester was crippled in *Jane Eyre*.[4] Additionally, Du Maurier's novel employs as part of its plot the very structure of romance which it performs; just as romance novels offer fantasy lives for women readers whose married lives seldom can compare to the sexual adventures they read about, so Rebecca's legend offers her successor a fantasy identification that lends glamour to her modest affect.

A generic hybrid of romance and mystery-thriller,[5] the novel *Rebecca* oscillates in its admiration of its ghostly central character, just as its narrator oscillates between her infatuation with the legend of Rebecca and her loyalty to her new husband. The narrator's movement between love and hate and the novel's accompanying movement between romance and crime marks a radical undecideability in the novel about the role of phallic femininity in both everyday married heterosexuality and in national life. For even as the narrator distances herself from Rebecca, she becomes more and more like her, and even as she disavows the legitimacy of Rebecca's polymorphously perverse femininity, she finds herself perfecting the feminine masquerade that secured her predecessor both power and lasting fame.

Joan Rivière, an English analyst who became one of the first translators of Freud's works into English, suggested in her 1929 case study "Womanliness as a Masquerade" that the performance of an exaggerated white femininity might help women disguise a masculine identification or lesbian desires. "Women who wish for masculinity," she writes, "may put on a mask of womanliness to avert anxiety and the retribution feared from men."[6] Queer theorists such as Judith Butler have been strongly influenced by Rivière's notion of feminine masquerade and have used her ideas to theorize the performativity of gender.[7] I would like to draw an analogy here between feminine masquerade and the performance of companionate married femininity, both of which consist of presenting to men the kind of woman who could never be mistaken for masculine or lesbian. I have argued elsewhere that Rivière's case study is striking in the way it maps the womanly masquerade's racial exchange, that is, the scapegoating that deflects attention away from transgressive lesbian sexuality by constructing the sexuality of black men as predatory and dangerous.[8] Other parts of her essay recognize the womanly masquerade's class instability. In these sections Rivière narrates incidences of bourgeois women's self-deprecation around servants and tradesmen; one "capable housewife . . . has a compulsion to hide all her technical knowledge" and "show deference to the workman, making her suggestions in an innocent and artless manner, as if they were 'lucky guesses.'"[9] Here feminine masquerade is clearly operating as a mechanism that helps the woman negotiate the grid where social expectations of gender deference and class authority contradict each other. In the end, female duplicity is both frightening and subversive; Rivière herself notes that "womanliness [i]s a mask, behind which man suspects some hidden danger."[10]

The social pressure placed on women to perform the mask of femininity in this era was exacerbated by the growing importance of sexual happiness in heterosexual marriage, a notion which gained increasing influence in the years between the world wars.[11] "Heterosexuality" first appears as a word in the dictionary at the beginning of an era when congresses for sex reform begin to proliferate.[12] The World League for Sexual Reform was established in 1928 under the auspices of German pioneer Magnus Hirschfeld and counted many prominent British reformers among its participants.[13] Birth control advocates, sex educators, feminists, and sex reformers joined forces to argue for what would eventually come to be known as "companionate marriage," which defined female sexual expressivity as heterosexually passionate yet bounded by marriage and monogamy, and as against the supposed female sexual reticence, indifference, and frigidity of an earlier era.[14] British and U.S. sex reformers of the 1920s defined a positive, healthy, and normal female heterosexual responsiveness against the absence of heterosexual desire—frigidity, lifelessness, static or suspended libido—which they saw as stemming from ignorance, dormancy, or trauma.[15] Companionate marriage discourse thus attempted to make itself respectable by colonizing female sexuality in the interests of national heterosexuality. By defining normal and national married sexuality against a vaguely apprehended frigidity coded as lesbian, companionate heterosexuality banished lesbianism as an alternative sexual possibility. Lesbianism, drained of sexuality, became another kind of national alterity, like alien ethnicity or marginalized racial identity.

Stepping into Rebecca's shoes at the start of her marriage, the narrator of Daphne Du Maurier's novel *Rebecca* encounters the repressed kinkiness at the heart of companionate married femininity. The narrator's oblique fascination with her sexually deviant predecessor's possessions signals the conflict of competing knowledges in her: that, on the one hand, Rebecca represents the most desirable and accomplished of feminine ideal; but that, on the other, her desire to know Rebecca, to have Rebecca, and to become Rebecca is a forbidden desire, punishable—as she will learn—by death. Shoes, especially, signify a notion of femininity as frivolous, commodified, and bourgeois at the same time as, serving as classic clichés of sexual fetishism, they mark a more general social ambivalence concerning female masquerade and phallic femininity. Rebecca's shoes haunt the unnamed narrator because they represent the knowledge, hovering just at the edge of the narrator's consciousness, of the phallic Rebecca's superb ability to pass for castrated, heterosexual, and "normal." As such, Rebecca's shoes mock the narrator's own inability to play the feminine game, to "do" beauty and class with the style of her predecessor, to make an upper-class femininity look easy and natural.[16] At the same time, Rebecca's shoes also suggest the inauthenticity of Rebecca's sexuality, the insincerity and hollowness of her character, and the falseness of a wealthy, powerful femininity as a national ideal. As literal accoutrements of feminine masquerade, Rebecca's shoes elicit the narrator's doubts about femininity in general, because they suggest both the power of Rebecca's seemingly ideal femininity and its "true" insincerity and lack. This narrative ambivalence about Rebecca's feminine masquerade operates, or attempts to operate, in the novel to delegitimate and dethrone the phallic woman's performativity, and to crown in its place the less showy, more "sincere" femininity of the middle-class, heterosexually responsive companionate wife.

Functioning as a kind of shorthand for fetishism, Rebecca's shoes signal moments in the novel when the narrator oscillates between a commonsense friendliness and a combination of nativist-inflected homophobia and misogyny, or lesbophobia, as well as jealousy. In these moments, readers' sympathies in the novel follow the shift in the narrator's attitudes, from admiration for Rebecca's sexual and social power to disgust at women who take up too much space, or are too sexual, or want to be like men. Shoe fetishism is usually associated with men and is classically read as a refusal to recognize sexual difference, and with it, a refusal to acknowledge male castration; Freud suggests that the fetish "saves the fetishist from becoming a homosexual, by endowing women with the characteristic which makes them tolerable as sexual subjects."[17] However, the shoe fetishist in *Rebecca* is its nameless female narrator, who remembers and memorializes the novel's phallic woman by remembering, imagining, and even wearing her shoes. Not only is the narrator's early fearful or insecure fetishism of Rebecca at the heart of her marriage, but even her later hateful and dismissive feelings toward Rebecca operate to make her marriage more passionate and sexually expressive. This suggests that it is in fact a lesbian fetishism that succeeds in making the narrator's husband more tolerable to her as a sexual subject.

Recent academic conversations about fetishism have emphasized that fetishism has long managed not only anxieties about gender difference but anxieties stemming from imperialism's interest in national ideologies of racial and sexual difference as well.[18] For Freud, the "shoe or slipper" paradoxically signifies the phallic woman *and* her castration, serving as both "a corresponding symbol of the *female* genitals" and, in the case of the foot, "a woman's penis, the absence of which is deeply felt."[19] Freud emphasizes that the self-interest of the fetishist lies in insisting on phallic femininity—that women have penises—in order that he might disavow his own castration: "If females, like other living creatures, possess a penis, there is no need to tremble for the continued possession of one's own penis."[20] Freud never questions his own reflexive belief in the correlation between masculine fear of sexual difference and castration anxiety—a correlation which more than suggests that simultaneous fears of male femininity and female masculinity lie embedded at the heart of masculine subject-formation. By thus refusing to recognize castration, Freud's fetishizing subject disavows his complicity with the social violence and oppression that secures his symbolic authority. Arguing that fetishism operates by replacing knowledge with belief, Slavoj Žižek marks this fetishistic moment as the moment where ideology exempts a body or substance from material laws, granting it instead a "sublime" body or essence that is secured by symbolic authority.[21] In other words, ideology itself operates fetishistically, by laminating belief over knowledge. Belief in ideology allows one to ignore the knowledge that one's power and dominance are unjust. Ideology makes the fetishizing subject feel better about dominating and oppressing others by rationalizing that oppression as, for example, a normative and thus defensible racism, sexism, or homophobia.

Feminists have argued, contra Freud, that not only can women also fetishize,[22] but that a specifically lesbian fetishism exists, operating as a kind of counterfetishism that functions less as a disavowal of masculine castration than as a disavowal "against personal debasement and the transformation of the woman's status."[23] Female fetishism thus resists what the masquerade *seems* to go along with on the surface. Like feminine masquerade, fetishism can also indicate phallic femininity, whose attributes the flirtatious and deferential masquerade disguises. Certainly, lesbian fetishism functions in *Rebecca* to signal the novel's ambivalence toward both phallic femininity and England's national imperial past and the relation to that past. With its myths of graciousness, wealth, and colonial romance, the national past bears the same relationship in the novel to a diminished Britain as the socially powerful sapphism of an earlier era bears to a contemporary feminine heterosexuality. For the most part, *Rebecca* renders this diminished national femininity as subservient and masochistic. But fetishism can never work just one way, and lesbian fetishism functions not so much outside other types of fetishism as within and alongside them. An analysis of fetishism in general and shoes in particular in *Rebecca* reveals some of the shifting, unstable, and simultaneous ideological and identificatory positions that fetishism of all types sets in motion.

In *Rebecca,* the history of this substitution of ideological belief for moral knowledge remains embedded in the fetishistic sublimity of Maxim's murdered first wife, whose body flickers as both feminine ideal and monstrous horror.[24] Rebecca's sexual perversity surfaces in the novel precisely when it is most needed to secure the narrator's belief in him—that is, with Maxim's revelation that he murdered Rebecca. Further, *Rebecca* also gestures toward the ways in which this sublime and sublimated body of phallic femininity functioned both to compensate Britain for her dwindling international influence and to compensate Britain's men for their wartime emasculation and postwar social irrelevance. Thus *Rebecca* seeks to resolve its fetishistic anxieties by deploying a culturally sanctioned nativism in tandem with lesbophobia, which in turn allows the narrator to disavow the humanity of her sexually perverse lesbian predecessor. Lesbophobia and jealousy allow the narrator's intense desire to both have and be Rebecca to give way to the "right" kind of belief, belief that the outrageous behavior Maxim attributes to Rebecca is true, belief that such behavior is inexcusable, belief that Maxim has done the right thing in killing his sexually perverse first wife. This disavowal, in turn, instantiates the narrator as an integral part of the heterosexual couple at the novel's center, which in turn justifies Maxim's having killed Rebecca, and justifies the narrator's complicity in the cover-up as crucial to the solidification of their marriage. Only Favell, Rebecca's cousin and sometime lover, voices unambivalent opposition to the symbolic law of patriarchal authority which justifies Maxim's actions to himself and his wife. An incestuous, alcoholic example of aristocratic degeneracy, he offers sexual perversity as its own kind of oppositional politics: "I'm a bit of a socialist in my way, you know, and I can't think why fellows can't share their women instead of killing them" (326).

For the most part, however, the disavowal practiced by Maxim and the narrator— the replacement of knowledge of Rebecca's humanity with the ideological belief that heterosexual monogamy must be assured at any cost—is contested in the novel more ambivalently through the novel's fetishistic fascination with Rebecca, a fascination which, like Rebecca's own motto, *Je reviens,* instantiates her return within the very mechanisms of repression that attempt to secure her prohibition and exile. So, too, narrative energy in the novel is fetishistic, shuttling between a backward-looking notion of ideal femininity from the past and the necessity of moving away from such femininity, along with the place it occupied in the past, in order to move forward into the future.[25] The story itself, which begins long after the events that will take place in the novel are over, takes the form of a backward look, commencing with the exile of Maxim and the narrator from Manderley and moving back through the occurrences that led up to that moment. Thus the narrative itself shuttles from past to present and back, its narrative tension springing from its fashioning as a tale of innocence and discovery told from the perspective of hard-won knowledge and experience. The negotiation of chronological ambivalence is present throughout the novel not only in the backward and forward movement of the narrative but in the stories the housekeeper, Mrs. Danvers, tells of Maxim's "backwards and forwards" pacing following Rebecca's death, as well as in the moment where the novel itself kicks free of Rebecca with Maxim's account of his murder of her, his rage kindled by the "backwards and forwards" movement of her sandal swinging in feigned nonchalance as she goads him into violence.

In Brontë's *Jane Eyre,* "backwards and forwards" links Jane's restless intellect to the mad rage of her predecessor at Thornfield, Rochester's first wife, Bertha Mason, the dark and foreign woman locked away in a hidden room. Du Maurier's rewriting of *Jane Eyre* as *Rebecca* is a literary backward glance as well as a narrative one. *Rebecca* transposes the colonial sexuality of *Jane Eyre*'s Bertha—a foreign sexuality which functions as a sign of her mixed-race degeneracy in Brontë's novel—into female polymorphous perversity and lesbianism. Thus *Rebecca* also justifies the demise of British imperialism by pointing to female perversity as a root cause of imperialism's excesses, suggesting by extension, albeit ambivalently, that the end of empire might not be such a bad thing.

Significantly, because the novel, in fetishizing Rebecca, also fetishizes the lost romantic past of English national wealth as epitomized by the leisure class for which Manderley serves as a kind of social center, readers are never allowed to look upon Manderley in ruins, except in the opening dream of the narrator, replete with its intimation of trauma and repression. Manderley offers the romantic allure of wealthy rural life as the allure of England in the heyday of empire, with social balls, servants, and beautifully appointed rooms and grounds. Rebecca's metamorphosis into a fetish also helps perpetuate the myth of Manderley's grandeur in ways similar to those in which nations perpetuate myths of pastness. Although Maxim maintains to the narrator that most of Manderley's splendor is a product of Rebecca's tastes, few characters in the novel seem to remember a Manderley before Rebecca. Thus Manderley's grandeur, which seems to always have existed in its present state, is synonymous with Rebecca's tasteful, masquerading femininity, even as Rebecca's iconic femininity becomes reduced to the objects she leaves behind. Like its mistress Rebecca, Manderley is made present in the narrative by means of the things belonging to and surrounding it. The narrator's ambivalent attraction to Manderley's grandeur and extravagant display, to its "luscious and over-proud" (109) flowers and conspicuously valuable art objects and its rooms filled with expensive clothes, bedding, and furniture, mirrors her attraction to Rebecca herself, whose sensibilities created such display in the first place.

However, rather than be transformed by love into an elegant lady, as was Cinderella, the narrator seems to more closely resemble the wicked stepsisters in the German folk versions of the Cinderella tale, sisters who—because they are impostors and social climbers forced to wear someone else's shoes—resort to slicing off bits of their feet in vain attempts to fit into prefabricated notions of feminine refinement. The narrator seems willing to suffer abuse for no apparent reason other than a sense of her own perverse and guilty feminine inadequacy. Strangely, she accepts Maxim's brusquely condescending proposal by offering, "I'm not the sort of person men marry" (51). Her sense of unworthiness is exacerbated in the novel by recurring tales from the lips of everyone she meets of the extraordinary competence of her predecessor Rebecca, whose taste, social flair, and beauty were legendary. Victimized by love rather than victorious in it, *Rebecca*'s narrator suffers her new husband's condescension and harsh rebukes, endures ridicule from the servants, and allows herself to be terrorized to the point of suicide by Rebecca's sapphic nursemaid Mrs. Danvers, who stays on as Manderley's housekeeper after Rebecca's death. In short, Rebecca's presence as an impossible ideal seems to feed the narrator's need for guilty self-abasement, offering her both a fantasized object of desire and a kind of deliciously masochistic reassurance of her own impossibility: "I could not help it if she came to me in thoughts, in dreams. I could not help it if I felt like a guest at Manderley, my home, walking where she had trodden, resting where she had lain. I was like a guest, biding my time, waiting for the return of the hostess" (137).

Yet while the narrator admires, and even adores, her predecessor, that admiration is tinged with horror. Rebecca's ambiguity—who she was, what she was like as a woman, whether Maxim loved her best—inspires this horror, which increases whenever the presence of Rebecca is most felt in the novel. This horror has everything to do with the narrator's own liminal class and gender at Manderley, and her own uncertainty about her role in a marriage she seems to have inherited from someone else. Remembering Manderley, a place whose name itself suggests either a feminized "man" or a phallicized woman, the narrator cannot help but think synonymously of Rebecca's feminine masquerade: "When the leaves rustle, they sound very much like the stealthy movement of a woman in evening dress, and when they shiver suddenly, and fall, and scatter away along the ground, they might be the patter, patter of a woman's hurrying footsteps, and the mark in the gravel the imprint of a high-heeled satin shoe" (9). Here the creepy effect of this Christabel-like moment is achieved not only through reference to Coleridge's lesbian witch—another enchantress who seduces a young girl unable to see through her disguise—but through the suggestion of Rebecca's fetishistic presence in her dress and her shoes. Through her own passionate relationship with Rebecca's belongings, the narrator comes to express both her desires and her rejection of those desires—for beautiful things, status and sophistication, the approval and admiration of other women, and even the love and recognition of Rebecca herself, who circles outside the text like an absent lover. In the novel's symbolic economy, the narrator's desire for Manderley and Rebecca becomes synonymous with her desire for an older, gracious Britain whose wealth rests on appropriation and violence, while her memory of Manderley and Rebecca is laced with fear and guilt. Yet the backward glance of apprehension is also one of memory, and memory functions in the novel to conjure the allure of what has been so violently repressed—the fetish of Rebecca.

Through the phallic flowers and echoing footsteps attributed to her, Rebecca becomes present in the narrative even before readers know much about her. The narrative opens with the combination of fantasy and exile present in the famous first line, "Last night I dreamed I went to Manderley again" (1), but although one suspects that this house might be an English house, what the text presents instead is the Cornish estate of Manderley reimagined by the narrator as a jungle landscape, complete with half-caste anxieties, intimations of sexual licentiousness, and undomesticated denizens atavistically reverting to wildness:

> Scattered here and again amongst this jungle growth I would recognize shrubs that had been land-marks in our time, things of culture and of grace, hydrangeas whose blue heads had been famous. No hand had checked their progress, and they had gone native now, rearing to monster height without a bloom, black and ugly as the nameless parasites that grew beside them. . . . The rhododendrons stood fifty feet high, twisted and entwined with bracken, and they had entered into alien marriage with a host of nameless shrubs, poor, bastard things that clung about their roots as though conscious of their spurious origin. (2–3)

Here the empire is in full racial and sexual revolt; "half-breed plants" go "marching," while nettles constitute "the van-guard of the army" (3). Female creatures left unhusbanded lose their beauty and class status, becoming black, phallic, ugly, nameless, parasitic, perverse, and oddly foreign, their sexual licentiousness muddling the carefully tended differences that constitute "culture" and "grace." Because femininity has become warlike and appropriative, a new self-doubt seems to mar the faith in nation and race that grants legitimacy to its female denizens; because of feminine sexuality run wild, the civilized order has become one of vast disparities, characterized by extremes of dominance and submission.

Later on in the narrative, which is to say, farther back from the opening of the novel in the chronology of the story, these plants more overtly trigger the narrator's anxiety concerning the relationship of feminine comportment to national aggression:

> I glanced at Maxim. He was smiling. "Like them?" he said.
> I told him "Yes," a little breathlessly, uncertain whether I was speaking the truth or not, for to me a rhododendron was a homely, domestic thing, strictly conventional, mauve or pink in colour, standing one beside the other in a neat round bed. And these were monsters, rearing to the sky, massed like a battalion, too beautiful I thought, too powerful, they were not plants at all. (65)

The seeds that Rebecca has sown transform formerly domesticated and feminized species into warlike Amazons. Once an example of Britannia's feminine phallic display, the revolt of her once-homely subjects also marks her castration, her shrinking political relevance, her loss of colonial territories, and the demise of her prestige. Racialized images such as these suggest both the foreignness of the phallic woman as well as her complicity in both Britain's imperially aggressive past and its demise.[26] Not plants but some other kind of plant, a plant that is not a plant but that is really something else, these plants signal not only the narrator's anxiety about serving as Rebecca's stand-in but her anxiety about what exactly she is standing in *for*.

If Rebecca stands, in some sense, for imperial Britain, evoking British majesty and accomplishment as well as the motherland's acquired foreign tastes, then one desire of the Cinderella plot would be that the narrator be transformed into Rebecca and thus become more the epitome of an aristocratic Englishness. This is certainly the first trajectory in the novel, for by immediately juxtaposing the narrator against the woman who employs her as a paid companion, the crude Mrs. Van Hopper, the narrator creates sympathy for her own unsophisticated and self-effacing feminine style while gesturing toward the necessity of becoming someone better able to stand up for herself.

At the same time, Mrs. Van Hopper, whose name suggests both her ungainly movements and her affinity with American gossip columnist Hedda Hopper, stands as a warning against women becoming too assertive, too autonomous, and too knowledgeable. Rendered in the text as a monstrous creature of appetites whose gluttony for food is matched only by her desire to know everything about the titled people who come to Monte Carlo, she fairly bristles with willful curiosity: "She would precede me to lunch, her short body ill-balanced upon tottering, high heels, her fussy, frilly blouse a complement to her large bosom and swinging hips, her new hat pierced with a monster quill aslant upon her head . . . while the other hand toyed with that inevitable lorgnette, the enemy to other people's privacy" (9–10). Mrs. Van Hopper's excessive embodiment is outrageous, bold, and fleshy. Medusa-like, she looks at, rather than looks away, and thus seeks to know more than she should about the people she fixes in her gaze. Her high heels, unlike the ghostly satin shoes of Rebecca, are graceless and awkward, her femaleness hyper-present and intrusive. She is not attractive, precisely because she lacks the kind of "domestic" and "conventional" unassuming femininity the narrator favors in women and rhododendrons. Her phallic, "tottering" high heels signal her inability to pull off the masquerade of femininity; indeed, her comic appeal depends upon readers' ability to easily apprehend the incommensurability of her coy, flirtatious affect with her shameless and omnivorous pursuit of intimate gossip.

Against her calculated and theatrical womanliness, the narrator's femininity appears natural, understated, and modest. One begins to doubt whether either Mrs. Van Hopper or her shoes really function here as fetishistic markers of disavowal, especially since Mrs. Van Hopper herself so obviously functions as a comical figure of failed femininity. Yet if Mrs. Van Hopper is what she seems, in spite of her best efforts, then who is it who is masquerading? The answer, surprisingly, is the narrator herself, whose duplicitous courtship with Maxim at Monte Carlo while Mrs. Van Hopper is sick in bed leads to a proposal of marriage. Masquerade—this time of a specifically classed femininity—serves to set up an ironic reversal where the humble Cinderella gets to triumph over the scheming old stepmother, yielding readers pleasure in the revelation of marriage they know is coming. Yet the narrator's duplicity, while less than sexually suspicious because heterosexual in its ends, still suggests the possibility of perversity, pointing to an affinity with the Rebecca who acted the part of a good wife in order to marry Maxim. The text sounds an additional ominous note when the narrator surreptitiously excises a dedication in Rebecca's handwriting from one of Maxim's books and burns it: "A new confidence had been born in me when I burnt that page and scattered the fragments. The past would not exist for either one of us, we were starting afresh, he and I. The past had blown away like the ashes in the wastebasket. I was going to be Mrs. De Winter. I was going to live at Manderley" (59).

Indeed, as the story unfolds, masquerade is linked not only with excessive and excessively passionate femininity but with inappropriate, even lesbian knowledge. In one instance, as the narrator unwittingly prepares to dress herself as Rebecca once did for the Manderley ball, she loses herself in a fantasy of being Rebecca, eliciting stern reproofs from Maxim: "I don't want you to look like you did just now. You had a twist to your mouth and a flash of knowledge in your eyes. Not the right sort of knowledge" (201). When pressed, Maxim links knowledge to deception, and deception to a perversity which both he and the text decline to name: "There is a certain type of knowledge I prefer you not to have. It's better kept under lock and key. So that's that" (202). Maxim's Bluebeard-like control of the narrator's actual knowledge is nearly subverted because he has no idea what she believes, or that she believes in an older model of masquerading femininity that he has been forced to see through and reject. The narrator's gradual assumption of the social responsibilities of an aristocrat's wife begin to mold her unconsciously into another version of Rebecca only underscores the textual message concerning the impossibility of reconciling a modern middle-class feminine respectability with the expectations of British aristocratic femininity. In such a milieu, all women might become Rebecca. More to the point, in order to be a good wife to Maxim, she must in reality begin to assume a feminine masquerade, which makes her resemble Rebecca far more than it makes her different from her.

Yet by emulating Rebecca, by giving way to her belief in the power of Rebecca's aristocratic, and therefore more legitimate, femininity, the narrator gives way to fears that her predecessor's "breeding, brains, and beauty" (272) will always decisively trump her own seemingly minor qualities of modesty, deference, and fidelity. Perceiving the narrator's class insecurity, Mrs. Danvers takes her to Rebecca's bedroom, which she keeps as a secret shrine to her former mistress. Mrs. Danvers arranges Rebecca's hidden bedroom as a play on hidden and revealed knowledge, with Rebecca's belongings peeping out from under each other, drawing the visitor into a quest for knowledge that seems contiguous with fetishizing Rebecca's expensive things:

> I had expected to see chairs and tables swathed in dust-sheets, and dust-sheets too over the great double bed against the wall. Nothing was covered up. There were brushes and combs on the dressing-table, scent, and powder. The bed was made up, I saw the gleam of white linen on the pillow-case, and the tip of a blanket beneath the quilted coverlet. There were flowers on the dressing-table and on the table beside the bed. Flowers too on the carved mantelpiece. A satin dressing-gown lay on a chair, and a pair of bedroom slippers beneath. For one desperate moment I thought that something had happened to my brain, that I was seeing back into Time, and looking upon the room as it used to be, before she died. . . . In a minute Rebecca herself would come into the room, sit down before the dressing-table, humming a tune, reach for her comb and run it through her hair. If she sat there I should see her reflection in the glass, and she would see me too, standing like this by the door. (165)

Mrs. Danvers, as lesbian foil to Maxim, arranges the room for spying, as if tempting the narrator to seek the knowledge her husband forbids her to have. In the passage, the narrator's initial desire for knowledge becomes a desire for Rebecca herself, until she longs for Rebecca to reenter the room, repossess her things, and really see her. Above all, Rebecca's unnamed and placeless successor desires that Rebecca recognize her as

FIGURE 1 ↗ Mrs. Danvers forces the second Mrs. De Winter's hands into Rebecca's shoes in the Hitchcock film version of *Rebecca* (1940).
Courtesy of Museum of Modern Art Film Stills Archive. Special thanks also to Melissa Bradshaw.

Maxim does not—as a grown woman, sensuous, desiring, and desirable. She longs to see Rebecca see her, and to have Rebecca tell her who she is.

The narrator's demoralizing fantasies of Rebecca's perfection are nurtured by the antipathy of Mrs. Danvers, who in one instance mimes the kind of cruel seduction Rebecca can no longer perform by using her former mistress's shoes, her words all the while expressing her own deeply physical admiration of Rebecca:

> "Look, this is her dressing-gown. She was much taller than you, you can see by the length. Put it up against you. It comes down to your ankles. She had a beautiful figure. 'Throw me my slips, Danny,' she used to say. She had little feet for her height. Put your hands inside the slippers. They are quite small and narrow, aren't they?" She forced the slippers over my hands, smiling all the while, watching my eyes. (168; see figure 1)

The impossible relationship between Rebecca's height and the size of her feet signifies the extent to which Rebecca's ability to inspire fantasy exceeds her physical and temporal limitations. Rebecca's shoes mark the beginning of the narrator's intimations that there is something unhealthy about loving Rebecca, yet the shoes also mark the limits of what the narrator can actually know about Rebecca. As sign of both the female phallus and its absence, Rebecca's shoes demand that the narrator love Rebecca or be loved by her. Seducer or seduced? Mrs. Danvers inquires of the narrator, knowing full well that there are no other subject positions to occupy around Rebecca. Placing the shoes over the narrator's hands—and hands are eroticized by lesbians—Mrs. Danvers seems to be offering the narrator the option of becoming like Rebecca; later, she strengthens this identification by suggesting suicide.

Further, in covering over the narrator's potentially—albeit disavowed—lesbian hands with the masquerade of fetishistic shoes, "Danny" challenges the narrator's attempt to resist knowing what she knows—that she is in love with Rebecca, or the idea of Rebecca, and that this is somehow wrong. Drawing the narrator into her own fetishistic world, Danny uses Rebecca's things to eroticize her own intimate relationship to Rebecca's person, while exploiting the narrator's fantasies of debasing herself before Rebecca's glamour and power. Thrusting Rebecca's shoes over the narrator's hands emphasizes not only the impossibility of the second Mrs. De Winter ever measuring up to her mythic predecessor, but that the differences between the kinds of women represented by Rebecca and the narrator amount to physical differences, such as the differences between hands and feet, as if the two women constitute two different species. Rebecca's slippers are "forced" over the narrator's hands in a kind of fetishistic lesbian rape, a rape where Rebecca's things take advantage of the narrator's desire, using and usurping her body in order that Rebecca might continue to have a sublime, valuable social body. Danny fetishizes Rebecca for the same reason Maxim does—to disavow castration at Rebecca's hands, and deny desiring the sexuality Rebecca withheld from each of them. By continuing as Manderley's feminine ideal, Rebecca continues to structure the subjectivities of its residents. The sexual and emotional appeal for Mrs. Danvers of Rebecca's things is apparent, as is the perversity the narrator attributes to such emotions: "I shall never forget the expression on her face. Triumphant, gloating, excited in a strange unhealthy way. I felt very frightened" (167).

The narrator's abasement, this reiteration of her unworthiness to be the great lady of Manderley, shifts at the very moment in the novel when her husband exposes the phallic sexuality of his first wife, as well as his role in expunging that sexuality from their home. When the boat that contains Rebecca's body reappears from the sea and Maxim confesses to the narrator that he murdered Rebecca because of her sexual infidelities, the narrator suddenly becomes confident and strong, determined to support her husband and believe his story of Rebecca's sexual insolence, resolved to lie for him before the law, if necessary. No longer enamored of Rebecca, given sudden permission to vent a jealous hostility toward her dead rival, the narrator helps Maxim expunge the memory of his first wife by vilifying her sexuality. With this expulsion, the narrator stabilizes her own unstable heterosexuality within a newly companionate marriage, while her husband in his turn covers over the memory of his sexual rejection and castration at his first wife's hands. Just as the narrator represses her own guilty desire to have and be the ideally accomplished Rebecca, so Maxim represses his part in her murder, as well as his role in the similarly national murders of others on the battlefields of the First World War, and thus his castration at the hands of Britannia more generally. As both of them turn away from their gender inadequacies, their sex life perks up significantly: "We began to kiss one another, feverishly, desperately, like guilty lovers who had not kissed before" (355).

This change in the narrator's sensibilities, loyalties, and identifications, accompanying as it does the novel's generic shift and Maxim's revelations about Rebecca's polymorphous perversity, signals a fetishistic ambivalence at the heart of both the narrator's femininity and the novel itself. For while the narrator's new hatred of Rebecca seems to intensify rather than diminish her rival's power, this intensity also operates to cement the narrator's marriage to Maxim. Indeed, it is at the moment of Maxim's revelations about Rebecca's sexual perversity that the narrator's most powerful and attractive fantasy of Rebecca—and the novel's most famous description of her—appears: "The real Rebecca took shape before me . . . Rebecca slashing at her horse; Rebecca seizing life with her two hands; Rebecca, triumphant, leaning down from the minstrels' gallery with a smile on her lips" (272). As the fervor of this portrait suggests, the narrator's supposed rejection of Rebecca is rooted in a profound apprehension of Rebecca's autonomous will and sexual power. Although she protests otherwise, the narrator's passion for Rebecca increases at the moment Rebecca's true nature is unmasked. At the same time, Maxim's revelations of Rebecca's wifely inadequacies eliminate the need for the narrator to mask her own competence any longer. Rebecca's exposure as sexually perverse reveals her femininity as merely a mask, taking the heat off the narrator's feminine performance by making it appear by contrast more authentic, thus allowing the narrator to master the situation without appearing unwomanly, and to assume an upper-class demeanor without appearing to be phallic or castrating.

In short, the narrator's fetishism of Rebecca is not resolved until Maxim reveals to her his first wife's indiscriminate sexual tastes, and even this only occurs because Rebecca's body resurfaces. Teaching the narrator to feel horror at sexual perversity, he initiates her reeducation as a proper wife. With the revelation by Maxim of the true nature of Rebecca's sexuality—a revelation he had previously censored as inappropriate knowledge—she must substitute apprehension of her husband's lust, duplicity, and murderousness with a belief that he has done the right thing to kill his first wife. She must turn away from her knowledge of Rebecca's power and accomplishments, and instead believe the story her husband tells her. This process operates by means of homophobia and misogyny—lesbophobia—evoked by the text's careful refusal to speak the sexuality that the narrator herself cannot know. And this she cannot know because she is not allowed to know and not know, to have knowledge of perversity yet maintain the innocence required of her to believe Maxim's version of his and Rebecca's sexual story.

As the narrative moves backward into the past, with Maxim's account of the murder fleshing out the details of Rebecca's personality that had been shrouded in mystery, Rebecca is finally unmasked, in ways the text does not perceive as being at all contradictory, as both a heterosexual nymphomaniac and as a lesbian. At this moment in the novel, all women suddenly appear to be suspiciously susceptible to lesbianism; Colonel Julyan's daughter, alluded to briefly in the text by her father, the local magistrate, as a girl who "ought to have been the boy" (294) in the family, presents readers with a type proximate to normalcy, and even to the law, a type which, while not yet sunk into vice and duplicity, nevertheless reveals a susceptibility to lesbianism. The novel links this daughter as a type to Rebecca, who also, in the words of the sapphic Mrs. Danvers, "had all the courage and the spirit of a boy" (243) and even "looked like a boy in her sailing kit, a boy with the face of a Botticelli angel" (278). Mrs. Danvers's own name functions less as a husband's patronym than as the masculine "Danny." As if all this is not enough to code Rebecca as a lesbian in spite of Maxim's stories of her heterosexual nymphomania, the narrator learns from "Danny" that Rebecca cut her hair short in an Amazonian gesture because it was "easier for riding and sailing" (169), that she was subsequently "painted on horseback" (169), and that Maxim hated the painting and refused to have it in the house. Finally, the "real" difference between Rebecca's sexuality and that of the narrator is both emphasized and elided when, believing that Maxim loved Rebecca, the narrator offers to yield her place to Rebecca's memory, to "be your friend and your companion, a sort of boy" (265), only to be told by Maxim that Rebecca "was not even normal" (271).

Yet for all the text's insistence on Rebecca's impotence as a feminine icon, it takes Rebecca's body to save the narrator from Rebecca's things, as if the horror of her flesh resurfacing from the depths of its repression is necessary to banish her sublimity at Manderley. After the crisis of the Manderley ball dress, which the evil Mrs. Danvers has made sure is the exact copy of the costume worn by Rebecca the previous year, Rebecca herself reappears, brought back by the discovery of her little boat at the bottom of the cove, with her still in its cabin. With the resurfacing of her remains, the question of Rebecca's social legitimacy is finally resolved to the narrator's satisfaction, first by Maxim's stories of Rebecca's sexual perversities, which lay to rest her moral status as feminine icon and justify his murder of her, then later by the doctor's report of her cancer and malformed uterus, which allows the narrator to dismiss her as a physical ideal as well.

As the narrator recalls Maxim recounting the story of Rebecca's murder, the narrative emphasizes that the thing he remembers most clearly is Rebecca's shoe, which, like the narrative itself, swings backward and forward:

> "Haven't we acted the parts of a loving husband and wife rather too well?" she said. I remember watching that foot of hers in its striped sandal swinging backwards and forwards, and my eyes and my brain began to burn in a strange quick way. "We could make you look very foolish, Danny and I," she said softly. "We could make you look so foolish that no one would believe you, Max, nobody at all." Still that foot of hers, swinging to and fro, that damned foot in its blue and white sandal. (279)

Rebecca's shoe turns the moment where Maxim shoots her into a kind of freeze frame, indicating his symbolic refusal to accept his helplessness at her hands and his disavowal of his greater castration by a society that demands the keeping up of appearances as the price of social respectability.

At this moment, substituting belief in his actions for the knowledge that what he has done is wrong, Maxim looks away from his own impotence and rejection as a lover by his first wife. Going "backwards and forwards to the cove" (280) for water to wash away her blood with "the window banging backwards and forwards," he also masters his castration at the hands of the nation in the Great War, musing, "I'd forgotten . . . that when you shot a person there was so much blood" (280). The equation between Rebecca's murder and Maxim's army service is clear; just as he killed for his country in the war, so he kills for his country and his social position in eliminating Rebecca. The question of his helplessness in either case is resolved by the narrator's insistence on his agency as a shared purpose, his loss of control as strength, his crime as just, and his manhood as untarnished and patriotic.

Joined in a conspiracy of duplicity and silence, the narrator and her suddenly humbled husband found a new companionate relationship based on their shared knowing, a knowing which is now not about lesbian knowledge but about violence as the price of heterosexual safety. The narrator even imagines that she was there with him at the murder, as his accomplice: "And the rain on the roof, I thought, he does not remember the rain on the roof. It pattered thin and light and very fast" (280). Later she reassures him, "We are the only two people in the world to know, Maxim. You and I" (283). Becoming ever more confident, the narrator feigns girlish innocence in the cause of their marriage, inventing plausible stories for Maxim to tell the police. Insisting that "I too had killed Rebecca" (284), and exulting that "it would not be I, I, I, any longer, it would be we, it would be us" (285), she turns the masquerade of femininity toward its proper married ends: "I would fight for Maxim. I would lie and perjure and swear, I would blaspheme and pray" (285). Monogamous loyalty to her husband becomes a virtue trumping all vice, imbuing her with the power and certainty she never had when she thought of Rebecca as an ideal woman. Although she insists that the truth has made her dispassionate, and that all her love has turned to Maxim's service, the vehemence with which she characterizes her former rival betrays her: "Now that I knew her to have been evil and vicious and rotten I did not hate her any more. She could not hurt me" (284–285).

Ironically, all of this serves not so much to expel Rebecca from the narrator's marriage to Maxim as to bind the three of them together more closely. Like the "malevolent ivy" (3) in the narrator's opening dream of Manderley's "lost garden" which "had thrown her tendrils" around beech and lilac and "made them prisoners," Rebecca's death serves both to cement their marriage and make Maxim and the narrator each other's prisoners. In her dreams, the narrator is Rebecca; Manderley's empty rooms now memorialize not Rebecca's things but the narrator's and Maxim's handkerchiefs, library books, pillows, cigarette stubs. She and Maxim are exiled forever from Manderley and England, compelled for the rest of their lives to try to forget the phallic femininity so integral to the English life they have lost. Nevertheless, that femininity, and the memory of that life, resurface again and again between them, in the silences of thoughts not spoken and newspaper stories not read aloud, and in dreams. Although the narrator claims that "we have no secrets now from one another" (6), she lies, for her peace of mind comes from a "secret indulgence" (7) not in the sexual excesses of her predecessor but in fantasies of Englishness: "Colour and scent and sound, rain and the lapping of water, even the mists of autumn and the smell of the flood tide, these are memories of Manderley that will not be denied" (7).

Rebecca's—and Manderley's—status as fetish at the end of the novel suggests both the inextricability of female sexual perversity from national heterosexuality and the destructive ends to which heterosexuality might go to ensure its own hegemony; indeed, the novel's last lines suggest both Maxim's murder of Rebecca and the narrator's burning of the page with Rebecca's dedication to Maxim: "The road to Manderley lay ahead. . . . But the sky on the horizon was not dark at all. It was shot with crimson, like a splash of blood. And the ashes blew towards us with the salt wind from the sea." This is the only information the novel provides about the burning of Manderley; readers of Brontë's *Jane Eyre* will know that Manderley's own Bertha Mason, the evil and lovesick lesbian Mrs. Danvers, has probably set fire to the house in a rage over Maxim's aquittal of the murder of his first wife. The resonance of this passage with the narrator's earlier immolation of Rebecca's handwriting, when in a fit of passion she burns the page from a book of poetry given to Maxim by Rebecca, suggests that somehow the narrator's repression of her own love for Rebecca is responsible for the burning of Manderley, just as Maxim's murder of Rebecca is responsible for their exile from England.

The nation has somehow become so queer that they must both leave it behind in order to maintain their companionate relationship, their exile reiterating both their fitness to publicly represent a bygone Englishness abroad and the marginalizing of that Englishness as secretly tainted. Displacing blame for what has happened to them, and to their gracious aristocratic lifestyle, onto Rebecca's polymorphous sexuality, the narrator and Maxim both turn her into a permanent fetish memorializing the failure of Britain to live up to its egalitarian ideals at home or abroad. Like Maxim's last memory of Rebecca frozen in the memory of her oscillating shoe, Rebecca stands as both fetish and rebuke at the end of the novel, indicative that patriotism and female sexual freedom are constantly at war with one other. However, because the narrator's desire for Rebecca eventually becomes not only a desire for Manderley but a recurring and insistent desire for Britain itself, the novel ultimately suggests that ideological belief can never completely write over the promise of inclusion that the nation offers to all its subjects, nor can it completely control the terms of that inclusion.

NOTES

1. Jonathan Ned Katz argues that this "newly heterosexualized" type of woman "made possible her opposite, a menacing female monster, 'the lesbian.'" See his *The Invention of Heterosexuality* (New York: Plume, 1996), 90.

2. Daphne Du Maurier, *Rebecca* (New York: Avon, 1971 [1938]), 233. All page numbers in parentheses in the text are drawn from this edition.

3. Tania Modleski argues that Hitchcock's film version of Rebecca "more or less explicitly declares itself to be a kind of feminine 'family romance.'" See *The Women Who Knew Too Much: Hitchcock and Feminist Theory* (New York: Methuen, 1988), 47.

4. Daphne Du Maurier, *The Rebecca Notebook and Other Memories* (New York: Doubleday, 1980), 23.

5. Alison Light points out that Rebecca is a generic hybrid of romance novel and crime thriller, and that the movement between the two genres in the story "marks out the distance which the girl and the reader have to travel in coming to understand Rebecca's significance as a seductive but ultimately tabooed expression of femininity" ("'Returning to Manderley'—Romance Fiction, Female Sexuality, and Class," *Feminist Review* 16 [summer 1984]: 10).

6. Rivière posits that heterosexual femininity is inseparable from the performance that produces it. This performance, according to Rivière, takes the form of a flirtatious, self-deprecating mask, which distracts powerful male figures from the woman's intellectual performance by substituting an equivocating heterosexual woman who eagerly solicits male approval. See Joan Rivière, "Womanliness as a Masquerade," in *Formations of Fantasy,* ed. Victor Burgin, James Donald, and Cora Kaplan (London: Routledge, 1986), 35.

7. See Judith Butler's discussion of both Rivière and Stephen Heath's reading of Rivière advocating the performativity of femininity in *Gender Trouble: Feminism and the Subversion of Identity* (New York: Routledge, 1990), 53.

8. Jaime Hovey, "'Kissing a Negress in the Dark': Englishness as a Masquerade in Virginia Woolf's *Orlando*," *PMLA* (May 1997): 393–404.

9. Rivière, "Womanliness as a Masquerade," 39.

10. Ibid., 43.

11. See Jeffrey Weeks, *Sex, Politics, and Society* (New York: Longman, 1981), 200. Weeks argues that sexual freedom cut both ways in this era: "On the one hand, there was undoubtedly a greater stress on sexuality as an aspect of the familial norm. On the other hand, we can detect the refinement of new forms of control on sexual behavior outside the norms." Christina Simmons shows that companionate marriage discourse blamed lesbianism "as the cause rather than the effect of women's resistance to heterosexuality" ("Companionate Marriage and the Lesbian Threat," *Frontiers* 4, 3 [1979]: 57).

12. Jonathan Ned Katz points out that "heterosexuality" appears in *Merriam-Webster* fourteen years after "homosexuality." Just as homosexuality was defined as "morbid sexual passion for one of the same sex," so "heterosexuality" was similarly defined as a "morbid sexual passion for one of the opposite sex." Katz also notes that "heterosexuality" is not defined as "normal sexuality" until 1934. See Ned Katz, *The Invention of Heterosexuality*, 92.

13. Weeks, *Sex, Politics, and Society*, 184.

14. On sexual reticence, see Ben Lindsey, *The Companionate Marriage* (New York: Boni and Liveright, 1927); Theodore Van De Velde, *Ideal Marriage: Its Physiology and Technique* (New York: Random House, 1930); and Floyd Dell, *Love in the Machine Age: A Pyschological Study of the Transition from Patriarchal Society* (New York: Farrar and Rinehart, 1930). On colonizing marriage for heterosexuality, see Christina Simmons, "Companionate Marriage and the Lesbian Threat," *Frontiers* 4, 3 (fall 1979): 55. See also Lillian Faderman, *Odd Girls and Twilight Lovers: A History of Lesbian Life in Twentieth-Century America* (New York: Columbia University Press, 1991), 90–91, and John D'Emilio and Estelle B. Freedman, *Intimate Matters: A History of Sexuality in America* (New York: Harper and Row, 1988), 257.

15. Among these sex reformers were Marie Stopes, Margaret Sanger, Theodore Van De Velde, Ben Lindsey, and Bertram Russell.

16. Tania Hammidi and Susan B. Kaiser argue that "upper middle-class markings" of "fashionable" white femininity in the contemporary United States operate as beauty standards that force lesbians to negotiate queer identities around and against them ("Doing Beauty: Negotiating Lesbian Looks in Everyday Life," in *Lesbians, Levis, and Lipstick: The Meaning of Beauty in Our Lives*, ed. Jeanine C. Cogan and Joanie Erickson [Binghamton, N.Y.: Harrington Park Press, 1999], 61).

17. Sigmund Freud, "Fetishism," in *The Standard Edition of the Complete Psychological Works of Sigmund Freud*, vol. 21, ed. James Strachey (London: Hogarth Press, 1961), 149–157.

18. See Robert A. Nye, "The Medical Origins of Sexual Fetishism" (13–30) and Kobena Mercer, "Reading Racial Fetishism: The Photographs of Robert Mapplethorpe" (307–329), in *Fetishism as Cultural Discourse*, ed. Emily Apter and William Pietz (Ithaca: Cornell University Press, 1993). See also Homi Bhabha, *The Location of Culture* (New York: Routledge, 1994) and Anne McClintock, *Imperial Leather: Race, Gender, and Sexuality in the Colonial Contest* (New York: Routledge, 1995).

19. Sigmund Freud, *Three Essays on the Theory of Sexuality*, ed. James Strachey (New York: Basic Books 1995), 21, fn.1 and 2.

20. Sigmund Freud, *An Outline of Psycho-Analysis*, ed. James Strachey (New York: Norton, 1989), 91.

21. Slavoj Žižek, *The Sublime Object of Ideology* (London: Verso, 1989), 18.

22. See Emily Apter, "Introduction," 1–9; Jann Matlock, "Masquerading Women, Pathological Men: Cross-dressing, Fetishism, and the Theory of Perversion, 1882–1935," 31–61; Naomi Schor, "Fetishism and Its Ironies," 92–100; and Elizabeth Grosz, "Lesbian Fetishism?" 101–115; all in *Fetishism as Cultural Discourse,* ed. Apter and Pietz. See also Lorraine Gamman and Merja Makinen, *Female Fetishism* (New York: New York University Press, 1994 and 1995); Kaja Silverman, *Male Subjectivity at the Margins* (New York: Routledge, 1992); and Laura Mulvey, *Fetishism and Curiosity* (Bloomington: Indiana University Press, 1996).

23. Grosz, "Lesbian Fetishism?" 112.

24. Some critics have seen Rebecca's hyperpresence as more pronounced in the film version of the novel than in the novel itself. Rhona J. Berenstein, writing about Hitchcock's famous adaptation of Du Maurier's story, argues that "the novel is more explicit in its associations of Rebecca and Fontaine's character with queerness" than is Hitchcock's film version, whose "very repression of the subject actually reinforces its presence as a relentless undercurrent" ("'I'm Not the Sort of Person Men Marry': Monsters, Queers, and Rebecca," in *Out in Culture,* ed. Corey K. Creekmur and Alexander Doty [Durham, Duke University Press, 1995], 248).

25. Modleski reads the narrator's attraction to Rebecca in the film version as a mother-daughter attraction, the story of "the heroine's attempt to detach herself from the mother in order to attach herself to a man" (*The Women Who Knew Too Much,* 50).

26. Alison Light points out that "the logic of Maxim's crime is, of course, blurred and it seems that Rebecca is responsible for his loss of home, authority, and even for the sunset of the Empire." See Light, "'Returning to Manderley,'" 20.

Power

$\mathcal{B}$rogans

ANTHONY BARTHELEMY

When I knew anything I was all dressed up in white. I had on a long white robe. I
had a golden belt about my waist and golden slippers on my feet.
—*Anonymous ex-slave's conversion narrative, quoted
in George Rawick, ed.,* The American Slave, *vol. 19*

The brogan is a humble shoe. Its makers and wearers alike are among those Christ
spoke of in the Beatitudes: the meek who have not yet inherited the earth; those
who still hunger and thirst after righteousness. The very word "brogan" encapsulates some
of the shoe's lowly origins. The *Oxford English Dictionary* tells us the word "brog" is an
Irish and Gaelic diminutive of "brogan," the Irish and Gaelic word for "shoe." And although
one might be inclined to think otherwise, the dictionary speculates that the term
"brogue," which is still used to identify the speech of the Irish, actually derived from
the word "brog" rather than vice versa. So the Irish were stigmatized by their footwear:
cheap, rough, unlined boots that suggested poverty and barbarism. Those who could
afford fancy shoes and boots maligned the wearer of the less delicate gear, assuming
the stiff and shoddy sole symbolized if not the soul of the wearer at least his or her character. Perhaps the connection included some suspicions by the ever-class-conscious English that the Irish must have had their feet in their mouths in order to speak the way
they did. Regardless of the exact derivation, the shoe and its wearer synthesized into

FIGURE I   ↗   Russell Lee, *Trash Collector* (1941).
Reproduced from the Collections of the Library of Congress.

Here I sit / With my shoes mismated / Lawdy—mercy! / I's frustrated!
—Langston Hughes, "Bad Morning"

one, *cap-à-pie* or, perhaps more precisely, *pie-à-cap*. What an interesting metaphor, the shod foot signifying the spoken word; together both recognize the poverty and difference, the marginality as the sociologists might say, of the possessor of the brog(ue). But the confusion of the material shoe with the airy nothingness of language provides us with a rather particular example of the way language helps to identify, to discriminate one class, race, or people from another. We are not actually talking about gait bondage here, but of a kind of foot-and-mouth disease that affects both the wearer and observer, speaker and auditor.

The history of the shoe's production on the Western side of the Atlantic mimics much of the social history of the shoe in the British Isles. One can find the same hardships, prejudice, and poverty associated with the American brogan. The manufacture of the brogan, in fact, documents the attempts by nineteenth-century factory workers to gain better working conditions, the entrance of women into the labor force, and the struggles of Irish and other immigrants to survive in the United States.[1] But the brogan in the United States also has a distinctly American history because it came to be associated with slavery and later the freedmen who struggled against the indifference and sometimes persecution of their countrymen and their government. And like so much of American history, the brogan and shoes themselves have been entangled in the great irony of this nation "conceived in liberty and with justice for all" yet whose constitution permitted the unfettered importation of slaves until 1808 and did not finally outlaw the practice of holding human beings as owned chattel until 1865.

From the late 1700s through the Civil War and beyond, shoe laborers in Danvers, Lynn, and other Massachusetts towns made brogans for southern slaves. Prior to the invention of the McKay Stitching Machine in 1862, most of the shoe industry in New England relied upon pieceworkers. As with any industry that depends on outsourcing, a standard model of production of brogans cannot be constructed. But the industry followed fairly common practices, and thus some features of the production followed a rather reliable paradigm. Usually uppers were sewn by hand and then returned to the shoe boss. The shoe boss consigned the sewn tops to a shoe binder. The binder then had the difficult task of attaching the stiff and hard sole of the shoe to the softer, more malleable uppers.

As was true of almost everything in the nineteenth century, labor differentiated itself with regard to gender. But strict gender demarcations never hold with regard to labor, and thus the shoe industry reflects both the tendency to offer women lower recompense for lower-skilled jobs as well as an indifference to gender when toil offered only subsistence wages. Frequently entire families worked as shoe binders, the husband receiving an allotment from the shoe boss and then depending on his wife and children to assist in the task. Some shoe bosses would give consignments of brogans to women. Because brogans were constructed from materials of inferior quality and designed for other than ladies and gentlemen, production of this coarse footwear did not require the kind of skilled workers necessary for making fine boots and fancy shoes; thus those employed in manufacturing the brogan usually received the lowest wages among shoemakers. And even when the binding work employed the whole family, the family earned wages based on piecework, not on the number employed in the work. Thus the younger and less experienced family members could work as long as their parents or older brothers and sisters but still increase only minimally the family income. In the case of women binders, the situation was often far worse. These women received the lowest wages in the industry, and sometimes they received no wages at all. Some shoe bosses offered the women only onions or store credit for their labor.[2]

Such worker exploitation characterized all shoe manufacturing in the United States during that period. Capitalists, such as Moses How, were eager to reorganize the process of shoe production, centralizing production in an effort to increase productivity and decrease worker remuneration. But not until after the Civil War was the reorganization of the industry completely centralized. And even when the steam engine factories came into existence in the 1870s, production procedures did not undergo an immediate revolution.

Yet even before the revolution in shoe production changed the industry, workers in Massachusetts began to be influenced by the social revolution that ignited around the issues of slavery and abolition. Ironically, impoverished shoe works laboring to produce cheap shoes for southern slaves would provide the model for the economic exploitation of blacks after emancipation. Consignments, store credits, agricultural bosses, and the other components of the sharecrop system already existed in the industrial North and created significant profits for owners and others not directly involved in the labor of production. However, the ferment of social change that erupted around the issue of chattel slavery provided the model for protest by the exploited shoe workers. In Lynn, Massachusetts, women workers organized the Lynn Female Anti-Slavery Society. Some workers, male and female alike, protested more aggressively and called their abolitionist employers hypocrites for working to end chattel slavery while profiting from "wage slavery." Some shoe workers, in fact, complained that their situation was worse than that of slaves in the southern states: "While they [shoe manufacturers] have been fighting against the slavery of the south, they have been grinding down the laboring men of the north, thereby enslaving them in a greater degree (in one sense) for the poor negro has a master, both in sickness and in health; while the poor white man is a slave as long as he is able to toil, and a pauper when he can toil no more."[3] The issue here is not the relativity of suffering but rather the fusion of the two struggles. As the shoe came to represent the wearer in the British Isles, the laborer wedded himself to the downcast wearer in the United States. The brogan again symbolized the lowest of the low, the untouchables who served, comforted, and threatened the Anglo-American elite. And, of course, as with any symbol, those condemned to wear the brogan created a mythology appropriate to its complex and multiple significations.

The first time I heard the word, it was pronounced "brogains," as it still frequently is in the black South.[4] It was in the 1950s, and "brogains" served frequently as the formulaic opening salvo in a game of the dozens. I listened as an older boy accosted another with: "Your mama wears brogains." "Your mama wears combat boots" was the ritualistic response. Thus the boys heralded a history we didn't know, but evoked images we did know. The first boy accused his opponent's mother of being poor, of perhaps having no sense of style. The first boy, of course, expected to be bested in this round. After all, what is to be won if you do not fight a worthy opponent? So the opponent insulted the initiator by declaring the latter's mother to be too masculine for a lady, perhaps even so masculine as to be "queer." In an odd way, poverty triumphed in this first round. A teenage boy could handle the stigma of poverty, but the other stigma, of course, reflected

FIGURE 2 ~ Marion Post, *Negro Rural Day Laborers* (1939).
Reproduced from the Collections of the Library of Congress.

I'm gonna put on my long white robes / Down by the
Riverside / Study war no more . . . / Gonna put on my golden
shoes / Down by the Riverside / Study war no more . . .
—Traditional Negro spiritual

back on the son. Black kids always understood that there was a certain dignity to poverty. Though none of us would admit to having ever seen a pair of "brogains," we were all pretty certain that at least one of our grandparents had worn this symbol of poverty. And only the most insecure of us would have been ashamed of that history. So at one time or another we all asserted that each others' mothers wore combat boots or brogains. But we all knew brogains were better.

Yet again this word, freed of its Irish history by way of its southern pronunciation, figured prominently in mapping the conjunction between foot and mouth, between speaker and auditor. What vital link joins the word and the foot? Perhaps, here again one recognizes the relationship between speech-act and action itself. In fact, a kind of metonymy exists that elevates both speech-act and action into something metaphysical, something beyond the individual to the group as a whole. As the game of dozens represents a special version of signifying, a repartee fraternal in nature, celebratory, and simultaneously inclusive and exclusionary, so "brogan" served as common ritual offering. Not a sacrifice that would be immolated on the altar, but rather a common text, a torah to unite all, an "In the beginning," to create not just a universe but its chosen people as well. And once the flesh is made word, the word must lavish itself on itself because love of the immateriality reflects the love of the material self. (Hip-hop wears brogains!)

So in the beginning was not the word, but once the word formed on the flesh of the tongue and expired forth between the flesh of the lips, the stories had to follow. The front porch or the back porch or the side steps or the kitchen table became the place where we heard of country cousins who arrived in "only brogains." Or how in "hard times" your father or someone else's wore "only brogains." Or how someone's in-law married into the family "with only a pair of brogains to his name." Or that someone didn't get his first pair of shoes until he got married. Or how so-and-so's feet were ruined from wearing brogains. Or how lucky one was during the depression even to get brogains. Or how so-and-so was so dumb he didn't know any better than to wear brogains to Christmas Eve Midnight Mass.

More important than these stories were the ones we did not hear, nor did perhaps our parents or maybe even our grandparents. The stories of brogans easing the steps of the freedmen walking from Texas to Virginia. The burlesque of the brogan perhaps freed the raconteur of the rough parts, the untanned parts of the story that no retelling could smooth over. The country cousin who might have worn brogans during the depression, regardless of his hardships, his persecution, even perhaps his death at the hands of a racist, could never dwell among the canonized in the seventh heaven. No one ever ascended into the realm of reverence and mystery as did our slave ancestors. Their endurance went beyond legend. Like Christ in the Garden of Gethsemane, they too sweated blood. So we did not hear the stories of their shod or bare feet but imagined them as we learned of slavery or heard the old folks whisper about so-and-so who was a slave. The whispers of separated families, of good or bad masters. The awe for the grand- or great-grandparent who survived the torments and indignities of having once been considered chattel. But the documentation animates the history, and this history confirms all the whispered and imagined things plus the unimagined and unimaginable.

At the end of the Civil War, the freedmen set forth on what historians have called "The Great Exodus"—the movement of masses of African Americans away from slavery into the unknown but long-dreamed-of promised land in the days of Jubilee. African American literature, both fiction and nonfiction, is full of the stories of this passage of jubilant freedman—W.E.B. Du Bois's *The Souls of Black Folk,* Earnest Gaines's *The Autobiography of Miss Jane Pittman,* Toni Morrison's *Beloved,* Margaret Walker's *Jubilee,* Booker T. Washington's *Up from Slavery,* and of course the hundreds and hundreds of personal testimonials of ex-slaves. But the road was long and frequently dangerous as night riders tormented, harassed, and lynched men, women, and children who sought to escape the plantation and all physical and emotional vestiges of slavery. And as with so much of the bloody history of slavery, many of the details surrounding these incidents have been lost or forgotten.

In *The Souls of Black Folk,* Du Bois finds the poetry of the moment as he describes the contraband who followed Sherman to the sea:

> Some see all significance in the grim front of the destroyer [Sherman], and some in the bitter sufferers of the Lost Cause. But to me neither soldier nor fugitive speaks with so deep a meaning as that dark human cloud [the escaping slaves] that clung like remorse on the rear of those swift columns, swelling at times to half their size, almost engulfing and choking them. In vain were they ordered back, in vain were bridges hewn from beneath their feet; on they trudged and writhed and surged, until they rolled into Savannah, a starved and naked horde of tens of thousands.[5]

Attempting military precision, General H. W. Slocum could not conceal his awe when he wrote of a similar situation on his march through Georgia:

> Negro men, women and children joined the columns at every mile of our march, many of them bringing horses and mules, which they cheerfully turned over to the quartermaster's department. I think at least fourteen thousand of these people joined the two columns at different points on the march; but many of them were too old and infirm, and others too young, to endure the fatigue of the march, and were left in the rear. More than one-half of this number, however, reached the coast with us. Many of the able-body men were transferred to the officers and subsistence department, and others were employed in the corps, as teamsters, cooks and servants.[6]

As an ex-slave, Annie L. Burton recalls a comparable scene and provides a more personal perspective:

> I saw all the slaves one by one disappearing from the plantation (for night and
> day they kept going) until there was not one to be seen.
>   All around the plantation was left barren. Day after day I could run down
> to the gate and see down the road troops and troops of Garrison's Brigade and
> in the midst of them gangs and gangs of negro slaves who joined with the
> soldiers, shouting dancing and clapping their hands. The war was ended, and
> from Mobile Bay to Clayton, Ala., all along the road, on all the plantations,
> the slaves thought that if they joined the Yankee soldiers they would be
> perfectly safe.[7]

These testimonies capture the joy and tragedy of the moment, the joy of freedom,
the uncertainty of the future. Each text exemplifies the old saw: "Be careful of what you
pray for." Nothing can be more frightening or portentous than facing with uncertainty
one's transcendent desire. A dark human shouting, dancing, and clapping constitutes
an oxymoron, and that is the only word that could describe the moment of jubilation
and anxiety faced by the freedmen who marched barefoot or shod in the shoe of their
servitude on the road to an inscrutable freedom. Let us consider the different perspectives
of the authors as we contemplate the emotions described in these passages.

Burton lived the moment. As she says, she would "run down to the gate and see
down the road." The spontaneity and the unforced emotion of the moment express both
Burton's wonder and that of the freedmen's.

Du Bois, on the other hand, represents from the distance of a scholar the history
that circulated as written or oral eyewitness testimony or anecdotal evidence from secondary sources. However, by 1903 the Sage of Great Barrington confronts what he views
to be the historiographic distortion of the importance of that historical moment. He
attempts to refocus attention away from the sympathy for the victors or the vanquished
to the triumph of human freedom, of human progress. From Du Bois's perspective the
military success is secondary to the freedom march.

By contrast, Slocum seems incredulous that men "cheerfully" surrendered animals, which they could have ridden, in order to join a "march." The general wants to
remind us that the Civil War was not the "Freedom War," as the slaves had come to call
the conflict.

Yet all these authors understand the significance of the sea of humanity that followed the army, and each recognizes the suffering and exultation that accompanied every
step along those dusty southern roads.

But alongside those savoring what must have seemed to them to be almost a biblical rapture marched thousands seeking not a new life unencumbered by the past, for

there on the road strode the displaced freedman, the chattel sold away from mother, father, husband, wife, brother, or sister. And these pilgrims chased not just the promise of the future; they also sought to catch up to their past. In one of the greatest testaments to family devotion, freedmen separated from family by the brutal economics of slavery marched alongside those rejoicing in their freedom. A Freemen's Bureau officer writes with wonder about the unprecedented attempts by freedmen to locate and reunite with their families: "They had a passion, not so much for wandering, as for getting together. . . . Every mother's son seemed to be in search of his mother, every mother in search of her children."[8]

The historical record provides enormous evidence of family members trying to reunite with others lost to them because of slavery's unimaginable cruelty. Annie Burton tells of her mother's efforts to reunite their family after a three-year absence. After being sold away from her children, the mother returned to claim them from her former mistress:

> My mother came for us at the end of the year 1865, and demanded that her children be given up to her. This, mistress refused to do, and threatened to set the dogs on my mother if she did not at once leave the place. My mother went away, and remained with some of the neighbors until supper time. Then she got a boy to tell Caroline [Burton's older sister] to come down to the fence. When she came, my mother told her to go back and get Henry and myself and bring us down to the gap in the fence as quick as she could. Then my mother took Henry in her arms, and my sister carried me on her back. We climbed fences and crossed fields, and after several hours came to a little hut which my mother had secured on a plantation.[9]

Any scrap of news, any slight yet hoped-for reference to a lost relative, could send a freedman on a journey in search of a beloved relative. Freed slave Mary Lindsay of Oklahoma told how an insubstantial hint sent her in search of her brother: "Some niggers tells me a nigger named Bruner Love living down west of Greenville, and I know that my brother Franklin, 'cause we call him Bruner. I don't remember how all I gets down to Grenville, but I knows I walk most the way and I finds Bruner."[10]

The dusty roads of the South were clogged with freedmen seeking wives, husbands, mothers, fathers, brothers, sisters, and other relatives. The human tragedy of slavery, the refutation of the lie propagated by slavery apologists that African Americans did not have emotional attachments to family and friends, became ambulatory in the years from 1860 well into the 1870s. So attests the reply of a South Carolina freedwoman named Delia to her former master's request that she remain on the plantation. "No Master," she said. "If I'm really free I must go and find my husband."[11] Tired feet testified to the pledges of the heart, pledges never recognized by the government or the patriarchal masters of the peculiar institution. Freedom for many manifested itself by shackling them to the road and the dream of reunification. And there to ease the steps of the few lucky enough to have any shoes at all was the brogan. Could so humble a shoe have such a noble history?

But the brogan does not find itself heralded in the history of this great progress of the South. No one says, "With only my brogans and hope I set out to find my wife." Perhaps nothing speaks more of this great silence, this void in the story of struggle, than the reality of the brogan itself. The shoe symbolized for the freedman what the Fifteenth Amendment to the Constitution sterilized into the phrase "previous condition of servitude." When asked what they wore while enslaved, the freedmen frequently report they were given brogans by their "masters." Hundreds of citations can be found in the massive collection of slave narratives compiled by the Federal Writers' Project (FWP) in the 1930s. Eighty-six-year-old Harry Johnson, recalling his life as a slave, told his FWP interviewer: "We wore what you call low-cut shoes; brogans we call 'em. De man I belonged to had 'em made."[12] "Old Boss provided brass-toed brogans for winter," Green Williams recalled at the age of seventy-seven.[13] Francis Willingham had a very clear memory of minute details of her life in slavery. The seventy-six-year-old Willingham complained to her interviewer:

> Slave gals' pantalettes warn't ruffled and tucked and trimmed up wid lace and 'broidery lak Miss Polly's chilluns' was. Ours was jus' made plain. Grown folks wore rough brogans, but me, I wore de shoes what Miss Polly's chillun had done outgrowed. Dey called 'em Jackson shoes, 'cause dey was made wid a extra wide piece of leather sewd on de outside so as when you knocked your ankles 'gainst one another, it wouldn't wear no holes in your shoes. Our Sunday shoes warn't no diffunt from what us wore evvyday.[14]

Deprived of a privilege even the poorest of the poor considered dignifying, Willingham, like other ex-slaves, laments more than forty years after his emancipation the lack of "Sunday best" during his years as chattel. But more important than even this splendid excess was the freedom that rendered all the vestiges of the past bondage superfluous, even if only for the elusive but gloriously brief moment of Jubilee. "Today, I shed the chains of bondage wearing the brogans that old master gave me." Such a statement seems almost surreal and trivializes the nearly eschatological solemnity of emancipation. General Slocum's surprise at the willingness of the slaves to surrender mules and horses to the quartermaster's department points out not his interest in the slaves' accoutrements but rather his own. Given the frequency with which former slaves refer to brogans, it is safe to surmise that the brogan, unheralded though it is, made the march to freedom and reunion. Perhaps the mention of the shoe was as irrelevant as pointing

FIGURE 3   ⌒   Arthur Rothstein, *Sharecropper Family* (1937).
Reproduced from the Collections of the Library of Congress.

I got shoes, you got shoes / All God's chil'en got shoes, / When I get to heaven gonna put on my shoes / And walk all over God's heaven.
—Traditional Negro spiritual

out that the slaves were black. The research of Helen Bradley Foster supports this fact. As she discovered from her exhaustive study of first-person slave narratives: "The most common footwear [during slavery] consisted of shoes made with wooden or thick leather soles pegged to a sturdy leather upper and often studded at the toe with brass tacks. This type of foot wear was known as 'brogans.'"[15]

The brogan was a hated symbol of slavery; even the shoe industry itself documented for posterity the disdain in which the freedmen held the brogue of their bondage. In 1888 New England shoe manufacturers complained of the loss of profits from the sale of brogans and were forced to acknowledge the stigma attached to the rough-hewn shoe. *The Shoe and Leather Reporter* lamented that African Americans refused to wear brogans. Some New England towns stopped making the brogan altogether. There was no profit to be earned from a shoe that African Americans, now made citizens by the Fourteenth Amendment, declined to wear because the brogan epitomized their previous state of debased servitude.[16] Like the bound foot in revolutionary China, the brogan symbolized the old order. And although the bound foot held a position of class ambivalence, it also signified unequivocally the subservience of women. The brogan may have accrued a certain status when compared to the bare foot of the bondman, but in freedom the shoe became an indisputable relic of a hideous and degrading past. African Americans may have had to wear the brogan while enthralled, but now they were free to reject it. But the rejection had nothing to do with shame in their poverty or a denial of their past; the rejection lay in their claim to their humanity, their assertion that they were not chattel, not beast, not subhuman. Only the luxury of a third generation of freedom could liberate the middle-class descendants of the bondmen from the shame of the shoe. Only that luxury allows for the embrace of the ambivalent signifier. As with the word "nigger" itself, its mysteries can be evoked with love and hate praise and derision.

On the heels of freedom followed the nadir, and by 1896 the path that the freed-men had embarked upon, one full of hope and promise, had forked into the fraud of "Separate but Equal." By 1914 Woodrow Wilson, the number-one fan of D. W. Griffith's *Birth of a Nation,* had extended official segregation throughout the federal bureaucracy. The raptorial Jim Crow circled the highway on which African Americans had set out in their search for full citizenship and "equal protection under the law," and no better than a buzzard, Jim Crow preyed upon and tormented black citizens as though they were mere carrion. It was in this environment that the brogan received its greatest infamy, serving as a symbol of "the Negro" in William Faulkner's 1932 novel *Light in August.* In fact, Faulkner's use of the brogan reconfirms its association with African Americans and certainly makes comprehensible the freedmen's wish to avoid wearing this humiliating symbol of their cruel bondage.

The novel's principal character, Joe Christmas, is suspected of being part African American, and thus, according to southern logic, he is African American. Like the freed-men some sixty years earlier, Christmas finds himself on the road trying to escape the police and a lynch mob eager to see him swing from a tree. In order to escape, Christmas trades his dress shoes for a pair of brogans being worn by a poor black woman, and this exchange allows the fugitive to throw the hound dogs off his scent:

> At last the noise and the alarms, the sound and fury of the hunt, dies away, dies out of his hearing. He was not in the cottonhouse when the man and the dogs passed, as the sheriff believed. He paused there only long enough to lace up the brogans: the black shoes, the black shoes smelling of negro. They looked like they had been chopped out of iron ore with a dull axe. Looking down at the harsh, crude, clumsy shapelessness of them, he said "Hah" through his teeth. It seemed to him that he could see himself being hunted by white men at last into the black abyss which had been waiting, trying, for

FIGURE 4 ↝ Russell Lee, *Cotton Pickers' Feet* (1938).
Reproduced from the Collections of the Library of Congress.

Be patient, weary body, soon the night / Will wrap thee gently in
her sable sheet, / And with a leaden sigh thou wilt invite / To rest
thy tired hands and aching feet.
—Claude McKay, "The Tired Worker"

thirty years to drown him and into which now and at last he had actually
entered, bearing now upon his ankles the definite and ineradicable gauge of
its upward moving.[17]

"The black shoes," writes the Mississippian, and surely the adjective in that
phrase refers to more than the color of those shoes. Faulkner, in fact, invokes the history of the shoe in the United States. It seems as though "the black shoes smelling of
negro" is one of those Faulknerian redundancies, for he gives the sense that only an excess
of words can properly convey the wealth of meaning, the prodigality of significance. With
Faulkner, the South's suffering, outrage, and wounded ego can never be adequately
expressed, and only redundancy can adequately capture the sense and sentiments that
can never be expressed. In the above quotation the narrative implies that the shoes themselves are infectious, and like the hematological fantasy of the one-drop theory, African-
ness itself can be caught from the shoes, their association with African Americans so
complete and ineradicable. So "the black shoes" lead Christmas to "the black abyss" that
was his destiny when the fatal drop or two forever cursed him to the fate of being a black

man in the United States. And now blackness, metonymically standing in for the race, is on the move again, but this time its movement is to destroy the bearer of blackness. It seems as though the brogan in *Light in August* can accomplish what white suprema-cists had predicted and hoped would happen to the freedmen: they would simply die without the benevolent oversight of a kind white master.

A few pages later, Faulkner, using almost the same words, repeats the curse of the brogan: "He [Christmas] thinks quietly, sitting on the seat, with planted on the dash-board before him the shoes, the black shoes smelling of negro: that mark on his ankles the gauge definite and ineradicable of the black tide creeping up his legs, moving from his feet upward as death moves" (339). But now death is no longer implied; it too is on the move, starting at the feet and creeping inevitably and cruelly up the body, which has no visible signifier of race other than the shoe itself. Oddly, this metaphor fails to recognize that death is our common fate, but here blackness seems to make it worse, to make it a particular punishment, like Ham's perhaps.

The exchange of shoes with a black woman intensifies the irony of this situation. As the bloodhounds follow Christmas's scent, they, in fact, follow an indisputably black person to what the author calls a "negro cabin" (329). And although Christmas has not set foot in this cabin, he has entered the circumscribed life of the African Ameri-can. In an odd way, the gendered structure of the incident—the woman is wearing her husband's brogans (329)—reminds one of the old slave classification law that declared the child "followed the condition of the mother." In Christmas's case, he follows the footsteps of his symbolic racial mother. Ironically, the scent of the black shoes liber-ates Christmas for a brief while. But as the bloodhounds track down his shoes now in the "negro cabin," the dogs will soon sniff out the criminal who was not allowed to fol-low the condition of his biological mother; he fills the shoes of his racially Othered father. The gauge of his blackness appears clearly on his feet, marked by the length of the man's brogans. In the postbellum South, brogans could never lead to freedom, no matter how far one marched in them. At some turn in the road, the lynch mob waited.

Characters from at least two of Ernest Gaines's novels wear brogans, and a look at these characters offers us some interesting contrasting views of the shoe and its wearer. In *A Lesson before Dying,* Jefferson, convicted of a murder he did not commit, awaits his execution in a 1940s Louisiana prison. During a visit by Jefferson's grandmother, the narrator describes the prisoner's approach: "The first thing you heard were the chains around his ankles, then Jefferson entered the room through the rear door, followed by the deputy. Jefferson wore the same brown wool shirt he'd had on a couple of days before. He had on a pair of faded denims and brogans with no laces. He was dragging his feet to keep the shoes on."[18] Jefferson's imprisonment represents the Old South's desperate effort to chain blacks to their historically denigrated state. His shoes symbolically underscore the fate that the racist society has dictated for him. Like Joe Christmas's, Jefferson's is a long death march. Although the state of Louisiana would have described the trial and investigation as "fair," it, like the rest of the southern states, if not the nation as a whole, viewed the Fourteenth Amendment to the Constitution as a private joke between white men, a no longer relevant bit of revenge by the victors of the Civil War on the vanquished. Thus everyone involved in the legal proceedings, including the judge and juror, knows and relishes his part in this lynch mob:

> She [his godmother] knew, as we all knew, what the outcome [of the trial] would be. A white man had been killed during a robbery, and though two of the robbers had been killed on the spot, one had been captured, and he, too, would have to die. Though he told them no, he had nothing to do with it, that he was on his way to the White Rabbit Bar and Lounge when Brother and Bear drove up beside him and offered him a ride. (4)

Jefferson's innocence remains insignificant to judge, jury, and the white community at large. Just as the brogans signify the hopelessness of his situation, Jefferson's static social position finds expression in the shackled feet too heavy to lift. Only in the end, after the black schoolteacher Grant is able to convince Jefferson of his humanity, of his manhood, is the innocent man able to walk like a man, even though that walk is in lace-less brogans to the electric chair. "Straight he walked," the deputy reports to the schoolteacher after the execution. "I'm a witness. Straight he walked" (254).

In *Of Love and Dust* a similar situation exists. Gaines again returns to the Louisiana of his birth and its racist criminal justice system. In this novel, Marcus, convicted of a murder he claims to have committed in self-defense, is paroled out as a bond servant to a white plantation owner. He is set to pull corn from the stalk during the harvest. He is to work under the supervision of the novel's narrator, Jim Kelly, and alongside two "punks," Freddie and John, who are the best corn pickers on the plantation. Marcus, however, refuses to wear the raiments of a convict or a plantation hand. Jim, bruised after a bad love affair, returns to the plantation and seems content to offer up his manhood as a sacrifice to the woman who abandoned him. Working in khakis and wearing a straw hat, Jim attempts unsuccessfully to convince Marcus to wear the khaki clothes all the other field hands wear. Freddie and John, however, accept their lot, and Jim approves of their dress: "I saw John and Freddie coming down the quarter. . . . There they were in their khakis and big straw hats and brogans, just giggling."[19] For Marcus the clothes and shoes are the livery of slavery and oppression, and he refuses to wear such "convict" clothes, preferring to pull corn in his silk shirts and fancy shoes, no matter how impractical and uncomfortable. Jim finds Marcus's indomitable spirit threatening and tries to find ways to break it, to make the unwilling plantation hand less proud, more like himself and John and Freddie:

> As I came farther down the quarter, I saw Playboy Marcus coming out the yard. He had on a short-sleeve green shirt and a pair of brown pants. No hat—not even a handkerchief around his neck. He had on a pair of brown and white dress shoes.
> "Where the hell you think you're going in that?" I asked him. (25)

Those in the livery of servitude grumbled but did not resist the racist oppression. Again, as in *A Lesson before Dying,* the brogan wearers suffer the continuing affronts that characterized the life of African Americans in Jim Crow America. The fact that Freddie and John are already not "real" men complicates our reading of the text. While the easy answer to this would be to brand the author homophobic, that would not address the complexities of the situation. In fact, one would be more accurate in saying that the sexual identity of Freddie and John is overdetermined. After all, Gaines's primary interest is resistance to racism. In both these novels, the author interrogates the notion of "manhood" in the context of resistance to systematic racism. Freddie and John's sexual behavior puts in relief the behavior of all the other black men on the plantation who do not act like men. In fact they are no different. The only "real" black man on the plantation is Marcus. Moreover, the fact that Freddie and John can work harder than any other men on the plantation proves that physical strength does not make the man. Nor does fashion, for Marcus, not Freddie and John, is the fancy dresser. By mutating the stereotypes, Gaines places the spirit of resistance above all else. The real black man contests the old order. Freddie and John do not; neither does the novel's narrator. They all fail to measure up.

Not until Jim learns to respect Marcus's spirit of resistance can he abandon both the mental and material raiments of servitude. He must unlace the brogans of his mind to be free. It does not really matter what he laces up on his feet. We never learn if Freddie and John make a similar transformation or whether they are happy to continue to wear the livery of servitude. But their sexual behavior is not the problem. For they too would become real men if they resisted the indignities that greet them solely because of their race.

Gaines and Faulkner together confirm the enduring legacy of the brogan and its continued association with the past slavery of African Americans. Yet both authors offer us drastically disparate views. Herman Beavers writes of these two very different southern writers:

> The African American novelist (and especially those born in the South) is invariably locked in an "engaging disengagement" with Faulkner; attracted to

his power of description and mastery of language, but repelled by his perpetuation of racial myth. One finds that this is most certainly the case for Ernest Gaines, especially since he has alluded to Faulkner's influence over "every Southern writer" who has followed him. But despite this, his task as a writer remains one of attempting to manifest an artistic vision of the South which is uniquely his own. This project takes on major dimensions when we consider the weight under which all African American writers labor in confronting the South as a site of fictional exploration. For African American Southern writing seems to move between two poles: the documentary and the transcendent. The former describes the degrading circumstances of Southern life, depicting the terror and violence, the political disenfranchisement and peonage, embodied in a segregated society. The latter attempts to situate African American folk culture as a resistant, coherent force out of which characters are able to manifest some semblance of either self-consciousness or self-recovery.[20]

In *Light in August* the brogan signifies the innate inferiority and the inescapable destiny of those who wear them. Joe accepts what Faulkner sees as his nature when he realizes the awesome and infallible signifying power of the shoes. Gaines's characters, on the other hand, understand that they must overthrow their oppressors, that they must not allow the shoe to shackle them to a self-loathing acceptance of peonage and inferiority, that perhaps they need to unlace themselves from the signifier in order to walk into their rightful humanity. As Foster observes:

> Clothing enables a human being to identify personal self and communal self, and that self in relation to those of other communities; and clothing is the most obvious, silent message by which a person communicates his or her self as an individual to others. Although particular items and styles of dress change over time and from place to place, the meanings that people give to clothes are universal. . . . But in a broader sense, clothing helps to regulate bodies within a socially constructed order; this was no less so during the time of slavery in the United States of America.[21]

It is within this ambiguous social order that the African American "reads" the brogan: the show of debased servitude, the symbol of passive acceptance, and the signifier of a vast human struggle to make whole a person, a family, and a community in a nation that saw only the fraud it nurtured beyond all reason.

Faulkner's use of the brogan here confirms the shoe's rigid association with African Americans, but I think it also hints at how the myth of the shoe has survived into the signifying game of dozens. As with all things that white America has used to denigrate and stigmatize African Americans, African Americans triumphantly claim the stigma and forge it into something that yet again signifies not only our survival but our triumph over the centuries of obstacles placed in our path. "Your mama wears brogains" embraces the opponent; it says "we are equals, now let's see who plays the game better." Even when it does not intend to, it recalls the Jubilee and the embrace of family separated not by fate but by man's cruelty. Who would care if his or her mama wore brogains to walk from Texas to Virginia just to say "I love you."

NOTES

1. For more information about the workers who made brogans and all workers in the shoe industry, see Mary H. Blewett, *Men, Women, and Work: Class, Gender, and Protest in the New England Shoe Industry, 1780–1910* (Urbana: University of Illinois Press, 1988); Paul G. Faler, *Mechanics and Manufacturers in the Early Industrial Revolution: Lynn, Massachusetts, 1780–1860* (Albany: State University of New York Press, 1981); and Harriet Silvester, *Tapley's Chronicles of Danvers: (Old Salem Village) Massachusetts, 1632–1923* (Danvers: Danvers Historical Society, 1923), 89–90.

2. Blewett, *Men, Women, and Work,* 61, 65, 81.

3. Faler, *Mechanics and Manufacturers,* 212.

4. I use the spelling "brogains" in an attempt to capture the pronunciation of the word in New Orleans and the black South.

5. W.E.B. Du Bois, *The Souls of Black Folk* (New York: New American Library, Signet Classic Edition, 1969), 59.

6. Quoted in Elizabeth Hyde Botume, *First Days amongst the Contrabands* (New York: Arno Press, 1968), 79.

7. Annie L. Burton, *Memories of Childhood's Slavery Days: Six Women's Slave Narratives* (New York: Oxford University Press, 1988), 35–36.

8. Quoted in Dorothy Sterling, ed., *We Are Your Sisters: Black Women in the Nineteenth Century* (New York: Norton, 1984), 311.

9. Burton, *Memories of Childhood's Slavery Days,* 12.

10. Quoted in Herbert G. Gutman, *The Black Family in Slavery and Freedom: 1750–1925* (New York: Random House, Vintage Books, 1976), 206.

11. Quoted in Sterling, *We Are Your Sisters,* 310.

12. George Rawick, *The American Slave: A Composite Autobiography,* supplement, series 2, vol. 6, Texas Narratives, pt. 5 (Westport, Conn.: Greenwood, 1979), 200; italics added.

13. Rawick, *The American Slave: A Composite Autobiography, vol. 13, Georgia Narratives,* pt. 4 (Westport, Conn.: Greenwood, 1972), 141.

14. Ibid., 155.

15. Helen Bradley Foster, *"New Raiments of Self": African American Clothing in the Antebellum South* (New York: Berg, 1997), 231–244 and 329.

16. Blewett, *Men, Women, and Work,* 148.

17. William Faulkner, *Light in August* (New York: Random House, Vintage International Edition, 1990), 331. Subsequent page references to this work are given in the text.

18. Ernest J. Gaines, *A Lesson before Dying* (New York: Knopf, 1993), 188. Subsequent page references to this work are given in the text.

19. Ernest J. Gaines, *Of Love and Dust* (New York: Norton, 1979), 33. Subsequent page references to this work are given in the text.

20. Herman Beavers, *Wrestling Angels into Song: The Fictions of Ernest J. Gaines and James Alan McPherson* (Philadelphia: University of Pennsylvania Press, 1995), 129.

21. Foster, "New Raiments of Self," 4.

Empty Shoes

ELLEN CAROL JONES

"We are the shoes, we are the last witnesses.
We are shoes from grandchildren and grandfathers.
From Prague, Paris and Amsterdam,
And because we are only made of fabric and leather
And not of blood and flesh, each one of us avoided the hellfire."
—*Moses Schulstein (1911–1981), "I Saw a Mountain"*

LAST WITNESSES

"Hear the shuffle of shoes left behind—that which remained," Yiddish poet Moses Schulstein counsels in "I Saw a Mountain."[1] The empty shoes of the victims of the Shoah—as at the death camps of Majdanek and Auschwitz-Birkenau—bear silent witness to the systematic attempt by the Germans and their collaborators to exterminate the Jews of Europe, as well as other groups of people the Nazis deemed threatening or inferior. In tracing the origins of the shoes "from grandchildren and grandfathers. / From Prague, Paris and Amsterdam," Schulstein inscribes the irreparable loss across time and space: intergenerational, international. Abject survivors of the abjection suffered by the men and women and children killed in the Shoah, the shoes—derelict, decaying—figure the abandonment of European Jewry by the West, the decomposition of a people under the Nazis (figure 1). Yitzhak Katzenelson's "The Song of the Murdered

197

FIGURE I ⌁ Shoes from victims of the Majdanek Concentration Camp,
Lublin, Poland.

On loan from the State Museum of Majdanek, Lublin, Poland, to the United States Holocaust Memorial
Museum. Courtesy of the United States Holocaust Memorial Museum Photo Archives.

Jewish People," written shortly before his death in Auschwitz in 1944, apprehends that loss as total:

> Never will a Jewish mother cradle a baby. Jews will not die or be born.
> Never will plaintive songs of Jewish poets be sung.
> > All's gone, gone. . . .
> Woe unto me, nobody is left. . . . There was a people and it is no more.
> > There was a people and it is . . . Gone. . . .[2]

How can we hear that song of a murdered people, hear the shuffle of those shoes left behind?

And how can we—who may be only witnesses to memory, not rememberers ourselves—hear the voices of those who survived, those whose survival is a life after "death"?[3]

> We, the rescued,
> From whose hollow bones death had begun to whittle his flutes,
> And on whose sinews he had already stroked his bow—
> Our bodies continue to lament
> With their mutilated music.[4]

How can we hear the mutilated music of their testimonies if the core of trauma is a void, an absence that is unrepresentable? "As if from one day to the next a chasm opened into which everything fell. . . . A wall of fog remained, through which I cannot penetrate," a survivor describes the experiencing of trauma. "There is nothing there . . . an . . . emptiness." The trauma is unrepresentable because the experience of the Shoah exceeded "the parameters that define human experience": "Anyone crossing these boundaries of the unspeakable cannot necessarily return."[5] To cross that border is to enter the void: "It is worse than memory, the open country of death."[6]

That erasure, that "wound without memory," is transmitted to the next generation; its void is inescapable, as a child of survivors laments: "I am a prisoner of an empty space."[7] The 1991 series of fourteen black-and-white photographs by German-Jewish artist Susanna Pieratzki, *Parents,* portrays her own parents, survivors of the Shoah. This cyclical series is intended to emphasize regeneration. Yet in their confrontation with her parents' past, the photographs also suggest that for the child of the survivor, the power of this empty circle is in its perpetuating itself, an eternal recurrence. The child's present is haunted by the parents' past; the child repeats, reenacts, the parents' pain.[8] Pieratzki's objective in the series is not to confront the actual horrors of the Shoah but "to show the deep-rooted human instinct to survive such dark times": "Despite the mental and physical weakness caused by the past, my parents, as well as many others like them, still possess within them this deep, hidden spark to build a new life and bring forth a new generation."[9]

That new generation is figured in *Birth* as a pair of baby shoes placed on the head of her father. Pieratzki photographs her father in profile; the baby shoes face forward (figure 2). The father looks inward; his countenance appears saddened by the burden of memory; his shoulders are slumped as if weighed down by the past. Appearing oblivious to the baby shoes precariously balanced on his head, he seems unhopeful for, or at least unaware of, the future they forecast. The baby shoes allude to the birth of his daughter, Susanna; their placement on his head suggests a parthenogenetic birth. Tellingly, they are empty. These shoes reappear in the elegiac *Remembrance,* the last photograph in the series, between shabbat candles that evoke a *yahrzeit* for a future lost to genocide (figure 3). (*Yahrzeit* is Yiddish for "year" [*yahr*] and "time" [*zeit*], marking the anniversary of death.) And as if to emphasize the figuring of life through shoes, in this series Pieratzki portrays *Death* as the soles of her parent's bare feet (figure 4). The subject is lying face down, but the only part of the body visible in the photograph are the wrinkled soles, the toes of the left foot contorted as if death has not yet released its victim from pain. Unlike Jeffrey Wolin's photographs of Shoah survivors—on which he inscribes their stories, surrounding the images of the survivors with their words filling the background—Pieratzki's photographs contain no text. Their backgrounds

FIGURE 2   ↢   Susanna Pieratzki, *Birth,* from *Parents* series, 1991,
14 black-and-white photographs, each 26.5 × 26.5 cm.
Copyright © Susanna Pieratzki. Reproduced with permission.

F I G U R E 3   ~   Susanna Pieratzki, *Remembrance,* from *Parents* series, 1991,
14 black-and-white photographs, each 26.5 × 26.5 cm.
Copyright © Susanna Pieratzki. Reproduced with permission.

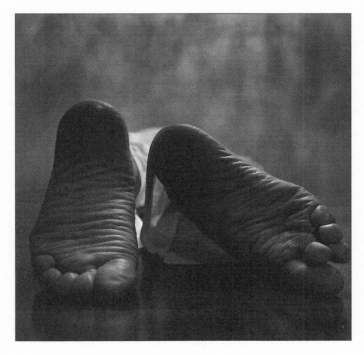

F I G U R E 4   ~   Susanna Pieratzki, *Death,* from *Parents* series, 1991,
14 black-and-white photographs, each 26.5 × 26.5 cm.
Copyright © Susanna Pieratzki. Reproduced with permission.

remain empty, as if the only stories they could record are not those of loss, of absence, but absence itself.

Witness to a devastation that can be recorded only as absence, the survivor comprehends rescue or reprieve from death as unique and eschatological. Simha Rottem ("Kajik"), a member of the resistance in the Warsaw ghetto, "circled the ruins" after the German attack on the ghetto, hearing only one woman cry out from the rubble, meeting only one man by the sewers: "At one point I recall feeling a kind of peace, of serenity. I said to myself: 'I'm the last Jew. I'll wait for morning, and for the Germans.'"[10] To wait for the Germans is to complete a destruction Primo Levi apprehends as already accomplished. Levi contrasts the docility of the other prisoners—broken, conquered—with the courage of an Auschwitz prisoner hung for allegedly taking part in the revolt by a few hundred men at Birkenau, in which one of the four crematoria was blown up. The man cries out to the other prisoners before his death: "*Kamaraden, ich bin der Letz!*" (Comrades, I am the last one!); the rebel is indeed the last one.[11]

For the survivors of the Shoah, the "unplaced and unplacatable memory"—or the beyond of memory—of the dead haunts the present.[12] To listen to that absence, that empty space, is to create a place for the exiled and for the disremembered, to act in memory (of): "Teach us, Forever Dead, there is no Dream but Deed, there is no Deed but Memory."[13]

THE OPEN COUNTRY OF DEATH

The decomposition of the Jews—their erasure, their annihilation—constituted for Reichsführer SS Heinrich Himmler "an unwritten and never-to-be-written page of glory" in Nazi history: "for we know how difficult we would have made it for ourselves if today—amid the bombing raids, the hardships and the deprivations of war—we still had the Jews in every city as secret saboteurs, agitators, and demagogues. If the Jews were still ensconced in the body of the German nation, we probably would have reached the 1916–17 stage by now." In this speech, delivered to *Schutzstaffel* officers at Posen (Poznan) on October 4, 1943, about a subject Himmler claims "we have never talked about . . . and never will" (what he infamously refers to as "the evacuation of the Jews" before juxtaposing that euphemism to a phrase he considers apposite, "the annihilation of the Jewish people"), the unspeakable and forever unspoken subject constitutes the "unwritten and never-to-be written page of glory" of "our history."[14] In such a desubjectification, the de-composed Jews comprise an inscription that thus must remain forever silent, forever absent.

The shoes' very presence signals the absence of those humans who once wore them, their materiality a metonymy for a corporeality obliterated. Part of Józef Szajna's 1969 art installation, *Reminiscences,* emphasizes that metonymy: worn and discarded shoes are strewn before a cutout silhouette of an anonymous victim composed of inmate snapshots, a wheel attached to the face as if a target. Large nails pointing upward on the floor between and around the shoes emphasize the vulnerability of the victims. And Marc Klionsky's 1962 *Pile of Shoes* is set before a barbed wire fence, the desolation of the shoes alluding to the fate of those imprisoned. Zinovii Tolkatchev's *Preparations for a Massacre,* part of his Auschwitz series of 1945, stresses that fate: camp uniforms are placed beside the pile of shoes in the foreground of the artwork to clarify the locale of the massacre. The legs of the living and the dead—those awaiting execution and those already murdered—form the background, the legs of the dead draping the pile of shoes. In Erich Brauer's 1973–74 painting of a Jew being gassed, *1944,* the relics or debris of the life lived appear to have exploded from the figure in the center of the painting, naked except for a cloth draping the torso as in early Renaissance depictions of the crucified Christ. Unlaced, derelict peasant's shoes—the iconographic shoes of the Holocaust—have fallen in the lower right corner of the painting.[15]

The status of the shoes as object, their materiality—precisely because that materiality remains merely figurative for the human—saves them from a fate reserved for humans so reified their very bodies were rendered into products. But prior to that ultimate reification of their victims, the Germans confiscated their money, other valuables, clothes, and shoes; the "Final Solution" produced over two thousand freight carloads of stolen goods. Systematic plunder accompanied systematic slaughter. Ordered by the Nazis and their Ukranian cohorts to clear out the undressing area at Treblinka, Abraham Bomba, a survivor of that death camp, was forced to carry bundles of victims' clothing "to the main place where there were big piles of clothes, of shoes, of other things." This "sorting place," states Richard Glazer, another survivor of Treblinka, "was buried under mountains of objects of all kinds. Mountains of shoes, of clothes, thirty feet high" (figure 5). The undressing area was soon cleared, Bomba testifies, "as though people had never been on that place. There was no trace, none at all, like a magic thing, everything disappeared." The entire process from arrival at Treblinka to death for a whole trainload of people took "two hours, two and a half hours, three hours," according to Franz Suchomel, SS Untersturmführer of the death camp. Even the death trains were financed by Jews forced to pay for their tickets or by confiscated Jewish property; in the Nazi government, "there was no budget for destruction."[16]

As the ghettos were successively "liquidated," German troops gathered the clothing and belongings of the dead to be sorted, often by Jews forced to live in ghettos

FIGURE 5 ⌒   Auschwitz women inmates sort through a huge pile of shoes
from the transport of Hungarian Jews. Auschwitz-Birkenau, Poland, May 1944.

Photo by Bernhard Walter. Yad Vashem Photo Archives, Jerusalem, Israel. Courtesy of United States
Holocaust Memorial Museum Photo Archives.

as yet not destroyed. *The Chronicle of the Łódź Ghetto* records on September 6, 1943,
under the heading, "Old Shoes":

> More old shoes have come into the ghetto. Twelve freight cars had been
> unloaded as of September 5. The old-shoe warehouse will be busy for many
> months just sorting out this vast quantity. Think for a moment of the various
> categories that need to be dealt with: (1) leather and other shoes; (2) men's,
> women's, and children's shoes; (3) right shoes and left shoes; (4) whole shoes
> and half shoes; (5) black shoes and brown shoes. Finally—and this is the
> hardest job of all—the matching pairs have to be ferreted out. Considering
> the mountains of second-hand shoes, one can hardly believe that such a job
> is possible.

Repercussions of theft were severe. On September 13, 1943, *The Chronicle of the Łódź
Ghetto* records the execution of a worker punished for taking scraps of leather to make
shoe laces:

> Today at 6 P.M., Icek Bekerman, 34 years old, was executed. Bekerman was a
> worker in the Leather and Saddlery Department, where he had misappropriated
> some scrap leather in order to make shoe laces. . . . Since, in wartime, the
> German authorities regard such thefts as sabotage, according to military law,

and punish offenders very severely, Bekerman was denied mercy. . . . The ghetto carpentry shop was required to supply the gallows; and the entire personnel of the leather and saddlery workshop and the shoe workshop was commanded to be present, along with delegations from all other workshops, so that the execution would serve as a deterrent. The offender's wife and two children were also driven to the place of execution to witness the death sentence carried out.

Ben Edelbaum, twelve years old at the time of Bekerman's execution, testified that the cries of Bekerman's wife and children "were the most terrifying lamentations I had ever heard."[17]

Abraham Sutzkever, in an untitled poem written in the Vilna ghetto on July 30, 1943, parallels the arrival of the shoes into the ghetto with the disappearance of the people who once wore them. The shoes as remains stand in for, take the place of, the bodies now lost. Sutzkever's own mother disappeared after her hiding place in the ghetto had been discovered; the poem addresses, through the synecdoche of the shoe, the void of loss: the loss of his mother, his father, his child, his community. "Every moment," Sutzkever writes, "I am more an orphan":

> Once, through a cobblestone ghetto street
> Clattered a wagon of shoes, still warm from recent feet,
> A terrifying
> Gift from the exterminators . . .
> And among them, I recognized
> My Mama's twisted shoe
> With blood-stained lips on its gaping mouth.
> —Mama, I run after them, Mama,
> Let me be a hostage to your love,
> Let me fall on my knees and kiss
> The dust on your holy throbbing shoe
> And put it on, a *tfillin* on my head,
> When I call out your name!
>
> But then all shoes, woven in my tears,
> Looked the same as Mama's.
> My stretched-out arm dropped back
> As when you want to catch a dream.

Ever since that hour, my mind is a twisted shoe.[18]

The Nazi crime against humanity attempted to erase the past and negate the possibility of the future; all traces of Nazi victims were to be obliterated. But in addition to immediate mass murder, the Nazis perfected a perverse version of slave labor that reduced "human beings to consumable raw materials from which all mineral resources were systematically extracted." The Nazis regarded the slave not "as a capital investment but as a commodity to be discarded and easily replaced. As one survivor put it, 'They oiled the machines; they did not feed the workers.'"[19] As the tide of the war turned against Germany after 1942, the inmates of the concentration camps became indispensable to the war economy. The number of forced laborers exceeded seven million; some of the "most respected German corporations had no scruples about using concentration camp slave labor. The well-known companies that lined up to receive workers included Flick, I. G. Farben, BMW, Siemens, Messerschmitt, Daimler-Benz, and Krupp. The decision to use slave labor was entirely voluntary."[20]

As Allied troops advanced in the closing months of the war, the SS attempted to efface all signs of the death camps. But when Soviet troops entered Majdanek on July 23, 1944, and Auschwitz-Birkenau on January 18, 1945, to take two examples, the commodities left behind communicated the fact of mass extermination (figure 6). Few prisoners—"1,000 living corpses," Roman Karman called the survivors—remained at Majdanek, but a storehouse of over 800,000 shoes narrated the fate of their owners. An eyewitness report of Majdanek after liberation by one of the thirty-four Western correspondents brought to the camp through the efforts of the Polish Committee of National Liberation describes this storehouse: "It was full of shoes. A sea of shoes. I walked across them unsteadily. They were piled, like pieces of coal in a bin, halfway

FIGURE 6   ⌁   A warehouse full of shoes and clothing confiscated from the prisoners and deportees gassed upon their arrival. The Germans shipped these goods to Germany. Auschwitz-Birkenau, Poland, after January 1945.

Photo by Lydia Chagoll. Courtesy of United States Holocaust Memorial Museum Photo Archives.

up the walls. Not only shoes. Boots. Rubbers. Leggings. Slippers. Children's shoes, soldiers' shoes, old shoes, new shoes. They were red and grey and black. Some had once been white."[21]

The Germans had registered 405,000 prisoners at Auschwitz, and at the last roll call had counted 67,012 prisoners, most of whom were forced to march to Wodzislaw in order to board freight trains to concentration camps at Gross-Rosen, Buchenwald, Dachau, and Mauthausen (almost one in four prisoners died during the forced march). Although the retreating SS officers blew up crematoria buildings, destroyed SS documents and I. G. Farben corporate documents at Auschwitz III (Buna-Monowitz), and burned twenty-nine storerooms, Soviet troops discovered in the six remaining storerooms 348,820 men's suits, 836,255 women's coats, 13,964 carpets, and more than 15,400 pounds of hair packed into paper bags to be shipped to Axis industries.[22] Property confiscated from victims had been sorted by camp inmates in the "Canada" section of Auschwitz and was often sent to Dachau for further sorting. Pastor Heinrich Grüber testified to the sight of railway freight cars full of clothes from Birkenau (Auschwitz II) arriving at Dachau: "We were shaken to the depths of our soul when the first transports of children's shoes arrived—we men who were inured to suffering and to shock had to fight back tears." He declared that later, when they saw yet more thousands of children's shoes, "this was the most terrible thing for us, the most bitter thing, perhaps the worst thing that befell us."[23]

Even though the SS had burned Treblinka and had planted pine trees to conceal Bełżec (both camps were closed in 1944 after most of Poland's Jews had been slaughtered), Soviet soldiers found "bones protruding from the ground."[24] At Treblinka, a survivor of the Warsaw ghetto, Dr. Adolf Berman, described the site: "a tremendous area of many kilometres, and all over this area there were scattered skulls, bones—tens of thousands; and piles of shoes—among them tens of thousands of little shoes." He picked up a pair of children's shoes, telling the court at the Eichmann trial in Jerusalem sixteen years later: "I brought it as a very precious thing, because I knew that over a million of such little shoes, scattered over all the fields of death, could easily be found."[25]

DEATH BEGINS WITH THE SHOES

"Death begins with the shoes; for most of us, they show themselves to be instruments of torture," Primo Levi claims in *Survival in Auschwitz* (34). Betrayed in 1943—possibly by one of the outcasts swamping the band of resistance partisans camped in the mountains of Italy who was searching for perhaps no more than a pair of shoes—Levi was detained in camps in Italy and eventually deported to Auschwitz in 1944. "Today, in our times, hell must be like this," Levi says of Auschwitz (*Survival in Auschwitz,* 22).

Divested of his property, including clothing and shoes, on arrival, he was forced to wear the uniform and wooden shoes or clogs, or broken-down boots with wooden soles, doled out to the "economically useful Jews" of the camps (non-Jewish inmates were permitted to wear leather shoes, albeit not their own). If the shoes hurt their feet, the inmates were allowed one opportunity to exchange one shoe: "If a shoe hurts, one has to go in the evening to the ceremony of the changing of the shoes: this tests the skill of the individual who, in the middle of the incredible crowd, has to be able to choose at an eye's glance one (not a pair, one) shoe, which fits. Because once the choice is made, there can be no second change" (Levi, *Survival in Auschwitz,* 46, 34).

The new arrivals quickly learned the rules, spoken and unspoken, of the camp; failure to do so ensured one would not survive: "We have learnt that everything is useful: the wire to tie up our shoes, the rags to wrap around our feet, waste paper to (illegally) pad out our jacket against the cold. We have learnt, on the other hand, that everything can be stolen, in fact is automatically stolen as soon as attention is relaxed; and to avoid this, we had to learn the art of sleeping with our head on a bundle made up of our jacket and containing all our belongings, from the bowl to the shoes" (Levi, *Survival in Auschwitz,* 33).

The story of Vladek Spiegelman's friend Mandelbaum, a new arrival from Sosnowiec to Auschwitz, illustrates the inmates' dilemma (figure 7): "But now, in Auschwitz, Mandelbaum was a *mess.* His pants were big like for 2 people, and he had not even a piece of string to make a belt. He had all day to hold them with one hand. . . . One shoe, his foot was too big to go in. This also he had to hold so he could find maybe [someone] with whom to exchange it. One shoe was big like a boat. But *this* at least he could wear. It was winter, and everywhere he had to go around with one foot onto the snow."[26] Mandelbaum, holding onto his clothes and his shoe, drops his spoon and spills his food; the spoon is stolen before he can bend to pick it up, the guards beat him when he asks for more soup. His dilemma is the stuff of pratfall comedy—"I hold onto my bowl and my shoe falls down. I pick up the shoe and my *pants* fall down . . ."—were it not that his plight is lived, not staged, and the turn of the screw is so vicious: "But what can I do? I only have two hands! My God. *Please* God . . . help me find a piece of string and a shoe that fits!" Below the frame of the comic—literally and figuratively—is Vladek Spiegelman's comment: "But here God didn't come. We were all on our own" (189). And so, although eventually Vladek is able to secure a spoon, a belt, and a pair of wooden shoes to fit Mandelbaum (figure 8), only a few days after that miracle ("My God. My God. My God . . . . It's a *miracle,* Vladek. God sent shoes through you") the Germans select Mandelbaum for "work": "*Nobody* could help this. So. It was finished with Mandelbaum. I never saw him more again" (194).

F I G U R E 7 ～ Art Spiegelman, *Maus: A Survivor's Tale* (1997).
Courtesy of Pantheon Books.

FIGURE 8 ⁊ Art Spiegelman, *Maus: A Survivor's Tale* (1997).
Courtesy of Pantheon Books.

Thus, despite all precautions, for the inmates of Auschwitz, anatomy (as well as *Selektion*) is destiny:

> And do not think that shoes form a factor of secondary importance in the life of the Lager. Death begins with the shoes; for most of us, they show themselves to be instruments of torture, which after a few hours of marching cause painful sores which become fatally infected. Whoever has them is forced to walk as if he was dragging a convict's chain (this explains the strange gait of the army which returns every evening on parade); he arrives last everywhere, and everywhere he receives blows. He cannot escape if they run after him; his feet swell and the more they swell, the more the friction with the wood and the cloth of the shoes becomes insupportable. Then only the hospital is left: but to enter the hospital with a diagnosis of "*dicke Füsse*" (swollen feet) is extremely dangerous, because it is well known to all, and especially to the SS, that here there is no cure for that complaint.
>
> (Levi, *Survival in Auschwitz*, 34–35)

In the camp, it is "rigorously forbidden to enter Ka-Be with shoes"; the *Kranken-bau,* or infirmary, like the other institutions of the camp, manufactures arbitrary rules for torture. But, as Levi remarks, since no "economically useful Jew" can be treated in the infirmary for more than two months without losing the status of usefulness, "it is enough to think of how many enter Ka-Be with shoes, and leave with no further need of them" (Levi, *Survival in Auschwitz,* 46). Paradoxically, it is the respite that Ka-Be offers the prisoners—"killed in our spirit long before our anonymous death"—that enables them to comprehend their fate: "No one must leave here and so carry to the world, together with the sign impressed on his skin, the evil tidings of what man's presumption made of man in Auschwitz" (Levi, *Survival in Auschwitz,* 55).

NARRATIVE DISPLACEMENT

"The Dachau Shoe" by W. S. Merwin, a story that foregrounds the mnemonic readjustments necessitated by unacknowledged responsibility—and, hence, unacknowledged guilt—for the Shoah, explores the displacements and fetishizations dictated by the refusal to mourn. Distancing by the first-person speaking voice both from the event and from its memorialization is signaled at the outset as the speaker hypercorrects his relationship to his "cousin Gene," insisting on a more distant connection: "(he's really only a second cousin)."[27] The narrative itself enacts the very processes of distancing and displacement the story implicitly critiques, as the speaking voice lists Gene's explanations but reveals little of what he explained or why he felt the explanations necessary. Gene's explanations rationalize his bringing home as a souvenir a shoe from Dachau but fail, in their obsessive repetition, not only to justify that act of specularizing and domesticating atrocity but also to disavow responsibility for the West's reaction to the plight of the Jews under the Nazis.

In Gene's rationalizations, the reality of the life lost is itself lost, so that the killing of the owner of the shoe merely guarantees that the shoe is now free for the taking, given that its new owners, the Germans, have been defeated:

> He explained he didn't steal it because it must have belonged to a Jew who was dead. He explained that he wanted some little thing. He explained that the Russians looted everything. They just took anything. He explained that it wasn't top quality to begin with. He explained that the guards or the kapos would have taken it if it had been any good. He explained that he was lucky to have got anything. He explained that it wasn't wrong because the Germans were defeated. He explained that everybody was picking up something. A lot of guys wanted flags or daggers or medals or things like that, but that kind of thing didn't appeal to him so much. He kept it on the mantelpiece for a while but he explained that it wasn't a trophy. (278)

The appeal to national affiliation and allegiance foregrounds the conventional portrayal of the Jew as one who has no national bounds. Jewish diasporic identity functions as an ethnic signfier that inevitably invokes the idea of national belonging "while simultaneously insisting on a counternarrative to the nation."[28] During the Shoah, as the Dachau shoe so poignantly demonstrates, the battle for German national assertion plays out diaspora to its ultimate: Jewish evacuation as Jewish annihilation.

The repetition of the explanations—graphically underscored by the obsessive repetitiveness of sentence structure—attempts to assuage guilt for the belatedness and inadequacy of the West's response to the Shoah; for the rehabilitation of the Germans "a few years later as the result of an unprincipled political game" fought over the bodies of the victims, as Primo Levi notes, and for the West's expedient realignment with the Federal Republic of Germany during the Cold War.[29] Collective identity is for Gene grounded in the temporal rhetoric of memory and in the fixed space of the nation-state form:[30]

> He explained that it's no use being vindictive. He explained that he wasn't. Nobody's perfect. Actually we share a German grandfather. But he explained that this was the reason why we had to fight that war. What happened at Dachau was a crime that could not be allowed to pass. But he explained that we could not really do anything to stop it while the war was going on because we had to win the war first. He explained that we couldn't always do just what we would have liked to do. He explained that the Russians killed a lot of Jews too. (278)

The narrative voice, in the concluding sentence of the story, privileges the explanations over what evokes them, the human life and violent death entailed in the shoe's history dissolved in story: "It's not that it's really a very interesting shoe when you come right down to it but you learn a lot from his explanations" (279). The attribution of value, then, is not to the shoe—and not to the shoe's original owner, the absent subject voided by the "explanations" that purport to bestow meaning. The shoe serves as cipher to be deciphered by the explanations. The narrative voice attests to the educative function of these explanations, but the story itself is silent about what has been learned.

Indeed, the traumatic event cannot be known as such. The Shoah remains the unassimilable core of Western history, of Western knowledge.[31] The traumatic event cannot be grasped in its positivity but can be constructed only retroactively, from its structural effects, as Gene attempts to construct the Shoah retroactively through the explanations the Dachau shoe as fetish—and as wound—elicits. The structural effects of a massive traumatic event such as the Shoah reveal that it "proactively contaminates all previous and subsequent events, compromising the healing ability of post-traumatic experience."[32] The imagery of genocide remains indelible, unassimilated, paralyzing. And long after the traumatic event occurred, the affect and all the effectivity of the event lie in "the distortions it produces in the symbolic universe of the subject: the traumatic event is ultimately just a fantasy-construct filling out a certain void in a symbolic structure and, as such, the retroactive effect of this structure."[33] The shoe as banal but sublime object thus serves as cipher in another sense as well, occupying the place of the impossible-real object of desire, masking an emptiness, a void.

"What happened at Dachau" cannot be spoken, in this story, less so because of the unspeakability of its horror than because of the psychological security of a euphemism that cannot name or refuses to name that trauma. What is spoken—the list of explanations—fetishizes the trauma. In "The Dachau Shoe" the repetitive explanations fail to perform the work of mourning.[34] Instead they guard against the return of the repressed. Sigmund Freud asserts in *Beyond the Pleasure Principle* that "the compulsion to repeat must be ascribed to the unconscious repressed." The resistance of the conscious and unconscious ego, operating under the sway of the pleasure principle, seeks "to avoid the unpleasure which would be produced by the liberation of the repressed." But that compulsion to repeat also recalls from the past "experiences which include no possibility of pleasure, and which can never, even long ago, have brought satisfaction even to instinctual impulses which have since been repressed."[35]

Freud's emphasis on the resistance of the conscious ego as well as the unconscious suggests, too, the possibility of a willed forgetting, one that parallels the postwar period

of deliberate collective amnesia concerning Nazi atrocities. After the public's immediate postliberation interest subsided, survivors could rarely find publishers for their testimonies. Voices of the victims were absent from the first histories of the camps, and
eventually the story of Nazi atrocities was severed from the larger narrative of the war
and itself ghettoized. For the liberators and others who had taken personal photographs
of the camps to bear witness to the atrocities, this period, from the late 1940s to the
late 1970s, impelled them to forget to remember: "Although many at first readily displayed their personal photos as evidence of what they had seen, keeping them in
accessible locations and retrieving them to stave off rumors of denial about the atrocities, they now took to hiding them. Snapshots of the camps were concealed in trunks,
basements, and attics."[36]

In Merwin's story, progressively hiding—almost burying—the shoe figures the act
of repression, and perhaps a willed forgetting:

> After a couple of years he put the shoe away in a drawer. He explained that
> the dust collected in it.
>   Now he has it down in the cellar in a box. He explains that the central
> heating makes it crack worse. (278–279)

And, tellingly, even though Gene retrieves the shoe to show it to a visitor "anytime you
ask"—if, indeed, the visitor asks anytime—his explanations, acting to counter the
repressed, return compulsively to the questions of the legitimacy of his owning it, of
its annulled use value, of its aesthetic surplus value as derelict object for display. These
questions displace doubts about the legitimacy of his responses and those of others during the Holocaust; they repress full acknowledgment of the deaths that could have been
prevented:

> He explains how it looks. He explains how it's hard to take it in, even for him. He
> explains how it was raining, and there weren't many things left when he got there.
> He explains how there wasn't anything of value and you didn't want to get caught
> taking anything of that kind, even if there had been. He explains how everything
> inside smelled. He explains how it was just lying out in the mud, probably right
> where it had come off. He explains that he ought to keep it. A thing like that. (279)

His explanations, then, return compulsively to questions of value—economic, political, ideological, ethical—with the unconscious desire to redeem empirical reality. But
nonfetishistic narrative requires the critical distinction between values and empirical
reality.[37] This distinction is one neither Gene nor the speaker can make, as both
attempt to redeem their responses to the Shoah through an object they deem valueless:
"It's a pretty worn-out shoe. It wasn't top quality in the first place, he explained" (278).
Thus the only yield available to the narrative fetishists of "The Dachau Shoe" in that
attempt to redeem the past is a return to the repressed.

SHARDS OF MEMORY

The careful attention of the narrative fetishists in Merwin's story to the aesthetics of the shoe and to its archival preservation—even as these serve to displace affect—parallels the museological concerns of curators both at the sites of Nazi concentration and death camps and at pedagogical museums, such as the United States Holocaust Memorial Museum in Washington, D.C., that have imported actual artifacts from the locales of destruction. Curators fear that the display of certain objects, such as the canisters of Zyklon-B, would make the museum or site into "a terrible cabinet of curiosities."[38] In the resurgence of memory work during the final two decades of the twentieth century—a resurgence that reconfigures Holocaust representation—the pictorial documents of the Shoah are troped as the "figure rather than the ground" for that representation. "Pictorial documents of history have become an independent metonymy: the mountains of eyeglasses, suitcases and hair take the place of the dead; they represent the dead in a cultural symbolic system, historicizing and thus relegating them to the distant past. An aesthetic ritual of mourning is created."[39] That troping also holds true for the display of artifacts in our postmodern memorial culture. Perhaps because the decaying shoes themselves are displayed as they were found, in piles, they recall the piles of corpses in the streets of the ghettos, in the death carts of the camps, in the mass graves. In these displacements, not only do the artifacts serve as metonymies for the dead, but also, in a double displacement, the pictorial documents of these artifacts serve as metonymies both for the dead and for the artifacts themselves. The visual frame for bearing witness becomes formulaic; the multiplicity of images of the immediate postliberation period, which underscored the complexity of the act of bearing witness, is laundered, and the images solidify into icons.[40]

The shoes of the Shoah—remnants, metonymies, monuments—are *lieux de mémoire.* They function as a historical trace, as a simulation of the past and its irretrievable loss, in an overdetermination of history and memory. That is, the vehicles of memory no longer actuate memory but are instead energized by memory itself. And because that memory is itself subject to diverse historicizations, the vehicles of memory are multiply configured. In museum displays or photographs or films such as the 1998 documentary *The Last Days,* the piles of abandoned, empty shoes signal for the viewer the enormity of the loss by metonymically materializing what had been rendered immaterial. Their resonance lies in their very materiality: remnants of what was to have been erased, expunged, these *lieux de mémoire* mark the *non-lieux de mémoire* of Europe and particularly eastern Europe as sites of massive death, absence. But because that materiality is deteriorating, the shoes also embody in their own process of disintegration the disembodiment of the people they symbolize. The very fragmentation of memory,

Salman Rushdie suggests, makes it so evocative for those who—also—remain: "The shards of memory acquired greater status, greater resonance, because they were *remains*; fragmentation made trivial things seem like symbols, and the mundane acquired numinous qualities."[41]

The pedagogical museums that attempt to "establish the physical reality of the Holocaust," as the United States Holocaust Memorial Museum attempts, reign over the "the palpable inaccessibility of its historical trauma."[42] They mark a cultural shift from a willed forgetting to remember to an obsessive, willed—but perhaps no more authentic—remembrance. Amassing artifacts from the concentration camps, the death camps, the Warsaw ghetto, the Evian Conference, and other sites to narrate an American version of the Shoah, the Holocaust Memorial Museum repeats the convention of metonymic displacement. Memory is not only prodded by the relic of the past but also reincorporated into it, even replaced by it. Relics as *memento mori* serve as "both metonymies and the authenticating evidence of our foothold in buried worlds"; "the place of origin becomes the matrix for the final return."[43] What are the goals of the museum's displaced stagings? "Are they attempting to mirror the realities, to act as supplements to the losses they stand in for, or do they function as barriers to the events? The artifact intrudes in the realm of the present through its hyperreality, through the utter concreteness it signals. It brings one closer to the historical real, supposedly closer to the tangibility of the events and to the experience of those who did and did not survive."[44]

Indeed, the museum planners termed these artifacts "object survivors," as if to strengthen their parallel to the human survivors enjoined by the Holocaust victims to live to tell their story.[45] But in their role to bear witness to the Shoah, the artifacts are doubly burdened: their provenance is to testify as historical proof; their abjection, to elicit empathy. Despite the historical authenticity of the object itself, "the artifact enacts its own absolute resignation to tell. There is no a priori guarantee that it can be enacted as evidence; rather, it attests to the trauma and the posttraumatic lacerations of the resurfacing of the events," a resurfacing enacted by the museum itself.[46] Such posttraumatic lacerations bear witness not only to the truth of the traumatic event but also to its incomprehensibility.

That is, the pedagogical museums of the Holocaust deploy actual artifacts to demonstrate the accessibility and comprehensibility of events so traumatic they remain not only historically irretrievable but also psychologically incomprehensible. Shoes, used by museums as such (im)possible evidence, constitute the quintessential traveling trope. As Jacques Derrida says of shoes deployed as object survivors, "They will have traveled a lot, traversed all sorts of towns and territories at war. Several world

wars and mass deportations. We can take our time. They *are there,* made for waiting."[47]
Four thousand shoes imported to the United States Holocaust Memorial Museum from
the death camp at Majdanek, Poland, a remnant of remnants, echo the far larger pile
at the site where the Germans confiscated them.[48] But that echo is inevitably a stylization, and, as Theodor Adorno claims, "through the aesthetic principle of stylization,
an unimaginable fate still seems as if it had some meaning; it becomes transfigured,
with something of the horror removed."[49] Horror, evoked by the pedagogical museum,
is nevertheless not located there. Through the artifacts, the pedagogical museum is
intended to connect to the center, the original sites of the Shoah, "so that Americans
could feel the 'shiver of contact,' could 'touch' the Holocaust at an outpost of memory."[50] Yet for the museum visitor viewing the exhibit, "that the experience becomes
aestheticized is inevitable; what is on display is not the horrific real, but artifactual remnants mandated to bring the viewer to a place of difficult approach, a place of fleet-
ing, overwhelming, and yet resistant empathy. The aestheticizing activities of the
museum must create bridges for guarded, imaginative projections and (im)possible wit-
nessings. . . . The metonymy is eerie, deadening; the theatrical effect materializes the
real into its evocation. The shoes thus become an empty yet elegant metonym. . . . One
of the stories at the museum thus reaches its crescendo on a highly aestheticized, albeit
somber chord."[51]

Such an aestheticization produces a loss. For one observer, the artifacts on site
at the death camps at Poland "carried a terrible immediacy" even as he acknowledges
the constructedness of their display: "In the barracks of shoes at Majdanek, I could only
go in a few feet. The smell and impact were overpowering, suffocating. I was stunned
by the power of the ruins and artifacts at Majdanek and Auschwitz, and the mass graves—
artifacts of a kind—at Chełmno." Viewing the "object survivors" at the United States
Holocaust Memorial Museum domesticates them, disempowers their effect—and
affect:

> Seeing and smelling the shoes, on either side of the visitor in a tower room on
> the third floor of the exhibit, I was, rather jarringly, taken back to Majdanek.
> And yet it was easier somehow to view these in the museum. The shoes were
> "visitors," and there was the sanctuary of recognizable space just outside.
> Even though they—and other artifacts—were skillfully woven into the fabric
> of an intense Holocaust narrative, their raw power and seemingly unmediated
> presence in the barracks at Majdanek were moderated. In both places, of
> course, the shoes served as props in a larger story. In Majdanek, however, the
> story was told within the total environment of the camp, an environment that
> seemed to collapse the distance between event and recollection of event, an
> environment in which the shoes were actually worn, taken off, left behind,
> and collected. They were less selected artifact—by definition something out

of place, put on display—than remnant, at home in the camp. In Washington, the shoes clearly had the status of artifact, and for me, at least, their presence as part of a narrative in the controlled environment of the museum domesticated them, made them "safer" to view.[52]

This aestheticization distances affect at the very moment the display attempts to invoke it. "The risk of aestheticizing here is directly linked to the project of historicizing to the point that artifactual display can become dangerously equated with inevitable cultural extinction. In this sense the United States Holocaust Memorial Museum in Washington, D.C., obliquely stands in as the silent other to the Nazi's Central Jewish Museum in Prague."[53] Yet such a critique must also take into account the public, dialogical, intertextual, and pedagogical aspects of the memorial space. *Lieux de mémoire* may materialize the immaterial, immortalize death, but they also metamorphose, generate, and recycle meaning.[54]

The imaginary dimension of phobic anxiety may explain in part why Hitler planned the Central Jewish Museum to commemorate a culture he planned to annihilate. This museum was to be staged "precisely on celebrating the remnants of extermination, on what they [the Nazis] willed to be the past": "Their institutionalized acts of genocide were to be knowingly and coyly muted beneath the elegant display of confiscated Jewish ceremonial and domestic artifacts as precious objects—an obscene ethnographic aesthetic based on the dialectic of extermination/preservation, in which one could not exist without the other."[55] Yet, paradoxically, the aesthetic ideology of the National Socialists in its negative sublimity could not tolerate "an inmixture of otherness in the self—a hybridization to which the fundamental contributions of Jews to German culture attested and which had to be exorcised through racial essentialism or hypostatization that made the other 'within' into a localized entity fully discrete and separate from the self. Hence the Jews formed a constitutive outside for the Nazi (one marking the inside in a way that is denied and repressed), thus becoming a phantasmatic cause of all evil and the projective carrier of the anxieties and ills of the modern world." Anti-Semitism invested the ideological figure of the "Jew" with its own unconscious desire, deploying that figure as the means to veil the inconsistencies of its ideological system. Hitler's plans for the museum anticipated not only the empirical fact of annihilation of the Jews but also "both the elimination of Jewish self-representation or memory and the retention of the Jew as a phantasm within the Nazi imaginary that was in some sense necessary for a paranoid, narcissistic, radically exclusionary, and inherently insecure type of internal solidarity."[56] Ideology, according to Jacques Lacan, designates "a totality set on effacing the traces of its own impossibility"; the anti-Semitism of Nazi ideology enacts that effacement to its extreme.[57]

Annihilated, effaced so that no name and no trace remain, the dead of the Holo-caust—through their deaths to which even their bodies cannot testify—reveal the absoluteness of their victimization. The witness disappears, leaving only ashes as bodily remains, a diaspora of ashes. These cinders are "a destruction of memory," the trace of the forgetting of forgetting, Derrida remarks, "one in which the very sign of destruction is carried off. . . . Everything is annihilated in the cinders."[58] The flame of *Geist* neither transforms nor consumes history; what remains, charred, resistant, are cinders.[59] And, for the survivor, only suffering remains; partial, fragmented memory remains.

REVENANT

The empty shoes of the Shoah testify to absence, forcing the viewer to acknowledge the need for restitution, for discharging a ghostly debt our mourning cannot discharge. Figured as remainder and remaindered, empty and emptied, silent and silenced, the shoes—as "object survivors" and as affect—are voiced through our representations. The shoes as remainder serve as demand for rendering: rendering that absence representationally, rendering that debt politically. But to whom can the debt be rendered? The shoes as remainder serve as revenant, as spectral reminder of absence.

The revenant functions doubly, ambivalently, like the angel of history Walter Benjamin famously pictures unable to restitute the ruined past as it is propelled into an abstract, abstracted future:

> His face is turned toward the past. Where we perceive a chain of events, he sees one single catastrophe which keeps piling wreckage upon wreckage and hurls it in front of his feet. The angel would like to stay, awaken the dead, and make whole what has been smashed. But a storm is blowing from Paradise; it has got caught in his wings with such violence that the angel can no longer close them. This storm irresistibly propels him into the future to which his back is turned, while the pile of debris before him grows skyward.[60]

The future, imbricated in the past, beckons toward what is not (yet).

Self Portrait, the initial painting of Samuel Bak's series *Landscapes of Jewish Experience,* reveals how, for the survivor, thinking the specter can signal toward the future only through a thinking of the past (figure 9). "My paintings," Bak states, convey "a sense of a world that was shattered, of a world that was broken, of a world that exists again through an enormous effort to put everything together, when it is absolutely impossible to put it together because the broken things can never become whole again."[61] At the outbreak of war in 1939, Vilna, the city in Poland where Bak grew up, was transferred to Lithuania. Occupied by the Soviet Union in June 1940 and by the Germans in 1941,

FIGURE 9   ⌐   Samuel Bak, *Self Portrait* (1995–1996). Oil painting. *Landscapes
of Jewish Experience* series.
Courtesy of Pucker Gallery, Boston, Massachusetts.

Vilna lost almost all of its Jewish population. Bak and his mother survived; his father
was shot a few days before Russian troops liberated the city in July 1944. *Self Portrait*
paints the artist as child, sitting in a sack "as if emerging from a cocoon of death," as
Lawrence Langer describes an image he notes seems allegorical but is not. This image
alludes to Bak's escape from the Vilna ghetto: "Sent with his son from the Vilna ghetto
to a labor camp nearby, Bak's father hid him in a sack, which he then dropped unob-
served from a ground-floor window in the warehouse where he was working. Through
an arranged plan, the young Bak was met by the maid of a relative who was raised as
a Christian and taken to a safe haven. The memory of that moment turns his expression inward in the portrait, making him virtually oblivious to his external environment," a blasted landscape of a ruined edifices, crematoria smoking on the horizon.[62]

   For the survivor of the Shoah, the revenant shadows the future. *Self Portrait* is a
"vivid reminder of the deathlife that is a vexing if paradoxical birthright" of the murder
of over nine million people, including a million and a half children: "no one's survival
can be detached from the loss of someone else."[63] Looming behind the seated child,

imprinted on canvas fragments like a collage nailed to the remains of a wood surface that may be a broken easel, is the ghost image of a frightened child forced from his home in the Warsaw ghetto after the revolt by the Jews in April 1943. This child's fear was captured for posterity by the most famous photograph of the Shoah: his hands are raised in surrender, the gun of a soldier trained on him.[64] The child, frightened and confused, also looks inward, his innocence incapable of comprehending the inhumanity of his oppressors. In Bak's painting, the image of the child is pieced together with tape, the unequal and rent shapes of the collage suggesting the fragility of the child's life. A further sign of that fragility is the mark Bak adds to the photograph: the trace of the Star of David formed on the child's coat by tape.

Behind the collage another board repeats the shape of the boy's arm and coat. Opposite this collage of the imprint of the Warsaw ghetto victim, at least three wood cutouts of his figure with raised hands, uncanny echoes, loom behind the artist-child. The first wood cutout is reversed, its props exposed. In the painted collage the Warsaw ghetto child's feet exceed the frame and, cropped, are not shown. Two empty and unlaced shoes, painted outside the frame of the imprinted ghost child, take the place of those feet. "The boy with his hands raised no longer has need of them, as his feet fade from flesh to painted wood. The feet of the child who was Bak are still hidden in the sack, not yet ready to pursue the arduous journey that will lead from life through death to art."[65]

The image of the Warsaw ghetto child, its collage painted in the faded rainbow colors of a broken covenant, returns in the final painting of Bak's 1994–97 series *Nuremberg Elegies, Elegy III,* reenvisioning Albrecht Dürer's 1514 engraving *Melencolia I* (figure 10). If Dürer's engraving portrays the inner problems of the artist, brooding over the absence of inspiration despite all the accoutrements of art and knowledge surrounding the winged genius of artistic creation, Bak's *Elegies* suggest the impossibility of art in a post-Holocaustal world. Dürer's engraving signals the mutability of time by depicting an hourglass half empty, appropriate to the artist in the middle of his life. But the Holocaust "transmutes mutability into annihilation. The atrocity of mass murder has no tragic dimension, its barbaric destructive power temporarily thwarting the basic impulses of the creative urge. . . . It is as if the murder of European Jewry has stripped the mystery from existence, leaving only the barren truth of a spiritual wreckage whose import is all too clear."[66] Yellow Stars of David, like fallen leaves, litter the ground. And as in *Self Portrait,* below the collage of the Warsaw ghetto child, where the feet of the child should have been, are empty shoes.[67]

In *Self Portrait* a blank canvas fills the space behind the cutout figures. Blank pages—held by the small stones, placed on grave markers, that for Jews commemorate the dead—are strewn before the painted, printed, and cutout images of the children,

FIGURE 10   ↝   Samuel Bak, *Elegy III* (1997). Oil painting. *Nuremberg Elegies* series.
Courtesy of Pucker Gallery, Boston, Massachusetts.

as if to plead, as Nelly Sachs does: "do not destroy the cosmos of words / do not dis-
sect with the blades of hate / the sound, born in concert with the breath."[68] The lace-
less, empty shoes also weight down the blank pages; like the commemorative stones,
they honor the dead (figure 11). Shapes of the blank pages echo the shapes of the pieces
of the collage, as if these torn pages, too, will be imprinted with the image of the child
lost in the Shoah. Or the pages may be *yisker biher,* literally "tombstones of paper": the
obligation, both religious and historical, to remember the dead of annihilated communities
and the collective and individual memorial books written by survivors to perform this
work of mourning. Finding it difficult to write under the extreme conditions in the Warsaw ghetto but considering his diary an "obligation" he is determined to fulfill with his
"last ounce of energy," Chaim Kaplan declares: "I will write a scroll of agony in order
to remember the past in the future."[69] Kaplan's scroll of agony, inscribing the traumatic

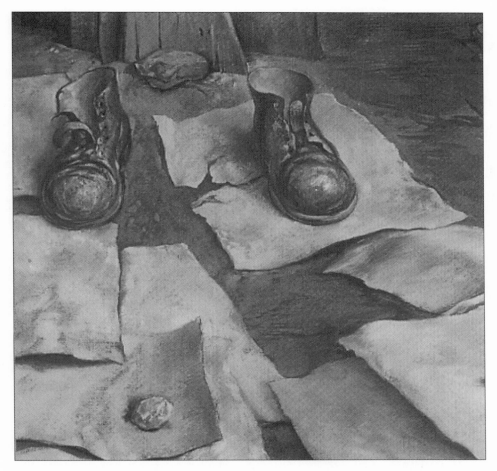

FIGURE 11 ⌁ Samuel Bak, detail of *Self Portrait* (1995–1996). Oil painting. *Landscapes of Jewish Experience* series.

Courtesy of Pucker Gallery, Boston, Massachusetts.

past for the future, enacts what Carolyn Forché images as a "revolt against silence": "The page is a charred field where the dead would have written / *We went on.*"[70] The dead would have written but cannot. Their story remains eternally in abeyance. Thus, in Bak's *Self Portrait,* both canvas and pages remain blank: for victims of the Shoah, both the dead and those who survived, the past is what is not, the future is what is not.

In no painting is that loss registered as poignantly as in Bak's 1997 *Absence* (figure 12). Spatial absence signals temporal absence. The blank face of the disembodied Warsaw ghetto child, recognizable by its angle and cap, is screwed or nailed to a derelict wood easel; the child's raised hands of surrender are figuratively cut out of the painting, represented by airy nothingness. Resting on a broken stone in front of the easel, where the remainder of the body should be represented but is not, are the iconographic

FIGURE 12   ⌐   Samuel Bak, *Absence* (1997). Oil painting.
Courtesy of Pucker Gallery, Boston, Massachusetts.

laceless empty shoes; and tumbled among broken stones below this "pair that is not a pair" are other broken shoes, some partly buried by the debris. This mound of broken stones and shoes recalls the mound of the broken tablets of the law in Bak's 1991 *Shema Yisrael,* shards that symbolize the covenant sundered between Yahweh and His people. In *Absence* fragments of the blue-and-white-striped cloth of the prisoners' uniforms and of the yellow Star of David are nailed to the easel; and behind the child's cap a piece of paper or cloth is nailed, the two *yods* that designate Adonai, the Lord, barely visible. What remains are only these shards.

Schulstein's "I Saw a Mountain" imagines the remainder as revenant. For him, a coming back to the ghost (*revenant au revenant*), a return, is figured as marching / voicing, marking the demand for justice as the demand to judge. The imperative of this mountain's judgment supersedes the imperative of divine commandment. And the insistence on the holy ground of the mountain of Jewish shoes rejects a holocaustal or sacrificial comprehension of the genocide of the Jews by echoing and interrogating the promise of deliverance made to Moses on Mount Horeb, when Yahweh called to Moses out of the burning bush, instructing him: "Draw not nigh hither: put off thy shoes from off thy feet, for the place wheron thou standest is holy ground" (Exodus 3:5; figure 13):

> I saw a mountain
> Higher than Mt. Blanc
> And more Holy than the Mountain of Sinai.
> Not in a dream. It was real.
> On this world this mountain stood.
> Such a mountain I saw—of Jewish shoes in Majdanek.
> Such a mountain—such a mountain I saw.
> And suddenly, a strange thing happened.
> The mountain moved. . . .
> And the thousands of shoes arranged themselves
>
> By size—by pairs—and in rows—and moved.
> Hear! Hear the march.
> Hear the shuffle of shoes left behind—that which remained.
> From small, from large, from each and every one.
> Make way for the rows—for the pairs,
> For the generations—for the years.
> The shoe army—it moves and moves.
>
> "We are the shoes, we are the last witnesses.
> We are shoes from grandchildren and grandfathers.
> From Prague, Paris and Amsterdam.
> And because we are only made of fabric and leather
> And not of blood and flesh, each one of us avoided the hellfire.
> We shoes—that used to go strolling in the market
> Or with the bride and groom to the *chuppah*,
> We shoes from simple Jews, from butchers and carpenters,
> From crocheted booties of babies just beginning to walk and go
> On happy occasions, weddings, and even until the time
> Of giving birth, to a dance, to exciting places, to life . . .
> Or quietly—to a funeral.
> Unceasingly we go. We tramp.
> The hangman never had the chance to snatch us into his
> Sack of loot—now we go to him.
> Let everyone hear the steps, which flow as tears,
> The steps that measure out the judgment."
>
> I saw a mountain
> Higher than Mt. Blanc
> And more Holy than the Mountain of Sinai.

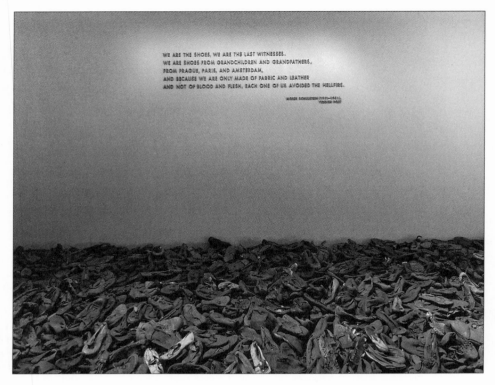

FIGURE 13 ↲ Shoes confiscated from prisoners at Majdanek Concentration Camp, Lublin, Poland. Quotation in English from Moses Schulstein, "I Saw a Mountain." Display, third floor of permanent exhibition, the United States Holocaust Memorial Museum, Washington, D.C.

Photo by Alan Gilbert. Permission from Alan Gilbert. Courtesy of the United States Holocaust Memorial Museum Photo Archives.

NOTES

I thank Susanna Pieratzki for permission to reproduce three of her photographs. I am indebted to Bernard Pucker, Pucker Gallery, Boston, for books and images of Samuel Bak's paintings. And I am indebted, for their conversations with me about "Empty Shoes," to the following people: Eleni Beja, Suzanne Ferriss, Georgia Johnston, Lucy McDiarmid, Edward Maloney, and, above all, Morris Beja. I dedicate this work to the Beja-Cohen-Stoller family.

1. Moses Schulstein, "I Saw a Mountain," trans. Mindelle Wajsman and Bea Stadtler, quoted in Michael Berenbaum, *The World Must Know: The History of the Holocaust as Told in the United States Holocaust Memorial Museum* (Boston: Little, Brown, 1993), 145–147. The word "holocaust" derives from "the Greek word for wholeburnt"; the sacrificial connotation of this term as "burnt offering," consistent with a Christian reading of Jewish history, is absent from the Yiddish word for the Nazi genocide of the Jews, *hurbn,* which connotes the violation of the continuity of life within the community, and from the Hebrew word for the genocide, *Sho'ah,* which connotes cosmic disaster, waste, and desolation (Sidra DeKoven Ezrahi, *By Words Alone: The Holocaust in Literature* [Chicago: University of Chicago Press, 1980], 2, 221; Vivian M. Patraka, "Situating History and Difference: The Performance of the Term *Holocaust* in Public Discourse," in *Jews and Other Differ-*

ences: *The New Jewish Cultural Studies,* ed. Jonathan Boyarin and Daniel Boyarin [Minneapolis: University of Minnesota Press, 1997], 55).

2. Yitzhak Katzenelson, "The Song of the Murdered Jewish People," quoted in Berenbaum, *The World Must Know,* 152.

3. Lawrence L. Langer, *Holocaust Testimonies: The Ruins of Memory* (New Haven: Yale University Press, 1991), 39.

4. Nelly Sachs (1891–1970), "Chorus of the Rescued," in *Art from the Ashes: A Holocaust Anthology,* ed. Lawrence L. Langer (New York: Oxford University Press, 1995), 643.

5. Dori Laub and Marjorie Allard, "History, Memory, and Truth: Defining the Place of the Survivor," in *The Holocaust and History: The Known, the Unknown, the Disputed, and the Reexamined,* ed. Michael Berenbaum and Abraham J. Peck (Bloomington: Indiana University Press, 1998), 810; survivor's testimony quoted on 805.

6. Carolyn Forché, *The Angel of History* (New York: HarperCollins, 1994), 13.

7. Quoted in Laub and Allard, "History, Memory, and Truth," 806.

8. Ibid., 808.

9. Susanna Pieratzki, artist's statement, October 1994, in *After Auschwitz: Responses to the Holocaust in Contemporary Art,* ed. Monica Bohm-Duchen (Sunderland, England: Northern Centre for Contemporary Art, 1995), 154. That this series addresses her parents' loss is particularly clear in *War:* her father, dressed in striped pajamas that recall the uniform forced on the concentration camp inmates, faces away from the camera. Eight wire hangers dangle behind his back, the number recalling the eight siblings Pieratzki's father lost in the Shoah (see Monica Bohm-Duchen, "Fifty Years On," in *After Auschwitz,* 143).

10. Claude Lanzmann, *Shoah: The Complete Text of the Acclaimed Holocaust Film* (1985; reprint, New York: Da Capo Press, 1995), testimony of Simha Rottem, 185.

11. Primo Levi, *Survival in Auschwitz: The Nazi Assault on Humanity,* trans. Stuart Woolf (New York: Simon and Schuster, 1996), 149–150. Originally published as *Se questo è un uomo,* 1958. Subsequent page references to this work are given in the text.

12. Langer, *Holocaust Testimonies,* 34.

13. W.E.B. Du Bois, *The Autobiography of W.E.B. Du Bois: A Soliloquy on Viewing My Life from the Last Decade of Its First Century* (N.p.: International Publishers, 1968), 423.

14. Heinrich Himmler, speech at Posen (Poznan), October 4, 1943: International Military Tribunal, Nuremberg, document PS-1919; quoted in *A Holocaust Reader,* ed. Lucy Dawidowicz (West Orange, N.J.: Behrman House, 1976), 132–133.

15. Ziva Amishai-Maisels, *Depiction and Interpretation: The Influence of the Holocaust on the Visual Arts* (Oxford: Pergamon, 1993),148; see figures 42–44 and 344; color plate 12.

16. Lanzmann, *Shoah,* testimony of Bomba, 37; testimony of Glazer, 30–40; testimony of Suchomel, 98; conversation between Raul Hilberg and Lanzmann, 134.

17. Łódź Chronicle, September 6, 1943, and September 13, 1943: Lucjan Dobroszycki, ed., *The Chronicle of the Łódź Ghetto, 1941–1944,* trans. Richard Lourie, Joachim Neugroschel et al. (New Haven: Yale University Press, 1984), 379, 381; Ben Edelbaum, *Growing Up in the Holocaust* (Kansas City: Edelbaum, 1980), 65–67, quoted in Martin Gilbert, *The Holocaust: A History of the Jews of Europe during the Second World War* (New York: Henry Holt, 1985), 610.

18. Abraham Sutzkezer, untitled poem, quoted in Langer, ed., *Art from the Ashes,* 568.

19. Berenbaum, *The World Must Know,* 108.

20. Ibid., 131.

21. Richard Lauterbach, "Murder, Inc.," *Time,* September 11, 1944, 36; quoted in Barbie Zelizer, *Remembering to Forget: Holocaust Memory through the Camera's Eye* (Chicago: University of Chicago Press, 1998), 55. Zelizer notes that in the photographic record of this death camp, the

emphasis was less on the remaining corpses of the victims of Nazi atrocity or on the wasted bodies of the survivors than on "the accoutrements of atrocity—gas cells, hanging ropes, furnaces, and
cans of Zyklon B, the gas used for extermination—while portrayals of enormous quantitites of objects
associated with the victims—mounds of shoes, passports, and luggage locks—suggested how widespread and systematic was Nazi brutality and how numerous its victims" (57).

22. Berenbaum, *The World Must Know,* 139, 184.

23. Testimony of Heinrich Grüber, Eichmann trial, May 16, 1961, session 41; quoted in
Gilbert, *The Holocaust,* 540–541.

24. Berenbaum, *The World Must Know,* 183.

25. Testimony of Dr. Adolf Berman, Eichmann trial, May 3, 1961, session 26; quoted in Gilbert,
The Holocaust, 765–766. Martin Gilbert adds: "A young child's shoe is now in a special display case,
as the final exhibit in the holocaust exhibition at Yad Vashem, in Jerusalem" (891–892, n. 53).

26. Art Spiegelman, *Maus: A Survivor's Tale,* vol. 1, *My Father Bleeds History* and vol. 2, *And Here
My Troubles Began* (New York: Pantheon, 1997), 189. Subsequent page references to this work are
given in the text.

27. W. S. Merwin, "The Dachau Shoe," in *American Gothic Tales,* ed. Joyce Carol Oates (New
York: Penguin, 1996), 278–279. Subsequent page references to this work are given in the text. "The
Dachau Shoe" (1969) is also collected in W. S. Merwin, *The Miner's Pale Children* (New York:
Atheneum, 1970).

28. Johannes von Moltke, "Identities on Display: Jewishness and the Representational Politics
of the Museum," in *Jews and Other Differences,* ed. Boyarin and Boyarin, 92.

29. Primo Levi, *The Drowned and the Saved,* trans. Raymond Rosenthal (New York: Simon and
Schuster, 1988), 203. Originally published as *Sommersi e i salvati,* 1986.

30. Jonathan Boyarin posits that our reified notions of objective and separate space and time
are "peculiarly linked to the modern identification of a nation with a sharply bounded, continuously
occupied space controlled by a single sovereign state, comprising a set of autonomous yet essentially identical individuals." To comprehend memory as embodied enables us to rethink concepts
of space, time, and the politics of memory, Boyarin claims: First, to focus on embodied memories
reveals "some of the hidden ways in which state ideologies appeal to organic experience and commonsense dimensionality to legitimize themselves," dictating "both the contents of appropriate 'memory' and the proper spatial borders of the collective." Second, to focus on embodied memories reminds
us that "our articulations of 'space' and 'time' are rooted in an organic world" in which the dimensions of space and time are not separated a priori (Boyarin, "Space, Time, and the Politics of Memory," in *Remapping Memory: The Politics of TimeSpace,* ed. Jonathan Boyarin [Minneapolis: University
of Minnesota Press, 1994], 2, 25–26).

31. Such unassimilability defines both the traumatic event and the Real. Jacques Lacan defines
the Real as both the "impenetrable kernel resisting symbolization *and* a pure chimerical entity which
has in itself no ontological consistency." The traumatic event is a "point of failure of symbolization,"
a ghost-effect that, like the Real, persists only as "failed, missed, in a shadow," dissolving itself at
the moment one tries to grasp it in its positive nature (Slavoj Žižek, *The Sublime Object of Ideology* [London: Verso, 1989], 169).

32. Laub and Allard, "History, Memory, and Truth," 801. See also Cathy Caruth, *Unclaimed Experience: Trauma, Narrative, and History* (Baltimore: Johns Hopkins University Press, 1996).

33. According to Lacan, the Real is the basis of the process of symbolization, both preceding
the symbolic order and "subsequently structured by it when it gets caught in its network." Lacan
comprehends symbolization as a process that empties "the fullness of the Real of the living body."
But the Real is "at the same time the product, remainder, leftover, scraps of this process of symbolization, the remnants, the excess which escapes symbolization and is as such produced by the
symbolization itself." Thus the Real, conceived as a starting point, as a basis, is "a positive fullness
without lack"; in contrast, the Real, conceived as "a product, a leftover of symbolization," is "the

void, the emptiness created, encircled by the symbolic structure" (Žižek, *The Sublime Object of Ideology,* 169–170).

34. Eric Santner contrasts the use of narrative as fetish with what Freud called *Trauerarbeit,* the "work of mourning": "Both narrative fetishism and mourning are responses to loss, to a past that refuses to go away due to its traumatic impact. The work of mourning is a process of elaborating and integrating the reality of loss or traumatic shock by remembering and repeating it in symbolically and dialogically mediated doses; it is a process of translating, troping, and figuring loss. . . . Narrative fetishism, by contrast, is the way an inability or refusal to mourn emplots traumatic events; it is a strategy of undoing, in fantasy, the need for mourning by simulating a condition of intactness, typically by situating the site and origin of loss elsewhere. Narrative fetishism releases one from the burden of having to reconstitute one's self-identity under 'posttraumatic' conditions; in narrative fetishism, the 'post' is indefinitely postponed" ("History beyond the Pleasure Principle: Some Thoughts on the Representation of Trauma," in *Probing the Limits of Representation: Nazism and the "Final Solution,"* ed. Saul Friedländer [Cambridge, Mass.: Harvard University Press, 1992], 144). See also Eric L. Santner, *Stranded Objects: Mourning, Memory, and Film in Postwar Germany* (Ithaca: Cornell University Press, 1990), and Sigmund Freud, "Mourning and Melancholia," 1915, 1917, in *The Standard Edition of the Complete Psychological Works of Sigmund Freud,* trans. and ed. James Strachey, vol. 14 (1914–1916) (London: Hogarth, 1957), 239–258.

35. Sigmund Freud, *Beyond the Pleasure Principle,* 1920, in *The Standard Edition of the Complete Psychological Works of Sigmund Freud,* trans. and ed. James Strachey, vol. 18 (1920–1922) (London: Hogarth, 1955), 20.

36. Zelizer, *Remembering to Forget,* 164.

37. Dominick LaCapra, *Representing the Holocaust: History, Theory, Trauma* (Ithaca: Cornell University Press, 1994), 201.

38. Edward T. Linenthal, *Preserving Memory: The Struggle to Create America's Holocaust Museum* (New York: Viking Penguin, 1995), 162.

39. Zelizer, *Remembering to Forget* 171; Gertrud Koch, "The Angel of Forgetfulness and the Black Box of Facticity: Trauma and Memory in Claude Lanzmann's Film *Shoah,*" *History and Memory* 3, 1 (spring 1991): 123. On postmodern culture as a memorial culture, see Pierre Nora et al., *Realms of Memory: Rethinking the French Past,* ed. Lawrence D. Kritzman, trans. Arthur Goldhammer, 3 vols. (New York: Columbia University Press, 1996–1998) and Andreas Huyssen, "Monument and Memory in a Postmodern Age," in *The Art of Memory: Holocaust Memorials in History,* ed. James E. Young (New York and Munich: Prestel-Verlag, 1994), 9–17.

40. Zelizer, *Remembering to Forget,* 160.

41. Salman Rushdie, *Imaginary Homelands: Essays and Criticism, 1981–1991* (London: Granta, 1992), 12.

42. Andrea Liss, *Trespassing through Shadows: Memory, Photography, and the Holocaust,* Visible Evidence Series, vol. 3 (Minneapolis: University of Minnesota Press, 1998), 69. The first quotation is from an interview Liss conducted on August 22, 1990, with Martin Smith, independent documentary film maker and the former director of the permanent exhibition program of the United States Holocaust Memorial Museum, Washington, D.C.

43. Sidra DeKoven Ezrahi, "Conversation in the Cemetery: Dan Pagis and the Prosaics of Memory," in *Holocaust Remembrance: The Shapes of Memory,* ed. Geoffrey H. Hartman (Oxford: Blackwell, 1994), 122.

44. Liss, *Trespassing through Shadows,* 70.

45. Linenthal, *Preserving Memory,* 145.

46. Liss, *Trespassing through Shadows,* 71.

47. Jacques Derrida, *The Truth in Painting,* trans. Geoff Bennington and Ian McLeod (Chicago: University of Chicago Press, 1987), 281.

48. "Once we knew that Majdanek had hundreds of thousands of shoes, we could ask for four thousand," Michael Berenbaum recalls of the museum's negotiations with camps in Poland (quoted in Linenthal, *Preserving Memory,* 147). Linenthal notes, "The museum made a point of not buying artifacts, partly in fear of creating what Martin Smith characterized as an 'obscene market'" (*Preserving Memory,* 152).

49. Theodor W. Adorno, *Noten zur Literatur,* vol. 3 (Frankfurt am Main: Suhrkamp Verlag, 1965), 125–127.

50. Linenthal, *Preserving Memory,* 154.

51. Liss, *Trespassing through Shadows,* 78.

52. Linenthal, *Preserving Memory,* 162, 163–164. The claim to authenticity at the memorial camps is compellingly made by the artifacts themselves: "the icons of destruction seem to appropriate the very authority of original events themselves":

> Guard towers, barbed wire, barracks and crematoria—abstracted elsewhere, even mythologized—here stand palpably intact. Nothing but airy time seems to mediate between the visitor and past realities, which are not merely *re*-presented by these artifacts but present in them. As literal fragments and remnants of events, these artifacts of catastrophe collapse the distinction between themselves and what they evoke. Claiming the authority of *un*reconstructed realities, the memorial camps invite us not only to mistake their reality for the actual death-camps' reality but also to confuse an implicit, monumentalized vision for unmediated history. (James E. Young, *Writing and Rewriting the Holocaust: Narrative and the Consequences of Interpretation* [Bloomington: Indiana University Press, 1988], 174–175)

However, the artifacts on site are not necessarily "at home"; shoes and other artifacts on display at Auschwitz I, for example, were imported from Birkenau (Auschwitz II), the killing center of the massive Auschwitz complex. The site of Auschwitz I itself is changed from the camp the Soviets liberated in 1945, reconstructed to its state after the initial German 1940–42 program to transform the Polish military barracks into a concentration camp. The standard guided tour of the memorial site does not include Birkenau, the principal site of the Judaeocide. Very few Jews deported to Auschwitz-Birkenau ever saw the infamous steel gate inscribed *Arbeit Macht Frei;* most deportees were marched or transported directly to their deaths at Birkenau. "Yet our memory," Dwork and Jan van Pelt write, "clings to the inscription above the gate as the modern version of Dante's *Lasciate ogni Speranza* ('Abandon all hope') at the entrance of his Inferno" (Debórah Dwork and Robert Jan van Pelt, "Reclaiming Auschwitz," in *Holocaust Remembrance,* ed. Hartman, 237); see also Debórah Dwork and Robert Jan van Pelt, *Auschwitz: 1270 to the Present* (New York: Norton, 1996).

53. Liss, *Trespassing through Shadows,* 79–80.

54. See Nora et al., *Realms of Memory;* and James E. Young, *The Texture of Memory: Holocaust Memorials and Meaning* (New Haven: Yale University Press, 1993).

55. Liss, *Trespassing through Shadows,* 79.

56. LaCapra, *Representing the Holocaust,* 104–105.

57. Žižek, *The Sublime Object of Ideology,* 49.

58. Jacques Derrida, "Passages—from Traumatism to Promise," in his *Points . . . : Interviews, 1974–1994,* ed. Elisabeth Weber, trans. Peggy Kamuf et al. (Stanford: Stanford University Press, 1995), 389, 391.

59. Jacques Derrida, *Of Spirit: Heidegger and the Question,* trans. Geoffrey Bennington and Rachel Bowlby (Chicago: University of Chicago Press, 1989) and Geoffrey H. Hartman, *The Fateful Question of Culture* (New York: Columbia University Press, 1997), 119.

60. Walter Benjamin, "Theses on the Philosophy of History," thesis 9, in his *Illuminations,* ed. Hannah Arendt, trans. Harry Zohn (New York: Schocken, 1969), 257–258. Benjamin critiques teleological interpretations of history: "This storm is what we call progress."

61. Testimony of Samuel Bak, tape HVT-618, Fortunoff Video Archive for Holocaust Testimonies, Yale University; cited in Lawrence L. Langer, "Essay," in Samuel Bak, *Landscapes of Jewish Experience: Paintings of Samuel Bak* (Boston: Pucker Gallery in association with Brandeis University; Hanover: University Press of New England, 1997), 2–3; and Lawrence L. Langer, *Preempting the Holocaust* (New Haven: Yale University Press, 1998), 81.

62. Langer, "Essay," in Bak, *Landscapes of Jewish Experience,* 21; and Langer, *Preempting the Holocaust,* 111. In its emphasis on interior visualization of memory, the expression Bak gives his self-portrait echoes that of a self-portrait painted in 1946, *Self-Portrait at the Age of Thirteen.* This work, painted when Bak was still in a displaced persons' camp, depicts only the head of the child surrounded by a wash of blue-and-black paint: "The boy-artist gazes wide-eyed in horror at the spectator, still seeing before him the hell he had witnessed" (Amishai-Maisels, *Depiction and Interpretation,* 5; color plate 1). Amishai-Maisels notes that a photograph of Bak as a boy before he entered the concentration camp is printed in Abraham Sutzkever's *Vilner Geta* (Paris: Farlag Ikuf, 1946), opposite page 132. Photographs of Bak from the displaced persons camp in Germany are printed in Dan Omer, "Ani Holekh u'Mitkaleph Yoter v'Yoter," *Prosa* 40–41 (July–August 1980): 59, 61. These photographs of the child before and after his experience of concentration camps clarify how the camps' horror effects a "hell in our memory." And as if to emphasize that hell in his own memory, his 1949 *Children* includes his self-portrait with the group of naked, skeletal children who appear doomed to untimely deaths. And, although Bak himself did not meet that doom, all the members of his family did, except his mother: on the day of their liberation, his mother and he walked through the smoke-filled streets of Vilna, "aware that we were among those fortunate few who had survived. I knew that my father had been shot in the camp from which my mother had managed to rescue me and escape herself. Later we learned that of the entire family, we were the only survivors" (Bak, "Notes from an Artist's Autobiography," *Israel Magazine,* 1974, 21, quoted in Amishai-Maisels, *Depiction and Interpretation,* 105; figure 147).

63. Langer, *Preempting the Holocaust,* 110.

64. Images of this child from the Warsaw ghetto occur in a series of four oils on linen that Bak painted in 1995: *Study I* depicts the face of the child in the window of a derelict dutch door. Spectral images of his upraised hands are imprinted on torn paper or canvas collages tacked onto the wood openings of the window. A nail pierces the palm of each hand. *Study B* also recasts details of Christ's crucifixion in its depiction of the child, "his palms nailed in a posture of permanent surrender to the will of God." *Study C* combines images of the child's face with broken wood cutouts of a faceless silhouette, the one in the foreground, riddled with bullet holes, in the striped uniform of the camp inmates. (Renato Guttuso also paints a faceless image of this Warsaw ghetto child, as well as echoes of the horse in Picasso's 1937 *Guernica,* in *The Triumph of War,* 1966.) *Study A* places a broken wood-and-stone cutout of the child against an intact but filthy brick wall. The palm of an upraised hand has a nail driven through it; the other palm is broken at the point the nail would have entered. The wood-and-stone clothing of the child open to reveal a self-portrait of the artist as a child. Echoing the stone arch framing that self-portrait is a broken arch, imprinted with two raised hands mirroring the Warsaw ghetto child's hands. Bak and his mother hid in a Benedictine convent twice during the Shoah, sheltered by Sister Maria Mikulska. The Catholic iconography of the dying Jesus, seen in the convent, was part of his early awakening to the power of art: "I was often startled by a life-size polychrome sculpture of a Jesus who had been tied to a pillar and was bleeding from all his wounds. I was seeing him in the corridor whenever I left our room. At my first encounter with this Jesus, I was so moved by his plight, that I almost threw up. This is how I learned something about art and emotions. I was asked by the nuns to express some of my emotions with crayons and watercolors on sheets of paper which they supplied. I painted for them scenes from the Bible and many angels. I was hardly seven years old and I developed an obsessive need to produce art. This obsession has stuck with me till this very day" (Patrick O'Donnell, introduction to Samuel Bak, *Angels from Elsewhere: The Paintings of Samuel Bak,* catalog from Lamont Gallery [Boston: Pucker Gallery, 1997], 6; *Study I* and *Study C,* 7; *Study A,* 18).

65. Langer, "Essay," in Bak, *Landscapes of Jewish Experience,* 22; and Langer, *Preempting the Holocaust,* 111–112.

66. Langer, "Essay," in Bak, *Landscapes of Jewish Experience,* 24; and Langer, *Preempting the Holocaust,* 115–116.

67. As in *Self Portrait* and *Elegy III,* a figure, like a ghost image, is painted on a wood easel in Bak's 1987 oil on linen, *Angels and Their Guardians.* A soldier with wood or metal wings stands next to a painting on wood of an exhausted soldier; and an exhausted man, wearing only one boot, sits before a fainter painting on canvas, of a winged soldier, tacked to a wood easel. This painting is cropped below the knee; in front of the easel are two unlaced boots (Bak, *Angels from Elsewhere,* 1997, 5).

68. Nelly Sachs, *Fahrt ins Staublose: Die Gedichte der Nelly Sachs* (Frankfurt: Suhrkamp, 1971), 152; translated and quoted in Langer, *Preempting the Holocaust,* 87.

69. Chaim A. Kaplan, *The Warsaw Diary of Chaim A. Kaplan* (New York: Collier, 1973), 30.

70. Forché, *Angel of History,* 69.

Red Shoes and Bloody Stumps

ERIN MACKIE

WITH THE FETISH

Shoes can tell us where a person has been and where she wants to go. Worn and tattered, shoes, like faces, are drawn into signatures, inscribed through time and experience with identity. New, sumptuous, and smart, shoes tell the story of desires, of aspirations written, not only on the heart and soul but, just as intimately, on the body. Shoes tell us the stories of who people are and who they would be. So in his tale "The Red Shoes," Hans Christian Andersen narrates the story of Karen, an orphaned pauper girl, as a progress through a series of red shoes. (This tale is reprinted in the appendix.) Karen begins life in wooden clogs stained with the blood of her chafed ankles; then she is given a pair of ragtag red shoes she wears at her mother's funeral; next, she acquires a pair of red moroccan dancing slippers; finally, she ends her life an amputee, her blood-red stumps fitted into a pair of prosthetic wooden feet fashioned for her by the state executioner.

The story told by Karen's successive pairs of red shoes hinges on inequities, ambitions, and charmed transfigurations rooted in class status. Karen aspires to transcend not merely the beggar status into which she is born, but also the genteel bourgeois status to which she is subjected by the old woman who adopts her. Yet while they speak of economic and material conditions, Karen's red shoes are charged, first by her

233

own prayers for transfiguration and then by the curses of an old soldier-sorcerer, with all the magical potency of the fetish charm. And while the tale chastises Karen's fetishization of the red shoes, it does so, as I will show, only through a kind of magical counterfetishization; the censure of Karen's fetishism itself works through fetish super-naturalism. Fixated on and in her red shoes, Karen seeks to fix the class inequities that bind her. Countering this aspiration by cursing her red shoes, the soldier-sorcerer (working with religion and the state) in turn wants to fix Karen's vain ambitions and reduce her to social conformity.

The use of magic to redress social wrongs and this dynamic contest of charm pitted against charm have analogues in actual fetish practices such as that in Haitian vodun, which calls such charms *wanga*. *Wanga* work not in some realm of spirit removed from history and the material world, but rather as supercharged interventions aimed at altering socioeconomic and political conditions. Here the logic involves a kind of homeopathic repetition that has an analogy in the way the successive pairs of red shoes in Andersen's story repeat, in order to correct, the (previous) condition they mark. As one vodun priest, Papa Mondy, puts it: "*Mo geri mo,* the dead cure death."[1] "The Red Shoes" opens with two deaths in quick succession: Karen's own social death as a pauper and then the death of her mother, which, leaving Karen an orphan, deepens the poverty of her social status. Each death is marked by red shoes that then reappear and repeat as talismans of death set against death.

"The Red Shoes" focuses on the simultaneously social and magical content of shoes. It establishes circuits of signification among originating trauma, desire (especially as aspiration), and fetishism, specifically where this fetish involves shoes and feet, not on the sexual but rather on the social and sacral functions of the fetish. In Andersen's story shoes operate primarily as fetishes of the sort we recognize as magical-religious rather than psychoanalytic-sexual.

The psychosexual articulation of fetishism is but one strand in a thick knot of fetish discourse. The logic of psychic wounds extends far beyond specifically psycho*sexual* processes to include sociohistorical traumas whose character and content would be occluded by being reduced to sexual fetishism. Karl Marx's analysis of the commodity fetish is a widely available discourse of nonsexual fetishization which, with its analysis of illusory value, is integral to the critical discourse of fetishism. But following the lead of anthropologist and cultural critic Michael Taussig, I want to analyze fetishism at work in "The Red Shoes" within a positive rather than negative register of value, one that affirms fetish work rather than disowns it. In his essay "*Maleficium*: State Fetishism," Taussig exhorts: "The task is neither to resist nor to admonish the fetish quality of modern culture but rather to acknowledge, even submit to, its fetish powers and attempt to chan-

nel them in revolutionary directions. Get with it! Get in touch with the fetish! This exhor-
tation points the way to an aptly critical, aptly synergistic, sociology of modernity."[2] In
relation to both psychoanalytic and Marxian notions, I believe that Taussig's injunction
to "get with the fetish" develops this affirmative rather than negative analysis of the fetish
by going beyond both the perimeters of their objects (i.e., the sexual and the commodity
fetishes) and those of their exclusively critical perspectives. Such an affirmative analysis gains critical power insofar as it admits the phenomenal validity, which is not the
ideological innocence, of a wide range of fetish practices. Rather than using the discourse of fetishism solely to expose "false" attributions of value, this stance acknowledges the nature and power of fetish, taking respectful recourse to what Marx described
as "the mist-enveloped regions of the religious world."[3]

Of course, Marx resorts to these regions in a spirit not of respectful acknowledgment
but of ironic dismissal, which he then aims against commodity fetishism. Marx's point
is to realize the true nature of value as human labor. The discourse of commodity fetishism
joins a long line of criticism aimed at the exposure of alleged misapprehensions of value,
initially the mistaken value West African peoples, bedeviled by a deficit of secular rationality, invested in ritual objects. In the arenas of economic, sociological, anthropological, and psychological thought, the discourse of fetishism has uniformly focused on the
critical identification of (allegedly) mistaken assignation of value.[4]

Such critical discourses are positivist insofar as they claim for themselves access
to values that, in contrast to those produced through fetishism, are fixed, stable, and
appropriately assigned. This kind of criticism works morally in Andersen's tale to mark
the red shoes as fetishes invested with Karen's overestimation of personal distinction
(as vanity) and social exaltation (as pride). The tale's lesson is not, therefore, "with" but
against the fetish.

But really getting with the fetish involves not the positivist assignation of
value—critical, social, and political—to concepts outside the fetish's logic, but the
recognition of the critical, even revolutionary, powers of the fetish itself. Indeed, one
way to talk about positivism lies in the identification of those notions it fixes against
the (false) fetishized values it critiques. Such notions (labor value, the phallus), insofar as they possess the magical potency of determinants of value, become fetishes in
their own right. Fetish is pitted against fetish in an interdependent logic where each
is "contaminated" with the talismanic trace of the other it would displace. In Andersen's tale the red shoes become fetishes of Karen's misplaced values, the shoes operating as a counterfetish to reveal and transgress what, from the perspective of an
underclass, beautiful, and ambitious young girl, is the bad juju of a socioreligious system fixed against her.

VOODOO CHILD

The fetish marks an originary event, a foundational moment in the formation of consciousness.[5] The event from which it follows and which it fixes brings together previously disparate, heterogeneous elements into a novel identity. Insofar as this novelty originates and defines the very horizon of identity and consciousness, it produces the sense of the fetish's self-evident value and its autonomous powers. The dynamic of the fetish "is precisely the power to repeat its originating act."[6] Since (exact) repetition is, strictly speaking, impossible, the act is repeated in a series of returns that fuels the machine of difference. So Andersen's tale moves through a succession of contiguous and mirroring, transformed and transformative sets of "red shoes": the bloody wooden clogs; the first scrappy red shoes pieced together for Karen by the widow; the second pair of red shoes, store-bought and fancy; and, at last, Karen's bloody, amputated stumps fitted into prosthetic wooden feet. The logic of repetition produces difference at an accelerating rate that finally hurls Karen toward amputation and heaven.

"The Red Shoes" opens: "Once, there was a little girl who was pretty and delicate but very poor. In the summer she had to go barefoot and in the winter she had to wear wooden shoes that rubbed her poor little ankles and made them red and sore." The initial trauma here is poverty at odds with both Karen's beauty and her delicacy, marred and violated as they are by the ugly, chafing wooden clogs. From the start and throughout the tale, this discrepancy is marked by her feet and shoes. In the red shoes she subsequently acquires, Karen's bloody clogs find a fetish that commemorates and redresses the inequities and social mortifications lived by the little girl. Lovely like Karen and red like her wounded ankles, the shoes embody her identity and so link its heterogeneous elements: her beauty and delicacy, on the one hand, and, on the other, her agonizing poverty. They mark, even as they are called upon to remedy, the discrepancy between her merit and her affliction. Karen's origins and identity lie in this disparity, and her aspirations take flight in her drive to amend it.

Giving the "little girl" a proper name with her first pair of red shoes, the narrative seals the bond between Karen's identity and her shoes. An old widow gathers scraps and makes some shoes: "They were meant for the poor little girl, whose name was Karen. Now on that very day that her mother was to be buried, Karen was given the red shoes." The street urchin in clogs is anonymous; the girl in red shoes is Karen. And the same two sentences that give her a name and shoes take away her mother. So just as Karen's bloody clogs mark a kind of social death, evidenced by her anonymity, her first pair of red shoes commemorate the death of her mother. Karen receives her shoes and her name, her identity, even as that identity is thrown open to displacement by its unmooring from any familial tie. The fetish fixes traumas of vulnerability and abandonment, first figured as being no one and next as having no one. The crippling disparity between merit and affliction is repeated in the disjunction of mother and child.

For the death of her mother restates in an intimate register the more general social matrix from which Karen emerges. As a figure for Karen's origins, everything about this ghostly mother signals want, abandonment, and absence. Her existence acknowledged only by the mention of her death that summons her as an already terminated presence, the mother appears twice, first as the shrouded contents of "the pauper's coffin," and then of the "pauper's grave" where Karen, driven by the hectic red shoes, wishes in vain to rest. Anonymous, invisible, inanimate, immured, Karen's mother figures the social death that begets and awaits Karen.

Her charm against this death is her red shoes. In ways that recall the wooden clogs and, at the same time, step away from them toward the next, fancier pair of red shoes, the composition of these first makeshift red shoes invokes and redresses the painful scarcity of Karen's origins. And the construction of these ragtag shoes literalizes the structure of the fetish which "is always a composite fabrication":[7] "In the same village there lived an old widow whose husband had been a shoemaker; and she sat sewing a pair of shoes from scraps of red material. She did her very best, but the shoes looked a bit clumsy, though they were sewn with kindness. They were meant for the poor little girl, whose name was Karen." The widowhood of the old woman recalls Karen's orphanage; her care for the poor little girl foreshadows the concern of another, much better off, old lady who subsequently appears on the scene to adopt Karen. Replacing the clogs, the widow's red shoes remedy Karen's wounded feet; transferring the bloodred from flesh to fetish, they invoke the trauma in order to heal it: *mo geri mo,* the dead cure death.

With the shoes the girl performs her first social act, an impropriety that establishes the transgressive trajectory of her red shoes: "Now on that very day that her mother was to be buried. Karen was given the red shoes. Though they weren't the proper color for mourning, she had no others, so she put them on. Raggedly dressed, barelegged, with red shoes on her feet, she walked behind the pauper's coffin." Karen, still innocent of their offense, wears the red shoes, so the narrator claims, because she "had no others." But Karen's view of her red shoes differs from that of the narration and of the old lady who soon adopts her. Certainly Karen has no others, but she experiences her new red shoes, "sewn with kindness," as plenitude (of care and comfort), rather than as lack (of appropriate black shoes). Far from feeling awkwardly improper in them, Karen senses that they invest her with irresistible charisma. Understanding her red shoes as talismans against poverty and loss, she "thought it was because of her new red shoes that the old lady had taken a fancy to her."

But she thought wrong. The old lady "declared that the shoes looked frightful and had them thrown into the stove and burned." Her response extends the notion that the shoes are improper into a suggestion that they are noxious and unclean; not only are they inappropriate for mourning, but they are in themselves frightful and even, like a dead body, contaminating. The red shoes present evidence of social injustice and moral inequity—Karen didn't do anything to "deserve" her poverty or her mother's death—beyond the reach of charity. Such signs of realities that remain resistantly immune to the rituals of charity, hygiene, and conformity sit uneasily with a benevolence inseparable from its myopic righteousness. The narrowness of vision I associate here with the old lady's charity is uncannily figured in her own literal near-blindness. Karen's origins, in her mother's body and in her red and tattered feet, must be obliterated before she can be affixed to the identity the old lady offers. The burning of the red shoes, then, initiates the old lady's program of social and moral hygiene and, as soon becomes apparent when the shoes jump right back into the tale, conjures the presences of the very trauma, wounds, and origins it would annihilate.

A dutiful parishioner, the old lady consults the minister about her adoption of Karen: "she went at once to the minister and spoke to him. 'Let me have that little girl, and I shall be good to her and bring her up'"—that is, she will transform her into a modest, grateful, obedient, and pious young lady. However, as we have seen at her mother's funeral, Karen's first, and all her subsequent, brushes with religion define her transgressive independence from them, rather than their hold on her. Karen is not, at this point, the minister's to give.

At her confirmation, the struggle between Karen's devotion to the red shoes and the pressure to conform to social and religious propriety comes sharply to the fore and escalates into a contest for Karen's very self. To draw out a pun inherent in the terms of the tale, this contest for Karen's soul is waged through her soles, through her dancing feet in their red shoes, which open paths to transformative mobility. But this mobility is appropriated by the agents of socioreligious control and, through a course of sorcery, is turned against Karen's desires onto a path that leads, more through exhaustion than abnegation, to the annihilation of mobility and its motive desires.

The red shoes rise phoenixlike from the ashes of the old lady's stove, reappearing in the next paragraph on a princess who passes through the village wearing "no crown on her head" but "a very pretty white dress and the loveliest red shoes, made from morocco." The image of the princess retrospectively reconfirms Karen's sense of the sovereign value of red shoes, any red shoes, all red shoes. Although she recognizes that the princess's shoes are "much prettier than the ones the old shoemaker's widow had made for Karen . . . [e]ven they had been red shoes, and to Karen nothing else in the world was so desirable." In a transfer that evokes this sovereign value of red shoes, the metonymic token of nobility (the crown) has passed from the princess's head to foot, where the red shoes connect her to Karen. Head and foot, crown and slipper, the princess and Karen, high and low meet as they pass through an exchange with one another. This image of the princess fixes the red shoes to a fantasy of social transcendence that would lead Karen from low to high, from rags to riches, from a little pauper in blood-stained clogs to a princess in red moroccan slippers. Generated by the red shoes, the desires this fantasy addresses are those structured by the originary discrepancy between Karen's merit and her affliction. And the beautiful princess not only has her red shoes but also has her real mother. Little wonder that "nothing else in the world was so desirable" as red shoes. Elevating Karen from pauper to princess, the red shoes, then, commemorate in order to fully redress her originating trauma: *mo geri mo,* the dead cure death.

The old lady's project, in direct opposition to Karen's fantasy, seeks to obliterate rather than commemorate Karen's origins. Two visions for Karen's future—as the princess in Karen's dreams or as the decent, ordinary girl in the old lady's scheme—are at this point established and set into competition when Karen arrives at her confirmation dressed just like the princess in a white dress and red shoes. Appearing not as the humble charity orphan but as the aspiring princess, Karen pays no attention to the service: "When the old bishop laid his hands on her head and spoke of the solemn promise she was about to make—of her covenant with God to be a good Christian—her mind was not on his words. The ritual music was played on the organ; the old cantor sang, and the sweet voices of the children could be heard, but Karen was thinking of her red shoes." The rituals of Christianity do not take. Fixed on the red shoes, Karen remains outside the charmed circle chanted around the communicants by the cantor. The shoes are the fetish posed against the fetishes of the church. At this liminal moment, the red shoes block Karen's ritualized assimilation into the identity proposed by the old lady and by conventional society at large. Communing with the red shoes, Karen is confirmed not in her identity as a Christian and congregation member, but simultaneously in that of her earlier self, the bloody-footed pauper girl, and that of the princess. For to Karen, it is in the image of the princess, not in the image of Christ, that all painful inequities and all traumatic loss are redeemed. At this moment, Karen's red shoes are at once the "frightful" markers of where she has been and the utopian talismans of where she would go. Her devotion to traversing the distance between these two points, and the tale's insistence not simply on the impossibility of this aspiration but on its sinfulness, are the crux of the rest of the story.

When Karen goes to take communion the Sunday following her nominal confirmation, she again wears the red shoes in defiance of the old lady's order that she wear black ones. The scandalized congregation had reported Karen's earlier transgression to the old lady, but because she cannot see she is tricked again. In church, Karen's shoes once more become the scandal of the congregation and her sole object of reflection: "When she knelt in front of the altar and the golden cup was lifted to her lips, she thought only of the red shoes and saw them reflected in the wine." The vision of her red shoes reflected in the consecrated wine effects a symbolic displacement of the blood spilled from Christ's wounds by that from Karen's own wounded feet, and so substitutes the promise of transcendence through identification with Christ's sacrifice with a different kind of fantasy involving a more worldly and social translation through the medium of the red shoes. Karen communes, then, not with the Holy Spirit but with the red shoes and so with her own origins and aspirations.

In effect Karen puts her red shoes—her own identity and ambitions—in the place of God himself, and so tempts the devil who promptly appears as an "old invalid soldier leaning on a crutch." He approaches Karen and the old lady on their way into church and begs to dust off their feet. Seeing Karen's shoes, he proclaims, "What pretty little dancing shoes!" Tapping them on the soles, he addresses the shoes: "Remember to stay on her feet for the dance." After the service, this old soldier reappears and repeats his address to the shoes: "Look at those pretty dancing shoes." The soldier's words are a sorcerer's charm, a *maleficium*. They infuse the shoes with a spirit of perverse and hectic motion that cancels Karen's agency: "His words made her take a few dancing steps. Once she had begun, her feet would not stop. It was as if the shoes had taken command of them. She danced around the corner of the church; her will was not her own."

The first red shoes had been fashioned to heal Karen's ankles rubbed raw from the wooden clogs. The second pair are chosen by Karen as instruments of social aspiration that would redress her social mortification; hexed by the soldier-sorcerer, they are magically refashioned as a cure for Karen's vain and proud ambition—her spiritual maladies. Charged with an ungovernable will to dance, the shoes make Karen the victim of her own aspirations for social mobility.

Before the soldier-sorcerer hexes them, the red shoes are Karen's identity and her desire. They possess a sovereign and unique value ("nothing else in the world was so desirable") and a talismanic power forceful enough to overcome poverty ("Karen thought it was because of her new red shoes that the old lady had taken a fancy to her") and override the claims imposed by church and society ("When . . . the golden cup was lifted to her lips, she thought only of the red shoes and saw them reflected in the wine"). Karen's will is, up to this point, fully identified with them; their value and powers mirror and protect her own.

The obvious problem is that the sovereignty of the red shoes challenges and displaces that of church and state. The soldier-sorcerer with his devilish red beard and his powerful magic steps in to drive Karen into an acceptance of the values, conventions, and identifications she has resisted with her red shoes. The religious-social system, having failed to win her soul through regular means, employs, in the person of this crippled soldier, the extraordinary and profane powers of sorcery to co-opt and redirect the powers of the fetish that resists it.

From this point, then, Karen becomes the old soldier's zombie. Her body labors not under the direction of her own agency but under that of the hexed shoes: "She danced! But when she wanted to dance to the left, the shoes danced to the right; and when she wanted to dance up the ballroom floor, the shoes danced right down the stairs and out into the street." Karen becomes as terrified by her red dancing shoes as the old lady was of those first red shoes. Their dance is "horrible and frightening"; far from being the most desirable thing in the world, the shoes are now pure torment. The extravagance of Karen's ambition is mocked in the maniacal capers of the shoes, which finally propel her toward debility and death.

Driven to exhaustion and despair, Karen seeks rest in the church, but her way is blocked by an angel who echoes the soldier's curse and confirms its ultimate source: "You shall dance . . . dance in your red shoes until you become pale and thin. Dance till the skin on your face turns yellow and clings to your bones as if you were a skeleton." Karen is danced to the brink of death. She dances day and night, night and day, and passing the funeral of the old lady who had cared for her, realizes her fate: "Now she felt that she was forsaken by all of mankind and cursed by God's angel."

The curse transforms Karen into a cripple like the old soldier-sorcerer. Surrendering to its power, Karen approaches the executioner and, echoing the old soldier's request to dust off her feet, begs him to cut them off. There is no other way to remove the furiously dancing shoes; the hex has recast Karen's psychosocial identification with her red shoes into a corporeal attachment to them. The executioner, like the soldier-sorcerer, is an operative of the church and state, and takes over when the kinder, gentler forms of domination fail. With her command "cut off my feet," Karen's will is cut down to a size that fits into the straitjacket of socioreligious conformity. Confessing her sins and losing her feet, at a single stroke Karen submits to the abbreviation of her will and her stature. Karen, her bloody stumps fitted into a pair of prosthetic wooden feet carved by the executioner, is returned to her origins in bloody ankles and wooden clogs with a difference that is at once an amplification of agony and a diminution of substance. The amputation of her feet is but a brutal literalization and repetition of earlier injunctions that Karen should take off her red shoes. The slash of the executioner's ax retrospectively marks the brutality of the previous mandates to conformity. Had Karen taken off her red shoes from the beginning, the deformation of her self and her desire would be no less certain, if perhaps less physically manifest, than it is as she hobbles on her bloody red stumps.

One thing, then, that this amputation suggests is the mutilation of the subject that may attend her suturing into the social group. The loss of her feet produces another trauma that initiates just such an assimilation. Karen reflects, "'Now I have suffered enough because of those red shoes,'" and resolves, "'I shall go to church now and be among the other people.'" This amputation does not so much dispel the red shoes as, once more, replicate and proliferate them.

At the close of the tale there are two sets of red shoes that appear simultaneously and confront one another: the bloody stumps in their prosthetic feet and the red shoes on the severed feet. These red shoes, severed from Karen's ankles, first dance away "into the dark forest" but then reappear to block Karen's entrance to the church as she hobbles up to the gate on her stumps and crutches: "when she walked up to the door of the church, the red shoes danced in front of her, and in horror she fled." Earlier in the story, the red shoes appear sequentially, one set replacing and recalling the last. Here this simultaneous appearance of the two sets of red shoes reinforces the sense that this tale is about competing fetishes, about a struggle over the determinates of origin, identity, and desire.

After appropriating the red shoes and turning them against her, the church and the state replace the red shoes with their prosthetic feet, which, in their turn, operate as a fetish commemorating Karen's repentance and rebirth into the very socioreligious order she had initially resisted with her red shoes. The bloody stumps in their wooden feet mark her traumatic consciousness of guilt and subjugation. Yet, the other red shoes, infused with a spirit of autonomy and resistance which is gruesomely intensified, even as it is divorced from Karen's will, by the soldier-sorcerer's dancing curse, dance on, the perfect magical fetish with powers all their own.

Both sets of red shoes incarnate with almost hyperbolic exaction the corporeal intimacy of fetishes, which, "although cut off from the body[,] function as its controlling organs" and are used "to achieve certain tangible effects (such as healing) upon or in service of the user."[8] The amputated feet are inseparable from the red shoes that control them even after they are severed from a living body. The wooden prostheses are perhaps even more inseparable from Karen's (absent) feet, for now they *are* her feet. Whereas the first pair of red shoes effect a transfer of blood and wounds from flesh to fetish, the final pair reverses this transfer by traumatically reinstating the wounds to the flesh and, simultaneously, fixing these wounds, these bloody stumps, to its own fabrication, the wooden prosthetic feet.

In "The Red Shoes" the dynamic of power that structures the action and the conflict is, on both sides of that conflict, uniformly determined by the magical logic of the fetish with its propensity toward repetition, mirroring, and displacement, rather than resolution. Accordingly, the resolution of the tale, and the final authorization of its moral, rely quite literally on a deus ex machina in the person of the angel who comes down and transports Karen, her heart bursting with joy, into heaven. This resolution does not substantiate any claim that the angel and the powers at his disposal work outside fetish magic, for this cannot be sustained in face of the angel's and the soldier's curses, but simply asserts their domination over Karen's fetish. This mastery is realized only in heaven, where the red shoes and Karen's soul are finally put to rest: "Her soul flew on a sunbeam up to God; and up there no one asked her about the red shoes," which, we must assume, still dance on below.

THOSE BLOODY SHOES

Some of the ways that Andersen's tale speaks not merely to general struggles involving traumatic origins, identity, and aspiration, but more particularly to those that typify careers in ballet are reinforced by the 1948 film *The Red Shoes*. Directed by Michael Powell and starring dancers Leonid Massine, Moira Shearer, and Robert Helpmann, the film allegorizes Andersen's "The Red Shoes" as the story of the life of a contemporary ballerina. This seems an obvious move: the ballerina, after all, is possessed by her passion for dancing, just as Karen is possessed by the charmed red shoes. In the frame story of the film *The Red Shoes,* the aspiring ballerina is torn between submission to the will of her director, the grandly autocratic Lermontov, and to that of her composer husband. She can either marry dance or a husband (not, as Lermontov insists, both), but there is no available option of an independent, self-directed existence. Her passion for dance puts her in the hands of Lermontov; her passion for her husband puts her dance career off limits.

An elaborately cinematographic performance of the ballet *The Red Shoes* stands at the center of the film and at the apex of the ballerina's career. In one scene, the ballerina dancing the part of Karen is confronted by the sinister shoemaker (danced by Massine, the ballet's counterpart to the soldier-sorcerer in Andersen's story) who has given her the fatally potent red shoes. As she stands transfixed by the shoemaker's sinister stare, the frame of the ballet slips and the conditions of the ballerina's real life assert themselves as the image of the shoemaker fades first into Lermontov's image and then into her husband's. Here the film reveals how the dancer is controlled and driven by another's will, the red shoes the instruments of this control.

Just as Karen is driven in a dance propelled by shoes that are at once insepar-able from her body and severed from her will in ways that violate both her autonomy and her body, so the ballerina is typically viewed and used as the instrument for the execution of another's will and design: her dance teacher's, her choreographer's, her director's. In a debased sense often conveyed by comparisons to trained animals, dancers exist to do the work set to them, most often by powerful men whose control of the dancer's body inevitably involves an extension into the psyche. Joan Brady, in her autobiographical account of her dancing career, records the comments of one of Balanchine's dancers: "We're animals here, all of us—big strong, stupid, domestic animals—like dogs."[9] Throughout her narrative, Brady comments on how the aspir-ing dancers quite consciously pretend to be actually mute, brutally stupid and mind-less, in order to convey that quality of blankness, of utter absence of individual will so valued by teachers and choreographers.

Rather like Karen, worked to death under the spell of the soldier-sorcerer, ballet dancers lead a zombielike existence. They are sometimes disparaged by jazz and mod-ern dancers, who despise their "herd instinct and mentality" and their lack of "lives or well-formed personalities."[10] Noting how the movie *The Red Shoes* is administered to ballet students as "a clear warning against romantic entanglements," Suzanne Gordon writes of the conflict between dance and life: "In the world of ballet, dancers are often discouraged from engaging in any activity that might draw their attention away from dance. Romantic attachments, friends, and family indicate a diminishing ardor."[11] Classical ballet serves as the limit case against which other forms of dance discipline may prove themselves "healthy," "balanced," and even "natural."

But the same features that provoke a peculiar mixture of pity and distaste for the ballerina also generate awe and even reverence. So Agnes de Mille eulogizes Anna Pavlova in a portrait that witnesses at once the ballerina's masochistic fanaticism and her irre-sistible charisma: "Bright little bird bones, delicate bird sinews! She was all fire and steel wire. There was not an ounce of spare flesh on her skeleton, and the life force used and used her body until she died of the fever of moving, gasping for breath, much too young."[12] Pavlova killed herself by dancing through a serious illness.

This maniacal drive, ending in injury, debilitation, and even death, recalls Karen's fate. Its cultivation is the central tenet of ballet training, which was defined in the nine-teenth century. In his history of the romantic ballet, Ivor Guest describes the lives of the dancers in the Royal Company in Paris. Like Andersen's Karen, most of these dancers were extremely poor, very ambitious little girls. One, whose story Guest recounts, was worse off even than Karen: "I had neither clogs for my feet, nor a shawl for my shoulders." She describes her early training, how her feet were forced into a box to produce turnout, how she was driven at the barre through exercise after exercise:

> When this toil was over, you might think I was allowed to rest. Rest! Does a dancer ever rest? We were just poor wandering Jews at whom M. Barrez incessantly shouted, "Dance! dance!" . . . And do not imagine that such brutal fatigues only last for a short time. They must continue for ever and be continually renewed. . . . The dancer personifies the fable of Sisyphus and his rock. She is like a racehorse which sacrifices repose, weight, and freedom for the rapid victories of Chantilly and the Champ de Mars.[13]

So this *petit rat* of the Paris ballet and all succeeding generations of ballet dancers suffer much the same fate that the angel dictates to Karen: "You shall dance . . . dance in your red shoes until you become pale and thin. Dance till the skin on your face turns yellow and clings to your bones as if you were a skeleton."

After Marie Taglioni fully incorporated pointe work into female ballet technique, the dancer worked in heavily blocked shoes that allowed her to move on the tips of her toes, thereby giving her legs an elongated extension through the feet. Radically abbreviating the body's connection to earth, dance on pointe creates an impression of weightless mobility, of magical, gravity-defying levity. Historically, pointe work allowed female dancers to develop a spectacular virtuosity competitive with the athleticism of male dancers. This virtuosity, in combination with their sociosexual value (dancers were prized courtesans), elevated female dancers to a place far above their male counterparts, a place that was not successfully challenged until Vaslav Nijinsky came on the scene at the turn of the twentieth century. Student dancers are fixed on the acquisition of their toe shoes, for this initiates them into the company of real dancers. Just as with Karen and her red shoes, so with dancers and their pointe shoes: "nothing else in the world [could be] so desirable."

Joan Brady describes the scene at the school of the San Francisco ballet: "After class, blood-stained tights and blood-soaked shoes were exposed and commented on. No tears were shed, but special fortitude drew special notice; the atmosphere was offhand Spartan."[14] And de Mille recalls how she learned to bind up her toes "so that they would not bleed through the satin shoes."[15]

Pointe shoes are, then, the central fetish of ballet; they mark the traumatic origins of every dancer's entry into serious training and her identity as a dancer, an identity pursued and confirmed through a discipline that excludes other identifications. Intimately sutured to the body through a long course of wounding and scarring, the shoes function, in William Pietz's words, "as its controlling organs."[16] The pointe shoes allow

the dancer to perform the magical feats required of her. The precious torment of wearing them is sacralized by rituals through which the dancer seeks, psychologically and
physically, to fix her feet to her red shoes. The ritualistic status of pointe shoes is witnessed in the story of a fan who bought a pair of Taglioni's for three hundred rubles and,
in an act of sacral devotion, "cooked them, and had them for supper."[17] This is shoe
fetishism of an emphatically eucharistic sort, recalling the scene of displaced communion
in Andersen's story where Karen "thought only of the red shoes and saw them reflected
in the wine" of the chalice.

Pointe shoes are designed to render the foot, in all its flat, earth-bound sprawl,
irrelevant; they take a foot and, standing it up, create from its horizontal extension a per-
pendicular column, a stump. Pointe shoes, then, perform a kind of illusory amputation.
Just as at the end of Andersen's tale, Karen, her connection to her mortality severed with
the amputation of her feet, is wafted up to heaven, so the ballet dancer on her stumps
strives toward transcendence. Driven to conquer all flesh-bound limitations, the dancer
is subjected to a strained tension between overcoming the body and being overcome
by the body so harshly disciplined and denied. What the ongoing prevalence of exhaustion, injury, debilitation, and anorexia in ballet subculture emphasizes is the expense
of a transcendence of the body purchased at the price of that body. Driven beyond its
capacities, the body performs the transgression of its own limits. This seems achingly
romantic and sublime; and it is. But like Karen, who loses her feet and her will before
she is translated to heaven, the ballerina makes a heavy sacrifice of body and spirit in
the pursuit of a performance that seems to so perfectly transcend all corporeality, all
ties to gravity and time, that when achieved, no one asks her about her red shoes.

NOTES

1. Quoted by Elizabeth McAlister, "A Sorcerer's Bottle: The Visual Art of Magic in Haiti," in
Sacred Arts of Haitian Vodou, ed. Donald J. Cosentino (Los Angeles: UCLA Fowler Museum of Cultural History, 1995), 319.

2. In *Fetishism as Cultural Discourse,* ed. Emily Apter and William Pietz (Ithaca: Cornell University Press, 1993), 229.

3. Karl Marx, *Capital,* vol. 1, in *The Marx-Engles Reader,* 2nd ed., ed. Robert C. Tucker (New
York: Norton, 1978), 321.

4. Apter and Pietz, *Fetishism as Cultural Discourse,* 9.

5. Ibid., 4.

6. Ibid., 7–8.

7. Ibid., 7.

8. Ibid., 10.

9. Joan Brady, *The Unmaking of a Dancer: An Unconventional Life* (New York: Harper and Row,
1982), 173.

10. Modern dancer quoted by L. M. Vincent in *Competing with the Sylph: Dancers and the Pursuit of the Ideal Body Form* (New York: Andrews and McMeel, 1979), 5.

11. Suzanne Gordon, *Off Balance: The Real World of Ballet* (New York: McGraw-Hill, 1983), 45.

12. Agnes de Mille, *Dance to the Piper* (Boston: Little, Brown, 1952), 43.

13. Ivor Guest, *The Romantic Ballet in Paris* (Middletown, Conn.: Wesleyan University Press, 1966), 25.

14. Brady, *Unmaking of a Dancer,* 18.

15. de Mille, *Dance to the Piper,* 54.

16. Apter and Pietz, *Fetishism as Cultural Discourse,* 10.

17. Janice Barringer and Sarah Schlesinger, *The Pointe Book: Shoes, Training, and Technique* (Hightstown, N.J.: Dance Horizons, 1990), 4.

Perception

The Slip in the Ballet Slipper: Illusion and the Naked Foot

GERRI REAVES

The reason I wasn't really pestered [by your repeated question "When can I go barefoot?"] was that you had several pairs of ballet shoes. Being partly colorblind, I paid little or no attention to their color. You apparently liked to wear the shoes, so when they were no longer suitable for studio use you wore them everyday.

—James B. Reaves, e-mail to author, October 1998

I have always wanted to be barefoot. And, I have never worn a pair of shoes that I was not eager to get off my feet. My childhood favorites were ones that allowed me to feel barefoot, flexible, and free but gave me the advantage of "clinging" nonskid soles. I remember a particular pair of shoes I wore at the age of ten or eleven: black and flexible, with a sole that enabled me to successfully leap over big gaps between logs in the woods and magically cling to the bark like a high-wire artist. I was a good jumper, and even at that age, I attributed my expertise, in part, to my comfy magic shoes, which in memory resemble black ballet slippers.

My earliest memories about going barefoot are associated with autonomy and freedom. My associations with ballet slippers are the same—a sort of protected, more stylish or private nakedness of the feet. A naked foot in a ballet slipper has, for me, always signified freedom, dance, autonomy, and, eventually, sexuality. These associations lead me to wonder, how does this relationship between the dainty yet highly functional ballet slipper and the dancer's body create and articulate our ideas about naturalness? In shape, flexibility, material, and, often, color, the shoe's purpose is to disappear—to cloak and render invisible the body part it enfolds, protects, and extends. Ballet at its best deceives us. The slipper slips; it lies.

The body's integration of the slipper and the resulting unfragmented dancer's line— a sweeping *arabesque,* say, or the glorious ellipsis of an *attitude*—ironically are dependent on the shoe's invisibility, even disintegration. In fact, the dancers in many professional ballet companies apply pancake makeup to their pointe shoes, as they do to their faces, to ensure that they continue the line of the body and create the illusion that shoes are flesh. The invisible foot at the end of a ballet dancer's leg conspires in a complementary anatomical unreality—that the leg begins not at the hip socket, but originates at the solar plexus and curves lusciously to the toe and into infinite space. Thus the ballet slipper celebrates a kind of artificial barefooted state that nevertheless contradicts the very abandon and sexuality we commonly associate with bare feet.

However, contrast this enigmatic foot with the naked foot of dance genius Isadora Duncan (1878–1927), modern dance pioneer Martha Graham (1894–1991), or even the contemporary "modern" dancers, who inherited these geniuses' rejection of ballet to forge a dance that glorifies the natural, unfettered body. Today's choreographers and dancers, such as Twyla Tharp, have created a hybrid of classical ballet and the modern American dance codified by Duncan, Ruth St. Denis, Graham, Doris Humphrey, and others. Of all the arts, dance articulates a cluster of sexual and cultural paradoxes about woman. The bare feet of early-twentieth-century modern dancers represented the "New American Woman" of this century. The strong, supple naked foot signifies freedom, sexuality, and abandon, and whether bare or shod, the dancer's foot is a synecdoche for the dancer's body. However, the elegantly bound ballet foot aspiring to invisibility evokes not only barefoot abandon but, conversely, the oppression of foot binding and the enhancement of sexual pleasure through the masochism associated with professional dance training. From the foot, we imagine the dancer's body.

THE BOUND BALLET FOOT

When one looks at the x-ray images of feet in the silk embroidered Chinese lotus shoe and in the satin pointe shoe, the resemblance is extraordinary (figures 1–3). Given the similarity between the deformed bones of a Chinese bound foot and the position of the bones in the foot of a ballet dancer, it is not surprising that a near duplicate of today's ballet foot existed centuries ago in China. Foot binding was widespread in China for hundreds of years, lasted well into this century, and was eradicated only after intense government campaigning.[1] Precious Thing, a concubine of Prince Li Yu, is credited

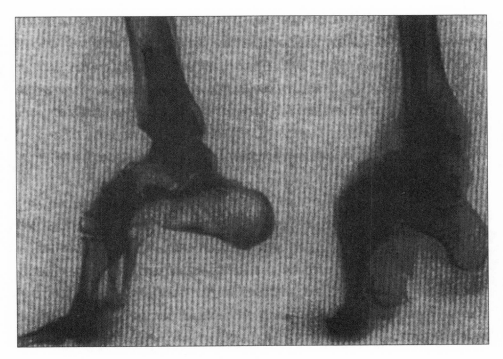

FIGURE 1 ↝ X-ray images of bound foot.

Reproduced courtesy of William A. Rossi, *Sex Life of the Foot and Shoe* (1976, Krieger Publishing, Malabar, Florida).

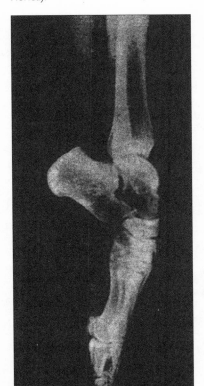

FIGURE 2 ↝ X-ray image of foot in pointe shoe.

Copyright © 1987. From Celia Sparger, *Anatomy and Ballet.* Reproduced by permission of Routledge, Inc.

FIGURE 3 ↝ This skeletal outline contrasts normal bone structure with that of the bound foot.

Reproduced courtesy of William A. Rossi, *Sex Life of the Foot and Shoe* (1976, Krieger Publishing, Malabar, Florida).

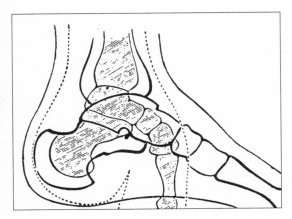

with originating the bound foot. As Beverley Jackson explains in *Splendid Slippers: A Thousand Years of an Erotic Tradition,* Precious Thing, centuries before Western ballerinas donned satin pointe shoes, "toe-danced" in "silk socks over which she wound long, narrow bands of silk to make her dancing more seductive."[2]

Even Western fetish publications often dramatize the sadomasochistic connection between foot binding—ballet style—and sexual pleasure. These connections demonstrate how the nonballet world easily mixes the ballet lexicon and the staples of fetishized fashion. For instance, a startling cover photograph for *Secret Magazine* literally equates ballet with foot binding. Black seamed stockings, more suited to a fashion model than a ballet dancer, grace the legs and feet, which do not exhibit the arch and strength of a dancer. Thick white satiny rope highlighted against black substitutes for the satin ribbons that characteristically bind a dancer's feet and ankles. The close-up floor-level camera angle from behind the insteps emphasizes the control of the photographer and viewer over the stationary bound subject; the photograph simulates a close-up facial "portrait": bound feet as dancer. The photograph also embodies the inherent contradiction between a pointe dancer's escape from gravity and the rope-bound legs. It calls attention to the model's inability to dance, to her submission to the prettily executed restriction, not to the freedom that dance signifies.

Many researchers, whether studying fetishism, fashion, or foot binding, have commented on the equation of the woman's foot with the female genitalia. William A. Rossi notes explicitly the "lotus foot" standing in for the vulva. In fact, the supremely fetishized Chinese bound foot "vied with the vagina itself as the organ of ultimate sexual pleasure."[3] The "deep cleft" created by breaking the arch and folding the four smaller toes underneath the foot created a "soft fleshy cleavage" that for the Chinese male was the "equivalent of the labia."[4] This cleavage or "crevice" could be treated as a "second vagina,"[5] or it could be used in creative masturbation scenarios.

Chinese women, primarily Han Chinese women, underwent this unspeakably brutal procedure to create the invaluable asset, the lotus foot, which would endow a woman with beauty, and therefore status and a marriage of material security. As Jackson surmises, "There is definitely a link between bound feet and sado-masochism centering around the pain the woman had to endure to achieve her tiny feet."[6]

A shoe can function androgynously as well, "as a symbolic substitute for the penis, and also for the vagina into which the phallic foot is inserted";[7] however, in dance the slipper and pointe shoe function as a second skin for the synecdoche of the foot. The concealing-revealing, intrusive-obtrusive ballet shoe is a unifier, a guarantor of coherence, and a diffuser of the threat of castration or loss of power. As C. Fred Blake speculates about foot binding and the sexuality of Chinese women, "The obtrusive and intrusive nature of feet allows them to represent the male organ. . . . Thus the obtrusive and extrusive nature of the womb and the obtrusive and intrusive nature of the feet each possess androgenic properties: Female gender therefore represents an essential androgynous ambiguity, one internal, the other external."[8] Implicit in seeing the dance slipper is seeing the foot's sexual cover or, as Mimi Pond playfully calls it, "a [totem] of Disembodied Lust."[9] The slipper-bound dancer's foot is both interior and exterior, thus creating the erotic tension associated with dance—the tension between part and whole, fragmentation and wholeness, control and freedom. Therefore, the slipper as a paradoxical signifier unifies pain, restrained beauty, and control, and it clothes in glossy satin the wounded feet that make ballet beautiful (figure 4).

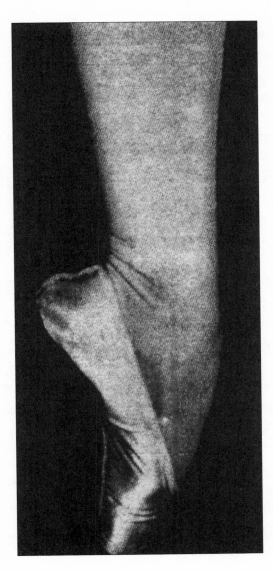

FIGURE 4

Image of foot in pointe shoe.

Copyright © 1987. From Celia Sparger, *Anatomy and Ballet.* Reproduced by permission of Routledge, Inc.

In addition to the genitalia, shoes can project other fetishized aspects of the female anatomy, for example, "the idea of cleavage or décolleteé associated with the bosom."[10] The sensitivity and vulnerability of one part of the body is easily transferred to the similarly sensitive and vulnerable part of the foot, with the appropriate part of the shoe assuming the name of the body part. In fashion, the foot becomes a "surrogate body" whose throatline, or instep, can be exposed like a woman's neckline.[11] By definition, the very word "slipper" is associated with undress, vulnerability, and sexual availability; it is a shoe that one easily slips or falls into or out of. Salvatore Ferragamo's "clear 'crystal' oval inserted into the sole" takes shoe fashion to new extremes of fetishism as it allows the wearer to flirtatiously expose the bottom of the foot by skillfully holding the foot at the right angle.[12] Mimi Pond notes the kinky thrill that "deep toe cleavage" and slingback shoes can give to both the wearer and the fetishist, for they are ways to convey a sexuality that "decent" women cannot otherwise openly express.[13]

Rossi traces even etymological links between eroticism and the foot, specifically, the "long inside arch" of a woman's foot: "Our word 'fornication' comes from the Latin *fornix,* meaning the arch of the vaulted chamber of ancient Roman brothels, or the arch of the aqueducts under which prostitutes and their clients 'fornicated.'"[14] Without the overexaggerated, signature arch of the ballet foot, ballet would not exist; without the hyperextended arch and the cleft of the "lotus"-like foot to fit and thus create the ballet slipper, the magic of the slipper would not exist. To the layperson, the exaggerated arch of the foot signifies ballet itself; the arch is the defining attribute, along with long legs, that can, by genetic default alone, assumes the layperson, make a woman a ballet dancer. In her autobiography, *Dancing on My Grave,* American ballerina Gelsey Kirkland records that some dancers go so far as to have plastic surgery to break the arch of the foot and realign the bones in a more perfect arch and pointe, a measure that parallels the tortures of foot binding. Early in her career, she noted the price that the relentless and demanding ballet technique had exacted: "Misguided and caught between excessive demands for turn-out and pointe, my feet had already begun to deform."[15]

The pointe shoe's fashion equivalents are, naturally, the bound foot and the foot in high heels. All three fulfill the criteria for a sexy shoe, the pointed phallic toe. Alison Lurie explains the popularity of high-heeled, narrow-toed shoes, which "are considered sexually attractive, partly because they make the legs look longer—an extended leg is the biological sign of sexual availability in several animal species—and because they produce what anthropologists call a 'courtship strut.'"[16] David Kunzle, in *Fashion and Fetishism,* remarks that "extremists . . . have raised the foot on tip-toe in a shoe blocked in the manner of a ballet-slipper." This "tip-toe boot, often rising to the crotch, represents a 'classic' if extreme form of fetish footwear, one which in the fetishist mind reduces the whole leg to a huge hyper-erect, hyper-constricted or engorged 'phallic' unit."[17] The "wobbling" or "quivering," "tottering" or "teetering" seen in the gait of someone in very high and slender heels not only resembles the "willow walk,"[18] the "golden lotus limp," or the "lotus gait,"[19] but mimics some ballet steps that fetishize the foot and emphasize its vulnerability. *Bourrées,* for example, are the tiny skimming steps that dancers take on pointe with vibrating and undulating legs; the willowlike malleability of the legs and feet contradict the usual arched straightness and strength of the legs in pointe work. In beats *sur le coup de pied,* or around the ankle, the delicate instep of one arched foot, a self-created cleft, rapidly beats against the other foot as it entwines the ankle.

Pointe shoes are in fact the natural extension of high-heeled shoes, which were the standard footwear of dancers before ballerina Marie Camargo, in 1726, abandoned them for the flat slipper to aid and better show off her jumping ability. She thus ushered in the age of the ballet slipper tied with ribbons. However, it was not until 1832 that Marie Taglioni became the first ballerina to perform *en pointe* and begin the Romantic Age of ballet, although prints from decades before portray ballerinas apparently balancing on their toes.[20]

THE BROKEN SLIPPER
AS SURROGATE BODY

Even as a child, I was hard on shoes. As an adult, I still keep shoes well past their "respectable" appearance. (I now think of the worn-out lilac Birkenstocks by the front door; they're at least eight years old.) The wearing-out process endears them to me. I have learned to buy two pairs of shoes when I finally find a pair I like, and I can spend more than a year looking for a particular type of shoes, a pair that allows my feet to basically "be themselves" and takes me everywhere everyday. I tend to look for the rare all-purpose shoe: comfortable, perhaps not "in style" but not glaringly "out" either, and suitable to wear with almost all my casual tropical wardrobe. Right now, that role is filled by the SAS three-strap sandals I bought last summer in Miami in both bone and black. Amazingly, they closely resemble sandals in an early 1950s *Vogue* ad; however, the compliments I get on those shoes pertain to comfort, never to style.

My tendency to use shoes beyond their presentable life also applies to my ballet slippers. I currently take two pairs to class: one broken-down comfortable pair for the *barre* work, and one "newer" pair for the center work. And sometimes when the floor just isn't right—too slippery or too resistant—in frustration I change back to my older shoes in the middle of an exercise. The pair for *barre* work is frayed, with holes on both sides of the toe area, holes large enough for my big toe to sometimes protrude. I have

to decide when class begins, which foot is more suited that day to deal with the dis-
advantage of the protruding toe: the stronger, better-arched left foot, or the right foot,
which needs much more help in balancing and turns?

The newer shoes are on the way to becoming the old ones; the linings are ripped
out, and the shoes are soft and endearingly stained with studio sweat and dirt. When
the old shoes become more a liability than a help—impossible to turn in, say—the new
shoes will replace the old. I then will again search for a new pair to begin breaking in.
I will take to dancewear shops my threadbare shoes from six years ago and urge the clerks
to please find ones exactly like them. The label has long been destroyed, and they will
have to guess at the maker by studying the design of the shoe, for I have forgotten it.
The store clerks seem embarrassed when they see me carrying around those old shoes
in a plastic bag, searching for duplicates of those perfect slippers.

Humans use clothes to define the body, set boundaries, enhance naturalness, or
defy nature. How does this idea translate into our relationship to shoes, particularly the
dance slipper meant to seamlessly continue the dancer's skin? First, autoeroticism, or
what Jennifer Craik calls the "frisson between bodies and clothes,"[21] plays a role in our
relationship to clothes, and by extension, shoes. Rossi is but one writer who attests to
the power of the bare foot: "The foot possesses and expresses the strange power of 'podolinguistics' or foot language—an innate ability to communicate feelings, attitudes,
desires, especially as sexual and psychosexual symbols."[22] However, commercial fashion rhetoric naturally insists on the powerlessness of the bare foot itself and its depen-
dence on shoes for power. This duality of secrecy and power, withholding and potency,
contributes to the paradox of barefootedness as a representation of freedom, revelation, vulnerability, and fear of pain and punishment—a kind of potency and impoverish-
ment at once. A *High Heels* ad in 1962 declares, "The bare foot . . . holds no secrets!"
But once covered, it becomes "mysterious" and "forbidding"—and therefore fascinating. The leather "is like firm, hard skin!"[23] Only in transforming itself into a "false" foot
with its flawless sexual cover can an invisible foot inspire and intrigue, the shoe fashion world implies.

While in dance we have the high-gloss, virginal, pink-rosebud ballet slippers of
adolescent fantasy, we also have the coveted image of beat-up ballet shoes. The popular ascendance of ballet companies such as the New York City Ballet and American
Ballet Theatre in the 1960s and 1970s, and films such as *The Turning Point* (1979) and
the trendy *Flashdance* (1983), were concurrent with the popularity of a series of dance
posters glorifying the ballet foot: feet in disintegrating shoes perched on ballet bars or
placed in contorted fifth positions, with ragged leg warmers wrapping the ankles.
These posters romanticized the "suffering for art" attitude the public often links with

ballet and deliberately redefined the glamour of ballet as a visceral physicality usually associated with athletics (hence the resulting concurrent dance-exercise craze).

Thus, the fleshlike leather or canvas second skin of the ballet slipper represents for the dance spectator a torture assumed to exist underneath, one that exceeds even the torture of stiletto heels. Just as our ideas about what constitutes the ideal nude form have dictated clothing fashions—the perfect body underneath the drapery—our fantasies about the ideal bare foot inform our design of shoes. Ballet slippers beautifully hide the ugliness of abused feet and transform that ugliness into perfect supernatural feet for the ballet goer's gaze: satin pink skin and a wondrous arch. In dance photographs and posters of the iconographic worn-out ballet slipper, fans vicariously witness and thrill to the masochism implied under the layer of shoe skin. Underneath this worship of bodily and technical perfection lies the awareness of the art form's violence that through relentless discipline achieves the most natural lyricism and tensile strength by unnatural means and illusion. For the amateur, the foot with the impossibly high arch, wrapped in a worn-out ballet slipper, represents simultaneously the pain of foot binding, the masochism of art, the sexuality of the naked foot, and the sadistic coercion that makes it possible.

The dancer abuses, breaks in, and beats up the ballet slipper, her surrogate body. *The Pointe Book: Shoes, Training, and Technique* details a number of tried-and-true methods for dancers to make the intractable pointe shoe their own. In addition to the rather mild tactics of molding them with the hands or stepping on the box of the shoe, dancers are known for "banging them in doors, whamming them with hammers, and having large men jump up and down on them," or even taking a utility knife to them.[24] A ballerina might spend up to two hours preparing a pair of shoes for wear, and she can go through hundreds of pairs a year, often wearing out more than one pair during a full-length ballet performance. Through force and sweat, the dancer accelerates the disintegration that results in the shoe's absorption by the dancer's body, its being owned by the foot. As the shoe's glue dissolves, its surfaces fray, and its inner cotton lining tears, it becomes the dancer's skin, an encasement that hides the individuality of the foot. The enclosed foot no longer differs from the leg, the other body part from which it extends; from the mirrored anatomy of the dancer's other foot; nor from the feet of other dancers of either sex.

This denial of difference is evident in the identical construction of male and female slippers, and in the prevalent practice of alternating right and left shoes so there are no "right" and "left" shoes, no natural opposition in the body. The forced symmetry or identical-ness of a dancer's right and left feet erases the eccentricities and physical abuses of the foot and masquerades them as the perfect naked extension of the leg.

The denial of anatomy is also revealed in the dancer's aspiration to have feet that are perceived not as callused dancer's feet at all, but like the most articulate, dexterous, and graceful of gloved hands. Just as the "turnout" at the hip, which is the foundation of ballet technique, unfolds, opens, and exposes the interior of the body—crotch to inner thigh to arch of the foot—ballet slippers turn the dancer's body inside out to represent the interior as exterior—the discipline, the wear, the strength—thus perfectly exemplifying Rossi's podolinguistics.

THE FAIRY TALE PRECEDENT: THE CASTRATED DANCER

Castration images and mutilation in fairy tales such as Charles Perrault's "Cinderella" (1697) and Hans Christian Andersen's "The Red Shoes" (1845) remind us of the "podosexual" nature of the dance slipper. (Both tales are reprinted in the appendix.) These images reinforce Freud and Jung's connections between foot mutilation, dreaming of forced removal of one's shoes, and castration.[25] Rossi observes that "the Cinderella fable has served not only to romanticize further the small-foot image, but to dramatize the degree of deformation and mutilation that women will submit to for this pedic ideal of sex attraction."[26] In these tales, dance symbolizes the young woman's freedom and autonomy, and the mutilation eventually desexualizes or controls her.

"Cinderella" and "The Red Shoes" have over time been stripped of the goriest details that might alarm children, but the original message was very clear: young women are willing to literally cut off toes, slices of heels, or even both feet to "fit in" the desirable shoe or the traditional role demanded of them.[27] However, the two tales offer different messages about the dance slipper and bare feet. "Cinderella" emphasizes the futility of self-mutilation and contortion to "fit" expectations; in the end, the natural foot does not lie, the tale argues. Karen, the young girl in "The Red Shoes," lusts after the red shoes, the freedom, and the sheer joy of dance they represent. Ultimately, her own desires turn on her, and she rejects the shoes—and, inevitably, the self they have given birth to.

In "Cinderella," the prince's future wife will be the young woman whose foot perfectly fits the glass slipper, a paradox of revelation, concealment, and fragility. Cinderella's uglier sisters are willing to resort to self-mutilation to achieve the illusion of the perfect fit/foot, but fail because their feet are simply too big or because bloodstains reveal the deception practiced to make the foot—and self—fit. While the glass slipper is not specifically a dance shoe, it is a slipper for the ball, a formal mating ritual for the prince who seeks the "perfect fit" of a wife.

In "The Red Shoes," Karen personifies woman as dance slipper, a woman who has dangerously and willfully slipped out of control. Karen's desire and the power of the magic slippers doom her. Intentionally courting danger, she insists on wearing the beautiful red dancing shoes and loves the power they give her; however, her village interprets that longing for self-expression as arrogance, vanity, and disobedience. Both the village and God damn her. When the shoes take on a life of their own, intent on dancing her to death, she appeals to the executioner for help:

> The shoes carried her across fields and meadows, through nettles and briars that tore her feet so they bled.
> One morning she danced across the lonely heath to a solitary cottage. Here, she knew, the executioner lived. With her fingers she tapped on his window.
> "Come out! Come out!" she called. "I cannot come inside, for I must dance."
> The executioner opened his door and came outside. When he saw Karen he said, "Do you know who I am? I am the one who cuts off the heads of evil men; and I can feel my ax beginning to quiver now."
> "Do not cut off my head," begged Karen, "for then I should not be able to repent. But cut off my feet!"
> She confessed all her sins, and the executioner cut off her feet, and the red shoes danced away with them into the dark forest.

The fairy tale ends with the executioner fashioning some wooden feet for Karen and teaching her a psalm for sinners. Her soul eventually flies "on a sunbeam up to God." The castration desexualizes Karen and eliminates her as a threat to the community. Rendered dance-less and her autonomy destroyed, she reaffirms her obedience to church control. Dance and desire become her sins, and she pays penance for the rest of her life.

THE DAMNATION
OF THE PERFECT DANCE

In the chapter "Breaking the Mirror" in her autobiography, ballerina Gelsey Kirkland defines another kind of self-mutilation, the self-discipline needed to reach what many dancers consider the pinnacle of success, becoming a principal dancer in George Balanchine's New York City Ballet. Her desire for artistic perfection and selfhood rivals the seduction Karen experiences in "The Red Shoes." The ballet world holds for Kirkland the seductive power that the red shoes hold for Karen. For art, Balanchine dancers risk "drown[ing] themselves in their own images, pushed by forces unseen":

> Throughout the early phases of my career, the mirror was my nemesis,
> seductive to the point of addiction. Stepping through the looking glass meant
> confronting a double who exposed all of my flaws and pointed out all of my
> physical imperfections. . . . Until the opposition between the images was
> resolved, I saw myself as a walking apology, unable to attain or maintain my
> constantly refined ideal of physical beauty. (72–73)

Like the prince who holds the glass slipper to receive the woman who is his perfect fit,
"Mr. B" holds the mirror for his ballerinas. Dancers must adopt a mind-set that enables
them to suffer the scrutiny of the multiple gazes under which a ballerina works, in the
case of Kirkland, Mr. B's, the world's recognized ballet authority until his death in 1983;
the public's; and her own, primarily an internalized version of Mr. B's. The gazes exercise control of a woman's body through the demand for perfection, and the demand is
seamlessly, unwittingly absorbed and met by the dancer. She transmutes the relentless
desires of others in learning to coerce her own body.

The ultimate endorsement for one of Mr. B's ballerinas was, according to Kirkland, a combination of romance, classical tribute, and co-opting of her body and tal-
ent for his art: "On a higher level, a dancer's dream was that he might fall in love with
her, that he might 'choreograph a ballet on her,' the expression used to describe what
happened when Mr. B placed a ballerina on the pedestal of his stage, using her as his
muse. Such a dancer became a fetish, whether he touched her or not" (50). Here, Kirkland defines the paradox of ballerina as both worshiped spectacle and defaced object.
Mr. B's chosen ballerina of the moment is, she insists repeatedly, the mere medium of
the choreography, literally "dance writing" (choreo=dance, graph=writing), Mr. B's art,
not her own.

Given the struggle Kirkland describes as inherent in the professional ballet world,
it is no surprise that ballet dancers are especially vulnerable to anorexia nervosa, a "tem-
pestuous warfare against [their] bodies."[28] According to Kirkland, the ballerina's daily
warfare is a wresting away of herself from herself so that she can become a component
in the revered choreographer's dream.

Kirkland's book is a primer in masochism for art's sake. She chronicles how her
ballet training effectively put herself in competition with herself as well as with other
dancers; she is well trained to be her own tormentor and inures herself to the pain. *The
Pointe Book,* clearly written to inform aspiring dancers about the realities of being a ballerina, nonchalantly mentions common practices that teach ballet students to develop
the masochism they will later need and to equate pain with beauty. Some teachers believe
it is an advantage for students to "develop calluses on their toes early in their pointe training."[29] And, "in England, a product called surgical spirit is used to deaden the top lay-

ers of the epidermis, which helps the dancer with tender feet get used to wearing pointe shoes."[30] A number of products, such as Ouch Pouches, Jelly Toes, and Eurotard's Pointe Comfort and Pointe Comfort Ultra Lites, employ high-tech polymers "to make performing more enjoyable and [to] possibly extend the life of your career," as the Pointe Comfort ad states ("Get to the Pointe!"). The claim that Ouch Pouches make "the serious dancer's life a little easier" masterfully hints that, with a little pampering, pain is bearable and normal ("Bunheads"). The marketing of pampering foot washes, sprays, and lotions tacitly admits to the foot torture involved in ballet work even as it suggests that pain, blisters, ripped toenails, and enlarged toe joints are just negligible sacrifices for wrapping one's feet in pink satin.

These foot devices and cosmetics convert the pain of ballet into a desired rite of passage for the young female dancer. Even the most innocent of young ballet dancers accept such seemingly minor initiations into pain as the price they must pay to enter ballet puberty—pointe work. In fact, the methodical conditioning necessary to endure pointe work echoes the pain Chinese girls experienced in adapting to the pain of foot binding. As Kirkland herself notes, "Pleasure and pain were inextricably connected and integral to the study of dance" (33).

The result of this degree of bodily contortion and acceptance of pain is that ballet technique can effectively fragment the dancer's body and alienate her from herself. As Kirkland remembers:

> I frequently received verbal corrections addressed to each part of my body in isolation, figuratively dismembering me and dispelling any semblance of grace. It was as if separate strings were arbitrarily attached to my head, arms, and legs; the teacher seemed to pull each without regard to the others, usually ignoring the torso entirely. Nevertheless, I forced my body to absorb the spastic effect of each correction. (33)

She condemns Balanchine's view of the human form as "essentially mechanical": "The body was a machine to be 'assembled'—the same word that he used to describe the process by which he created his ballets" (45). Ultimately, the glory that Mr. B offered his beautiful muse was her "defeminization" (56), which echoes Karen's foot castration in "The Red Shoes." Kirkland went so far as to "reassemble" herself through "a risky course of plastic surgery and silicone injections, major dental realignments and gruesome medical procedures" (57–58). The elegant slipper masks the brutal physical reality behind the ultimate goal of pointe work, "to make it seem effortless," to make the dancer an airborne being immune to the limitations of age and pain. Kirkland unwraps her wounded feet and lays her shoes before us.

BARE FEET AND FEMALE
CORPOREAL PLEASURE

I'm guessing, but I think the main reason you were almost continuously nagging . . .
me about going barefoot was not really because you wanted to go barefoot, but
to have the option to go or not go seemed to be the important issue—and still
does.
                                          —James B. Reaves, e-mail to author, October 1998

The techniques of the barefoot Isadora Duncan and Martha Graham, the two
most important early-twentieth-century "modern" dancers, are distinctly antifetishistic
when contrasted with contemporary ballet training and fairy tales, such as "Cinderella" and "The Red Shoes," which inform our idea of the dancer. The modern dance
pioneered by Duncan and Graham sets a new precedent, dance based on the dancer-
choreographer's self-discovered aesthetic and ideal. Duncan's dance draws on Greek
classical tradition and glorifies the body's natural beauty and intelligence; Graham's
extends the body's natural capabilities of breath, contraction, and release, and movement thus emanates organically from the spine and the center of the body, not from
the limbs (figures 5–6). Both women wrenched away from the predominantly male
choreographers and dance directors the right to invent woman's ideal movement and
relationship to her own body. Duncan and Graham revolutionized our attitudes toward
bare feet and woman's body, and their dance techniques offer a sensual counterpoint
to the masochism of the ballet slipper.

Martha Graham's codified "modern dance," which she forged in the 1920s and
1930s and worked on until her death in her nineties, evolved into the United States's
woman-centered response to the centuries-old ballet tradition. For example, in a
famous 1932 photo from her "Satyric Festival Song," there is no pretense of being airborne. She uses rather than defies gravity. Her bare feet palpably press into and away
from the floor. The energy surges from her arched bare foot through the lines of her body,
traverses the horizontal lines of her dress, and continues even to the tips of her flying
hair. Graham technique foregrounds the dancer's connection with the floor, the body
moving naturally and freely underneath flexible clothes that emulate the body rather
than contain it; as in many of her dances, the clothing becomes an integral part of the
dance, not a mere body adornment.

But it was really Isadora Duncan who first freed the body for modern dance (figure 7). She encountered outrage and shock when she danced barefoot and bare legged
in her instinctive revolt against constraints on the mind, body, and spirit. Duncan's art
onstage constituted indecency and scandal. Her freeing of the dancer's body is usually
cited as an influence on Serge Diaghilev's avant-garde Ballet Russe, which included

FIGURE 5 ☙ Modern dancer and choreographer Alyce Bochette illustrates characteristics of modern dance.

Photo by James Brock.

FIGURE 6   ↵   Modern dancer and choreographer Alyce Bochette illustrates
characteristics of modern dance.
Photo by James Brock.

premier dancer Vaslav Nijinsky; however, that influence took effect before the company's performances in Paris. In her autobiography, *My Life,* Duncan pinpoints the actual beginning of her liberating influence on Russian ballet, which in fact began during her first visit to Russia in 1905: "There were many quarrels for and against my ideals; and one duel was actually fought between a fanatic *balletoman* and a Duncan enthusiast. It was from that epoch that the Russian ballet began to annex the music of Chopin and Schumann and wear Greek costumes; some ballet dancers even going so far as to take off their shoes and stockings."[31] For her, the body's freedom from clothes takes on an almost religious passion. When no less a figure than Cosima Wagner, widow of composer Richard Wagner, objected to her transparent tunic, Duncan said, "I was adamant. I would dress and dance exactly my way, or not at all" (*My Life,* 157).

Duncan and the modern dancers and choreographers who continued her legacy set the stage for a major shift in twentieth-century women's fashion—what Anne Hollander calls "a new style of female corporeal pleasure, one more visibly expressive of what women had always liked about their own bodies, the physical feel of flexibility and articulation in both limbs and torso even without vigorous activity, the sense of

FIGURE 7 ~ Isadora Duncan in *Iphegenia at Aulis* (London, 1908).

Reproduced courtesy of Dance Collection, the New York Public Library for the Performing Arts, Astor, Lenox, and Tilden Foundations.

subtle muscular movement and the strength of bones under smooth skin, the rhythmic shift of weight."[32]

In contrast to the mechanical and dismembering Ballanchine technique as experienced by Kirkland, Duncan offers a clichéd yet genuinely felt ideal of the human body:

> The human body has through all ages itself been the symbol of highest beauty. I see a young goatherd sitting surrounded by his flock, and before him rose-tipped of the sun, stands the Goddess of Cyprus, and she smiles as she reaches her hand for the prize which she knows to be hers. That exquisitely poised head, those shoulders gently sloping, those breasts firm and round, the ample waist with its free lines, curving to the hips, down to the knees, and feet—*all one perfect whole.*[33]

At the crux of Duncan's dance is not only the freedom of the body epitomized by bare feet and legs, but a virulent antiballet sentiment that predates by decades Kirkland's scathing analysis of Balanchine's training. She laments that the feet of girls studying ballet "are being tortured into deformed shapes" (*Art,* 73). She attacks the supreme achievement of ballet technique, the illusion that dancers are airborne: "All the movements of our modern ballet school are sterile movements because they are unnatural: their purpose is to create the delusion that the law of gravitation does not exist for them" (*Art,* 56). For her, ballet is doomed because it works not only against natural physical laws but against "the natural will of the individual" (*Art,* 55) as well and does not acknowledge the body as a natural instrument.

Her reaction to watching Anna Pavlova, the leading classical ballerina of the day, at practice demonstrates that Duncan, like Kirkland, valued the totality of the dancer, the interdependence of mind, body, and spirit. For Duncan, this amalgamation was a spiritual truth that must be manifest in her dance: "For three hours I sat tense with bewilderment, watching the amazing feats of Pavlowa [sic]. She seemed to be made of steel and elastic. Her beautiful face took on the stern lines of a martyr. She never stopped for one moment. The whole tendency of this training seems to be to separate the gymnastic movements of the body completely from the mind" (*My Life,* 165).

Duncan answered the martyrdom of ballet with self-indulgence and pleasure, the very sins embodied by the red shoes. She danced literally barefoot and pregnant (and out-of-wedlock to boot) to double the scandal of her revealing dress and bare feet. She enjoyed food and wine and did not hesitate to expose her body when she began to gain weight in her later years. In a passionate political statement, she once bared her breast while dancing to "The Marseillaise." Unlike ballet, she contended, *her* dance would not die as it was made (*Art,* 55).

CONCLUSION: HIGH-TECH BARE FEET

My lover has high arches and somewhat delicate feet. They always look clean and vulnerable, and he likes to go barefoot and wear open sandals.... He appreciates the calluses and toughness that my barefoot dancer's life has given my feet. And, like at least two of my other lovers before him, he has studied dance to share my joy in flexible, naked, strong feet.
—*Author's unpublished narrative, October 1998*

So what are the alternatives to the glamorized masochism of the bound foot and the ballet slipper? Unsurprisingly, it is the marketplace that offers a perfect compromise that resolves the opposition between ballet and modern dance and bridges the gap between bare and bound feet. As the polar opposite of the pointe shoe and lotus shoe, the "Sole Protection" foot thong by Bloch is not really a shoe but a device named for a scant piece of clothing associated only with genital coverage. Available in two "flesh" shades (light and dark), the skimpy leather-and-elastic thong closely resembles a cross between the tiniest of bikini bottoms and a minuscule jock strap. The advertisement's imperative "Turn without Tears" alluringly promises the delight of nearly naked feet minus the pain associated with professional dance. The foot thong also preserves the sexualized image of the shoe but adorns the foot, almost invisibly; it is high-tech barefootedness.

The floating modern dancers in Bloch's series of "Sole Protection" advertisements depict the magical goal of ballet, but *as we would dream it*: not bound in clothes and shoes, but barefoot, free of all but the lightest of clothes—Duncan's scandalous transparent tunic perhaps? Or, in one case, only three thongs—two for the feet and a dance belt for the genitals. The dancers in the series hover aloft without effort; the almost palpable air cushions and supports them. They are suspended and still; the streaming hair of female dancers diffuses into and enlarges space. Dancers extend hands as if to invite all viewers to join in the dances on air. Their feet and legs exhibit classical dance lines and strength; however, the dancers are free of all constraining clothes that would detract from the wholeness of the image, the sense that the movement originates from within them, that it is *their own* dance originating in the moment. Space, too, becomes part of the dance moment, which gives the sensation of the top of a breath. White space asserts itself as a dancer, curving around the dancer and shimmering on bare skin.

Bloch's foot thong is the dance slipper taken to its evolutionary perfection. It is both a practical symbol of the foot-genital equation traceable through fashion history, and a vestigial symbol of the interdependence of Chinese foot binding and sexuality, freedom and dance. Its design suggests the free spirit of Duncan and the stunning technical perfection of classical ballet. Here, the shoe becomes the dancer's skin that connects the "sole" of the dancer with the earth, even as the dancer escapes gravity.

NOTES

1. For a brief history of the eradication of foot binding, see William A. Rossi, *The Sex Life of the Foot and Shoe* (Ware, Hertfordshire: Wordsworth Editions, 1989), 43–44.

2. Beverley Jackson, *Splendid Slippers: A Thousand Years of an Erotic Tradition* (Berkeley: Ten Speed Press, 1997), 12.

3. Rossi, *Sex Life of the Foot and Shoe,* 29.

4. Ibid., 30.

5. Jackson, *Splendid Slippers,* 108.

6. Ibid., 110.

7. Valerie Steele, *Fetish: Fashion, Sex, and Power* (New York: Oxford University Press, 1996), 106.

8. C. Fred Blake, "Foot-binding in Neo-Confucian China and the Appropriation of Female Labor," *Signs: Journal of Women in Culture and Society* 19, 3 (1994): 676–712. Blake describes the intrusive-obtrusive aspect of foot binding as mirroring "a world in which males intrude as husbands and obtrude and extrude as sons."

9. Mimi Pond, *Shoes Never Lie* (New York: Berkeley, 1985), 13.

10. Rossi, *Sex Life of the Foot and Shoe,* 91.

11. Steele, *Fetish,* 111.

12. Ibid., 111.

13. Pond, *Shoes Never Lie,* 97.

14. Rossi, *Sex Life of the Foot and Shoe,* 68.

15. Gelsey Kirkland, *Dancing on My Grave* (Garden City, N.Y.: Doubleday, 1986), 33–35. Hereafter cited in the text.

16. Alison Lurie, *The Language of Clothes* (New York: Random House, 1981), 227.

17. David Kunzle, *Fashion and Fetishism: A Social History of the Corset, Tight-Lacing, and Other Forms of Body-Sculpture in the West* (Totowa, N.J.: Rowman and Littlefield, 1982), 17.

18. Rossi, *Sex Life of the Foot and Shoe,* 32.

19. Jackson, *Splendid Slippers,* 121.

20. Janice Barringer and Sarah Schlesinger, *The Pointe Book: Shoes, Training, and Technique* (Princeton, N.J.: Princeton Book Co., 1991), 2–3.

21. Jennifer Craik, *The Face of Fashion: Cultural Studies in Fashion* (New York: Routledge, 1994), 116.

22. Rossi, *Sex Life of the Foot and Shoe,* 5.

23. Quoted in Steele, *Fetish,* 101.

24. Barringer and Schlesinger, *The Pointe Book,* 39.

25. Blake, "Foot-binding," 676 and Rossi, *Sex Life of the Foot and Shoe,* 231.

26. Rossi, *Sex Life of the Foot and Shoe,* 160.

27. The Cinderella Project web site (http://www-dept.usm.edu/~engdept/cinderella/inventory. html) is a comprehensive source of the many versions of the fairy tale over hundreds of years. Director Michael Powell's 1947 film *The Red Shoes,* starring dancer Moira Shearer, is a fascinating, Academy Award–winning film adaptation of that fairy tale.

28. Kim Chernin quoted in Susan B. Kaiser, *The Social Psychology of Clothing: Symbolic Appearances in Context,* 2d ed. rev. (New York: Fairchild Publications, 1997), 104.

29. Barringer and Schlesinger, *The Pointe Book,* 24.

30. Ibid., 25.

31. Isadora Duncan, *My Life* (New York: Liveright, 1927), 172. Hereafter cited in the text as *My Life*.

32. Anne Hollander, *Sex and Suits* (New York: Knopf, 1994), 136.

33. Isadora Duncan, *The Art of the Dance* (New York: Theatre Arts Books, 1969), 67, emphasis added. Hereafter cited in the text as *Art*.

The Modern Foot

JANET LYON

Rummaging around on the Internet recently, I came across a 1914 pamphlet titled *The Barefoot League: Being a Tete a Tete on the Virtues and Delights of Barefoot Walking, between You and Your Brother in Life*.[1] Its author (presumably the "brother" of the subtitle), one James Leith Macbeth Bain, brought out his tract in London with the Theosophical Publishing Company, publisher of such esoteric works as *The Astral Plane, Its Scenery, Inhabitants, and Phenomena* and *Man Visible and Invisible: Examples of Different Types of Men as seen by Means of Trained Clairvoyance*.[2] These titles suggest something of the new age–modernist eccentricity to be found in Bain's pamphlet. The Theosophical Society had been founded in 1875 as a kind of sociological church of spiritualism (or a "Wisdom-Religion," as leader Annie Besant glossed it) and by 1914 its adherents, hailing mostly from the elite or educated classes, were combining Eastern mysticism and Western reform into an amalgam of feminism, socialism, sexology, occultism, vegetarianism, and other strands of nonconformist and antistatist dissent. James Leith Macbeth Bain was, as his insistently Scots name suggests, a self-ordained outsider; his pamphlet—gentle in tone, addressed mildly to "the Children of the Sun"—quietly introduces a new venue for reform: barefootedness.

The logic runs something like this: if you're reading his pamphlet in the first place, you must be a "true lover of freedom"; if you love freedom, you perforce love nature; and if you love nature (dually personified herein as "He, the good Father of our spirit,"

272

and "She, the good Mother of our earthly days"), you'll embrace barefootedness. Why? Because barefootedness ensures contact with the earth and the sun. Not only that; it is *through the soles of the feet* that humans receive "the finest of the sun's energy [and] also the virtues of the body of our earth in all its manifold richness and power." The sole of the foot is, in other words, both a nutritional and a spiritual membrane; to deny contact between the foot and the earth is to ensure the deformation of body and soul. On this logic, the shoe is an impediment to all levels of human development, though the agreeable Bain prefers to extol the virtues of the bare foot rather than to condemn the vice of the shoe.

In what follows I offer a brief and perhaps slanted discussion of the significance of the bare foot for debates about modernity in the modernist moment of 1914, for Bain is neither the first nor the last to advocate barefootedness at this time. (He is, however, probably its most energetic proselyte, his efforts having led him from the Highlands of Scotland to the Vegetarian Home for Destitute Children in Liverpool.) For my part, I am sympathetic to Bain's concerns, and especially to his descriptions of the bodily ecstasy produced by cool grass or warm rocks underfoot. But I am also alive to the uncanny aesthetic appeal of shoes, even the most pointy, pinching, and imprisoning of shoes. And if Bain and the other barefoot advocates mentioned herein are even remotely right about the physical and psychical benefits of bare feet—that is to say, if bare feet, or even barely shod feet, invigorate the body and soul—then how is one to account for this hypnotic allure, for so many generations of modernity's women, of the impractical, foot-deforming, outrageous shoe? Must we throw up our hands at the contradiction and follow the stern critics of modernity—Thorstein Veblen, Max Horkheimer, Theodor Adorno, Mary Daly, et al.[3]—in their dismissal of extravagant footwear as the stigmata of conspicuous consumption or the tainted sequela of mass culture? Must we agree, finally, that fancy shoes are little more than the pedal symptoms of a tortured unconscious and false consciousness?

Well, no, I don't think so. Besides, to put the shoe problematic in these terms is to put it too strongly. The gentle Bain actually says nothing at all about extreme shoe styles in his tract; he's off on a theosophical curl of smoke, far from the reticulation of fashion, dress reform, and decorative art that was so evident in London and Paris in 1914. And even if he *had* been aware of the truly fabulous shoes available in his time—the five-inch Cromwell heels, the pink satin Hellstern slippers, the forty-eye Bally walking boots—he couldn't have convincingly made the case that the pleasures of walking barefoot were necessarily antithetical to the joy of gorgeous shoes.

For fabulous shoes are indeed a joy. Think of the shoe as a sonnet, for a moment—as an expressive form bound by certain conventions and necessities (heel, vamp,

counter, toe box, throat). Like an excellent sonnet, the fabulous shoe works the equivalent of its requisite fourteen lines into unconventional beauty or wit, making subtle
cultural connections, playing with its materiality, extending the genre. When metal mesh
is overlaid onto a cerulean cigarette heel, or an ankle strap is twined out of dark green
and cream leather ribbing, an unusual aesthetic note is struck—one that often has to
do with the shoe's domain in the contact zone between the human and the earthly (precisely the zone valorized by Bain). To this add the fact that a pair of shoes are mirror
images of each other; once set to walking, a pair of shoes begins a chiasmatic rhythm
that never quite completes its own image. If those shoes are fabulous, you can bet that
the space between them is filled with desire.

   All of this is to say that not even the indelible sensual delights produced by bare
feet on cool slate or soft moss can undo a genuine, bone-bred attraction to pointy, thin-
soled, clunky, heavy-soled, high-rise, low-slung footwear. And not even the dire health
warnings about foot deformations issued by polemicists in the *querelle des chaussures*—
like chiropodist Samuel B. Shulman—will disappear a devotion to velvet stiletto
pumps or cutaway lamé T-straps. Shulman's 1949 declaration that "footgear is the greatest enemy of the human foot" came at the conclusion to his survey of a large number
of impoverished rickshaw pullers in India and China.[4] His data told him that these men
were lucky to be shoeless, for it was only their bare feet that made them capable of
"trotting a rickshaw on hard pavement for many hours each day . . . without pain or
pathology." Even a minimal investigation into the condition of twentieth-century
rickshaw pullers suggests that most would have been delighted by the opportunity to
actually *own* a pair of shoes; it seems doubtful, however, that Shulman offered them
this option.[5] Instead Dr. Shulman, apparently pleased that the subjects of his study had
made a virtue out of a necessity, closes his disturbingly cheerful treatise by admonishing
his Western readers to "learn from primitives the pleasure and painlessness of going
barefoot" (figure 1).

   This is a predictable choice of words, of course; and the association of barefootedness with blissfully undeveloped primitivism that undergirds Shulman's argument in 1949
is pervasive as well in 1914, thanks, not least, to the acute intersection of colonial activity and modernist culture in the prewar metropoles. Interestingly, however, the association of barefootedness and primitivism is absent in Bain's argument. Far from
understanding the desire for dermal contact with the earth and sun as the desire for a
return to the model of the noble savage, Bain characterizes it as a sign of the "supra-
normal sensitiveness" possessed by "the more finely evolved of our race." (It seems worth
pointing out here that "our race," in Bain's account, is an evolving tribe of "children of
the sun" who will communicate telepathically and fly about in "the clouds of the new

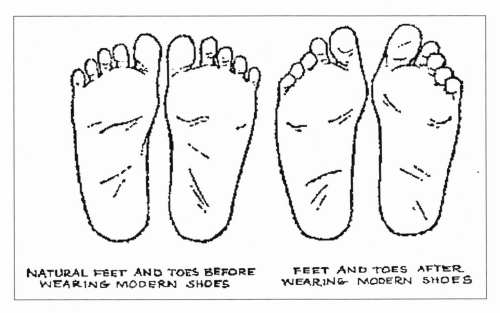

NATURAL FEET AND TOES BEFORE WEARING MODERN SHOES

FEET AND TOES AFTER WEARING MODERN SHOES

FIGURE 1   ↝   A 1961 illustration of the ills of modern feet.

From Simon J. Wikler, D.S.C., *Take Off Your Shoes and Walk* (Devin-Adair). Reprinted at http://www.lexica.net/pfbc/toysaw.htm.

heaven and the new earth"—if we play our developmental cards right.) Perhaps Bain is consciously performing a disidentification from the primitivism associated with decadence and devolution in the sociological writings of the time; perhaps, that is, the moral weight he places on barefootedness is meant to disable any easy elision of a bare-foot Briton with a colonial stereotype. But I would suggest that there's something else in Bain's argument for "natural" bare feet that helps to clarify the modern aesthetic worship of "unnatural" footwear.

James Leith Macbeth Bain's tract is of a piece with a long tradition advocating a kind of renegade barefootedness for Westerners—one that includes Jean Jacques Rousseau's Émile, who is encouraged to "run about barefoot all the year round, upstairs, downstairs, and in the garden."[6] But the peculiar intensification of this nonconformist naturalism toward the end of the nineteenth century produced a number of social formations that seem especially emblematic of modernism's negotiations with modernity. Bain's "Barefoot League," for example, is undoubtedly connected to the dress reform movement that had begun in earnest a generation earlier, a movement supported by suffragettes, renegade physicians, and cultural futurists, among others, and one which joined the rationalism of modern utility to a nostalgia for premodern synthesism. The "flesh-less diet" that he advocates in his tract is part of a vegetarian platform popular among alternative reformists. And his claim that barefootedness breeds "hardihood, sweet, strong, sane, chaste, noble hardihood," comes at a time when these hygienic traits are felt by many to be especially wanting in the metropole—when modern mechanization threatens to subsume individualism and eviscerate the human spirit, as Edwardian writers were fond of pointing out.

But the tract's focus on the foot—the naked, natural foot, "graceful and finely muscular"—has a particular aesthetic meaning in the cultural moment of 1914. That the naked foot had been an especially potent metonym for sexualized perfection was evident twenty years earlier in George Du Maurier's blockbuster novel *Trilby,* about an eponymous artist's model whose "astonishingly beautiful feet" trigger a tragic, cross-class love affair, as well as a lamentation by Du Maurier's narrator about the widespread spoiling of modern feet by leather shoes—since, as he puts it, "lovely slender feet" have the power "to suggest high physical distinction, happy evolution, and supreme development; the lordship of man over beast, the lordship of man over man, the lordship of woman over all!"[7] A generation later saw the lordship of some women over all, both in the militant suffrage movement and in the peak of the so-called barefoot dancing movement, pioneered by the likes of Loïe Fuller, Isadora Duncan, and Maud Allan.

Their barefoot dance—a.k.a. modern dance, Greek dance, natural dance, aesthetic dance—challenged not only the received laws of classical dance but also the broader laws of social decorum, which insistently linked the naked foot to obscene exhibitionism. Trilby may have had lovely feet, but it was precisely their naked loveliness that sealed her fate as a "fallen" artist's model (and thus made her easy prey for the creepy Svengali). Famous barefoot dancers, for their part, were squarely connected to a whole nexus of sexual taboos, no matter how assiduously they may have theorized their bareness as "spiritual freedom," "Attic grace," "oriental power," or "organic balance." Maud Allan's barefoot performance as Salomé in 1908, for example, both shocked and fascinated the London public. She wore nothing above the waist but pearl breastplates (and nothing below the skirt but bare legs and feet [figure 2]), and her hypnotic portrayal of Salomé's dance of desire drew scandalous tributes like the following: "Miss Allan is such a delicious embodiment of lust that she might win forgiveness with the sins of her wonderful flesh."[8] As with many of the famous barefoot dancers of the time, Allan's body stood in as a kind of cipher for the progress and the decadence of the modern, representing simultaneously the development and the downfall of high culture, the mysticism of the "Orient" and the athleticism of the West, the freedom and the horror of modern sexuality.

Isadora Duncan, who aimed to establish her own respectability somewhat more securely than did Allan, deliberately disrupted the semiotic link between obscenity and the "natural," barefoot body. In her writings and interviews she placed barefoot dance

FIGURE 2 ♪ Maud Allan as Salomé, London, 1910.
Public Record Office, London. Ref: COPY 1/550.

alongside the ideals of "nudity, childhood, the idyllic past, flowing lines, health, nobility, ease, freedom, simplicity, order, and harmony"[9]—in other words, within a concept
that could be easily opposed to the "primitive savagery" of other forms of undressed display. She deliberately codified her brand of barefoot dance as the cultural harbinger of
a new world. Like Bain's barefoot program, in which "vital contact" with the earth yields
"the most real communion with the Innermost o' our cosmic Being," Duncan's program
insists that "true dance must be the transmission of the earth's energy through the body."[10]
Unlike Bain's, however, her new world was a citation of and an embellishment on an
imagined premodern civilization of Greek perfection, one whose restitution through har-
monious dance would adumbrate the development of a truly modern culture—a culture distinct from bourgeois philistines and backward primitives alike. From this
perspective, barefoot dance was part of a utopian program that could deflect the instrumental ills of modernity by restoring a long-lost organic cultural equilibrium.

Bain seems to have known something about the censure of the barefoot dancer:
for all of its utopianism, his advocacy of barefoot walking displays no ignorance of the
complicated semiotics of bare feet. He is, in fact, acutely concerned with the social risks
incurred by the casual walker who goes barefoot, especially if that walker is a "delicately
bred and sensitive woman" whose unshod condition would likely elicit sexual attention
from "hooligans." He urges barefoot ladies to walk with male partners, in order to shield
themselves from the fury of public opprobrium, and to avoid walking on "holidays or
such times as the mob are at leisure, especially Sunday, when the demon of English
respectability and high religiosity flaunts its unloveliness everywhere, unabashed even
by its own hideousness." He knows firsthand that the naked foot, and even the sandaled
foot acts, in 1914, as a kind of social lightning rod, drawing clucks of horror from the
censorious, wolf whistles from the lascivious, and smiles of approval only from a small
but enlightened band of Bohemian brethren.

Bain's advocacy of bare feet registers a basic oscillation in modernist culture between
the progressive and the regressive, the civilized and the primitive, the cooked and the
raw. Like so many other icons in the culture—modernist art, modern music, modernist
poetry—the bare foot tends to be seen either as a tool and banner of enlightened liberation or as a sign of premodern degradation.

This multivalence is further complicated by the colonial climate in which it
takes shape, for it is possible to surmise, from Bain's tract, that to identify as barefoot
is to be part of an unofficial alliance against the metropole. Bain tells us that the English are scandalized by bare feet much more than the Scottish or the Welsh or the Irish
(who, as colonized constituents of the Celtic fringe, presumably have less of a stake in
codifying the signifiers of "civilization"). In this connection it is worth recalling the Theo-

sophical Society's ties with anti-imperialist movements and spiritual institutions in India. Theosophy's founder, Madame Helena Blavatsky, took her orders from mysterious Indian mahatmas, and Annie Besant, the leader of the movement from 1907 to 1933, was headquartered most of those years in Madras, where she was an outspoken activist for Indian nationalism and self-governance. The bare foot may, from this perspective at least, be something of a covert costume of nativism among Anglo sympathizers—a form of affective affiliation with the colonized of the empire (especially the colonized who were deemed to be particularly spiritual), and a form of disaffiliation from empire itself.

The bare foot may also be a distinct citation of the kind of premodern folk culture that was celebrated in the theatrical works of some of Bain's near contemporaries like August Strindberg, Fyodor Sologub, and Hugo von Hofmannsthal.[11] The freedom associated with barefoot peasantry in these plays—the sensual pleasure of treading grapes, the abandon of dancing in moonlight—bears the symbolic force of a Dionysian power unavailable to the civilized classes of modernity.

If, in fact, we may surmise that Dionysus is the god of bare feet—and certainly Duncan was one of many in her generation who raved about Nietzsche's Dionysus— then perhaps we have Apollo to thank for the dubious gift of shoes. Shoes provide structure, protection, boundaries; shoes seal off the lower extremities from the excremental earth and complete those costumes by which "bodies are made social and given meaning and identity."[12] What could be more Apollonian? Nietzsche himself equated Apollo with contemporary imperialism, nationalism, order—in short, with the affective implementations of instrumental modernity. In this calculus, bare feet are to Dionysian excess what shoes are to Apolline restraint.

But must the shoe itself be understood as the converse of the bare foot? Must it be consigned to the normative category of the instrumental, according to which any non-utile shoe gets equated with excess, waste, vanity, decorative meaninglessness? No, no, no. And this, finally, is my point about the relation between shoes and modernity. Instead of framing the modern shoe in a functionalist narrative—a narrative about the shoe-as-protection, or the shoe-as-replacement/fetish, or the shoe-as-commodity—we ought to consider the shoe (the fabulous shoe, at least) as a thrilling response to the ambivalence of modernity, to its relentless shuffle between liberation and disciplinization.[13] For if, as sociologists of modernity have argued, modernity itself is constituted by the tension between the liberating forces of modern autonomy and the restraining forces of modern disciplinary governance, then surely we must be able to identify cultural artifacts produced by that conundrum. The fabulous shoe, I would argue, is one of them.

Let me put it more plainly: in the extreme fashion of the fabulous shoe, we find a mediation of the modern tension between liberty and discipline. For the very fact of the shoe is a fact of discipline, confinement, Apollonian caution and control; but the extraordinary variability and emphatic beauty of the shoe produces a dialectical expression of liberation, aimed directly as a counter to the deadening functionalism of modernity. Imagine a shoe that looks like an Easter basket! or sparkles with ruby grapes! or ties off to the side in navy and white like a rakish sailor suit! Imagine a shoe that doesn't make you labor-worthy or sensibly grounded—a shoe whose corkscrew heel snaps right off at the first sign of coercion. Imagine a shoe—it doesn't have to be expensive or rare—a shoe that stands you up on the balls of your feet so that you tower above everyone else.

Imagine a shoe that is just as scandalous as a bare foot.

NOTES

1. Posted at http://www.barefooters.org/key-works/barefoot_league.html. All subsequent references to this pamphlet are to the Web edition, and therefore page numbers are not used.

2. Both of these titles are by C. W. Leadbeater and published in London, the first in 1895, the second in 1902.

3. I might well add Sigmund Freud to this list. He began to theorize the fetish at around the time of Bain's pamphlet, and in any case the symbolic overdetermination of the foot fetish was bound to leak out into Edwardian discussions of bare feet. As far as I have been able to determine, however, Freud had no eye for fashion and was largely unreceptive to the actual aesthetic properties of the shoe. Pumps, mules, slingbacks, and platforms were merely the foot soldiers in Freud's expanding empire of psychic symptoms.

4. Samuel B. Shulman, "Survey in China and India of Feet That Have Never Worn Shoes," *Journal of the National Association of Chiropodists* 49 (1949): 26–30. Posted at http://www.barefooters. org/medicine/j_natl_assoc_chir-49.html.

5. See, for example, Rob Gallagher, *The Rickshaws of Bangladesh* (Dhaka, Bangladesh: University Press, 1992), especially chapter 2, "Rickshaw History: The Hand-Pulled Rickshaws," 25–42. Gallagher reports that in Singapore, where rickshaw use peaked in the early 1920s, less than 2 percent of all pullers owned their own rickshaws; pullers lived in acute poverty and "appalling accommodations, sometimes 16 men to a room" (34). For that matter, it's easy enough to find photos of rickshaw pullers with bandaged feet. See, for instance, *Memsahibs Going Visiting, Ceylon, c. 1925,* plate 7, in Lawrence James, *The Rise and Fall of the British Empire* (New York: St. Martin's, 1994).

6. Jean Jacques Rousseau, *Émile,* trans. Barbara Foxley (London: Everyman, 1966), 104.

7. George Du Maurier, *Trilby* (Oxford: Oxford University Press, 1998), 15–16.

8. Quoted in Philip Hoare, *Oscar Wilde's Last Stand: Decadence, Conspiracy, and the Most Outrageous Trial of the Century* (New York: Arcade, 1997), 76. See chapter 4, "Salomania," for a cultural analysis of Allan's performance.

9. Ann Daly, *Done into Dance: Isadora Duncan in America* (Bloomington: Indiana University Press, 1995), 89.

10. Quoted in Deborah Jowitt, "Images of Isadora: The Search for Motion," *Dance Research Journal* 17, 2 and 18, 1 (1985–86): 27.

11. See Harold B. Segel, *Body Ascendant: Modernism and the Physical Imperative* (Baltimore: Johns Hopkins University Press, 1998), 91–98, for a discussion of these plays. See also Segel's discussion of Isadora Duncan, 80–90.

12. Joanne Entwistle and Elizabeth Wilson, "The Body Clothed," in *Addressing the Century: 100 Years of Art and Fashion,* ed. Peter Wollen (London: Hayward Gallery, 1998), 108.

13. See, e.g., Peter Wagner, *A Sociology of Modernity: Liberty and Discipline* (London: Routledge, 1994), especially parts 1 and 2.

Wearing It Out

LAURA MULLEN

> Touching scenes demand touchproof foundation.
> —*Tina Earnshaw, makeup artist (*Titanic*), quoted in a* Vogue *ad (January 1999)*

> Is Bliss then, such Abyss,
> I must not put my foot amiss
> For fear I spoil my shoe?
> —*Emily Dickinson*

tepping out on the thin air of an error in the authorized version of "Cinderella" (see appendix), we seek our footing where an apparently small faux pas opens an abyss our heroine is forced to recognize herself in—forever? The accepted tradition, as Marina Warner notes, tells us "that the . . . slipper in Perrault's 'Cinderella' was originally made of *vair,* fur or ermine"; material misheard to harden as *verre,* or glass.[1] Lucid about the pun's effective exile of the animal in exchange for "beauty, distilled and purified," Warner counts the ways "the glass slipper works to dematerialize the troubling aspects of [Cinderella's] nature, her natural fleshiness, her hairy vitality, and so give a sign of her new, socialized value," but is less accountable to the cost of woman's participation in that particular economy. For the stiff slipper that arose in the slippage of what Warner calls Perrault's "masterstroke" is still the dazzling form that rules us; the only one we mostly, still, get to dream about, or watch ourselves dreaming about. In the cold brilliancies given back to us briefly (for having loved our father, for having sat quietly down in the ashes after our mother's disappearance), we see, if we can't touch, the value an admiring gaze gives us. For a while at least—until the glass says someone else is fairer, and the shoe, as we say, is on the other foot. But how "perfect" they are indeed, the glass shoe, mirror, coffin, all the glittering display cases we can, by holding our breath or cutting *something* off, just about fit—as long as we don't kick up a fuss about how little room's been left us to live, much less dance.

This essay, then, is another attempt by a stepsister (and very material girl) to squeeze into—so as to wear out—the narrow glass bequeathed us by the master's stroke for what has become our self-regard (*Am I too . . .?*).[2] The essay means to draw attention to the message of its medium: the many footnotes meant to make us reflect on the cost—paid or pain in advance—of a textual surface kept smooth and small. What got lost in translation was a much more flexible and warmer model—animal, yes, but also anima—which, if less eloquent on the subject of "socialized value," has potentially a lot more to say about

FIGURE 1 ✑ Courtesy of Rikki Ducornet.

pleasure. But to get back from blisters to bliss requires not only an ear to the ground, as it were, but a hard look at what claims a certain transparency: looking itself.

     Perrault wrote an earlier fable in which a troublesome poet (who speaks too frankly) is killed and transformed (becoming "poli, clair et brilliant") into a mirror. The author's vision of "Cinderella" is arguably our tale of vision, for his deafness to his own *langue* leaves us in a world where seeing is not precisely believing but is precisely the primary mode of the "search" for truth.[3] It is worth touching on the fact that "Cendrillon, ou la Petite Pantoufle de Verre" engages almost no other sense. The cinders have no warmth, the ashes no grittiness. Our heroine does her sisters' hair for the ball, but if there is a softness as it flows through her skillful hands, the subject never comes up; "elle les coiffa parfaitement bien," and that—apparently—is "'all ye need to know'"—as Keats will say his vase insists. The tears she cries choke her speech but are neither wet nor hot; nor is the "pantoufle de verre" as cold and rigid as the smallest act of imagination insists it must be. It is as though all sensation vanished with the sensuous satisfaction the fur slipper held out.

     Indeed, "glass" taking more than one gloss, the slippers slipped into the title of Perrault's rewrite might be read as projected materializations of the gaze they enhance.[4] A gaze whose singular and increasing importance forms the subject(s) of much of Perrault's oeuvre and is acknowledged here in the author's anticipation of the ways in which Enlightenment science will brighten nineteenth-century police techniques: what Cinderella steps out of at the fatal hour is at once the "clue" and the glass under which its secret is revealed. (Indeed, functioning so perfectly to sign identity in the search for truth-as-bride, might not the slipper also be seen—from where we stand—as fingerprint or double he[e]lix?)[5] It goes without saying that size is both medium and message: the smaller the clue, the more miraculous the expansive wealth of information gathered from it, and the more eloquent the mute testimony to the largeness of vision, as well as what we call the "penetration," of the one who recognized it.[6] Which brings us to the prince ("the glass of fashion . . . / Th' observ'd of all observers" as another poet names him)[7] or calls our attention to the fact that we have been looking at him all along; for the story of seeing is, of course, the story of the observer—the site where the sharp-edged limits of a perspective come to light.[8]

The foot owes its preference as a fetish—or a part of it—to the circumstance that the inquisitive boy peered at the woman's genitals from below, from her legs up; fur and velvet—as has long been suspected—are a fixation of the sight of the pubic hair, which should have been followed by the longed-for sight of the female member.[9]

                                                                              —*Sigmund Freud*

Within the confines of what we might think of as a story for children, the "cas-tration" of woman is magic done in "the twinkling of an eye"; it is, as Luce Irigaray per-ceives, *the* effect of that gaze which, as primary power play, *"is at stake from the outset."*[10] Woman is consigned to the role of failed reflection by a man's re-membrance of a boy's glance, a glance which failed to get what it—in the poverty of its desire—"longed" for: itself mirrored back. Fairy tale on top of fairy tale, Freud's adds a shimmer to Perrault's, showing up the limits of a representational practice that insists on sameness, and which can only recognize difference as excess or lack. Looked at like this, it seems obvi-ous that the fear of the fur is the fear of the female genitalia, the site of anxieties Per-rault's test tube does not dematerialize but tries to distance and contain. The cost of this effort is re-marked in those versions of the story in which—the stepsisters having cut off parts of their feet to try to fool the fool with no memory for faces awhile—the glass slipper fills with blood to become itself an "open wound."[11] Displayed as safe simil-itude, verifiable in *verre,* the foot disappearing into *vair* makes visible the edge of the visible world—while enacting its own *jouissance.* In contrast, of course, the glass slip-per offers the member up for inspection, stepping neatly away, at the same time, from any reference to the sensual, though it might go on speaking of a purely reproductive sexuality. (Sparkle as she does, it is nonetheless "clear" to the viewer that the girl for-merly of the cinders is now, as the song goes, as cold as *glâce.*)

At this (freezing) point we might begin to feel that what Warner calls "the terms of . . . recognition and acceptance" are too high, or that our heroine, at least, has paid too much.[12] For, as Irigaray puts it (putting a foot down, we might say, right where it needs to be put):

> Woman takes pleasure more from touching than looking, and her entry into a
> dominant scopic economy signifies, again, her consignment to passivity: she is
> to be the beautiful object of contemplation. While her body finds itself thus
> eroticized, and called to a double movement of exhibition and chaste retreat
> in order to stimulate the drives of the "subject," her sexual organ represents
> *the horror of nothing to see.* A defect in this systematics of representation and
> desire.[13]

A "defect" which, if seen otherwise ("In the night where smooth is fair"), makes the sys-tematics look pretty lame and its masters go limp.[14]

To list what gets lost under the wave of the wand with which a threatening dif-ference is made invisible could take quite a while. "Almost everything," as Hélène Cixous notes, "is yet to be written by women about femininity: about their sexuality, that is, its infinite and mobile complexity."[15] In the slipper stolen away by a slip of the pen, however, we have a symbol of some of the things we could still say: about desire and pleasure, joie de vivre, the wide variety of ways to know and be in the world, and our deep entanglements with Otherness. For while the fur slippers—especially as a link to past versions of the tale, in which the godmother is an animal—make compassion manifest (feeling *for* and *with* coming close to feeling *as* where it's the godmother's own skin, practically, in which Cinderella is dressed), the glass slippers, in contrast, are all ambition, eloquent—by imitation—of little more than the wealth they are meant to attract; we might say what they "stand for" is an increasing hardness—of the heart.

Replacing "the hairy animal" with the exemplary, if immaterial, princess, the conversion narrative seeks to set us clearly on one side or the other of those transparent boundaries holding in place the usual series of suspect dichotomies (animal/human, nature/culture, body/mind, etc.). *For whose benefit?* As Perrault tells it, "Cendrillon" takes its displayed place on the pedagogue's bookshelf as yet another story about desensitization to the violent self-sunderings such lines in the (burning) sand require of those who toe them.

So here she is, our heroine, in the clearing the switch of a couple of letters made, still hobbling around the ballroom, *clink, clink, clink,* a bright smile held in place over feelings she is learning to ignore the existence of. By every standard of measurement made available to her, she's a success: denuded and provably "human," the fact that her foot is *like his* something the prince can be lucid about. If there's the "horror of nothing to see" higher up, at least her supervisor's seeing everything now—twinkle toes doing just that, stars of the televised and silenced foot. Dazzling advertisement for the money shot, she is packaged for consumption: she is a dish, as we say, but also *dished.*

Stop looking at me like that—I mean it—and try this: make a fist and wedge it into, yes, a wine glass. Doesn't your hand look like some kind of scientific exhibit? (The fragile label inked with the Latin name is all that is lacking.) But how does it feel? Aren't your knuckles starting to hurt? Would you like to (put the other hand in a matching glass) try a handstand? Nervous? The glass gets moist. Steamed up, as we say, meaning, I've had about enough of this!

Breath catching in her throat, our heroine (on her knees at the sale rack), holds up someone's more sensible version in Lucite, just "her" size—only to notice the little air holes discreetly punched in the plastic and be, breathing again, reminded of the flesh, the facts. *This isn't the shoe* I *lost.* Setting out to be understood by way of what is literally under her standing, what will she find, now, to please herself?

NOTES

Special thanks to artist and author Rikki Ducornet for her illustration to this essay. Her most recent novel is *The Fanmaker's Inquisition.* Ducornet confides that at one point she dreamed incessantly that the men she was fond of were giving her shoes—gorgeous shoes!

1. Marina Warner, *From the Beast to the Blond* (New York: Farrar, Straus and Giroux, 1995), 361–362.

2. "The rejection, the exclusion of a feminine imaginary certainly puts woman in the position of experiencing herself only fragmentarily, in the little structured margins of a dominant ideology, as waste, or excess, what is left of a mirror invested by the (masculine) 'subject' to reflect himself, to copy himself" (Luce Irigaray, *This Sex Which Is Not One* [Ithaca: Cornell University Press, 1985], 30).

3. "Le Miroir, ou la Métamorphose d'Orante" (1661) appears along with "Cendrillon, ou la Petite Pantoufle de Verre" in Charles Perrault, *Contes* (Paris: Editions Gallimard, 1981). The attention paid mirrors and glass within "Cendrillon" reflects many of the doublings the narrative deals with: doubled daughters of a second wife, the stepsisters are set apart from our heroine not only by their duplicities but by the mirrors in their bedrooms, "ou elles se voyaient depuis les pieds jusqu'à la tête," reflected wholenesses they give the whole of their time to before a ball that occurs twice. In a word, the "paire de pantoufles de verre" might serve as a metonymy for the pairing and repairing necessary where almost nothing goes unmated. For a fuller description of the emphasis on the visual in Perrault, see Philip Lewis, *Seeing through the Mother Goose Tales* (Stanford: Stanford University Press, 1996).

4. Commentators seem to be in agreement that the story—as far back as its steps can be traced— hails from China, where the emphasis on the smallness of the shoe takes on a literally painful significance.

5. Accessory after the fact and detective's tool, what is arrested by the slipper is a slippage of identity directly referenced by the fairy tale's substitutions of social roles for names, as well as via its doublings and replacements. This slippage most evidently affects the female figures (the arrival of the second wife and the new daughters establishes Cinderella's nickname, location, status, and apparent replaceability in the family syntax), whereas the male figures are relatively stable (neither the father nor the prince can be replaced, except insofar as the latter replaces the former in what we might call, for lack of a better word, our heroine's heart). Such an uneasy flux is halted only by what the story must emphasize as the decidedly nonarbitrary linkage of a signified (Cinderella) to its signifier (her slipper), so as to sign further. But the signifier of Cinderella's uniqueness can only be read, as difference, in the context of a language that calls such uniqueness into considerable doubt. Tried on, or, rather, attempted, by women of decreasingly lower rank, the shoe will reveal real worth inside apparent unworthiness, by way, however, of what is usually classed as mere appearance. Here the body produces itself as truth effect (against the sad evidence of sale racks decimated by previous Cinderellas): our heroine has the only foot this slipper will fit. Isn't this in fact the essence of the shell or shoe game we shill out for? The purchase (if we're lucky or early or . . .) of an individuality we must at once believe in the uniqueness of while also swearing allegiance to the promise that everyone else can—on credit if need be—also own. In the perfect bourgeois bedtime story the commodity steps forth, transcendent, to sign for what is "sans prix" (as the first "Moralité" attached to Perrault's tale puts it).

6. In this economy it comes as no surprise to see that he who sings out at the sight of "nothing," as Freud does, becomes the country's one-eyed king. Speaking of which, that "Gentilhomme" taking around the transparent slipper in the prince's place—holding out nothing at all, apparently (it's more *pantomime* than *pantoufle*)—might be enacting my favorite feminist joke:

> "Why are women so bad at math?"
> "I dunno, why?"
> "Because they've always been told this"—hands held apart, oh, say the length of a Golden Lotus shoe—"is nine inches."

Do I digress? Suffice to say that what's sought for the slipper's tight fit isn't motion but meat.

7. Where Prince Charming is harming and hamming: *Hamlet,* act 3, scene 1, in *The Complete Works of Shakespeare* (New York: Gannis and Harris, 1953), 689.

8. "For the problem of the observer is the field on which vision in history can be said to materialize, to become itself visible. Vision and its effects are always inseparable from the possibilities of an observing subject who is both the historical product and the site of certain practices, techniques, institutions and procedures of subjectification" (Jonathan Crary, *Techniques of the Observer* [Cambridge, Mass.: MIT Press,1992], 5).

9. "Fetishism" (1927), in *The Standard Edition of the Complete Psychological Works of Sigmund Freud,* ed. James Strachey with Anna Freud, vol. 21 (London: Hogarth Press, 1953–74), 152–157. Where "Cinderella" becomes clear as glass—or apparently transparent—Bruno Bettelheim puts his foot in it: to his eyes the story is "overtly . . . only about sibling rivalry of girls" and "covert[ly]" allusive to "castration anxiety" (the slipper is one of the "many and varied defenses" protecting the feminine psyche "from such imagined deficiency"). But no little bird has to tell us that Bettelheim has cut off whatever won't fit (the author's sex, for starters) to get into Freud's shoes, and his account pays painfully for its attempt to pass itself off as true. Bettelheim uses the story of the glass slipper to get down "the royal road to the unconscious mind" in a pair of glasses that "permit us to form a new and richer view of ourselves and the nature of our humanity." This "view" depends for its lucidity on our belief in the fairy tale of a natural, universal "humanity"; if we *actually* desired what we've been *told* we desire, it would work—but how well does the "you" fit, really? See his *The Uses of Enchantment* (New York: Knopf, 1976), 266–273.

10. Luce Irigaray, "Another 'Cause'—Castration," from *Speculum of the Other Woman* (1974), reprinted in *Feminisms,* ed. Robyn R. Warhol and Diane Price Herndl (New Brunswick, N.J.: Rutgers University Press, 1997), 431.

11. "So now [she] must put her foot into the hideous receptacle, this open wound, still slick and warm as it is, for nothing in any of the many texts of this tale suggests the prince washed the shoe out between the fittings" (Angela Carter, "Ashputtle or the Mother's Ghost," in *Burning Your Boats* [New York: Penguin, 1997], 394).

12. "But what is applauded and who sets the terms of the recognition and acceptance are always in question" (ibid., 362).

13. Irigaray, *This Sex Which Is Not One,* 26.

14. Fulke Greville, from "Caelica," section 56: "Cupid did best shoot and see / In the night where smooth is fair." The poem makes suggestive connections between sight, impotence, and pedagogy. *Selected Poems of Fulke Greville* (Chicago: University of Chicago Press, 1968), 84.

15. Hélène Cixous, "The Laugh of the Medusa," reprinted in *New French Feminisms,* ed. Elaine Marks and Isabelle de Courtivron (New York: Shocken, 1981), 256. At this point it might be better to say that almost everything has yet to be *read,* for some of what can be said certainly has been, by writers like Gertrude Stein and Emily Dickinson (for instance), and *is* being said by authors such as Cixous herself, Rikki Ducornet, and—at the head of a list that keeps wonderfully lengthening— Carole Maso, to whom I owe my first sight of the Cixous quote as well as a long view of the possibilities experimental writing by women has opened and keeps opening.

Postscript

Big Feets; or, How Cinderella's Glass Slippers Got Smashed under the Heel of a Size Ten Doc Marten

TODD LYON

It's 1971. I'm in Alexander's in the Milford Post Shopping Center, trying on a pair of high-heeled platform shoes made of crinkly blue patent leather. They're the highest shoes I've ever walked in. Way racy for the seventh grade.

"They make your feet look *tiny*," says my older, therefore cooler, sister.

I wear about a size eight back then, so this is a major compliment. We refer to any shoes over size five as "gunboats." The shoes I'm trying on have chunky heels and a quarter-inch platform; the length of the foot is perceived as being as long as the distance from the back of the heel to the tip of the toe—about seven inches.

Tiny.

We, that is, me and the other girls hitting puberty in numbers so large that for the next few years we'll be railroaded into crappy "temporary classrooms" that look a *lot* like trailers, aspire to tiny foothood. Never mind that the models we worship in magazines are tall and skinny and have long feet that look like femurs on whippets. We carry cultural vestiges. To us, little feet are feminine, wifely. I have read *The Good Earth* by Pearl Buck, and I know that she was cruelly mocked by Chinese women for the humongousness of her size four feet. And, although my mother never let me have a Barbie doll, I have also put in time staring at the tiniest shoes in the world—smaller than the nail on my pinkie—made of microscopic strips of white plastic. They fit Barbie's toeless feet as perfectly—whoosh!—as a Cinderella story.

Come to think of it, it was probably the tale of Cinderella—the stinkin' Disney version, in my case—that was lurking beneath my fervent belief in the superiority of small feet. Those ugly stepsisters were clodhopping, clumsy, flat-footed. They galumphed and flapped from here to there on big ol' dogs—and they probably had corns and hammertoes, too. Even their title, "stepsisters," defined them as noisy-walking girls, girls for whom the word "coarse" might be whispered, haughtily, by those with superior social graces.

Ah, but Cinderella—she floated. Her feet were so small that they barely touched the ground. When the love-crazed prince went from door to door with Cinderella's glass slipper—that's how they always referred to her shoes, you know, not "pumps" or "mules" or even "footwear," but "slippers"—what he was really looking for was the woman with the smallest feet in the kingdom. Those tiny feet were the very definition of refinement. It wasn't her sparkling conversation, fashion sense, or dancing skills that deemed Cinderella queenly and desirable. It was her teeny-weeny, eensy-beensy little feet.

So I was all aflutter when the blue platform shoes turned out to have a tinifying effect on my size eights.

But there was something else I liked about them. It was 1971, remember, and at home I had Janis Joplin's album, *Got Them Ol' Kosmic Blues Again Mama*. So I'd seen R. Crumb's underground comix, and I knew that Crumb loved big feets. He loved thick-boned, high-assed, braless women who used parking meters as walking sticks. Crumb drew them as if he were a sidewalk, worshiping the huge pounding underbottoms of hobnail boots; his pen licked the heels of chunky platform shoes like these.

The Crumb women were a bit like my oldest, and therefore coolest, sister. She and her friends wore manly shoes—army boots, Frye boots, work boots, cowboy boots—and laughed at girls with hairdos and culottes who wore slingbacks and little white Keds. One of her best friends, Olivia, had a pair of boots with stacked wooden heels and thick brown leather uppers that laced all the way up to her knees. She wore them with Boy Scout shorts and white undershirts of the kind that I, in seventh grade, was still wearing, shamefully, under my blouses.

My oldest sister and her friends were musicians and revolutionaries. They went to Black Panther rallies and snuck into concerts. They weren't saving themselves for marriage. They didn't give a damn how big their feet looked in shoes. They were women who could dance but were more interested in *marching*. In spite of their college educations, they worked as laborers—motel maids, truck drivers, bartenders.

I bought the blue platforms with my mother's charge plate and a permission slip, and let me tell you: I should have been crowned Miss Shoes 1971. I was a Cinderella girl and an R. Crumb woman, all at once. In those platforms I was tall as a model and as shiny as a blessed soul at Sunday School. I could pound pavement and strike fear in the heart of linoleum, I could crush tiny white Keds under one heel, and yet, for all their electric blue power, those shoes made my feet look small.

————

Clowns have big feets. They have to. I think it's a law or something. Except in France, where anybody could put a black dot under each eye and call themselves a clown or maybe a "clown artist," big feets are one of the main things that separate clowns from the rest of the population. Example: If you see a stunning woman in a chic outfit walking down the street, you might think, "Ooh, a powerful executive." But if she's wearing fourteen-inch yellow foam rubber shoes with floppy flowers on the toes, you can be pretty sure she's a clown.

Same goes for hicks. Anybody could wear a pair of faded overalls and a straw hat, maybe even chew on a piece of hay, and look perfectly at home in the pages of a J. Crew catalog. Add an oversize pair of work boots with one huge throbbing toe sticking out the end, however, and you've got yourself a genuine hick.

Big feets are an important part of what makes clowns and hicks "funny." It's a code: anybody with big, knobby dogs has probably been raised going barefoot, which is how their feets got so big in the first place. Maybe the big-footed have been working in the fields, or living in a hollow log and eating skunk cabbage and squirrel meat. Even if our feet are just inches smaller than theirs, we can, in relief, laugh at them, knowing that we've got class and they don't.

It's pretty easy to trace all of this cultural coding of feets back to worker/gentry tension. But now it's 1999 (a year claimed by Prince, who looks great in high heels), and big feets aren't so funny anymore. Foot Locker, the athletic shoe emporium, has a pair of basketball star Shaquille O'Neil's sneakers on display in one of its stores. They're size twenty-four or something, big enough for two litters of puppies to be born in. The kids gather around, gawking in awe, wondering if, someday, they'll have what it takes to fill them. Nobody laughs.

In Japan, avant-garde style setters have taken to wearing extremely long shoes. These shoes look like the pointy-toed shoes that British Mods wore in the 1960s, but they're way, way longer. They're so long that, with each step, they actually fold in the middle. The first time I ever saw a pair of these was on a home videotape made by a woman from Japan. The footage was of a flea market in Kyoto, and the camera was focusing on kitchy displays of toys laid out on a table. But in the background I noticed the unmistakable flap and slap of a pair of clown shoes walking by. I asked her to rewind the tape and play the footage again, then again, and pumped her for information: Is this a joke?

(No, it's the height of style.) Why are these clown shoes considered stylish? (I don't know.) Does this reflect a desire for Westernization? Have rich Japanese people, many of whom have their hair permed and their eyes "done" to look more Western, come to associate big feets with American culture or somehow with modernism?

After a while, the Japanese woman stopped answering my questions.

———————

On Eighth Street in downtown Manhattan, the grooviest shoe stores display women's size tens in their windows. It's really hard to tell them apart from the men's styles because, in addition to being big, the women's shoes are mostly variations on traditional men's styles: loafers, wing tips, work boots, hiking boots, engineer boots. Though many of these women's fashions have a feminine twist to them—the heel is higher or the laces are smaller—there are at least two kinds of shoes that break all boundaries between men and women, workers and gentry, rich and poor: athletic shoes and Doc Martens.

And what do these two styles have in common? Utility.

Athletic shoes are so blatantly utilitarian that they've been stripped of their skin. We see the engineering that goes into each shoe; we're exposed to the padding, the air pockets, the arch supports. Like modern art and Dave Letterman's TV show, these shoes have no secret backstage area. No attempt at illusion is made. Decorative sleight of hand is banished. The shoes themselves are machines for the feet, and the one who wears these shoes is the machine operator.

Most athletic shoes are really big, compared to, say, a pair of twee Pappagalos. This is because they're thickly padded. High-topped basketball shoes, designed to absorb shock and promote speed, have so many layers of engineering in them that they look like La-Z-Boy recliners—without the upholstery.

But bigness of foot doesn't seem to be a problem for sporting women. When she was in the sixth grade, NWBA star Rebecca Lobo Mim once told a friend that she wanted to be six-foot-seven. Her friend told her she was crazy, because if she was that tall she wouldn't be able to date guys. "Yeah," Rebecca replied, "but if I were six-foot-seven I could dunk."

If Rebecca had a Cinderella dream, it didn't involve glass slippers or the tiny feet that went into them. Her golden carriage came in the form of an undefeated season; her prince came in the form of a big fat contract.

Doc Martens don't apologize, either. They're made of industrial-strength leather and feature thick, air-cushioned soles. These heavy-duty boots and shoes first became popular with kids in Britain in the early 1960s; before that they were strictly for workmen, who bought them because they were comfortable and virtually never wore out. Linda O'Keefe notes that "by the '70s male and female club kids and punk rockers around the world had discovered the boots' defiantly quirky, almost brutal simplicity."[1]

I myself resisted buying Doc Martens for years and years, because I wasn't a squatter and didn't own a skateboard. I thought I didn't have enough piercings to pull them off. And anyway, I'm over forty and figured I'd need a fake ID to buy them. But then, in a funky little store, I spotted a pair that I couldn't resist trying on. They were dead black, with shining red flames climbing up the toes. The shaved-headed she-clerk brought them to me in a box so big it could have held the hearts of a dozen enemies.

The boots were heavy and smelled darkly of rubber and leather. I fit them over my size ten dogs, laced 'em up, and planted myself in front of a mirror. Because the mirror was on the floor, tilted back in a worshipful pose, it made my feet look twice as big as my head. The mirror told me I was the most grounded and powerful woman in the land. In these indestructible boots I could ride motorcycles, jump over mountains, pound sidewalks, hike the tundra, kick anybody that got in my way. I could dance all night and, at the stroke of midnight, run down the stairs. No matter how long that staircase or how fast I ran down those steps, these shoes would stay on my feets, protecting and empowering me, happily ever after.

I bought them with a credit card, and now I get the sense that, when I'm not looking, they make my high heels feel bad about themselves.

NOTE

1. Linda O'Keefe, *Shoes: A Celebration of Pumps, Sandals, Slippers, and More* (New York: Workman, 1996), 280.

Appendix

Cinderella, or the Little Glass Slipper

CHARLES PERRAULT

Once there was a gentleman who married, for his second wife, the proudest and most haughty woman that was ever seen. She had, by a former husband, two daughters of her own humor, who were, indeed, exactly like her in all things. He had likewise, by another wife, a young daughter, but of unparalleled goodness and sweetness of temper, which she took from her mother, who had been the best creature in the world.

No sooner were the ceremonies of the wedding over than the stepmother began to show herself in her true colors. She could not bear the good qualities of this pretty girl, and the less because they made her own daughters appear the more odious. She employed her in the meanest work of the house: she scoured the dishes, tables, etc., and scrubbed madam's chamber, and those of misses, her daughters. She lay up in a sorry garret, upon a wretched straw bed, while her sisters lay in fine rooms, with floors all inlaid, upon beds of the very newest fashion, and where they had looking glasses so large that they might see themselves at their full length from head to foot.

The poor girl bore all patiently, and dared not tell her father, who would have rattled her off; for his wife governed him entirely. When she had done her work, she used to go into the chimney corner, and sit down among cinders and ashes, which made her

Reprinted from *The Blue Fairy Book*, ed. Andrew Lang (New York: Random House, 1959), 96–104.

commonly be called *Cinderwench;* but the youngest, who was not so rude and uncivil as the eldest, called her Cinderella. However, Cinderella, notwithstanding her mean apparel, was a hundred times handsomer than her sisters, though they were always dressed very richly.

It happened that the King's son gave a ball, and invited all persons of fashion to it. Our young misses were also invited, for they cut a very grand figure among the quality. They were mightily delighted at this invitation, and wonderfully busy in choosing out such gowns, petticoats, and headclothes as might become them. This was a new trouble to Cinderella; for it was she who ironed her sisters' linen, and plaited their ruffles; they talked all day long of nothing but how they should be dressed.

"For my part," said the eldest, "I will wear my red velvet suit with French trimming."

"And I," said the youngest, "shall have my usual petticoat; but then, to make amends for that, I will put on my gold-flowered manteau, and my diamond stomacher, which is far from being the most ordinary one in the world."

They sent for the best tirewoman they could get to make up their headdresses and adjust their double pinners, and they had their red brushes and patches from Mademoiselle de la Poche.

Cinderella was likewise called up to them to be consulted in all these matters, for she had excellent notions, and advised them always for the best, nay, and offered her services to dress their heads, which they were very willing she should do. As she was doing this, they said to her:

"Cinderella, would you not be glad to go to the ball?"

"Alas!" said she, "you only jeer me; it is not for such as I am to go thither."

"Thou art in the right of it," replied they. "It would make the people laugh to see a cinderwench at a ball."

Anyone but Cinderella would have dressed their heads awry, but she was very good, and dressed them perfectly well. They were almost two days without eating, so much were they transported with joy. They broke more than a dozen laces in trying to be laced up close, that they might have a fine slender shape, and they were continually at their looking glass. At last the happy day came; they went to court, and Cinderella followed them with her eyes as long as she could, and when she had lost sight of them, she fell a-crying.

Her godmother, who saw her all in tears, asked her what was the matter.

"I wish I could—I wish I could—"; she was not able to speak the rest, being interrupted by her tears and sobbing.

This godmother of hers, who was a fairy, said to her, "Thou wishest thou couldst go to the ball; is it not so?"

"Y-es," cried Cinderella, with a great sigh.

"Well," said her godmother, "be but a good girl, and I will contrive that thou shalt go." Then she took her into her chamber, and said to her, "Run into the garden, and bring me a pumpkin."

Cinderella went immediately to gather the finest she could get, and brought it to her godmother, not being able to imagine how this pumpkin could make her go to the ball. Her godmother scooped out all the inside of it, having left nothing but the rind; which done, she struck it with her wand, and the pumpkin was instantly turned into a fine coach, gilded all over with gold.

She then went to look into her mousetrap, where she found six mice, all alive, and ordered Cinderella to lift up a little the trap door, when, giving each mouse, as it went out, a little tap with her wand, the mouse was that moment turned into a fine horse, which altogether made a very fine set of six horses of a beautiful mouse-colored dapple gray. Being at a loss for a coachman:

"I will go and see," says Cinderella, "if there is not a rat in the rattrap—we may make a coachman of him."

"Thou art in the right," replied her godmother. "Go and look."

Cinderella brought the trap to her, and in it there were three huge rats. The fairy made choice of one of the three which had the largest beard, and, having been touched with her wand, he was turned into a fat, jolly coachman, who had the smartest whiskers eyes ever beheld. After that, she said to her:

"Go again into the garden, and you will find six lizards behind the watering-pot. Bring them to me."

She had no sooner done so but her godmother turned them into six footmen, who skipped immediately behind the coach, with their liveries all bedaubed with gold and silver, and clung as close behind each other as if they had done nothing else their whole lives. The fairy then said to Cinderella:

"Well, you see here an equipage fit to go to the ball with; are you not pleased with it?"

"Oh, yes!" cried she. "But must I go thither as I am, in these nasty rags?"

Her godmother only just touched her with her wand, and, at the same instant, her clothes were turned into cloth of gold and silver, all beset with jewels. This done, she gave her a pair of glass slippers, the prettiest in the whole world. Being thus decked out, she got up into her coach; but her godmother, above all things, commanded her not to stay till after midnight, telling her, at the same time, that if she stayed one moment longer, the coach would be a pumpkin again, her horses mice, her coachman a rat, her footmen lizards, and her clothes become just as they were before.

She promised her godmother she would not fail to leave the ball before midnight; and then away she drives, scarce able to contain herself for joy. The King's son, who was told that a great princess, whom nobody knew, was come, ran out to receive her; he gave her his hand as she alighted from the coach, and led her into the hall, among all the company. There was immediately a profound silence. The people stopped dancing, and the violins ceased to play, so attentive was everyone to contemplate the singular beauties of the unknown newcomer. Nothing was then heard but a confused noise of:

"Ha! how handsome she is! Ha! how handsome she is!"

The King himself, old as he was, could not help watching her, and telling the Queen softly that it was a long time since he had seen so beautiful and lovely a creature.

All the ladies were busied in considering her clothes and head-dress, that they might have some made next day after the same pattern, provided they could meet with such fine material and as able hands to make them.

The King's son conducted her to the most honorable seat, and afterward took her out to dance with him; she danced so very gracefully that they all more and more admired her. A fine collation was served up, whereof the younger prince ate not a morsel, so intently was he busied in gazing on her.

She went and sat down by her sisters, showing them a thousand civilities, giving them part of the oranges and citrons which the Prince had presented her with, which very much surprised them, for they did not know her. While Cinderella was thus amusing her sisters, she heard the clock strike eleven and three quarters, whereupon she immediately made a courtesy to the company and hasted away as fast as she could.

When she got home she ran to seek out her godmother, and, after having thanked her, she said she could not but heartily wish she might go next day to the ball, because the King's son had desired her.

As she was eagerly telling her godmother whatever had passed at the ball, her two sisters knocked at the door, which Cinderella ran and opened.

"How long you have stayed!" cried she, gaping, rubbing her eyes and stretching herself as if she had been just waked out of her sleep; she had not, however, any manner of inclination to sleep since they went from home.

"If thou hadst been at the ball," said one of her sisters, "thou wouldst not have been tired with it. There came thither the finest princess, the most beautiful ever was seen with mortal eyes; she showed us a thousand civilities, and gave us oranges and citrons."

Cinderella seemed very indifferent in the matter; indeed, she asked them the name of that princess. But they told her they did not know it, and that the King's son was very uneasy on her account and would give all the world to know who she was. At this Cinderella, smiling, replied:

"She must, then, be very beautiful indeed; how happy you have been! Could not I see her? Ah! dear Miss Charlotte, do lend me your yellow suit of clothes which you wear every day."

"Ay, to be sure!" cried Miss Charlotte. "Lend my clothes to such a dirty cinder-wench as thou art! I should be a fool."

Cinderella, indeed, expected well such answer, and was very glad of the refusal; for she would have been sadly put to it if her sister had lent her what she asked for jestingly.

The next day the two sisters were at the ball, and so was Cinderella, but dressed more magnificently than before. The King's son was always by her, and never ceased his compliments and kind speeches to her; to whom all this was so far from being tiresome that she quite forgot what her godmother had recommended to her; so that she, at last, counted the clock striking twelve when she took it to be no more than eleven; she then rose up and fled, as nimble as a deer. The Prince followed, but could not overtake her. She left behind one of her glass slippers, which the Prince took up most carefully. She got home, but quite out of breath, and in her nasty old clothes, having nothing left her of all her finery but one of the little slippers, fellow to that she dropped. The guards at the palace gate were asked if they had not seen a princess go out.

Who said: They had seen nobody go out but a young girl, very meanly dressed, and who had more the air of a poor country wench than a gentlewoman.

When the two sisters returned from the ball Cinderella asked them if they had been well diverted, and if the fine lady had been there.

They told her: Yes, but that she hurried away immediately when it struck twelve, and with so much haste that she dropped one of her little glass slippers, the prettiest in the world, which the King's son had taken up; that he had done nothing but look at her all the time at the ball, and that most certainly he was very much in love with the beautiful person who owned the glass slipper.

What they said was very true; for a few days after, the King's son caused it to be proclaimed, by sound of trumpet, that he would marry her whose foot the slipper would just fit. They whom he employed began to try it upon the princesses, then the duchesses and all the court, but in vain; it was brought to the two sisters, who did all they possibly could to thrust their foot into the slipper, but they could not effect it. Cinderella, who saw all this, and knew her slipper, said to them, laughing:

"Let me see if it will not fit me."

Her sisters burst out a-laughing, and began to banter her. The gentleman who was sent to try the slipper looked earnestly at Cinderella, and, finding her very handsome, said it was but just that she should try, and that he had orders to let everyone make trial.

He obliged Cinderella to sit down, and, putting the slipper to her foot, he found it went on very easily, and fitted her as if it had been made of wax. The astonishment her two sisters were in was excessively great, but still abundantly greater when Cinderella pulled out of her pocket the other slipper, and put it on her foot. Thereupon, in came her godmother, who, having touched with her wand Cinderella's clothes, made them richer and more magnificent than any of those she had before.

And now her sisters found her to be that fine, beautiful lady whom they had seen at the ball. They threw themselves at her feet to beg pardon for all the ill-treatment they had made her undergo. Cinderella took them up, and, as she embraced them, cried that she forgave them with all her heart, and desired them always to love her.

She was conducted to the young Prince, dressed as she was; he thought her more charming than ever, and, a few days after, married her. Cinderella, who was no less good than beautiful, gave her two sisters lodgings in the palace, and that very same day matched them with two great lords of the court.

The Red Shoes

HANS   CHRISTIAN   ANDERSEN

*O*nce, there was a little girl who was pretty and delicate but very poor. In the summer she had to go barefoot and in the winter she had to wear wooden shoes that rubbed against her poor little ankles and made them red and sore.

In the same village there lived an old widow whose husband had been a shoemaker; and she sat sewing a pair of shoes from scraps of red material. She did her very best, but the shoes looked a bit clumsy, though they were sewn with kindness. They were meant for the poor little girl, whose name was Karen.

Now on that very day that her mother was to be buried, Karen was given the red shoes. Though they weren't the proper color for mourning, she had no others, so she put them on. Raggedly dressed, barelegged, with red shoes on her feet, she walked behind the pauper's coffin.

A big old-fashioned carriage drove by; in it sat an old lady. She noticed the little girl and felt so sorry for her that she went at once to the minister and spoke to him. "Let me have that little girl, and I shall be good to her and bring her up."

Karen thought it was because of her new red shoes that the old lady had taken a fancy to her. But the old lady declared that the shoes looked frightful and had them thrown

Reprinted from *A Treasury of Hans Christian Andersen,* trans. Eric Christian Haugaard (New York: Barnes and Noble Books, 1993), 231–236.

into the stove and burned. Karen was dressed in nice clean clothes and taught to read and to sew. Everyone agreed that she was a very pretty child; but the mirror said, "You are more than pretty, you are beautiful."

It happened that the queen was making a journey throughout the country, and she had her daughter, the little princess, with her. Everywhere people streamed to see them. When they arrived at a castle near Karen's village, the little girl followed the crowd out there. Looking out of one of the great windows of the castle was the little princess. So that people could see her, she was standing on a little stool. She had no crown on her head but she wore a very pretty white dress and the loveliest red shoes, made from morocco. They were certainly much prettier than the ones the old shoemaker's widow had made for Karen. But even they had been red shoes, and to Karen nothing else in the world was so desirable.

Karen became old enough to be confirmed. She was to have a new dress and new shoes for this solemn occasion. The old lady took her to the finest shoemaker in the nearby town and he measured her little foot. Glass cabinets filled with the most elegant shoes and boots covered the walls of his shop. But the old lady's eyesight was so poor that she didn't get much out of looking at the display. Karen did; between two pairs of boots stood a pair of red shoes just like the ones the princess had worn. Oh, how beautiful they were! The shoemaker said that they had been made for the daughter of a count but that they hadn't fit her.

"I think they are patent leather," remarked the old lady. "They shine."

"Yes, they shine!" sighed Karen as she tried them on. They fit the child and the old woman bought them. Had she known that they were red, she wouldn't have because it was not proper to wear red shoes when you were being confirmed. But her eyesight was failing—poor woman!—and she had not seen the color.

Everyone in the church looked at Karen's feet, as she walked toward the altar. On the walls of the church hung paintings of the former ministers and their wives who were buried there; they were portrayed wearing black with white ruffs around their necks. Karen felt that even they were staring at her red shoes.

When the old bishop laid his hands on her head and spoke of the solemn promise she was about to make—of her covenant with God to be a good Christian—her mind was not on his words. The ritual music was played on the organ; the old cantor sang, and the sweet voices of the children could be heard, but Karen was thinking of her red shoes.

By afternoon, everyone had told the old lady about the color of Karen's shoes. She was very angry and scolded the girl, telling her how improper it was to have worn red shoes in church, and that she must remember always to wear black ones, even if she had to put on an old pair.

Next Sunday Karen was to attend communion. She looked at her black shoes and she looked at her red shoes; then she looked at her red shoes once more and put them on.

The sun was shining, it was a beautiful day. The old lady and Karen took the path across the fields and their shoes got a bit dirty.

At the entrance to the church stood an old invalid soldier leaning on a crutch. He had a marvelously long beard that was red with touches of white in it. He bowed low toward the old lady and asked her permission to wipe the dust off her feet. Karen put her little foot forward too.

"What pretty little dancing shoes!" said the soldier and, tapping them on the soles, he added, "Remember to stay on her feet for the dance."

The old lady gave the soldier a penny, and she and Karen entered the church.

Again everyone looked at Karen's feet, even the people in the paintings on the wall. When she knelt in front of the altar and the golden cup was lifted to her lips, she thought only of the red shoes and saw them reflected in the wine. She did not join in the singing of the psalm and she forgot to say the Lord's Prayer.

The coachman had come with the carriage to drive them home from church. The old lady climbed in and Karen was about to follow her when the old soldier, who was standing nearby, remarked, "Look at those pretty dancing shoes."

His words made her take a few dancing steps. Once she had begun, her feet would not stop. It was as if the shoes had taken command of them. She danced around the corner of the church; her will was not her own.

The coachman jumped off the carriage and ran after her. When he finally caught up with her, he grabbed her and lifted her up from the ground, but her feet kept on dancing in the air, even after he managed to get her into the carriage. The poor old woman was kicked nastily while she and the coachman took Karen's shoes off her feet, so she could stop dancing.

When they got home, the red shoes were put away in a closet, but Karen could not help sneaking in to look at them.

The old lady was very ill. The doctors had come and said that she would not live much longer. She needed careful nursing and constant care, and who else but Karen ought to give it to her? In the town there was to be a great ball and Karen had been invited to go. She looked at the old lady, who was going to die anyway, and then she glanced at her red shoes. To glance was no sin. Then she put them on; that too did no great harm. But she went to the ball!

She danced! But when she wanted to dance to the left, the shoes danced to the right; and when she wanted to dance up the ballroom floor, the shoes danced right down the stairs and out into the street. Dance she did, out through the city gates and into the dark forest.

Something shone through the trees. She thought it was the moon because it had a face. But it was not; it was the old soldier with the red beard. He nodded to her and exclaimed, "Look what beautiful dancing shoes!"

Terrified, she tried to pull off her shoes. She tore her stockings but the shoes stayed on. They had grown fast to her feet. Dance she did! And dance she must! Over the fields and meadows, in the rain and sunshine, by night and by day. But it was more horrible and frightening at night when the world was dark.

She danced through the gates of the churchyard; but the dead did not dance with her, they had better things to do. She wanted to sit down on the pauper's grave, where the bitter herbs grew, but for her there was no rest. The church door was open and she danced toward it, but an angel, dressed in white, who had on his back great wings that reached almost to the ground, barred her entrance.

His face was stern and grave, and in his hand he held a broad, shining sword.

"You shall dance," he said, "dance in your red shoes until you become pale and thin. Dance till the skin on your face turns yellow and clings to your bones as if you were a skeleton. Dance you shall from door to door, and when you pass a house where proud and vain children live, there you shall knock on the door so that they will see you and fear your fate. Dance, you shall dance. . . . Dance!"

"Mercy!" screamed Karen, but heard not what the angel answered, for her red shoes carried her away, down through the churchyard, over the meadows, along the highways, through the lanes: always dancing.

One morning she danced past a house that she knew well. From inside she heard psalms being sung. The door opened and a coffin decked with flowers was carried out. The old lady who had been so kind to her was dead. Now she felt that she was forsaken by all of mankind and cursed by God's angel.

Dance she must, and dance she did. The shoes carried her across fields and meadows, through nettles and briars that tore her feet so they bled.

One morning she danced across the lonely heath until she came to a solitary cottage. Here, she knew, the executioner lived. With her fingers she tapped on his window.

"Come out! Come out!" she called. "I cannot come inside, for I must dance."

The executioner opened his door and came outside. When he saw Karen he said, "Do you know who I am? I am the one who cuts off the heads of evil men; and I can feel my ax beginning to quiver now."

"Do not cut off my head," begged Karen, "for then I should not be able to repent. But cut off my feet!"

She confessed her sins and the executioner cut off her feet, and the red shoes danced away with them into the dark forest. The executioner carved a pair of wooden feet for her and made her a pair of crutches. He taught her the psalm that a penitent sings. She kissed the hand that had guided the ax and went on her way.

"Now I have suffered enough because of those red shoes," thought Karen. "I shall go to church now and be among other people."

But when she walked up to the door of the church, the red shoes danced in front of her, and in horror she fled.

All during that week she felt sad and cried many a bitter tear. When Sunday came she thought, "Now I have suffered and struggled long enough. I am just as good as many of those who are sitting and praying in church right now, and who dare to throw their heads back with pride." This reasoning gave her courage, but she came no farther than the gate of the churchyard. There were the shoes dancing in front of her. In terror she fled, but this time she really repented in the depth of her heart.

She went to the minister's house and begged to be given work. She said that she did not care about wages but only wanted a roof over her head and enough to eat. The minister's wife hired the poor cripple because she felt sorry for her. Karen was grateful that she had been given a place to live and she worked hard. In the evening when the minister read from the Bible, she sat and listened thoughtfully. The children were fond of her and she played with them, but when they talked of finery and being beautiful like a princess, she would sadly shake her head.

When Sunday came, everyone in the household got ready for church, and they asked her to go with them. Poor Karen's eyes filled with tears. She sighed and glanced toward her crutches.

When the others had gone, she went into her little room that was so small that a bed and a chair were all it could hold. She sat down and began to read from her psalmbook. The wind carried the music from the church organ down to her, and she lifted her tear-stained face and whispered, "Oh, God, help me!"

Suddenly the sunlight seemed doubly bright and an angel of God stood before her. He was the same angel who with his sword had barred her entrance to the church, but now he held a rose branch covered with flowers. With this he touched the low ceiling of the room and it rose high into the air and, where he had touched it, a golden star shone. He touched the walls and they widened.

Karen saw the organ. She saw the old paintings of the ministers and their wives; and there were the congregation holding their psalmbooks in front of them and singing. The church had come to the poor girl in her little narrow chamber; or maybe she had come to the church. Now she sat among the others, and when they finished singing the psalm they looked up and saw her.

Someone whispered to her: "It is good that you came, Karen."

"This is His mercy," she replied.

The great organ played and the voices of the children in the choir mingled sweetly with it. The clear, warm sunshine streamed through the window. The sunshine filled Karen's heart till it so swelled with peace and happiness that it broke. Her soul flew on a sunbeam up to God; and up there no one asked her about the red shoes.

SELECTED BIBLIOGRAPHY

Agins, Teri. *The End of Fashion: The Mass Marketing of the Clothing Business.* New York: William Morrow, 1999.

All about Shoes: Footwear through the Ages. Toronto: Bata, 1994.

Barthes, Roland. *The Fashion System.* Trans. Matthew Ward and Richard Howard. New York: Hill and Wang, 1983.

Baudrillard, Jean. *For a Critique of the Political Economy of the Sign.* Trans. Charles Levin. St. Louis: Telos Press, 1981.

Benstock, Shari, and Suzanne Ferriss, eds. *On Fashion.* New Brunswick, N.J.: Rutgers University Press, 1994.

Breward, Christopher. *The Culture of Fashion: A New History of Fashionable Dress.* Manchester and New York: Manchester University Press, 1995.

Brownmiller, Susan. *Femininity.* New York: Simon and Schuster, 1984.

Craik, Jennifer. *The Face of Fashion: Cultural Studies in Fashion.* New York: Routledge, 1994.

Davis, Fred. *Fashion, Culture, and Identity.* Chicago: University of Chicago Press, 1992.

Evans, Caroline, and Minna Thornton. *Women and Fashion: A New Look.* London: Quartet Books, 1989.

Ewen, Stuart. *All Consuming Images: The Politics of Style in Contemporary Culture.* New York: Basic Books, 1988.

Gaines, Jane, and Charlotte Herzog, eds. *Fabrications: Costume and the Female Body.* New York: Routledge, 1990.

Garber, Marjorie. *Vested Interests: Cross-Dressing and Cultural Anxiety.* New York: Routledge, 1992.

Hollander, Anne. *Seeing through Clothes.* 1975. Reprint, Berkeley: University of California Press, 1993.

———. *Sex and Suits.* New York: Knopf, 1994.

Jackson, Beverley. *Splendid Slippers: A Thousand Years of an Erotic Tradition.* Berkeley: Ten Speed Press, 1997.

Kaiser, Susan B. *The Social Psychology of Clothing and Personal Adornment.* New York: Macmillan, 1985.

Kaiser, Susan B., Howard G. Schutz, and Joan Chandler. "Cultural Codes and Sex-Role Ideology: A Study of Shoes." *American Journal of Semiotics,* 5, 1 (1987): 13–34.

Kroker, Arthur, and Marilouise Kroker, eds. *Body Invaders: Panic Sex in America.* New York: St. Martin's Press, 1987.

Kunzle, David. *Fashion and Fetishism: A Social History of the Corset, Tight-Lacing, and Other Forms of Body-Sculpture in the West.* Totowa, N.J.: Rowman and Littlefield, 1982.

Lurie, Alison. *The Language of Clothes.* New York: Random House, 1981.

Mazza, Samuele. *Cinderella's Revenge.* San Francisco: Chronicle Books, 1994.

"Millennium Icon: The Shoe." *Miami Herald* Web site (http://www.herald.com), September 30, 1999.

O'Keefe, Linda. *Shoes: A Celebration of Pumps, Sandals, Slippers, and More.* New York: Workman, 1996.

Pond, Mimi. *Shoes Never Lie.* New York: Berkeley, 1985.

Rossi, William A. *The Sex Life of the Foot and Shoe.* 1977. Reprint, Ware, Hertfordshire: Wordsworth Editions, 1989.

Rubenstein, Ruth P. *Dress Codes: Meanings and Messages in American Culture.* Boulder: Westview Press, 1995.

Steele, Valerie. *Fetish: Fashion, Sex, and Power.* New York: Oxford University Press, 1996.

———. *Shoes: A Lexicon of Style.* New York: Rizzoli, 1999.

Wilson, Elizabeth. *Adorned in Dreams: Fashion and Modernity.* Berkeley: University of California Press, 1985.

ANTHONY BARTHELEMY is an associate professor of English at the University of Miami. He is the author of *Black Face, Maligned Race: Africans in English Drama from Shakespeare to Southerne* and other essays on race and early modern culture. Barthelmy prefers to be barefoot on the beach rather than shod. He does, however, buy the same type shoe in black and brown once a year.

SHARI BENSTOCK is associate dean of the College of Arts and Sciences and a professor of English at the University of Miami. She is the author of *Women of the Left Bank* (1986), *Textualizing the Feminine* (1991), *"No Gifts from Chance": A Biography of Edith Wharton* (1994), and coauthor of *Who's He When He's at Home: A James Joyce Directory* (1980). She has edited five volumes of work in feminist theory and gender studies, autobiography, and modernism, and is coeditor of the "Reading Women Writing" series at Cornell University Press. Although she has several closets full of shoes, she prefers to be shoeless and is known to her intimates as "the Barefoot Contessa."

CHRISTOPHER BREWARD is a reader in historical and cultural studies at London College of Fashion, the London Institute. He is the author of *The Culture of Fashion* (1995) and *The Hidden Consumer* (1999) and has published on the cultural history of fashion in several journals and edited collections. He is currently working on a history of London as a center for the production and consumption of clothing.

JULIA EMBERLEY is the author of *The Cultural Politics of Fur* (1997). She teaches at the University of Northern British Columbia, where she directs the graduate program in gender studies.

SUZANNE FERRISS teaches literature and gender studies at Nova Southeastern University. She has published articles on Romantic poetry and drama, travel literature, women writers, critical theory, and film. She is a proud member of the Imelda Club.

LORRAINE GAMMAN is a senior lecturer in cultural studies and product design at Central Saint Martins College of Art and Design, London. She is the coeditor of *The Female Gaze: Women as Viewers of Popular Culture* (1988), coauthor of *Female Fetishism: A New Look* (1994), and author of *Gone Shopping: The Story of Shirley Pitts, Queen of Thieves* (1996). She is currently researching the subject of visual seduction.

TACE HEDRICK is an assistant professor of English and women's studies at the University of Florida. She teaches U.S. Latina/o literature, feminist theory, and comparative American modernisms, and is currently working on a book, *Mestizo Modernism: New World Modernists and Race, Gender, and Nationalism*. She has published articles on Latin American and Brazilian poetry and fiction, bilingual poetry, and U.S. Anglo as well as third-world women writers. She recently visited Cuba, where she found that the revolution notwithstanding, Cubanas are still very attached to their high heels.

JAIME HOVEY is an assistant professor in the English department at the University of Illinois at Chicago. Her book *The Lesbian Janus: Nationalism, Sexuality, and Queer Female Modernism* is forthcoming. She wears a size ten men's shoe and buys her pumps at transvestite boutiques (really).

ELLEN CAROL JONES teaches Irish studies and women's studies at Saint Louis University. She has edited *Joyce: Feminism / Post / Colonialism* (1998), as well as four volumes for *Modern Fiction Studies: The Politics of Modernism* (1992), *Virginia Woolf* (1992), *Feminist Readings of Joyce* (1989), and *Feminism and Modern Fiction* (1988, coeditor). She has published articles on Virginia Woolf and on James Joyce.

JANET LYON teaches in the Department of English, the Women's Studies Program, and the Unit for Criticism and Interpretive Theory at the University of Illinois, Urbana-Champaign. She is the author of *Manifestoes: Provocations of the Modern* (1999). She and her sister, contributor Todd Lyon, own 108 pairs of shoes between them.

TODD LYON is a writer and artist living in New Haven, Connecticut. Her most recent book is *The Intuitive Businesswoman* (2000). Both she and her sister, contributor Janet Lyon, have weirdly long, prehensile toes with which they can pick up small objects.

ERIN MACKIE is an associate professor in the English department at Washington University, St. Louis, where she teaches eighteenth-century literature and culture, feminist thought, and cultural studies. She is the author of *Market à la Mode: Fashion, Commodity, and Gender in "The Tatler" and "The Spectator"* (1997) and editor of *The Commerce of Everyday Life: Selections from "The Tatler" and "The Spectator"* (1998). She loves and fears shoes but prefers to dance barefoot.

LAURA MULLEN teaches creative writing and literature at Colorado State University. She is the author of *The Surface* (1991), *The Tales of Horror* (1991), and *After I Was Dead* (1998). Charles Jourdan made the fishnet-and-leather platforms she owns two pairs of; in Spain she looks for the Muxart label; with the royalties from her first book she bought green lizard cowboy boots.

GERRI REAVES is an assistant professor of English at Texas Wesleyan University. She has published critical work, fiction, and creative nonfiction. Her book *Mapping the Private Geography: Autobiography, Identity, and America* is forthcoming. Her passions are birds, dance, and South Florida's natural environment, where she roams barefoot as often as possible.

MAUREEN TURIM is a professor of English and film studies at the University of Florida. She is author of *Abstraction in Avant-Garde Films* (1989), *Flashbacks in Film: Memory and History* (1989), and *The Films of Oshima Nagisa: Images of a Japanese Iconoclast* (1998). She has also published over fifty essays on theoretical, historical, and aesthetic issues in cinema and video, art, cultural studies, feminist and psychoanalytic theory, and comparative literature. She is currently working on a book, *Desire and Its Ends: The Driving Forces of Recent Cinema, Literature, and Art*. She loves looking at all styles of absurdly decorative shoes, a favorite being a 1931 Perugia fish-shaped stiletto made for Jourdan of France, but she desires for her own feet more high-style options that don't sacrifice comfort, à la Emma Hope.

JANICE WEST studied at the Royal College of Art and part-time at Cordwainers Technical College. She is a researcher, writer, lecturer, and curator. Among her recent books is *Made to Wear: Creativity in Contemporary Jewellery* (Lund Humphries, 1998).